The Semantics of Case

The phenomenon of case has long been a central topic of study in linguistics. While the majority of the literature so far has been on the syntax of case, semantics also has a crucial role to play in how case operates. This book investigates the relationship between semantics and case-marking in the languages of the world, exploring a range of phenomena in which case-assignment is affected by (or affects) meaning. By bringing together data from a wide range of languages, representing different language families, a cross-linguistic picture emerges of the correlation between case and meaning. Different approaches to the phenomena are considered, including both syntactic and semantic analyses, and the question is raised as to whether case can be treated as meaningful, ultimately helping us shed light on the broader connections between grammar and meaning and, moreover, grammar and human cognition.

OLGA KAGAN is based at Ben-Gurion University of the Negev. She is the author of the books *Semantics of Genitive Objects in Russian* and *Scalarity in the Verbal Domain*.

KEY TOPICS IN SEMANTICS AND PRAGMATICS

'Key Topics in Semantics and Pragmatics' focuses on the main topics of study in semantics and pragmatics today. It consists of accessible yet challenging accounts of the most important issues, concepts and phenomena to consider when examining meaning in language. Some topics have been the subject of semantic and pragmatic study for many years, and are re-examined in this series in light of new developments in the field; others are issues of growing importance that have not so far been given a sustained treatment. Written by leading experts and designed to bridge the gap between textbooks and primary literature, the books in this series can either be used on courses and seminars, or as one-stop, succinct guides to a particular topic for individual students and researchers. Each book includes useful suggestions for further reading, discussion questions, and a helpful glossary.

Already published in the series:

Meaning and Humour by Andrew Goatly

Metaphor by L. David Ritchie

Imperatives by Mark Jary and Mikhail Kissine

Modification by Marcin Morzycki

Semantics for Counting and Measuring by Susan Rothstein

Irony by Joana Garmendia

Implicatures by Sandrine Zufferey, Jacques Moeschler and Anne Reboul

The Semantics of Case by Olga Kagan

Forthcoming titles:

Frame Semantics by Hans C. Boas

Proper Names and Direct Reference by Gregory Bochner

Semantics and Pragmatics in Sign Languages by Kathryn Davidson Zaremba

Attitude Reports by Thomas Grano

Propositional Logic by Allen Hazen and Jeffrey Pelletier

Indirect Speech Acts by Nicolas Ruytenbeek

The Semantics of Case

OLGA KAGAN

Ben-Gurion University of the Negev, Israel

CAMBRIDGE
UNIVERSITY PRESS

University Printing House, Cambridge CB2 8BS, United Kingdom

One Liberty Plaza, 20th Floor, New York, NY 10006, USA

477 Williamstown Road, Port Melbourne, VIC 3207, Australia

314-321, 3rd Floor, Plot 3, Splendor Forum, Jasola District Centre, New Delhi - 110025, India

103 Penang Road, #05-06/07, Visioncrest Commercial, Singapore 238467

Cambridge University Press is part of the University of Cambridge.

It furthers the University's mission by disseminating knowledge in the pursuit of education, learning and research at the highest international levels of excellence.

www.cambridge.org
Information on this title: www.cambridge.org/9781108403474
DOI: 10.1017/9781108236867

First published 2020
First paperback edition 2022

A catalogue record for this publication is available from the British Library

Library of Congress Cataloging in Publication data
Names: Kagan, Olga, 1977– author.
Title: The semantics of case / Olga Kagan, Ben Gurion University of the Negev, Israel.
Description: Cambridge ; New York : Cambridge University Press, 2020. | Series: Key topics in semantics and pragmatics | Includes bibliographical references and index.
Identifiers: LCCN 2019053941 (print) | LCCN 2019053942 (ebook) | ISBN 9781108416429 (hardback) | ISBN 9781108236867 (ebook)
Subjects: LCSH: Grammar, Comparative and general – Case. | Semantics.
Classification: LCC P240.6 .K34 2020 (print) | LCC P240.6 (ebook) | DDC 401/.43–dc23
LC record available at https://lccn.loc.gov/2019053941
LC ebook record available at https://lccn.loc.gov/2019053942

ISBN 978-1-108-41642-9 Hardback
ISBN 978-1-108-40347-4 Paperback

To Edit Doron,
who has been a mother to me in the world of linguistics

Contents

Figures

Tables

Acknowledgments

It took several years for this book to be born, and many more years of thoughts and research on the nature of case that preceded the actual writing. Over these years, many people helped me by discussing, commenting, sharing ideas, criticizing and encouraging. I am very grateful to them all.

I would like to begin by expressing my deep gratitude to Professor Edit Doron, who, tragically, passed away this year. I intended to dedicate this book to her long before this happened, although, unfortunately, now I will not be able to show it to her. I first met Edit during my B.A. studies, and both my M.A. and Ph.D. theses were written under her supervision. She was a wonderful person and a dedicated scientist, and without her, I wouldn't have become the researcher I am.

I want to thank not only those people who helped me during my work on this specific book but also everybody who commented, participated in discussions, inspired and encouraged me during my work on the Ph.D. dissertation and the subsequent book *Semantics of Genitive Objects in Russian*. As is clear from the title, that project was very strongly related to the semantics of case as well, although, unlike the present book, it concentrated on two specific uses of a particular case in a particular group of languages (primarily Russian, but also Balto-Slavic more broadly).

I am very grateful to Barbara Partee and Vladimir Borschev for invaluable discussions of non-canonical genitive case in Russian and for their comments on my papers written at different stages of this work. I am indebted to Barbara Partee for being so supportive and generous, for commenting on my work at its different stages and for sharing with me her papers and ideas.

I wish to thank Donka Farkas for her invaluable help during my stay at UC, Santa Cruz, and for inspiring discussions of a range of topics in semantics, including case and mood. My thanks also go to Pranav Anand and Judith Aissen for our conversations during this period.

I am also deeply indebted to Malka Rappaport Hovav for her insightful comments, advice and support. Malka is a wonderful person and teacher, and I have learnt a lot from her. I also owe a lot to Anita Mittwoch for her comments and suggestions and for our inspiring conversations about aspect.

I wish to thank Elena Anagnostopoulou and Christina Sevdali for organizing a wonderful conference "On the Place of Case in Grammar" which brought together so many bright linguists investigating case in different languages from different perspectives. This conference significantly enriched my vision of the topic. I also thank the audience of this conference for the important comments on my presentation and subsequent discussions.

Conversations with my colleagues on various topics in syntax and semantics, including case, aspect, modality, mood and specificity were, of course, invaluable. I wish to thank Hana Filip, Idan Landau, Arik Cohen, Tova Rappoport, Aviya Hacohen, David Erschler, Ivy Sichel, David Pesetsky, Paul Kiparsky, Miriam Butt, Steven Franks, Louise McNally, Manfred Krifka, Fred Landman, Susan Rothstein, Yael Sharvit, Anna Szabolcsi, Ede Zimmerman, Anastasia Giannakidou, Asya Pereltsvaig, Monica Alexandrina Irimia, Yael Greenberg, Sergei Tatevosov, Scott Grimm, Lavi Wolf, Zarina Levy-Forsythe and Oria Ytzhaki for the discussions we conducted.

I am very grateful to Madzhid Khalilov for the discussion of case in Bezhta and for sharing with me his native-speaker judgments. And I wish to thank David Erschler for his help with complex transliteration matters.

I am grateful to the audiences of IATL 21, FDSL 6, SALT 17, FASL 17, Linguistic Evidence 2010, The Second Budapest Linguistics Conference, IATL 33, Ben-Gurion Linguistics Colloquium, Tel-Aviv University Linguistics Colloquium, Linguistics Departmental Seminars at Hebrew University of Jerusalem, the Linguistics Colloquia at New York University, University of California, Santa Cruz, University of California, Los Angeles, and the LLCC Center at Hebrew University of Jerusalem for important and inspiring comments and questions.

My thanks also go to the students who attended my seminars "On the Semantics of Case" and "Differential Object Marking": the preparation of these courses and the discussions that took place during the lectures contributed greatly to the work on the present book.

Of course, this work wouldn't have been possible without my numerous consultants, who provided their native-speaker judgments in different languages. Unfortunately, naming all of them wouldn't be possible, but I am grateful to everybody, and would particularly like to mention Zarina Levy-Forsythe (Uzbek), Madzhid Khalilov (Bezhta), Anya Ago and Satu Vallineva (Finnish), Pavel Caha (Czech), Franc Marušič (Slovenian), Joanna Zaleska and Robert Rothstein (Polish), Boban Arsenijevic, Donka Torov and Mirjana Dedaic (Serbo-Croatian), Oria Ytzhaki and Lavi Wolf (Modern Hebrew).

I'm also indebted to Dana Reznikov for her help with the Finnish data.

Finally, I would like to thank my husband Evgeny and my son Yoni, who would have received more attention if I hadn't been working on this book and other projects! And, of course, I am deeply indebted to my parents, who have always encouraged my aspiration toward self-realization.

Abbreviations

ABL	ablative
ABS	absolutive
ACC	accusative
ADESS	adessive
AgrOP	object agreement phrase
ALL	allative
AOR	aorist
AP	adjectival phrase
APPROX	approximative
AspP	aspect phrase
CL	clitic
COM	comitative
CP	complementizer phrase
DAT	dative
DEC	declarative
DOM	differential object marking
DP	determiner phrase
DSM	differential subject marking
EC	existential commitment
ECM	exceptional case-marking
EL	elative
ERG	ergative
ESS	essive
F	feminine
GEN	genitive
GenNeg	Genitive of Negation
ILL	illative
IMP	imperfective
IMPV	imperative
INDIC	indicative
INESS	inessive

INF	infinitive
INSTR	instrumental
L	ligature marker
LOC	locative
M	masculine
NEG	negation
NEUT	neutral
NOM	nominative
NPI	negative polarity item
NQP	negative quantifier phrase
NONFIN	non-finite
NP	nominal phrase
NPST	non-past tense
OBL	oblique
OT	Optimality Theory
P	preposition
PART	partitive
PASS	passive
PERF	perfective
PF	phonological form
PFC	potential for change
PL	plural
POSS	possessive
PP	prepositional phrase
PPTCP	past participle
PRES	present tense
PROG	progressive
PST	past tense
PTCP	participle
REFL	reflexive
SC	small clause
SG	singular
Spec	specifier
SUBJ	subjunctive
TP	tense phrase
TRA	translative
V	verb
v	little v functional head
VALL	verbal allative
VP	verb phrase

1 Introduction

1.1 INTRODUCTION

Does case have meaning?

Typically, within the minimalist framework, we expect the answer to be negative. Case is regarded as an uninterpretable feature whose checking constitutes a necessary condition for the licensing of nominal phrases (noun phrases (NPs) or determiner phrases (DPs)). This is a syntactic phenomenon which has morphological realization (e.g. case suffixes) in some languages but not in others. Relation to meaning is either totally absent (with structural cases like the nominative) or present to a very limited degree, when associated with theta-role assignment (with inherent case checked e.g. by prepositional heads).

Indeed, in many instances, it is easy to see that case-checking depends on the purely syntactic configuration, the structural position in which the DP appears, rather than on semantic considerations. For instance, over the centuries, nominative marking has been associated with both subjecthood (a syntactic function) and the thematic role of an agent (a semantic notion linked to the theta-grid of the verb). This duality is not surprising, given that subjecthood is, in general, associated with agentivity, in the sense that the most prototypical subjects are agents. However, it is not difficult to choose among these two notions as far as case-marking is concerned. While agentive subjects of finite clauses are indeed generally nominative (in nominative-accusative languages), the same case characterizes subjects that bear other thematic roles, such as experiencer (1a), instrument (1b) and theme (1c), or even subjects like dummy *it* in (1d), which carry no semantic meaning and fulfill an exclusively grammatical function.

(1) a. John loves Mary.
    b. This key opens the door easily.
    c. The ball rolled down the hill.
    d. It is getting dark.

Moreover, an agent does NOT appear in the nominative case in passive sentences, in which it no longer occupies the position of the subject, or in those instances in which it functions as the subject of a non-finite clause:

(2)   a.   This house was built *(by) Jack.
      b.   *(For) John to jump off the roof would be unwise.

The ungrammaticality of the sentences in (2) without *by* and *for* is due to the fact the proper names cannot check their case feature. Nominative checking is unavailable despite the agentivity.

What we conclude is that the presence (and licensing) of the nominative is dependent on syntactic relations (specifically, the nominal must appear in the specifier position of a finite tense head (T head)) and not on semantics. In many languages, the same conclusion is drawn regarding accusative case of objects (but see Chapters 4 and 5, which address the semantic consequences of accusative marking in a range of languages).

But, at the same time, numerous linguistic phenomena reveal that case is strongly interrelated with semantics and pragmatics, even if we put aside the issue of theta-role assignment. This is particularly evident in case alternations, a phenomenon whereby a DP can be marked by two morphologically distinct cases in what looks like the same construction, and the choice of case has clear consequences for meaning. Several examples are provided below.

In Finnic languages, a direct object may appear in either the accusative or the partitive case, as illustrated by the Finnish minimal pair in (3). The contrast is interrelated with the aspectual properties of the clause and with the interpretation of the nominal.

(3)   FINNISH
      a.   Join   veden.
           drank$_{1.SG}$ water$_{ACC}$
           'I drank the water.'
      b.   Join   vettä.
           drank$_{1.SG}$ water$_{PART}$
           'I drank some water / I was drinking water.'

Accusative marking of the object *veden* 'water' in (3a) results in a telic, or bounded, interpretation of the VP: the subject has finished drinking (up) the contextually relevant amount of water. In turn, (3b), with a partitive object, may receive an unbounded/progressive reading: the subject was engaged in the process of drinking water, but no information is provided as to whether this event has ever reached a natural endpoint. Alternatively, the sentence may report a completed event, but in that case, the partitive form is reflected in the semantics of the object: it receives an indefinite, quantificational, pseudo-partitive meaning (*some (amount of) water*, rather than *the water*).[1]

More generally, Finnic languages exhibit an object case alternation which correlates with (or is affected by) verbal aspect and, in certain instances, has consequences for the semantic properties of the nominal (see e.g. Lees 2015 and references therein, and Chapter 4). This correlation does not necessarily mean that the relation between case and semantics is direct; it could potentially be mediated by the syntax. Still, it is an empirical fact that morphological form and meaning are interrelated; further, from the perspective of the hearer, the case of the object allows to determine certain semantic properties of the sentence, such as its aspect.

Yet another object case alternation, quite widespread in world languages, is differential object marking (DOM). Rather than potentially receiving two different cases, within this phenomenon, an object of the verb may either be case-marked or remain unmarked. The contrast, again, is strongly interrelated with meaning. Depending on the individual language, the choice between the two variants is determined by such properties as animacy, the +/−human distinction, definiteness and specificity (see e.g. Aissen 2003, de Swart 2003, and Chapter 5). For the sake of illustration, consider the minimal pair in (4):

(4) KANNADA

    a. naanu pustaka huDuk-utt-idd-eene
        I$_{NOM}$ book   look.for-$_{NPST}$-be-$_{1.SG}$
        'I am looking for a book.'

    b. naanu pustaka-vannu huDuk-utt-idd-eene
        I$_{NOM}$ book$_{ACC}$ look.for-$_{NPST}$-be-$_{1.SG}$
        'I am looking for a book.'

                                                   (Lidz 2006)

The object in (4a) is unmarked for case, whereas its counterpart in (4b) appears in the accusative form. This contrast correlates with a truth-conditional difference. The accusative object in (4b) obligatorily

---

[1] In fact, the two interpretations are compatible, rendering the third reading of the sentence: the subject was engaged in the process of drinking some undefined amount of water which has not been referred to previously in the discourse. In other words, the quantificational interpretation of the DP is compatible with the unbounded reading of the clause.

receives a specific, wide-scope reading: there is a particular book that the subject is looking for. In turn, the caseless nominal in (4a) can receive both a wide- and a narrow-scope interpretation. The sentence may mean that the speaker is looking either for a specific book or, roughly, for any book.

Further, in some instances, a change in the form of the nominal creates fine semantic distinctions which are very difficult to pinpoint, even though native speakers of the language intuitively feel that some contrast is present. For example, consider the following minimal pair exhibiting the instrumental/nominative opposition on a sentence-initial adjunct:

(5) RUSSIAN

    a. Soldatom   Boris   ne   imel   žalosti.
       Soldier$_{INSTR}$ Boris   NEG   had   compassion
       'When Boris was a soldier he was not compassionate.'

    b. Soldat,   Boris   ne   imel   žalosti.
       Soldier$_{NOM}$ Boris   NEG   had   compassion
       'Being a soldier, Boris was not compassionate.'

                                             (Geist 2006, ex. 26)

The difference in meaning, although elusive, seems to be a matter of restricting those situations in which Boris has no compassion (see Geist 2006). According to (5b), he was not compassionate in general, which results from (or at least is interrelated with) the fact that he is a soldier. (5a), however, asserts that Boris is not compassionate in those situations in which he functions as a soldier but suggests that there exist alternative roles that he fulfills and/or alternative times when he does not act as a soldier. The implicature is that in these situations, he may very well be compassionate.

This contrast constitutes part of a more general nominative/instrumental opposition, observed in some Slavic languages, including Russian and Polish, which has been linked in the literature to the distinction between individual-level and stage-level predication. Instrumental case on predicates is associated with stage-level, impermanent properties, which hold in particular situations or during a limited temporal interval, whereas the nominative is more likely to be used with permanent properties (see e.g. Geist 2006, Citko 2008, and Section 7.1 of Chapter 7). In Uralic languages, it is the essive case that correlates with stage-level semantics (see de Groot 2017 and references therein, and Section 7.2 of Chapter 7).

Other case alternations are indeed associated with theta-role distinctions or with features of which thematic roles are composed. But even in these instances, the relation is somewhat more complex than originally assumed for inherent/lexical case, which is assigned due to a (potentially) idiosyncratic requirement of a given lexical head. Consider the following illustration of the nominative/ergative alternation in Urdu/Hindi (Butt 2006b, ex. 4):

(6) URDU/HINDI

    a. **ram** $\quad$ $k^h\tilde{a}$s-a
       Ram$_{M.SG.NOM}$ $\quad$ cough-$_{PERF.M.SG}$
       'Ram coughed.'

    b. **ram=ne** $\quad$ $k^h\tilde{a}$s-a
       Ram$_{M.SG=ERG}$ $\quad$ cough-$_{PERF.M.SG}$
       'Ram coughed **(purposefully)**.'

While above, differential **object** marking has been briefly discussed, here, we deal with an instance of differential **subject** marking: the subject of a clause may either remain morphologically unmarked (which is taken to be the nominative case form in (6)) or appear with an overt ergative case-marker. Just as with DOM, the case contrast correlates with a difference in meaning. Specifically, the addition of the ergative marker brings in the meaning component of intentionality: the action of coughing was performed by the subject on purpose. This property is, of course, an inherent component of agentivity. An ergative subject gets interpreted as an agent.

A very different phenomenon within which a case alternation is also related to theta-role assignment is found in German. Spatial prepositions in this language take either dative or accusative complements. Crucially, there exist prepositions which allow for both – with clear consequences for the truth conditions of the sentence. Specifically, in such alternations, the accusative variant of the prepositional phrase (PP) is interpreted as a goal and the dative one as a location.

(7) GERMAN

    a. Alex $\quad$ tanzte $\quad$ in $\quad$ dem $\quad$ Zimmer.
       Alex $\quad$ danced $\quad$ in $\quad$ the$_{DAT}$ $\quad$ room
       'Alex danced in the room.'

    b. Alex $\quad$ tanzte $\quad$ in $\quad$ das $\quad$ Zimmer.
       Alex $\quad$ danced $\quad$ in $\quad$ the$_{ACC}$ $\quad$ room
       'Alex danced into the room.'

                              (Zwarts 2006, ex. 2a–b)

For instance, in (7a) above, the complement of the preposition *in* 'in' appears in the dative case (as reflected in the form of the definite article). As a result, the whole PP is interpreted as a location: the event of dancing took place in the room. In turn, in (7b), the same DP is marked with the accusative case. Crucially, the sentence contains the same preposition *in*, but this time the form of its complement is different. The PP receives the thematic role of a goal. The dancing event is entailed to proceed along a path which begins outside of the room and ends in the room.

In such instances, a particular case is not merely required by a preposition which assigns to its complement a fixed thematic role. Rather, the state of affairs is more complex: more than one case is available, and different forms are accompanied by different meanings. (For further details and additional languages exhibiting similar contrasts, see Section 3.6 in Chapter 3 and Section 4.3 in Chapter 4.)

Finally, before completing this introductory section, it is worth pointing out that a correlation between case and meaning can be observed in the absence of an alternation as well. Consider, for example, the translative case in Uralic languages. Translative marking systematically characterizes adjectival and nominal predicates in sentences that entail a change of state. This is illustrated in (8) for Finnish:

(8) FINNISH
     Toini   tuli   sairaaksi.
     Toini   became   ill$_{TRA}$
     'Toini became ill.'

                                                    (Fong 2003)

This sentence entails a change of state due to the presence of the verb *tulla*, which, in this context, is best translated as 'become'. Toini is entailed to undergo a shift from healthiness to sickness. The new state which he enters at the endpoint of the event is denoted by an adjectival phrase (AP) predicate that contains the translative suffix *-ksi*. In general, the translative is systematically observed in sentences that entail a change of state. It is unacceptable in a sentence like (9), whose meaning is purely stative and non-dynamic and which, consequently, does not denote a change:

(9) *Toini   oli   sairaaksi.
     Toini   was   ill$_{TRA}$
     'Toini was ill.'

In other words, even in the absence of a case alternation, a link between case and a certain meaning component can be established. Moreover, the case-marked phrase need not bear any thematic role (as it need not be an argument).

(In fact, the view presented here for the sake of illustration is somewhat simplified. In Finnish, there do exist environments in which the translative is possible with no entailment of an actual change; arguably, however, those examples do involve dynamics and/or a **potential** change. See Chapter 7 for a detailed description of the data and a proposed analysis.)

The phenomena illustrated above raise a series of questions regarding the nature of case. Can it have meaning and make a contribution to the truth conditions of a sentence, or does it always correspond to an uninterpretable feature? If the latter is true, then in what way are the semantic components observed above contributed? If the relation between case and meaning is indirect, mediated by the syntax, then which syntactic elements are responsible for the interface with semantics? On a more descriptive level, which semantic and pragmatic phenomena can, cross-linguistically, be reflected by case-marking?

The goal of this book is to look into some of these questions. A range of semantic case-related phenomena from different languages will be considered. We will discuss both the intricacies of the data and the linguistic approaches to the phenomena that have been proposed in the literature. It is important to emphasize that the question of whether case is primary and meaning secondary, or vice versa (i.e. whether case determines meaning or rather meaning affects case-marking) is to a considerable degree subject to theory-internal considerations. In this book, we will be interested in those phenomena within which morphological marking correlates with semantic or pragmatic properties, empirically speaking. The more specific nature of the case–meaning relation will be addressed in the course of the discussion of linguistic analyses.

1.2 WHAT IS CASE?

In the previous section, we saw examples of various case alternations. But **what is case**, to begin with? It turns out that, despite (or maybe even due to) the important role that it plays in the linguistic theory, case is not easy to define. Intuitively and pre-theoretically speaking, we deal with a morpho-syntactic phenomenon whereby a noun (and often some of its associates) appears with different marking depending on the position it occupies in a sentence and on the role it fulfills. To illustrate, in (10a) below,[2] the nominal phrase *laatikko* 'a/the box'

---

[2] www.kaleva.fi/uutiset/ulkomaat/musta-laatikko-on-oikeasti-oranssi/275483/, accessed May 27, 2018.

functions as the subject of the sentence and appears in the nominative case, which is a classic case of subjects (unless we are dealing with an ergative language, see Section 1.4.2). In contrast, in (10b) the same nominal denotes a goal toward which the motion of the mouse is directed. As a result, it appears in a different form, in this instance, the illative one (illative is a case of goals). In turn, *hiiri* 'a/the mouse' occupies the subject position in this example and therefore receives nominative marking.

(10)   FINNISH

   a. Musta   **laatikko**   on   oikeasti   oranssi.
      But   box$_{NOM}$ is   really   orange
      'But, in fact, the box is orange.'

   b. Hiiri   juoksi   **laatikkoon**.
      mouse   ran   box$_{ILL}$
      'A/The mouse ran into the box.'

Formulating a single definition of case is challenging at the very least, given considerable contrasts between different types of cases, as well as the fact that the very term *case* can be used in somewhat different senses. As we will see below, some cases are purely grammatical, whereas others reflect semantic relations; further, in some languages, nominals in different cases are distinguishable morpho-phonologically, whereas in others, we deal with a purely syntactic phenomenon with no, or almost no, morphological realization.

Tentatively, case can be defined as the marking of the nominal that reflects its **relation to other elements in the sentence**. Thus, Blake (2001:1) defines case as "a system of marking dependent nouns for the type of relationship they bear to their heads." Concentrating on overtly reflected case, Butt (2006a:4) states that "One good hypothesis is that explicit case marking is useful for the establishment of the *semantic roles* of nouns (and pronouns) and their *syntactic* relationship to the verb." Similarly to Butt, Grimm (2005:8) relates to both syntax and semantics in his definition and proposes to "conceive of case as a morphological means of marking arguments for syntactic, semantic and/or pragmatic content."

Case may be determined by the purely syntactic function of the nominal (e.g. subject versus direct object versus indirect object), which also means marking the syntactic relation in which the nominal stands to the verb (and other lexical and functional elements in the sentence). But it may be also interrelated with semantics, as discussed in Section 1.1 above and as illustrated in (10b), in which the illative form provides information regarding the spatial relation which holds between the box and the mouse and regarding the change this relation undergoes in the course of the event. The range of semantic notions to which case-marking is sensitive turns out to be much wider than prototypical examples may suggest.

While the minimalist approach considers case as a primarily syntactic phenomenon, the cognitive framework places much more emphasis on the semantic and pragmatic side. The following list of assumptions is listed by Janda (1993:15) as an integral part of the cognitive approach to case:

(i) Case is always meaning-bearing.
(ii) Case meaning has a constant objective moment that can be subjectively applied.
(iii) Case meaning involves the organization of rather than the specification of information.
(iv) Case meaning is not essentially different from lexical meaning in structure.

While the present book concentrates primarily on the generative linguistic framework, reference to cognitive semantic approaches will also be made.

Further, within the minimalist framework, it has been proposed that, in certain instances, a case feature may be (construed as) semantic/interpretable (see e.g. Svenonius 2002, 2006, Richards 2013). Further, de Swart and de Hoop (2018:11) argue that case-markers "may impose typing restrictions on their arguments." Under this view, case does play a role in **semantic** relations.

In order to understand the nature of case better, it is not sufficient to concentrate on its defining features which are shared by all or almost all of its instances. Rather, it is essential to consider different case systems and the various distinctions and classifications that have been made in the literature on the topic. This is what Sections 1.3–1.5 are dedicated to.

1.3 ABSTRACT VERSUS MORPHO-SYNTACTIC CASE

1.3.1 Abstract and Morphologically Realized Case

One very important distinction that we have to bear in mind is between **morpho-syntactic** and **abstract** case. In many languages, the form of a noun (and possibly its associates) varies depending on the syntactic position in which it appears / the grammatical function it fulfills / the thematic relation in which it stands to other elements in the sentence, etc. For instance, the form of the subject differs from that of the object, the form of the direct object differs from that of the indirect object, and so on. In other words, case distinctions are reflected in the morpho-phonological properties of the nominal. To illustrate, in Russian, the DP *Masha* appears in the nominative case form (*Masha*) when it occupies the subject position of a finite clause (11a), in the accusative form (*Mashu*) in the object position (11b) and in the dative form (*Mashe*) when it functions as an indirect object (oblique complement) of the verb *dat'* 'give' (11 c).[3]

(11) RUSSIAN
    a. **Maša**   učit   lingvistiku.
       Masha$_{NOM}$ studies   linguistics$_{ACC}$
       'Masha studies linguistics.'
    b. Dima   poceloval **Mašu**.
       Dima$_{NOM}$ kissed   Masha$_{ACC}$
       'Dima kissed Masha.'
    c. Ivan   dal   **Maše**   knigu.
       Ivan$_{NOM}$ gave   Masha$_{DAT}$ book$_{ACC}$
       'Ivan gave Masha a book.'

Languages in which nominals exhibit this kind of paradigm have morphologically reflected case and are sometimes referred to as *case languages*. It is worth noting that while in Russian, case is morphologically realized via suffixation, other case languages use additional devices. Suffixation is indeed quite widespread; however, some languages use, e.g. case prefixes or case clitics.[4]

In English, unlike Russian, exactly the same form of the DP is found in the subject, object and oblique positions (unless this DP is a pronoun):

(12) ENGLISH
    a. **John** studies linguistics.
    b. Mary kissed John.
    c. Mary gave a book to **John**.

---

[3] (11) does not illustrate the complete case paradigm, but rather only provides several examples.

[4] In fact, under Caha's (2009) approach, case is realized as a suffix, rather than a prefix, only if the nominal constituent undergoes movement.

Thus, English (almost) lacks morphological realization of case, with the exception of its pronominal system (e.g. *he* versus *him* versus *his*) and possessive noun phrases (*John* versus *John's*). Then do we conclude that in this language, case is virtually absent?

The generally accepted answer in generative linguistics is negative. Case is present, even though it is typically not morphologically realized. The subject *John* in (12a) carries the nominative case feature, whereas the object *John* is (12b) carries the accusative feature. The contrast is present on the syntactic level but it remains covert, without being reflected in the morphology and, consequently, at phonological form (PF). Hence, syntactically, case is present in both English and Russian, but it is only in Russian that we can hear it.

Abstract case constitutes a syntactic feature which is present on a nominal phrase and (if uninterpretable) needs to be checked. The specific value of this feature (nominative, accusative, genitive, etc.) depends on the syntactic (and sometimes also thematic) relation in which the nominal stands to other elements in the sentence. The checking of this feature constitutes a crucial condition on the licensing of the nominal. This rule, referred to as Case Filter, is formulated in its original version in (13):

(13)   Every lexical NP must be assigned case
                                                          (Chomsky and Lasnik 1977).

Today, case-checking, rather than case-assignment, is assumed to take place, but the essence of the condition remains the same.[5] An overt nominal phrase must check its case feature, independently of whether the latter receives a morphological realization; otherwise, ungrammaticality results. In English, this rule explains the unacceptability of such sentences as (14):

(14)   *John is proud Mary.

No element in the sentence can check the case feature of *Mary*. *Proud* is an adjective, and adjectives do not carry case features. The sentence does not contain a transitive verb nor any of those functional

---

[5] Additional issues that have been raised include the question of whether Case Filter should be applied to NPs or DPs (or both), and whether case always constitutes an uninterpretable feature. The general assumption is that it is uninterpretable; however, as pointed out above, in some of the recent literature, it is proposed that it may, in fact, be interpretable in some sense or other (e.g. Svenonius 2002, 2006, Richards 2013). This issue is interrelated with the question of whether or not case may have meaning, which will be addressed in the following chapters.

projections associated with verbs that could do the case-checking job
(e.g. vP (little v phrase), AgrOP (object agreement phrase), AspP (aspect
phrase), etc.). The finite T head checks the nominative feature of the
subject. The only way for *Mary* to check its case is via the insertion of
the preposition *of*:

(15)   John is proud of Mary.

In (15), the P head successfully checks the case of its complement.
Examples of this kind reveal that the notion of (abstract) case and the
condition in (13) are relevant for languages like English, in which case
is not typically reflected in the morphology.

How is abstract case related to the morphological case form of
a nominal? The latter is often understood to be an overt realization
of abstract case, reflected at PF. For instance, Vainikka and Maling
(1996:180) state that "morphological case is one possible instantiation
of Abstract Case." Legate (2008:55) claims that "abstract Case features
are determined syntactically and realized in a postsyntactic morphological component." Indeed, in a prototypical situation, case morphology conforms to the abstract case feature carried by the nominal.
Thus, a DP that appears in an accusative form carries an accusative
case feature, etc. However, certain discrepancies exist as well. The
most trivial instance is a language with no or poor case morphology.
Here, a morphologically unmarked nominal is case-marked on the
abstract syntactic level. However, even for case languages, an analogous mismatch is possible. Arguably, this is observed within differential object marking (DOM). In DOM languages, a direct object may be
either marked or unmarked for case, depending on a range of factors.
However, Case Filter, which applies universally, requires all these
nominals to have case, irrespective of the form. This means that the
unmarked objects either bear an accusative case feature (i.e. the same
one as their marked counterparts) or a different case feature (e.g. the
partitive one, see e.g. Belletti (1988) and Vainikka and Maling (1996)
for a discussion of abstract partitive case). In any event, they are caseless morphologically but do carry an abstract case feature. To illustrate, López (2012) provides a detailed syntactic analysis explaining in
what ways *a*-marked and unmarked objects in Spanish satisfy their
case requirement. While the mechanism differs quite considerably in
the two instances, ultimately, Case Filter is satisfied with both types of
nominals. Yet another example is discussed by Legate (2008). She
argues that in several ergative languages (Walpiri, Niuean, Enga and
Hindi), both the nominative assigned by T and the accusative assigned

by v are realized as a morphological default, specifically, the absolutive, since these languages do not have nominative and accusative case morphology. In other words, the same form corresponds to two distinct abstract cases. (See Section 1.4.2 for a discussion of ergativity and split ergativity.)

In this book, we will concentrate mainly on case languages and on those phenomena that are reflected in the morphological form of the nouns. However, abstract case will be no less relevant, especially when issues of case-checking are raised.

1.3.2 Morphology and Case Syncretism

Finally, it is essential to relate to case syncretism and the distinction between **purely morphological** and **morpho-syntactic** case (it is the latter that will be of major importance in the present book). Again, the distinction is partially a matter of one's terminology, but there is an important reason to relate to the syntactic component even when non-abstract, overt realization of case is involved. The classification underlying traditional case paradigms (which will largely be followed here) is based not only on the purely morpho-phonological form of a noun but also on the distribution and/or function of the cases (Blake 2001). In other words, when we determine the (morphologically expressed) case of a lexical item, we consider not only the inflectional suffix it contains[6] but also the function it fulfills in the sentence. This is particularly evident in instances of so-called case syncretism, or neutralization, when in certain declensions (or even more broadly) different cases happen to be realized by the same morphological form. To illustrate, in Russian, a singular noun of the first declension receives the same morphological suffix in the dative and in the locative/prepositional case. This is illustrated in (16) below:

(16) a. Ira pomogla **Maše**.
         Ira helped Masha$_{DAT}$
         'Ira helped Masha.'

      b. Ja vižu v **Maše** mnogo xorošego.
         I see in Masha$_{LOC}$ much good
         'I see many good things in Masha.'

Why do we not conclude that the DP *Maša* appears in the same case in (16a) and (16b)? The reason has to do with the fact that when we consider a wider set of data, it turns out that the complement of the verb *pomoč* 'help' does not appear in the same case as the one of the

---

[6] Obviously, as mentioned above, this might not be a suffix but a prefix, clitic, etc.

preposition *v* 'in'. We see this clearly when plural nouns or nouns belonging to the second declension are considered, e.g.:

(17) a. Ira   pomogla **devočkam**   / **mal'čiku**   / **malčikam**
          Ira   helped   girl$_{PL.DAT}$ boy$_{SG.DAT}$ boy$_{PL.DAT}$
          'Ira helped the girls / the boy / the boys.'

      b. Ja   vižu   v   **devočkax**   / **mal'čike**   / **mal'čikax**
          I   see   in girl$_{PL.LOC}$ boy$_{SG.LOC}$ boy$_{PL.LOC}$
          mnogo   xorošego.
          much   good
          'I see many good things in the girls / the boy / the boys.'

If we want to make generalizations about case-assignment properties of the heads in question across declensions and number, we have to conclude that the verb *pomoč* 'help' assigns dative case and the preposition *v* 'in', the locative/prepositional one. This view is also in line with the fact that the complement of *help* receives the thematic role of a benefactive, and benefactives appear in the dative case in numerous languages of the world. And the complements of locative prepositions, quite naturally, receive the locative case in many Indo-European languages, which also holds for the locative uses of *v* 'in' and *na* 'on' in Russian. We will thus conclude, following the traditional approach, that *Masha* appears in different cases in (16a) and (16b), but for this noun (and, more generally, for singular nouns of this declension), the dative and the locative/prepositional forms happen to be phonologically identical.

Further evidence that it is important to recognize case distinctions across declensions even in instances of syncretism of the kind illustrated in (16) comes from agreement facts. Blake (2001:21) shows this for Latin. In this language, a genitive–dative syncretism is observed in certain declensions. For instance, *dominae* 'mistress' can be either genitive singular or dative singular. Crucially, in dative-case positions it will modified by a dative adjective (e.g. *tristī* 'sad') and in genitive-case positions, by a genitive adjective (e.g. *tristis* 'sad'). Since adjectives in Latin agree in case with the noun they modify, the difference in the adjectival forms reveals that the nouns appear in different cases, too, even though the forms of the latter happen to be homophonous.

To sum up, even when talking about morphological case paradigms (rather than purely abstract case features), we do take into account not only the form of the lexical item but rather the interaction between form and function. A more detailed discussion of this approach to case distinctions, referred to as **the distributional approach**, can be found in Blake (2001:19–22). It is important to emphasize that case syncretism of the kind illustrated above is probably non-accidental, and various accounts have been proposed for why some cases but not others get morphologically realized via the same form (see e.g. Jakobson 1957/1971, 1984, Blake 2001, Baerman 2008, Caha 2009, Starke 2017 and references therein). However, the issue will not be raised in this book. Here, we will take it for granted that *Masha* appears in the dative in (16a) and in the locative/prepositional in (16b) and concentrate on the semantic components that accompany the assignment of these cases.

1.4 CASE SYSTEMS

1.4.1 Examples of Case Systems

With the distinction between abstract and morpho-syntactic case being established, we can move on to the specific case distinctions that are made by individual languages.

When the number of cases in a given language is discussed, it is typically the morphological paradigm that is considered. A language may distinguish between two case forms (e.g. Persian and Aleut) as well as between ten cases and more (e.g. Hungarian and Pitjantjatjara). Some Daghestanian languages have been claimed to contain about fifty cases, but, as argued by Comrie and Polinsky (1998) and as we will see in Chapter 3, a different kind of calculation is probably more appropriate, which renders numbers around fourteen or fifteen (quite impressive, too!).

Let us now consider several specific examples.

As mentioned above, Persian is a language with a two-way case distinction, roughly, one between a subject-form (nominative) and an object-form (accusative). It is worth noting that this is a DOM language (see Krifka and Modarresi 2016 and references therein), which means that not all objects receive accusative/object marking.

Some Germanic languages, including Icelandic and German, have four cases: nominative, accusative, dative and genitive. If we relate to the most basic, prototypical uses, then these are: the case of the subject, the case of the object, the case of the indirect object and the case of the possessor, respectively. But, of course, this generalization is quite simplified, and in fact, the range of case uses is wider. For instance, genitive, dative and accusative are all checked by certain prepositions. The interaction of spatial preposition with dative and accusative forms in German is discussed in some detail in Chapters 3 and 4.

Proceeding to a higher number of distinctions, Tables 1.1 and 1.2 illustrate the case systems of Ukrainian (7 cases) and Finnish (15 cases, although not all of them equally productive). Each table lists the cases, provides examples of nouns appearing in the corresponding forms and specifies the basic functions of the cases. Again, descriptions of cases are brief, pre-theoretical and only relate to their most prototypical uses. Further, for some cases, English counterparts with such functional elements as prepositions or inflectional suffixes are provided.

The last three cases are highly restricted in their distribution and are therefore illustrated with a different noun, with which they are compatible. Note that the comitative case is generally accompanied by a possessive suffix, e.g. -ni 'my' in *taloineni* above.

Among particularly rich case systems is the one found in Kayardild, a language spoken in Australia, which is reported to contain twenty-one cases. These are divided by Evans (1995) into so-called nominal and verbal cases. The latter provide the original noun with verbal properties, as a result of which it agrees with the (main) verb in such features as tense, mood and polarity. This is illustrated in the following example from Evans (1995:162), where the phrase *that cave* is marked with past tense. (See Evans 1995 and Round 2009 for more information on the Kayardild case system.)

(18)   ngada   warra-jarra   dathin-kiiwa-tharra   ngilirr-iiwa-tharr
       1$_{\text{SG.NOM}}$ go$_{\text{PST}}$ that$_{\text{VALL.PST}}$ cave$_{\text{VALL.PST}}$
       'I went to that cave.'

Table 1.1 *Ukrainian case system (the noun* kniga *'book')*

Case	Form	Function	Parallels with English functional elements
nominative	kniga	subject	
accusative	knigu	object	
genitive	knigi	possessor	a/the book's
dative	knizi	indirect object	to a/the book
instrumental	knigoju	instrument	with a/the book
locative	knizi	with some prepositions	
vocative	knigo	addressee	

Table 1.2 *Finnish case system (the noun* ihminen *'man' and the noun* talo *'house' for the last three cases; based in part on Korpela 2015)*

Case	Form	Function	Parallels with English functional elements
nominative	ihminen	subject	
accusative	ihmisen	object	
genitive	ihmisen	possessor	a/the man's; of a/the man
partitive	ihmista	object; complement of a quantifier; complement of a preposition	
essive	ihmisena	stage-level predicate, a temporary property or otherwise relativized property	as a man
translative	ihmiseksi	change of state	(turn) into a man
illative	ihmiseen	goal, internal	into a man
inessive	ihmisessa	location, internal	in a man
elative	ihmisesta	source, internal	from in(side of) a man
allative	ihmiselle	goal, external	to a man
adessive	ihmisella	location, external	on a man
ablative	ihmiselta	source, external	from on a man
instructive	taloin	instrument	with (the use of) a house
abessive	talotta	without	without a house
comitative	taloineni	together	(together) with my house

1.4.2 Ergative and Accusative Languages

In addition to the number (as well as existence versus non-existence) of morphological case distinctions, languages differ in terms of morpho-syntactic alignment, a system that distinguishes (or unifies) the arguments of transitive and intransitive verbs. Consider the following three types of arguments: **the subject of a transitive verb**, **the object of a transitive verb** and **the subject of an intransitive verb**. Which of these will appear in the same case and which will receive a separate marking?

In **nominative-accusative** (or accusative) languages, such as Japanese, Russian and German, the subject of an intransitive verb receives the same marking as the subject of a transitive one. Both appear in the nominative case. In contrast, the object of a transitive verb receives a different, accusative, form.

In contrast, in **ergative-absolutive** (or ergative) languages, such as Basque and Inuit, the subject of an intransitive verb receives the same marking as the **object** of a transitive verb. They appear in the absolutive case. This time, it is the subject of a transitive verb that gets special marking (ergative).

It is worth noting that nominative and absolutive are cases which correspond to the citation form of the noun.

Crucially, languages of the world do not limit themselves to the two systems defined above. In fact, additional types of alignment are observed, including the mixed type of **split ergativity**, exhibited, for example, by Hindi, Walpiri and Georgian. Split ergativity characterizes those languages which show the ergative-absolutive pattern in some constructions but not in the others. The type of alignment may depend on a range of characteristics, including tense and aspect (e.g. in some languages, arguments of perfective verbs conform to the ergative-absolutive pattern and those of imperfective verbs, to the nominative-accusative one) or the thematic properties of the subject. In the latter case, agentive subjects of intransitive verbs receive the same marking as the subjects of transitives, whereas non-agentive ones are marked like objects instead. This shows us that the assignment of the ergative case is in some instances sensitive to semantics, an issue that will be discussed further in Section 1.6.2.

1.4.3 Case Hierarchies

Looking at the broad cross-linguistic picture of case distinctions, Blake (2001:156) proposes that cases can be ordered along the following hierarchy:

(19)   nom   acc/erg   gen   dat   loc   abl/instr   others

The scale contributes the following prediction. "If a language has a case listed on the hierarchy, it will usually have at least one case from each position to the left" (Blake 2001:156). In other words, a "lower" case implies the presence of the "higher" cases, but not vice versa. For instance, a language that has genitive case is expected to have the accusative or the ergative, and also the nominative (a term that also stands here for the absolutive). But the presence of the genitive tells us nothing as to whether the same language will have, e.g. the dative or the locative.

Blake further points out that in a system with a relatively small number of cases, the lowest case in the hierarchy will plausibly fulfill many roles, functioning as a kind of 'elsewhere' case.

Certain exceptions to the above generalization, or gaps, can be attested, but a close look at the data provides a principled explanation for their presence. For instance, in Nanai, the genitive case is absent despite the presence of "lower" cases such as dative and locative. This is due to the fact that the possessor relation is expressed by bound pronouns. Alternatively, an impression of a gap is created when the same case unifies the functions fulfilled in many languages by distinct cases (e.g. the accusative takes on itself the roles typically associated with the dative).

Blake proposes that there is a reasoning behind the scale in question, as it reflects "a hierarchy of functions or relations" (p. 159). Universally, some functions are more likely to be reflected morpho-syntactically, whereas others are often expressed lexically.

A largely similar (although not identical) hierarchy is defended by Caha (2009) in his dissertation, which is devoted to the topic of case syncretism. He refers to it as **Case sequence**, whose original version is represented in (20):

(20) nom acc gen dat instr com(itative)

The sequence itself constitutes part of the Universal Case Contiguity hypothesis, which states that "[n]on-accidental case syncretism targets contiguous regions in a sequence invariant across languages" (p. 20). For instance, the hypothesis allows for the nominative-accusative and the accusative-genitive syncretism (i.e. identity of case forms) but not for the nominative-genitive syncretism to the exclusion of the accusative.

It can be seen that Caha's case sequence contains the comitative, a case that expresses the meaning of accompaniment (e.g. in Hungarian and Chukchee). The comitative is not included within Blake's hierarchy (or, more precisely, is subsumed under "others"). The basic version of the case sequence also lacks some of the cases discussed by Blake, but in the course of the thesis Caha introduces various refinements of (20) while looking at a range of world languages. For instance, the scale for some Slavic languages, such as Russian and Slovene, includes the locative/prepositional case (Caha uses the term *prepositional*), which comes between the genitive and the dative.

In addition to accounting for case syncretism patterns, Caha employs the sequence in (20) to make the following prediction regarding the case suffix inventory of a language: "If a given case in the Case sequence is a suffix, all cases to its left (if present in the language) are also suffixed" (p. 43). For instance, if a language has an instrumental case suffix, it will have a dative suffix as well, as long as the dative function is expressed in this language at all. But, crucially, the dative will not be expressed by a preposition.

1.5 STRUCTURAL, INHERENT, LEXICAL AND SEMANTIC CASE

One prominent division of cases into distinct groups, particularly important for our purposes, is one between structural, inherent, lexical and semantic cases. This division is based on such factors as whether the given case is syntactic, semantic or idiosyncratic in nature, its productivity and the kind of configuration in which it is assigned/checked. Originally, a distinction between two types, structural and inherent, or structural and non-structural, was introduced (Chomsky 1981, 1986). At a later stage, it was argued that the system should be further enriched by the addition of the lexical and semantic types (e.g. Butt and King 2005, Woolford 2006). These distinctions are addressed in the following subsections.

1.5.1 Structural versus Inherent Case

As far as the relation between case and meaning is concerned, a crucial distinction has been introduced between structural and inherent case (see Chomsky 1981, 1986). Structural case is defined in morpho-syntactic terms; it is a realization of abstract case assigned to a DP in a particular syntactic configuration. In contrast, the licensing of inherent case is closely related to the assignment of a thematic role by the head which selects the DP in question. An example of structural case is nominative, assigned to the DP which occupies the subject, specifier of T(ense)P, position, as illustrated in (21a) for English and in (21b) for Russian:

(21) a. ENGLISH
        John loves Mary.
      b. RUSSIAN
        Maša   ljubit Mišu.
        Masha$_{NOM}$ loves   Misha$_{ACC}$
        'Masha loves Misha.'

In English, the DP *John* receives abstract nominative case. The subject *Maša* in the Russian example receives abstract nominative case as well, but it is also accompanied by a morpho-phonological realization. In both instances, the nominative is structural.

In turn, inherent case is illustrated in English by the genitive (22a), which is realized by the marker *of* and assigned e.g. by such verbs as *persuade* and *approve* to their complements (Chomsky 1986). Yet another example is the dative case that marks goals in some Germanic languages, as illustrated in (22b):

(22) a. ENGLISH
          Mary approves **of Bill's behavior**.
      b. ICELANDIC
          þeir   gáfu   **konunginum**   ambáttina.
          they$_{NOM}$ gave   king-the$_{DAT}$ slave-girl-the$_{ACC}$
          'They gave the king the slave-girl.'

                          (Maling 2002, ex. 44a, quoted by Woolford 2006)

Let us consider the contrast between inherent and structural case in more detail.

Most crucially, structural case is purely syntactic (or morpho-syntactic) in nature; it is supposed to be totally independent of semantic relations. In contrast, inherent case is strongly interrelated with thematic relations (e.g. *recipient* or *goal* in 22b). For the independence of structural case from semantics, let us consider again the example of the nominative. This case is received by any nominal that occupies the subject position ([spec, TP]) of a finite clause, no matter which semantic relations hold between this DP and other elements in the sentence. This is revealed in several ways. Firstly, nominative subjects can bear different thematic roles. Thus, the subjects in (23a–d) receive the theta-roles *agent, experiencer, instrument* and *theme*, respectively.

(23) a. Moriarty murdered many people.
      b. Moriarty hates Sherlock.
      c. The key opened the door.
      d. The door was opened with the old key.

Second, a nominative DP in a raising construction does not even constitute an argument of the closest verb; rather, it receives a thematic role from a lower verb, in the clause in which it is base-generated. In contrast, its case is assigned or checked by the higher T.

(24) Sherlock seems to ignore John.

In (24), *Sherlock* stands in a thematic relation with the verb *ignore*, not *seems*.

Third, the nominative case appears on dummy subjects, which are semantically empty:

(25)   a. It is cold outside.
       b. It is Sherlock who solved the case.

To sum up, the appearance of the nominative case is independent of
theta-role assignment or other semantic relations, which reveals that
this case is structural.

Turning to the relation between non-structural case and thematic
roles, illustrated in (22) above, it can be further exemplified by the
systematic checking of genitive case by source prepositions in Russian
(26a) and by illative and allative case-marking on goal DPs in Finnish
(26b).[7]

(26)   a. RUSSIAN
           iz   /   s   /   ot   /
           from (inside of)   /   from (the top of) /   (away) from   /
           iz-za   /   iz-pod   korobki
           from-behind   /   from-under   box$_{GEN}$
           'from (behind/under) the box'
       b. FINNISH
           Hiiri   juoksi   laatikkoon/laatikolle.
           Mouse   ran   box$_{ILL/ALL}$
           'A/the mouse ran into/onto the box.'

Here, case-marking is clearly linked to theta-role assignment. (26a)
reveals that, in Russian (as well as in some other Indo-European
languages), the genitive is systematically assigned to the object of
source prepositions. In (26b), (overt) adpositions are absent, but the
DP *laatikko* 'box' is interpreted as a goal due to the case form in which it
appears. Both sentences illustrate case patterns which correlate with
the assignment of certain thematic roles.

Let us now consider some of the additional (although related) differences between structural and inherent case. While the latter accompanies theta-role assignment, the former is interrelated with
agreement. Empirically speaking, across languages, nominative subjects tend to trigger agreement on the verb, whereas their counterparts in other cases, such as dative, typically co-occur with a verb in its
default, non-agreeing form. Formally, within the minimalist
approach, the same functional head, T(ense) or Infl(ection), is responsible for the checking of the nominative case and subject agreement
features. Analogously, the projection responsible for the checking of
structural accusative case is often taken to be AgrOP, which, in turn, is

---

[7] See Chapter 3 for a detailed discussion of local cases.

also the locus of checking object agreement features in those languages in which such a phenomenon is observed.

Yet another distinction originally introduced between the two case types has to do with the stage at which the assignment takes place. Inherent case was claimed to be assigned at D-Structure, and structural at S-Structure. This contrast was well motivated. Inherent case is a matter of head–complement relations and gets assigned in the position in which the DP is base-generated and receives its thematic role. If it undergoes movement from this position, its case is not affected – because it has already been assigned at D-Structure. Indeed, non-structural cases are known to be preserved under A-movement (i.e. movement to those positions where the DP could potentially receive a different case) (see Woolford 2006 and references therein).

In contrast, structural case is linked to S-Structure. If a nominal undergoes A-movement, it is at the landing side that it will get such a case, not in its original, base-generated, thematic position. For instance, subjects of passive sentences appear in the nominative, which they get in [spec, TP] and not in the object position where they are base-generated as internal arguments. The same holds for arguments of unaccusative verbs. Similarly, subjects that undergo raising receive the nominative case in the higher clause to which they move rather than in their original locus. Such constructions demonstrate that a structural case is assigned after A-movement takes place, specifically, at S-Structure.

Today this distinction cannot be maintained, given that the differentiation between D-Structure and S-Structure has been abandoned. However, possibly, the contrast in question can be represented in a different way. For instance, Woolford (2006) proposes that non-structural case is licensed in a relatively low position, within the vP phase, whereas structural case can be licensed higher (e.g. in [spec, TP]).

Additionally, structural case is systematically checked by functional heads, such as T, AgrO, etc. In turn, inherent case can, arguably, be licensed by lexical heads, such as V or P. This issue, however, depends on the way **inherent** case is defined. As we will see below, certain instances of non-structural case are sometimes analyzed as not inherent either. We turn to this topic in the next two subsections. Table 1.3 summarizes the contrasts between structural and inherent case discussed above.[8]

---

[8] See also Woolford (2006) for a review of tests determining whether a given case is structural or not, as well as for criticism of some of these tests.

Table 1.3 *Structural versus inherent case*

Structural case	Inherent case
purely syntactic	related to meaning via thematic roles
related to the checking of agreement features	related to Θ-role assignment
assigned at S-Structure	assigned at D-Structure
licensed by a functional head	(sometimes) licensed by a lexical head

1.5.2 Inherent versus Lexical Case

The structural/inherent distinction is very important, as it captures a striking contrast between different case types – crucially, a purely syntactic one as opposed to one that is linked to thematic relations. It has been proposed, however, that the two-way dichotomy is insufficient. One reason has to do with the fact that non-structural cases do not seem to form a homogeneous group.

Compare, for example, Icelandic dative case-marking in (27a) and (27b). (Both examples are quoted in Woolford 2006.)

(27)   ICELANDIC

    a. Bátnum   hvolfdi.
       Boat$_{\text{DAT}}$ capsized
       'The boat capsized.'

(Levin and Simpson 1981, ex. 1b)

    b. þeir   gáfu   konunginum   ambáttina.
       they$_{\text{NOM}}$ gave   king-the$_{\text{DAT}}$ slave-girl-the$_{\text{ACC}}$
       'They gave the king the slave-girl.'

(Maling 2002, ex. 44a)

The dative case in (27b) is assigned to the goal or recipient argument; this is an instantiation of a regular, systematic, predictable pattern, which is observed in the presence of numerous predicates. In Icelandic, with ditransitive verbs, the goal DP argument consistently receives dative case (although if the goal is realized as a PP, the case of the embedded nominal may be different).

In contrast, (27a) illustrates an instance of a much less systematic or productive phenomenon. Here, a particular lexical head idiosyncratically selects a DP in the dative case.[9]

---

[9] The question of whether the dative is purely idiosyncratic in such instances is subject to debate, however. For instance, Smith (2001) argues that such uses are at least compatible with the meaning of the dative case, and that the datives in

Analogous contrasts are observed in other case languages. In Russian, for example, recipient arguments systematically, with a wide range of verbs, appear in the dative. This phenomenon is as regular as the one illustrated in (27b) for Icelandic. In contrast, the Russian verbs *torgovat'* 'sell', 'trade', *pravit'* 'rule' and *vladet'* 'own' select instrumental complements under what seems to be a purely idiosyncratic requirement. After all, the complements of these verbs do not constitute instruments (or e.g. comitatives) in any obvious sense, as is illustrated by the VPs in (28):[10]

(28) RUSSIAN

    a. torgovat'   cvetami
       trade   flowers$_{INSTR}$
       'to sell flowers (as an occupation)'

    b. pravit'   stranoj
       rule   country$_{INSTR}$
       'to rule a country'

    c. vladet'   firmoj
       own   company$_{INSTR}$
       'to own a company'

Woolford (2006) captures the distinction illustrated above by arguing that non-structural case should be divided into two subtypes: **inherent** and **lexical**. Under this division, the notion of **inherent** case becomes more restricted than under the approach addressed in the previous subsection. Now this is the case that is strongly interrelated with theta-role assignment and characterized by strong regularity. Both these properties characterize the goal or recipient dative observed above. In addition, inherent case can be illustrated by the ergative. The assignment (or checking) of this case is quite systematic, and we see a considerable degree of regularity; semantically, the ergative is associated with the theta-role of an agent or, more broadly, with external thematic roles. Cases with such characteristics are analyzed as inherent.[11] This view of the ergative is further employed in Sheehan's (2017) syntactic analysis of ergative alignment.

---

    sentences like (27a) are semantically "motivated by the potential for energy they manifest as a result of their movement" (p. 147). More broadly, the view of lexical cases as purely idiosyncratic and semantically unmotivated is often debatable.

[10] But see Smith (1999:424) for a proposal that the instrumental with such verbs as in (28b,c) is semantically motivated and linked to the notion of domination.

[11] Baker and Bobaljik (2017) compare the inherent and dependent case analyses of the ergative and argue in favor of the latter. Dependent case theory is a syntactic approach which takes the case of a nominal to depend on the presence (or absence) of a higher or lower nominal in the same syntactic domain (see Marantz 1991, Baker 2015). Dependent case is a type of structural case according to Baker (2015).

In turn, **lexical** case is idiosyncratic, irregular, and is lexically selected by individual heads, e.g. the verb *vladet'* 'own' in (28 c). It is this kind of case that is assigned/checked in examples like (28) and (27a).

Woolford further argues that inherent and lexical cases are licensed by different (kinds of) heads. Inherent case is licensed by little v (a functional head) and lexical case by such lexical heads as V or P.

It is worth noting that the regular and productive nature of inherent case (under the present definition) makes it in some sense similar to the structural one, which, too, is characterized by these qualities. It is therefore unsurprising that debate arises regarding the status of some such cases. For instance, as discussed by Woolford (2006), the ergative is treated as a structural case by some researchers (e.g. Davison 2004) and as a non-structural one (inherent within Woolford's terminology) by others (e.g. Mohanan 1994, Nash 1996).

The contrast between inherent and lexical case, based on Woolford's (2006) distinction, is summarized in Table 1.4.

DISCUSSION

As mentioned above, in Russian, all source prefixes take a complement in the same, genitive, case:

(26)   a.   iz   /   s   /   ot   /
            from (inside of) /   from (the top of) /   (away) from /
            iz-za   /   iz-pod   korobki
            from-behind   /   from-under   box$_{\text{GEN}}$
            'from (behind/under) the box'

Should this "source genitive" be analyzed as inherent or lexical case within Woolford's (2006) approach? Can this case be trivially classified within this system, or does it pose a problem for the dichotomy?

(Hint: The "source genitive" is plausibly interrelated with the assignment of a particular thematic role. At the same time, it licensed by a lexical P head.)

Table 1.4 *Inherent versus lexical case*

Inherent case	Lexical case
related to meaning via thematic roles	lexically required by a given head
regular and productive	idiosyncratic
licensed by a functional head (little v)	licensed by a lexical head

1.5.3 Semantic Case

Partially in line with Woolford (2006) as discussed above, Kiparsky (1998), Butt and King (2005), Butt (2006a, b) and Kagan (2013), among others, point out that certain cases pose a problem for the classical two-way structural versus inherent distinction. However, they concentrate on those instances when a case has properties of a structural one but, at the same time, is clearly related to certain semantic notions. In such situations, the term *semantic case*, used by Butt and King, can be applied.[12]

Cases that, at least at first glance, do not fall neatly within the structural/inherent classification, include, for example, the Finnish partitive (as argued by Kiparsky 1998) and the Russian Genitive of Negation (as claimed by Kagan 2013). Both phenomena will be discussed in detail in the following chapters. Meanwhile, I just mention briefly the mixed nature of their properties.

Both the partitive and the Genitive of Negation have the following characteristics of structural case:

(i) Their assignment is productive and systematic (even though the precise rules capturing the patterns may not be easy to formulate).

(ii) They alternate with other structural cases, specifically, nominative and accusative, a property that does not characterize inherent cases (see Vainikka and Maling 1996).

(iii) Their appearance is not linked to any particular thematic role.

(iv) They mark internal arguments of a very wide range of verbs, and their licensing seems to depend on the syntactic configuration, rather than on a presence of any particular lexical head.

At the same time, these cases are strongly interrelated with certain semantic characteristics (albeit not theta-roles), which determine whether they or their accusative or nominative counterparts are to be used. Thus, the partitive in Finnish is strongly associated with atelicity and indefiniteness, and Genitive of Negation with such

---

[12] In fact, the way semantic case is defined by Butt and King (2005) has much in common with Woolford's (2006) definition of inherent (as opposed to lexical) case. Indeed, inherent case within Woolford's classification shares certain properties with structural case (as pointed out above, its assignment/checking is regular, productive and linked to a particular functional projection) and, at the same time, it is associated with a particular semantic content. See also Blake (2001:31–33) for an overview of an earlier established distinction between grammatical (syntactic) and semantic cases.

interrelated properties as indefiniteness, non-specificity, narrow scope and absence of existential entailment/presupposition.

Of course, the possibility is left open that these are still structural cases checked by functional heads which are, in some way or other, associated with particular semantic characteristics, e.g. Asp(ect) or Neg(ation). Such a view will indeed be considered in the following chapters. Still, the contrast between structural case as a purely syntactic phenomenon, and inherent case, which is dependent on semantic relations, gets blurred.

1.6 CASE-MARKING AND THEMATIC ROLES

The fact that the grammatical form of a nominal is interrelated with thematic roles has been known since ancient times (see e.g. discussion in Grimm 2005, Butt 2006a and Blake 2001), although the specific term *thematic role*, of course, did not exist then. This relation is even reflected in the names of many cases, such as *instrumental*, *dative*, *locative*, etc. As mentioned above, within generative linguistics, this link is addressed primarily in the context of inherent case.

Detailed research into all the case-thematic role relations that are attested in all the languages of the world falls beyond the scope of the present study. In the following chapters, this area of investigation is represented by two (broad) topics. Firstly, Chapter 2 is devoted to cross-linguistic uses of the dative case and their analyses. While the approaches vary considerably, some being semantically and others syntactically oriented, thematic roles such as goal, recipient and beneficiary and/or their components clearly play a substantial role in the distribution of this case. Secondly, Chapter 3 considers spatial cases, namely, cases that represent a range of local relations in numerous languages. While the semantic nuances vary considerably, the thematic roles of location, source and goal are definitely among the major semantic concepts conveyed with the help of such case forms.

In this section, I briefly discuss several instances of case-thematic role relation in order to present a somewhat wider picture of the phenomenon. The list of relations presented below is, again, not exhaustive, the goal being rather to "give a taste" of the phenomenon.

1.6.1 Instrumental

The fact that instrumental case is interrelated with the thematic role of an instrument (or means) is, in fact, revealed by the very term. Unsurprisingly, this function is often regarded as the basic or (proto) typical one for this case (see e.g. Wierzbicka 1980:4, Blake 2001:154,

Narrog 2011 and references therein). Indeed, many languages mark instruments with the instrumental, as is illustrated in (29a) and (29b) for Russian and Manipuri, respectively:

(29) a. RUSSIAN
          Dima   otkryl   dver'   ključom.
          Dima$_{NOM}$ opened   door$_{ACC}$ key$_{INSTR}$
          'Dima opened the door with a key.'
      b. MANIPURI
          məhak-nə   thaŋ-nə   u   kəki
          he.$_{NOM}$ knife-$_{INSTR}$ tree   cut
          'He cut the tree with a knife.'

                    (Chelliah 1997:128 and Bhat and Ningomba 1997:104–106,
                                        as quoted by Narrog 2011:593)

This case marks not only the most prototypical instruments of the kind illustrated above but also various types of means, e.g. vehicles, as in the Manipuri example in (30).

(30) a. RUSSIAN
          Oni   priexali   poezdom.
          they   came   train$_{INSTR}$
          'They arrived by train.'

                                            (Wierzbicka 1980:110)

      b. MANIPURI
          əy-nə   bəjar-də-gi   bas-nə   laki.
          I.$_{NOM}$ market-$_{LOC-GEN}$ bus-$_{INSTR}$ came
          'I came from the market by bus'
              (Bhat and Ningomba 1997:105, as quoted by Narrog 2011:593)

However, the relation between the instrumental case and the thematic domain is not limited to instrumenthood, even if the latter is widely defined. Crucially, in a range of languages, within certain configurations, the same case also marks agents. This is illustrated in (31a) for Hindi and (31b) for Russian.

(31) a. HINDI
          Anjum-ne   (mazdurõ-se)   makaan   ban-vaa-yaa.
          Anjum-$_{ERG}$ (labourers.$_{INSTR}$)   house   make-vaa.$_{PERF.M.SG}$
          'Anjum had a house built (by the labourers).'
                                            (Ramchand 2011:65, ex. 30)

      b. RUSSIAN
          Kniga   napisana   (Sašej).
          book$_{NOM}$ written   Sasha$_{INSTR}$
          'The book has been written (by Sasha).'

(31a) is a causative construction in which the instrumental is assigned to the so-called intermediate agent. (31b) is a passive construction in which the demoted agent appears in the instrumental case.

It should be pointed out that agents and instruments share an important property: they are both **causes**. It thus seems that the instrumental case tends to mark causes which, for some reason or other, fail to appear in the subject position and to receive the corresponding (nominative or ergative) case.

Of course, it is also important to emphasize that the uses illustrated above do not exhaust the range of functions that are cross-linguistically available to instrumental nominals. Our current goal has been to illustrate the phenomena in which the relation between case- and theta-assignment is particularly evident. In Chapter 7, a considerably different, predicative, use of the instrumental will be addressed. The chapter also contains references to different accounts of this use. See Narrog (2011:599) for a semantic map representing the various sub-meanings of the instrumental and the relations between these meanings. Wierzbicka (1980) provides a detailed discussion of the instrumental in Russian, listing seventeen uses of this case. Analyses addressing the different functions of the instrumental are further proposed by Janda (1993), Dabrowska (1994) and Smith (1999), among others.

1.6.2   Ergative

While in some languages, ergative marking is mainly a matter of the syntactic configuration, this case is often associated with the semantic notion of agentivity, and here, the relation is much tighter than that between agentivity and the nominative case in nominative-accusative languages, discussed at the beginning of this chapter. As pointed out by Palancar (2011:562), "In semantic terms, ergatives mark NPs that typically play the role of agents in the transitive event rendered by such [transitive] clauses."

Ergative marking of an agent is illustrated in (32) below for Basque:

(32)   BASQUE
       (Miren=e-k) liburu bat   irakur-r-r   d-u-Ø
       Mary$_{=L\text{-}ERG}$ book one$_{ABS}$ read.$_{L\text{-}PRF}$ 3.ABS-UKAN('have')3.SG.ERG
       'Mary has read a book.'

                                    (Palancar 2011:562, based on Manandise 1988:8)

The relation between agentivity and ergative marking becomes evident in the instances of case alternations. For instance, consider the example from Urdu/Hindi discussed in (6) and repeated below:

(33) URDU/HINDI

    a. **ram**   kʰãs-a
        Ram$_{M.SG.NOM}$ cough-$_{PERF.M.SG}$
        'Ram coughed.'

    b. **ram=ne**   kʰãs-a
        Ram$_{M.SG=ERG}$ cough-$_{PERF.M.SG}$
        'Ram coughed **(purposefully)**.'

(Butt 2006a, ex. 4)

In (33), the subject *ram* may appear either with or without overt marking. In the former instance it is glossed above as ergative and in the latter, as nominative (the same form can also be referred to as absolutive, see Section 4.2). Crucially, ergative marking adds the intentionality meaning component (the action was performed on purpose). Note that this component is not contributed by the lexical semantics of the verb and is absent if the subject appears in the nominative form.

A similar contrast from the Northeast Caucasian language Bats is provided in (34):

(34) BATS

    a. as   waxi
        I $_{ERG}$ drowned
        'I drowned myself.' [on purpose]

    b. so   waxi
        I$_{ABS}$ drowned
        'I got drowned.' [accidentally, involuntarily]
        (from Polinsky and Nedjalkov 1987, quoted by de Swart 2003:54)

While in (33) and (34), an absolutive/ergative (or nominative/ergative) alternation is illustrated, (35) shows the dative/ergative contrast. Again, the ergative subject is associated with a higher degree of control/volitionality, as is discussed below.

(35) URDU/HINDI

    a. nadya=ne   zu   ja-na   hɛ
        Nadya$_{F.SG=ERG}$ zoo$_{M.SG.OBL}$ go-$_{INF.M.SG}$ be$_{PRES.3.SG}$
        'Nadya wants to go to the zoo.'

    b. nadya=ko   zu   ja-na   hɛ
        Nadya$_{F.SG=DAT}$ zoo$_{M.SG.OBL}$ go-$_{INF.M.SG}$ be$_{PRES.3.SG}$
        'Nadya has to go to the zoo.'

(Butt and King 2005, ex. 3)

Both sentences have modal semantics, but the precise nature of modality is different. The sentence with an ergative subject is interpreted

as expressing a desire and the one with a dative subject, necessity/
obligation. This contrast has been accounted for via the link between
ergative marking and the property of volitionality (e.g. Butt and King
1991, 2005, Grimm 2005). The latter, in turn, constitutes a component
of agentivity. Roughly, in the absence of volitionality and/or control,
the modal relation between Nadya and the proposition *Nadya go to the
zoo* is interpreted as one of necessity (35b). In contrast, in the presence
of the ergative marking (35a), the subject is understood to be more
agent-like, and the relation is taken to be one of desire. Although not,
strictly speaking, an agent, the subject of (35a) still possesses certain
agentive properties. (See Dowty 1991 for the notions of Proto-Agent
and Proto-Patient, and the discussion of features into which thematic
roles can be decomposed in Chapter 2.)

More generally, the ergative case is associated with such agentivity-
oriented properties as volitionality, intentionality and control (see e.g.
Langacker 1991, Butt and King 2005, Grimm 2005, Butt 2006a,b, 2012, de
Swart 2003, Malchukov and de Hoop 2011, etc.). For a syntactic approach
to the ergative formulated within the dependent case theory, see Marantz
(1991), Baker (2015), Baker and Bobaljik (2017) and references therein.

1.6.3 Dative

The present subsection and the following one involve a brief illustration of topics that will be extensively discussed in Chapters 2 and 3,
respectively.

Dative case-marking is cross-linguistically associated with several thematic roles, such as: goal, recipient, experiencer and benefactive. The
corresponding uses of this case are illustrated in (36) for Modern
Hebrew[13]:

(36)   MODERN HEBREW

    a. Dani   tas   le-london.   GOAL
        Dani   flew $_{DAT}$.London
        'Dani went to London by plane.'

    b. Dani   natan   et   ha-sefer   le-dina.   RECIPIENT
        Dani   gave   ACC   the-book $_{DAT}$.Dina
        'Dani gave a book to Dina.'

---

[13] The status of the marker *le-* in Hebrew is, in fact, debatable: it can be analyzed as
a dative case-marker or as a preposition. The two approaches are unified if *le-* is
treated as a prepositional case. (In fact, the same holds for the Spanish *a*.)
Importantly for our purposes, the uses illustrated in (36) characterize dative nominal in numerous languages, including ones in which the syntactic status of dative
markers is less questionable. Relevant examples will be provided in Chapter 2.

    c. kar   li   EXPERIENCER
       cold I_{DAT}
       'I feel cold.'

    d. Dani   kana   le-Dina   simla.   BENEFACTIVE
       Dani   bought $_{DAT}$-Dina   dress
       'Dani bought a dress for Dina.'

1.6.4 Illative and Elative

The assignment of local/spatial cases is linked to such thematic notions as goal, location and source. In fact, the range of spatial concepts these forms represent is considerably wider, as will be discussed in Chapter 3. Below, we illustrate the phenomenon via Finnish sentences with an illative (goal) case and an elative (source) one:

(37) FINNISH

    a. Hiiri   juoksi   laatikkoon.
       mouse   ran box_{ILL}
       'A/The mouse ran into the box.'

    b. Hiiri   juoksi   laatikosta.
       mouse   ran box_{EL}
       'A/The mouse ran out of the box.'

Note that the examples above do not contain (overt) adpositions. Rather, the relations that hold between the motion events and the box are reflected in the case system.

    To sum up this section, case is indeed quite strongly associated with a wide range of thematic roles, including recipient, experiencer, benefactive, goal, source, location, instrument and agent, and with semantic concepts that are in some way or other interrelated with such thematic notions (e.g. volitionality and control). However, as we will see in the following chapters, the range of semantic phenomena that are reflected in case-marking is not limited to this area.

1.7 STRUCTURE OF THE BOOK

The book is organized as follows. Chapters 2 and 3 are dedicated to cases whose presence is interrelated with theta-role assignment. Chapter 2 concentrates on the dative. As mentioned above, this case, observed in a wide range of languages, is systematically linked to a particular set of thematic roles, including, for example, recipient and benefactive. We will consider different uses of this case, different semantic components and syntactic constructions which are accompanied by its assignment, and some of the analyses that have been proposed in the literature on dative nominals (including both semantic and syntactic approaches).

Chapter 3 is devoted to the interaction between case and spatial relations. We will consider those spatial notions that can be conveyed via case-marking, including configuration (the relation between figure and ground, e.g. IN versus ON versus UNDER), directionality (e.g. goal versus source versus location) and distality and see in what ways such distinctions are made within case systems of languages belonging to different families. Special attention will be devoted to Nakh-Daghestanian languages, which exhibit particularly rich inventories of local cases and one of which (specifically, Tabasaran) has even entered *The Guinness Book of Records* as a language that has the highest number of nominal cases. We will also consider some non-spatial uses of local cases. Finally, the chapter addresses the topic of semantically meaningful interactions of cases and spatial prepositions in such languages as Ancient Greek, German and Russian. We will consider ways in which case selection by a spatial preposition depends on the directionality specified by the prepositional phrase.

Chapters 4 through 6 are largely devoted to different types of object case alternations, phenomena which have received considerable attention in the linguistic literature and whose investigation contributes greatly to our understanding of the interaction between case and meaning. Chapter 4 deals with the relation between case and aspect. While aspect (e.g. telicity or boundedness distinctions) is often conceptualized as a verbal property, in fact, we know that it can be affected by additional material that appears in a VP (e.g. an object, a goal PP, or – if we are dealing with temporal delimitation – even an adjunct). Moreover, it has been claimed that even the subject may affect the aspectual nature of the clause. Compare, for example, *The train crossed the border* and *John crossed the border*. *The train*, but not *John*, constitutes the incremental argument: parts of the crossing event correspond to parts of the train getting to the other side (see Dowty 1991, Jackendoff 1996, Krifka 1998 for the special aspectual properties of verbs like *cross*). Therefore, it is probably not extremely surprising that aspect may be morphologically reflected not only on the verb (as e.g. in English and Russian) but also on the object (as in Finnish). We will consider several Finnic languages in which accusative object case alternates with the partitive, where the former correlates with a bounded interpretation of the VP, and the latter with the unbounded one (with the relevant sense of boundedness as well as challenges to this approach discussed in the chapter). This phenom-enon does not exhaust the interdependence of case and aspect, how-ever. We will see that the accusative case, cross-linguistically, marks those types of adjuncts that function as event delimiters, and consider analyses that unify case-related properties of such adjuncts with those of direct objects. Finally, we will address the question of whether accusative marking of complements of goal prepositions, illustrated in (7) above and further described in Chapter 3, is due to the more general link between accusative case and boundedness.

In Chapter 5, we turn to (asymmetric) differential object marking (DOM), which is found in a wide range of languages and involves an opposition between a marked and an unmarked direct object. The form depends on such properties as the +/–human distinction, ani-macy, definiteness and specificity. While in some languages, only one property seems to play a role, in others, an interaction of character-istics is at work. The general tendency is for the more prominent, or individuated, objects to be marked, and for the less prominent ones to remain without morphological case. Given how cross-linguistically widespread the phenomenon is, its emergence must be supported by certain principles of universal grammar. We will discuss the possible reasoning behind DOM and consider both analyses that have been proposed for individual languages and accounts whose goal is to capture the broad cross-linguistic picture.

It should be pointed out that while the book does not contain a separate chapter dedicated to differential **subject** marking, the topic of case-assignment to subjects and its sensitivity to semantics is addressed in different chapters throughout the book. For instance, the interaction between ergative marking and volitionality, control and agentivity has been illustrated and discussed in Section 1.6.2. Chapter 2 discusses dative subjects, among other types of dative nom-inals, Chapter 3 relates to the phenomenon whereby a subject is marked with a spatial case, etc.

Chapter 6 is devoted to yet another object case alternation that has intrigued linguists for many decades: the genitive/accusative alternation in Slavic languages. First we will concentrate on the so-called Genitive of Negation and Intensional Genitive in Russian, two types of genitive case-assignment to objects which have been argued by Neidle (1988) and Kagan (2013) to constitute instances of a single phenomenon. In Russian, objects of certain intensional predicates, as well as (base-generated) objects in negative clauses, may appear either in the accusative or in the genitive case. The phenomenon turns out to be quite complex and challenging, given the wide range of properties that affect case selection, including animacy, definiteness, specificity, number, the abstract/concrete and mass/count distinctions, verbal aspect, lexical characteristics of the individual verbs, etc. We will consider several analyses that have been proposed for this phenomenon and then address the question of whether it can be unified with DOM, in spite of the fact that in its framework, both versions of the object are morphologically marked. The chapter then turns to Partitive Genitive, which, too, involves a genitive/accusative alternation, but differs from the other two types both in terms of the environments in which it is licensed and in some of its semantic characteristics. Again, different approaches to this phenomenon will be considered, including one that takes the genitive case to be assigned/checked by a phonologically empty quantifier (Pesetsky 1982) and one that treats Partitive Genitive arguments as instances of a measure construction (Khrizman 2011). We will see that all the genitive/accusative alternations in Slavic share with DOM sensitivity to the property of individuation, with accusative marking being systematically associated with a higher degree on the individuation scale.

Phenomena of a different kind are considered in Chapter 7, which is devoted to predicate case. While nominal and adjectival predicates in sentences like *John is nice* or *John became a teacher* may appear in the same case as the subject (e.g. the nominative if we are dealing with a finite clause in a nominative-accusative language), alternative forms are possible, often associated with particular semantic characteristics either of the predicate or of the whole sentence. These include the instrumental case in Polish and Russian and the essive in Uralic. Both cases have been associated with stage-level properties, i.e. their marking becomes more likely if the property denoted by the predicate is impermanent, entailed to hold at a delimited temporal interval. In Slavic, instrumental-checking has also been linked to the presence of an extra functional projection, e.g. Asp(ect)P (Matushansky 2000), which allows for the emergence of the stage-level reading. In addition to temporal delimitation, both the instrumental and the essive are argued to be compatible with other kinds of relativization, e.g. the property may be ascribed to an argument only under one of the roles it fulfills (as illustrated in the "soldier" example in (5)) or only in a certain salient possible world (which differs from the actual one). Yet another predicate case we will consider is the translative, whose marking is licensed in the presence of the semantic components of change (along the property denoted by the case-marked phrase) or force exertion.

Finally, in Chapter 8, a cross-linguistic picture of the relation between case and meaning is sketched on the basis of the discussion of the individual phenomena. The chapter also summarizes the major generalizations and conclusions drawn in the different chapters. Broad questions on the relation between case and semantics and the role of syntax as a mediator between these linguistic components will be addressed.

Before we proceed, it is important to point out that a huge amount of highly valuable work has been dedicated to the research on different cases in a wide variety of languages. Unfortunately, the scope of the present study does not allow us to relate to all this work, all the languages or even all the cases. Definitely no disrespect is meant in such instances.

FURTHER READING

Blake's (2001) book *Case* (the first edition was published in 1994) presents an excellent resource on such topics as case inventories, distinctions that have been made in the literature between different case types, various existing approaches to the topic, including case feature analyses, the distribution of case morphemes and the historical development of case systems. It also proposes the implicational case hierarchy discussed briefly in Section 1.4.3.

The Oxford Handbook of Case (2011), edited by Andrej Malchukov and Andrew Spencer, is a very important source on any topic related to case. This volume includes numerous articles which address the topic from different perspectives, including syntactic, morphological, psycholinguistic and etymological ones. A separate part of the book is devoted to papers that deal with case systems of different languages; yet another part involves cross-linguistic overviews of individual cases, such as accusative, ergative, dative, instrumental. In general, the cross-linguistic empirical coverage is very rich. Different theoretical approaches to case are addressed as well.

Caha's (2009) dissertation presents an influential approach to case and is largely devoted to the topic of case syncretism. The research covers a wide spectrum of languages. It is argued that cases are composed of universal features, each of which corresponds to a terminal node on the tree.

Baker's (2015) *Case: Its Principles and Its Parameters* develops in detail the theory of dependent case. Under this approach, originated by Marantz (1991), the case of an NP is not determined merely by the position the nominal occupies, the grammatical function it fulfills or the relationship it bears to a functional case-assigning head. Rather, case also depends on the other NP that is present, higher or lower, in the relevant syntactic domain. Baker (2015) provides an in-depth analysis of the dependent case phenomenon in a wide range of languages, discussing such dependent cases as, e.g. ergative, accusative, dative and oblique.

Butt's *Theories of Case* (2006a) constitutes an excellent resource on case and the theories that have been proposed to capture this phenomenon. Crucially for our purposes, the book addresses the semantic components of case-marking. The book includes practical exercises.

Lingua 121.1, published in 2011 and edited by Klaus von Heusinger and Helen de Hoop, constitutes a special issue that is devoted to *Semantic Aspects of Case Variation*. This is a collection of articles that deal with different instances of the interaction between case and meaning in a variety of world languages.

2 Dative Case

Dative is a cross-linguistically widespread oblique case which is observed in a wide range of constructions and is associated with a set of semantic interpretations. The most prototypical position in which it is checked is that of an indirect object, but the distribution of dative marking is by no means limited to nominals with this grammatical function. Thus, we find dative subjects, dative complements of prepositions and even non-argument datives. Crucially for our purposes, (a) dative case-marking is strongly interrelated with the assignment of certain thematic roles and/or with certain features of which theta-roles are composed and (b) the range of meanings with which this case is associated repeats itself in a wide range of languages, including genetically unrelated ones. The fact that all these meanings are systematically linked to the same case suggests that we are not dealing with a mere coincidence/homonymy; rather, a common semantic core that unifies all the uses becomes at least plausible.

Below, I begin by listing the meanings/uses with which the dative is associated. Given the rich distribution of this case in some languages, the list will not be exhaustive, but I hope to relate to most salient, cross-linguistically observed uses.

2.1 THEMATIC ROLES

Dative case is associated with a range of thematic roles, which include mainly the following.

(i) Goal
The argument denoting an entity to which motion is directed, one that constitutes the endpoint of a path.

(1) a. KANNADA   (Amritavalli 2004:4)
         maisuur-ige   obbaru   hoodaru
         Mysore.$_{DAT}$ a.person   went
         'Someone went to Mysore.'

    b. HEBREW
         Dani   tas   le-London
         flew   flew $_{DAT}$-London
         'Dani went to London by plane.'

    c. JAPANESE   (Fukuda 2007:166, ex. 2b)
         Gakusei-ga   yane-#o/ni   nobor-ta.
         Student.$_{NOM}$ roof.$_{ACC/DAT}$ climb.$_{PERF}$
         'Students climbed to the roof.'

Not all languages allow dative marking on inanimate goals, as we
will see below. Still, this use of dative is exhibited by such typo-
logically different languages as Kannada, Hebrew, Japanese and
Tabasaran.[1]

(ii) Recipient
The argument that receives something. A particularly natural candidate for dative case-assignment given that the very term *dative* is
derived from a verb meaning 'give', and an event of giving, naturally,
involves a recipient.

(2) a. RUSSIAN
         Vasja   dal   knigu   Maše.
         Vasja   gave   book$_{ACC}$ Masha$_{DAT}$
         'Vasja gave a book to Masha.'

    b. HEBREW
         Dani   natan   et   ha-sefer   le-dina.
         Dani   gave   ACC   the-book $_{DAT}$-Dina
         'Dani gave a book to Dina.'

    c. GERMAN   (McFadden 2002, ex. 13)
         Hans   hat   seinem   Bruder   ein   Buch   gegeben.
         Hans   has   his$_{DAT}$ brother   a   book   given
         'Hans gave his brother a book.'

    d. JAPANESE   (Zushi 1992, example 13a)
         John-ga   Mary-ni   hon-o   age-ta
         John.$_{NOM}$ Mary.$_{DAT}$ book.$_{ACC}$ give.$_{PST}$
         'John gave Mary a book.'

---

[1] Comrie and Polinsky (1998) state that in Tabasaran, dative "occupies an inter-
     mediate status between grammatical and local case" (p. 110).

e. HUNGARIAN   (based on Rákosi 2006:129, ex. 83)
Küld-t-em   egy   kis   pénz-t   Kati-nak.
send.$_{PST-1.SG}$ a   little   money.$_{ACC}$ Kate.$_{DAT}$
'I have sent a little money to Kate.'

Given that the marking of indirect objects probably constitutes the most prototypical use of dative case syntactically speaking, it is not surprising that it is associated with the goal and recipient theta-roles. It is precisely these roles that indirect objects are prototypically assigned.

In addition to the languages illustrated above, the recipient use of the dative is observed in Tabasaran, Armenian, Latvian, Hungarian, Kannada and Hindi, among many others.

(iii) Beneficiary and Maleficiary
Dative may also mark a DP referring to an individual (or entity) on whose behalf / to whose benefit an action is done, or one who is harmed by it. This use is also referred to as *dativus commodi/incommodi*, the dative of benefit/harm. It is observed in such languages as Hungarian, Russian, Polish, Ancient Greek, Icelandic, Hebrew, French.

(3) a. RUSSIAN
        Dima   ispëk   Lene   tort.
        Dima   baked   Lena$_{DAT}$ cake$_{ACC}$
        'Dime baked Lena a cake.'

    b. POLISH   (Dabrowska 1997:35)
        Krystyna   zaśpiewała   Oli   piosenkę.
        Krystyna   sang   Ola$_{DAT}$ song$_{ACC}$
        'Krystyna sang a song for Ola.'

    c. HEBREW
        afiti   lax   uga.
        Baked$_{1.SG}$ you$_{DAT}$ cake
        'I baked you a cake.'

    d. HUNGARIAN   (Rákosi 2006:133)
        A   fokhagyma   jó   a   hangszalag-ok-nak.
        the   garlic   good   the   vocal.cord.$_{PL-DAT}$
        'Garlic is good for the vocal cords.'

    e. ICELANDIC   (Jónsson 2000:78)
        Ég   bakaði   mér   köku
        I   baked   me$_{DAT}$ cake$_{ACC}$
        'I baked myself a cake.'

    f. FRENCH   (Boneh and Nash 2010, ex. 13e)
        Jeanne   **lui**   a garé   sa   voiture.
        Jeanne   3S.DAT   parked   3.POSS   car
        'Jeanne parked her/his car for her/him.'

(iv) Experiencer

Further, in many languages, dative case marks nominals referring to individuals who experience an emotional, physiological or perception state. This phenomenon is illustrated in (4) below:

(4) a. RUSSIAN
         Maše   nravitsja   Dima.
         Masha$_{DAT}$ likes   Dima$_{NOM}$
         'Masha likes Dima.'

     b. HEBREW
         kar   li.
         cold   me$_{DAT}$
         'I feel cold.'

     c. KANNADA (Amritavalli 2004:8)
         avan-ige   bar-uvud-ikke   ista-villa.
         He-$_{DAT}$ come-$_{NONFIN-DAT}$ liking-$_{BE.NEG}$
         'He does not like to come.'

     d. ICELANDIC   (Bayer 2004:52)
         Henni   var   kalt
         her$_{DAT}$ was   cold
         'She felt cold.'

     e. NEPALI (Bickel 2004:79)
         malā-ī   bhut   saṅga   ḍar   lāg-yo.
         I-$_{SG.DAT}$ ghost with   fear   perceptible-$_{PT.3.SG.M}$
         'I was afraid of the ghost.'

Dative experiencers are found in such diverse languages as Russian, German and Icelandic, Kannada, Hindi, Hebrew, Tabasaran, Kathmandu Newar (a Newar language) and Lhomi (a Tibetan language). It is also worth noting that in some languages which lack dative, the same form is used to mark recipients, goals and experiencers (e.g. lative in Tsez, see Comrie 2004). In other words, the same semantic roles as listed above are unified by identical morphological marking.

In some instances, it is specifically dative case-assignment that allows us to identify the DP as bearing the experiencer theta-role. Consider, for example, the contrast in (5):

(5) RUSSIAN

     a. Maša   xolodna.
         Masha$_{NOM}$ cold$_{F.SG}$
         'Masha is cold.'

     b. Maše   xolodno.
         Masha$_{DAT}$ cold$_{NEUT.SG}$
         'Masha feels cold.'

(5a), with a nominative subject, ascribes to Masha the property of being cold (plausibly in a metaphorical sense of being indifferent and impassionate). (5b) contains the same argument and the same predicate, but this time, the former appears in dative case and there is no agreement between the two (rather, the adjective appears in the default, neuter singular form). The two grammatical properties are interrelated: in Russian, as in many other languages, only nominative arguments trigger agreement on the verb. Here, Masha is interpreted as an experiencer to whom the property of feeling cold is attributed.

Within the generative approach, this need not mean that dative case itself has meaning. It is possible that the two sentences differ in their syntactic structure, which, in turn, results both in the semantic contrast and in the different case-marking. But, in any event, the form of the argument correlates with a particular meaning and plays a crucial role in the way the hearer interprets the sentence.

Superficially, it seems that with some predicates allowing the dative/nominative alternation, case does not affect meaning, and the argument is interpreted as an experiencer independently of its form. This state of affairs seems to hold for the adjective *spokojna* 'calm', apparently, due to the lexical semantics of the predicate:

(6) RUSSIAN

   a. Lena   spokojna.
       Lena$_{\text{NOM}}$ calm$_{\text{F.SG}}$
       'Lena is calm.'

   b. Lene   spokojno.
       Lena$_{\text{DAT}}$ calm$_{\text{NEUT.SG}}$
       'Lena feels calm.'

However, even here, a contrast in meaning is available. Intuitively, (6b) is associated with a reduced degree of Lena's control over the situation. For instance, (6a) may be asserted in a context in which she behaves in a calm manner (which may, in fact, constitute a very difficult task for her). (6b) is not acceptable in such a context, as it relates exclusively to Lena's internal state which, crucially, is understood not to depend on her will. Thus, Lena is clearly an experiencer in (6b), but the thematic role of this argument in (6a) is somewhat more questionable. Schoorlemmer (1994) proposes, for an analogous pair of sentences with the predicate *vesel* 'merry', that a nominative subject receives a "modificational/predicational" thematic role, whereas its dative counterpart is an experiencer (p. 139).

Let us now briefly consider the syntactic behavior of the dative nominals under discussion. One question that is often raised in the context of dative experiencers is their grammatical status. Are these subjects or rather indirect objects which, in many languages, undergo movement to a sentence-initial position? In the latter case, what is the precise nature of this position? To illustrate, consider (6b) above. On the one hand, the DP appears to the left of the predicate (as subjects in an unmarked word order do in Russian); also, intuitively, it seems to constitute an analogue of the DP *Lena* in (6a), which is clearly a subject. On the other hand, *Lene* in (6b) lacks two important properties of prototypical subjects: it does not appear in the nominative case and does not trigger agreement on the predicate. (The two properties are, as mentioned above, interrelated.) Moreover, in sentences like (4a), dative experiencers even co-occur with a nominative argument (the stimulus). The latter constitutes a natural candidate for the role of the subject, despite its non-standard position.

Given this state of affairs, the grammatical status of the dative DP has to be determined on the basis of additional syntactic properties, often language-specific ones, which distinguish subjects from DPs bearing other grammatical functions. These include the licensing of subject-oriented anaphors, binding the null subject of a gerund, being conjoined with a nominative subject, being postposed in a construction with an expletive, etc. The results of applying such tests to dative experiencers turn out to be quite complex. First, they vary from language to language; for instance, Bayer (2004) shows that such datives pass certain subjecthood tests in Icelandic but not in German (although he claims that in both languages, these DPs constitute external arguments). Rákosi (2006) also mentions this difference between Icelandic on the one hand and German, as well as Dutch, Italian, Spanish and Rumanian, on the other. Rákosi further argues that in Hungarian, dative experiencer arguments are not subjects.

Second, native-speaker judgments sometimes vary even within a specific language, different tests may point in different directions, and the results altogether are not clear-cut. Unsurprisingly, opposite claims are made in the literature. For instance, Schoorlemmer (1994) and Kondrashova (1994) argue that in Russian, dative experiencer arguments of adjectival predicates are grammatical subjects. In contrast, Komar (1999) argues against this view.

2.2 ADDITIONAL ENVIRONMENTS

In a range of additional dative constructions, the use of this case is less obviously related to any particular theta-role. However, a deeper investigation of these phenomena typically takes us back to the thematic roles discussed at the beginning of this chapter. Several such constructions are illustrated below. All of them involve dative case which is at least arguably semantically motivated.

2.2.1 Modal Predicates

One well-attested use of the dative is exhibited by individual-type arguments of modal predicates. Thus, certain modal predicates, often adjectival, but sometimes also verbal, co-occur with dative DPs. The latter denote the subject/experiencer of the necessity or possibility state, for example the individual who is obliged or allowed to participate in a particular kind of event.

(7) a. RUSSIAN
        Mne   nado   domoj.
        Me$_{DAT}$ need   home
        'I need to go home.'
    b. HEBREW
        asur   li   linsoa   habayta.
        prohibited   me$_{DAT}$ go   home
        'I am not allowed to go home.'
    c. HUNGARIAN (Rákosi 2006:133)
        Niná-nak   új   cipő-k   kell-enek.
        Nina$_{DAT}$ new   shoe$_{PL}$ need$_{3PL}$
        'Nina needs new shoes.'
    d. ICELANDIC (Barðdal 2011:65)
        Honum   var   ekki   auðið   að . . .
        him$_{DAT}$ was   not   possible   to
        'He didn't have the chance to. . .'

It should be emphasized that not all modal predicates license dative arguments; some of them are accompanied by the more prototypical nominative subjects:

(8) HEBREW

    a. dana   yexola   linsoa   le-xeifa.
        Dana$_{NOM}$ can   go $_{DAT}$-Haifa
        'Dana can/may go to Haifa.'
    b. mutar   le-dana   linsoa   le-xeifa.
        allowed $_{DAT}$-Dana   go $_{DAT}$-Haifa
        'Dana is allowed to go to Haifa.'

Both sentences above express possibility, but different modality types are involved. (8a) is most likely to assert that Dana can go to Haifa given the circumstances, that is, circumstantial modality is involved. More generally, *yaxol* 'can' is one of the most basic possibility modals in Hebrew which is compatible with a wide range of readings. In contrast, *mutar* 'allowed' is limited to a deontic interpretation, hence (8b) means that Dana is allowed to go to Haifa (e.g. by her parents). While *yaxol* takes a nominative subject, *mutar* combines with a dative argument.

In general, datives seem to be associated more closely with deontic and bouletic modality than with epistemic and circumstantial ones. The argument of such modals may be analyzed as an experiencer or (meta-phorical) recipient of a modal state. Indeed, Rákosi (2006) treats this phenomenon together with (a certain subtype of) experiencer dative.

In this context, it is also worth mentioning dative subjects of infini-tival clauses which do not contain an overt modal but still receive a modalized meaning:

(9) RUSSIAN
     Mne   zavtra   rano   vstavat'.
     Me$_{DAT}$ tomorrow   early   wake.up$_{INF}$
     'I have to wake up early tomorrow.'

Although (9) does not contain an overt necessity operator, it receives a deontic modality interpretation: the speaker has to wake up early tomorrow. The source of this semantic component is subject to debate: for instance, while Kondrashova (1994) takes it to be contrib-uted by a phonologically empty modal operator, in her later work, she proposes, building on Stowell (1982), that the modal meaning comes from the infinitive itself (Kondrashova 2009).[2] (See also Pesetsky and Torrego 2004 on the distribution of realis and irrealis infinitives.)

Kondrashova (1994) argues convincingly that the dative DP in such sentences functions as the subject, and Komar (1999) agrees with this approach to the syntax of datives in infinitival clauses.

[2] The latter proposal is quite important, given that Russian non-finite clauses have been argued to contain dative subjects irrespective of their semantics. Dative is analyzed as the structural case assigned to (or checked on) the external argument by a non-finite T, in the same way as the structural nominative is assigned/checked by a finite T. Convincing evidence has been provided for treating the PRO subject in Russian control structures as dative, rather than caseless (see e.g. Franks 1995 and references therein). The data thus seem to point to the existence of a purely structural dative case which is not semantically motivated. However, if non-finite T itself is taken to contribute modal semantics, the whole approach to dative infinitive sentences needs reconsideration. I leave further investigation of this issue to future research.

2.2.2 Possessor Dative

Under the use illustrated below, a dative DP is interpreted as a possessor of another event participant. The dative phrase does not constitute a core argument of the verb.

(10) a. FRENCH (Boneh and Nash 2010, ex. 20a)
Marie   lui   a mis   la   main   sur   l'épaule
Marie   3SG.DAT   put   the   hand   on   the-shoulder
(*de son frère).
(of 3.POSS brother)
'Marie put a hand on her/his shoulder (affecting her/him).'

  b. GERMAN   (Deal 2017, ex. 53, taken from Lee-Schoenfeld 2006)
Er   ruinierte   mir   die   Wohnung.
he   ruined   me$_{DAT}$ the   place
'He ruined my place.'

  c. HEBREW
dani   Savar   le-moSe   et   ha-yad.
Dani   broke $_{DAT}$.Moshe ACC   the-arm
'Dani broke Moshe's arm (thereby affecting Moshe).'

  d. SPANISH (Cuervo 2003:77)
Pablo   le   besó   la   frente   a   Valeria.
Pablo   CL.DAT   kissed   the   forehead   DAT   Valeria
'Pablo kissed Valeria on the forehead', 'Pablo kissed Valeria's forehead'

To illustrate, the speaker is interpreted as the possessor of the place in (10b), due to the presence of the dative DP *mir* 'me'. In (10c), the broken arm is understood to be Moshe's (while in the absence of the dative DP the sentence would be most naturally interpreted as reporting Dani's breaking his own arm).

Sentences like (10) are also said to exhibit **external possession**. They can be minimally contrasted with **internal possession** sentences, in which the possessor appears, in a more traditional way, within the same DP as the possessee, often in the genitive form. For instance, (11a) and (11b) below illustrate internal possession, whereas (12a) and (12b) constitute their external possession counterparts:

(11) a. FRENCH   (Deal 2017, ex. 2a)
J'ai   pris   sa   main
I. have   taken   his   hand
'I took his hand.'

  b. RUSSIAN
Ja   položila   ruku   na   ego   plečo
I   put   hand   on   his$_{GEN}$ shoulder
'I put my hand on his shoulder.'

(12) a. FRENCH   (Deal 2017, ex. 1a)
          Je   lui   ai   pris   la   main.
          I   he$_{3.SG.DAT}$ have   taken the   hand
          'I took his hand.'
      b. RUSSIAN
          Ja   položila emu   ruku   na   plečo.
          I   put   him$_{DAT}$ hand   on   shoulder
          'I put my hand on his shoulder.'

An interesting observation about this construction, which has fasci-
nated linguists for several decades, has to do with the fact that the
dative behaves like a semantic argument of the possessee noun but
a syntactic argument of a verbal head (although, as mentioned above,
it is not a core argument of the V). In order to capture this discrepancy,
a **possessor raising** approach has been put forward, first formulated
as a transformational analysis and then changed in accordance with
the more recent developments of the generative theory (see e.g.
Landau's 1999 account of this phenomenon in Modern Hebrew). The
central idea behind this approach is that the external possessor (realized in many languages as a dative DP) is merged as an internal one,
inside the theme DP, and then undergoes movement to an external
position. (See Deal 2017 for a detailed overview.)

While rich evidence from a range of languages supports the movement approach (the support comes, e.g. from the sensitivity of external possession to island effects), a semantic observation poses
a challenge. It turns out that sentences exhibiting external possession
and their internal possession counterparts are not (or not always)
semantically equivalent. Subtle differences in meaning can be
observed, often related to the fact that dative possessors are understood to be affected by the event reported in the clause. Such an
affectedness meaning component does not characterize their genitive, internal, counterparts. To illustrate, consider the following contrast in Hebrew, described by Siegal and Boneh (2015):

(13) a. ben   šel   ariel   sharon   nixnas   la-politika.
          Son   of   Ariel   Sharon   entered $_{DAT}$.the-politics
          'A son of Ariel Sharon entered into politics.'
      b. #nixnas   le-ariel   sharon   ben   la-politka.
          entered $_{DAT}$-Ariel   Sharon   son $_{DAT}$.the-politics
          'A son of Ariel Sharon entered into politics, affecting him.'

While (13a), which contains an internal possessor, merely asserts that
Ariel Sharon's son entered into politics, (13b) with a dative possessor
DP further informs the hearer that Ariel Sharon is affected by this

eventuality. Given that Ariel Sharon is no longer alive, the second sentence, unlike the first one, is unacceptable.[3]

In order to reconcile the semantic non-equivalence with evidence for syntactic movement, some researchers have argued for a hybrid approach according to which the possessor is merged in a DP-internal position and undergoes movement to a thematic position. As a result, in addition to bearing the role of a possessor, it receives a second semantic role, which captures the contrast in meaning between internal and external structures. For instance, Lee-Schoenfeld (2006) argues that German possessor datives move to the specifier of $v_{BEN/MAL}$, which assigns to them the role of the affectee. Hence the affectedness interpretation which, intuitively, characterizes these arguments.

Alternative approaches to possessor datives, which unify them with additional uses of the dative case, are discussed in Section 2.3.1. The reader is also referred to Deal 2017 for a detailed discussion of syntactic approaches to external possession in a wide range of languages.

Finally, it is worth pointing out that in some languages, dative possessors are also found in the more standard possessive construction, in sentences of the "I have a book" kind. This is illustrated in (14):

(14) a. STANDARD SPOKEN TIBETAN (Bickel 2004, ex.17b; from Tournadre 1996:76)
khoṅ-la   deb   maṅ.po   yod-red.
3SG-DAT   book.$_{NOM}$ many   be.$_{ASSERTIVE.DISJUNCT}$
'He has got many books.'

b. KANNADA   (Amritavalli 2004:16)
avan-ige   aidu   makkaLu   iddaare
He.$_{DAT}$ five   children   are
'He has five children.' (Lit. 'to him five children are.')

Amritavalli (2004) argues that dative DPs in Kannada sentences like (14b) are not true subjects. Rather, these are benefactive datives whose case is checked/assigned by the possessive BE. This approach unifies such nominals with the datives illustrated in (3) above.

2.2.3 Co-Referential Dative Constructions (CDC)

Co-referential dative constructions involve a dative pronoun or pronominal clitic that is co-referential with the subject of the sentence. The appearance of the dative does not affect the truth conditions, but

---

[3] See also Cuervo (2003) for contrasts between external and internal possessives that are not based on affectedness.

rather has a pragmatic effect (Boneh and Nash 2010). The meaning component added in the presence of a co-referential dative relates to the way the subject experiences the event. It is specified that the subject perceives it positively, with "joy and easy-goingness" (Boneh and Nash 2010).

(15) a. HEBREW   (Boneh and Nash 2010, ex. 26a)
         rakadti   **li**   kol   ha-layla 'im   baxur   maksim
         danced$_{1.SG}$ me$_{.DAT}$ all the-night with guy charming
         'I danced me all night long with a charming guy.'
     b. RUSSIAN   (Boneh and Nash 2010, ex. 28a)
         Maša   guljala   sebje   po   gorodu
         Masha   strolled   REFL.DAT   around   town
         'Masha was strolling around the town.'
     c. SYRIAN ARABIC   (Boneh and Nash 2010, ex. 27a)
         salma   ra?ṣet-**l-a**   šway.
         Salma   danced$_{.3SF}$-to$_{.3SF}$ a little
         'Salma (just) danced a little (it's a minor issue).'

2.2.4 Ethical Dative

Ethical dative is yet another type of non-core non-truth-conditional dative. It typically appears on first- and second-person pronouns and indicates that its referent, who is introduced separately from event participants, exhibits interest or experiences some feelings toward the event. Janda (1997) emphasizes the subjective nature of such pragmatic uses of cases and proposes that in such instances, basic case meanings are applied "to domains other than perceived objective reality" (p. 13). Languages in which ethical dative is observed include German, Latin, Czech, Hebrew and Hungarian, among others.

(16) a. LATIN   (originally from Horace, quoted by Rákosi 2008:413)
         Quid   mihi   Celsus   agit?
         what   I$_{DAT}$ Celsus   does
         'What is Celsus doing, I wonder?'
     b. HUNGARIAN   (Rákosi 2008:413)
         Ez   meg   mi-t   csinál   itt   nek-em?
         this   and   what$_{ACC}$ does   here   DAT.1.SG
         'And what (the hell) is this one doing here?'

As can be seen from the translations, the speaker does not constitute an event participant in either (16a) or (16b). Rather, the first person singular dative pronoun indicates that the speaker experiences certain emotions toward the reported event.

2.2.5 Affected Dative

Although the concept of affectedness accompanies many kinds of datives mentioned above, sometimes affected dative is discussed as a separate category. Thus, Cuervo (2003) in her analysis of Spanish datives has a chapter devoted to "dative applicatives," dative arguments that combine with causative and inchoative verbs as illustrated in (17) below:

(17) SPANISH (Cuervo 2003:105)

A	Emilio	se	le	quemaron	las	tostadas.
DAT	Emilio	REFL	CL.DAT	burnt.$_{PL}$	the	toasts

'The toasts burnt on Emilio.'

2.2.6 Reduced Agentivity

Dative subjects may alternate with nominative or ergative ones in some languages, in which instances of dative marking are associated with reduced agentivity, lack of control and/or volitionality. In some cases, this contribution is essentially equivalent to turning the subject into an experiencer, and thus such uses seem to belong to Section 2.1, where the relation between the dative and specific theta-roles was discussed. In other examples, it is less obvious whether a shift from an agent to an experiencer takes place, but the degree of agentivity clearly becomes lower.

This phenomenon has been illustrated for Russian in (6), repeated below as (18) for the sake of convenience:

(18) RUSSIAN

a. Lena spokojna.
Lena.$_{NOM}$ calm.$_{F.SG}$
'Lena is calm.'

b. Lene spokojno.
Lena.$_{DAT}$ calm.$_{NEUT.SG}$
'Lena feels calm.'

(18a) may be used to report Lena's internal state or the way she behaves. In both instances, intuitively, she seems to have a certain degree of control over the situation. (18b) clearly reports her feelings, and here, control is absent. The state does not depend on Lena's desires (even though it is presumably perceived positively by her), it just comes about. Lena may be an experiencer in (18a), but even in that case (18b) is perceived as involving less control on the part of the subject.

While in (18), the dative alternates with the nominative, which is presumably a purely structural, non-semantic, case, in (19) the alternation is between the dative and the ergative. The latter, as discussed in Chapter 1, is strongly associated with agentivity. Therefore, in the ergative/dative contrast, a non-trivial question is raised as to whether it is the ergative that increases the degree of agentivity or the dative that reduces it (or both).

(19)   URDU/HINDI   (Butt and King 2005, ex. 3)

    a. nadya=ne   zu   ja-na   hε
       Nadya$_{F.SG=ERG}$ zoo$_{M.SG.OBL}$ go-$_{INF.M.SG}$ be$_{PRES.3.SG}$
       'Nadya wants to go to the zoo.'

    b. nadya=ko   zu   ja-na   hε
       Nadya$_{F.SG=DAT}$ zoo$_{M.SG.OBL}$ go-$_{INF.M.SG}$ be$_{PRES.3.SG}$
       'Nadya has to go to the zoo.'

Both sentences indicate that a certain relation holds between Nadya and the proposition *Nadya goes to the zoo* and both involve modality. However, (19b) with a dative subject indicates necessity/obligation, whereas (19a) with the nominative marking entails a desire. Even though the subject of *want* is not an agent, a higher degree of control is presumably reflected in the ergative version. (See Butt and King 2005 and Section 1.6.2 of Chapter 1 for further discussion of this example.)

2.3 DATIVE CASE: ANALYSES

The present section concentrates on several approaches to the dative case that have been proposed in the linguistic literature. Subsection 2.3.1 is devoted to those analyses that are primarily syntactic in nature (although they do capture certain semantic characteristics of dative nominals via the syntax–semantics interface). One of these approaches treats (certain uses of) the dative as assigned by the functional applicative head and the other by a phonologically empty preposition. In Subsection 2.3.2 I turn to an approach that relates more directly to semantics and takes dative case-marking to be interrelated with the presence of certain theta features. A review of Rákosi's analysis of Hungarian datives is followed by a discussion of the way in which a theta-oriented analysis can be formulated in order to capture Russian data.

It is important to emphasize that the analyses under discussion have been developed to account for somewhat different uses of the dative case and concentrate on different languages. Given the richness of the phenomenon, it is possible that more than one analysis is needed in order to capture the wide range of facts. The complexity of the dative is reflected in the fact that it is difficult to determine whether it is inherent or structural, and arguably, both types of datives are observed. As Landau (2010:21) points out: "The dative case is more complex, being structural in specific languages and contexts (e.g., double object constructions in English and Japanese, Romance causatives) and inherent in others (Romance double object constructions)."

2.3.1 Syntactic Approaches

2.3.1.1 *An Applicative Head*

The licensing of non-core datives is often associated in the recent literature with the presence of an applicative projection. This is a functional projection in whose specifier position a (dative) DP is merged. The latter is "structurally and semantically related to a constituent c-commanded by it" (Boneh and Nash 2010:1). Thus, an Appl head introduces an extra argument into the structure. Further, due to the semantic properties of this head, it is responsible for the experiencer/affectedness flavor that accompanies the interpretation of the DP. Thus, Boneh and Nash (2010) propose that "[a]ffectedness is the intrinsic interpretable feature of Appl" (p. 13).

Applicative heads are claimed to merge in different positions, which accounts for the variation that can be observed in the properties of non-core datives both cross-linguistically and within a given language. Thus, Pylkkänen (2000, 2002/2008) argues that a distinction should be made between **low applicatives** and **high applicatives**. The former denote a relation between two individuals, the direct object and the applied object (i.e. the argument introduced by Appl). The latter denote a relation between the applied object and the event (in line with the original proposal in Marantz 1993, on which Pylkkänen builds). Low applicative heads attach below the VP projection and high ones, above it (and below VoiceP, which introduces the external argument, following Kratzer 1994; see the structures in (21) below). Pylkkänen employs this distinction to account for a contrast between English and Chaga[4] constructions containing a benefactive. In English, a benefactive argument (also referred to by Pylkkänen as an applied object) is licensed with transitive verbs (which renders a double object construction) but not with unergative ones:

---

[4] Chaga is spoken in Tanzania and belongs to the Niger-Congo family.

(20) a. I baked a cake.   b. I baked him a cake.
      c. I ran.   d. *I ran him. (i.e. ran for him)

                                            (Pylkkänen 2000:197)

In contrast, in Chaga both kinds of constructions are acceptable.
Pylkkänen explains this difference by proposing that English has
only low applicatives, whereas Chaga also uses high ones. Since
a low applicative relates the benefactive argument to the direct object,
it is compatible with a transitive verb but not with an unergative one
(there is no direct object with the latter, which presumably results in
a type mismatch). In turn, a high applicative relates the benefactive to
the event argument, in which case it is not essential how many
individual participants are involved in the event. The following structural distinction between the two types (or, more precisely, two positions) of Appl is proposed:

(21)   (a) *High applicative* (Chaga)

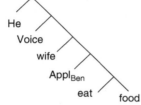

        (b) *Low applicative* (English)

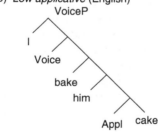

                                            (from Pylkkänen 2000:199)

Cuervo (2003) puts forward an applicative analysis to account for
a range of uses of the dative in Spanish. She argues that the specific
semantic role a given dative DP receives depends on a number of
factors, including the position of the applicative head (high or low),
the kind of head that takes it as the complement, as well as the type
of event denoted by the vP. She distinguishes three kinds of low
applicative heads: Low-Appl-TO, Low-Appl-FROM and Low-Appl-AT.
The former two are dynamic and the last one is static. The specifier of

Low-Appl-TO hosts applied recipients, the specifier of Low-Appl-FROM, applied sources (Pylkkänen's source applicatives), and Low-Appl-AT introduces dative possessors. The three types of datives are illustrated below (note that 22b is provided as an example of an applied source but can also be analyzed as involving possessor dative):

(22)   SPANISH   (Cuervo 2003:69–73)
  a. **applied recipient**
Pablo	le	pasó	un	mate	a	Andreína.
Pablo	CL.DAT	passed	a	mate	DAT	Andreína
     'Pablo handed Andreína a mate.'
  b. **applied source**
Pablo	le	robó	la	bicicleta	a	Andreína.
Pablo	CL.DAT	stole	the	bicycle	DAT	Andreína
     'Pablo stole the bicycle from Andreína.'
  c. **dative possessor**
Pablo	le	admira	la	paciencia	a	Valeria
Pablo	CL.DAT	admires	the	patience	DAT	Valeria
     'Pablo admires Valeria's patience.'

In turn, high applicatives host, for example, experiencers and ethical datives, and take a vP as their argument. Further, Cuervo argues for the existence of a third type, affected applicatives, which introduce affected datives in inchoative and causative constructions. The latter are analyzed as bi-eventive structures in which vP_{BE} is embedded under a dynamic predicate v_{DO} or v_{GO}. The applicative head takes vP_{BE} as its complement, thereby relating the dative argument to the result state, and the other vP is merged above it. Thus, ApplP appears between two little v projections.

Boneh and Nash (2010), who analyze data primarily from French, argue against the existence of low applicatives. However, they do maintain the view that applicatives may merge on different levels, although under their approach, all applicatives are high. Specifically, benefactive datives are merged above VP but below vP, and co-referential datives above vP but below TP. Moreover, the authors entertain the possibility that ethical datives are introduced by an Appl head which is merged even higher in the structure, possibly above TP. Thus, different types of non-core datives correspond to different levels at which an applicative head can be inserted into the structure.

In contrast, Siegal and Boneh (2015) argue for a unification of all truth-conditional non-core datives, at least in Hebrew. They claim that benefactive and malefactive datives, possessor datives and maybe even ethical datives (under some approaches to the latter) constitute

special instances of the same category, which they term affected
datives. The dative phrase denotes an affected participant in
a separate eventuality which is causally related to the event denoted
by the clause.

To sum up this subsection, the applicative approach to the dative
case is quite prominent in the recent literature. This approach takes
the dative nominal to be introduced into the structure via the applicative projection. The latter is also responsible for the affectedness-
related semantics associated with the DP. The analyses formulated
within this framework differ, sometimes quite considerably, in
terms of the number of Appl heads, the positions they occupy and
the range of additional factors that affect the semantic role of the
dative nominal.

2.3.1.2   An Empty Preposition Analysis

In his monograph *The Locative Syntax of Experiencers* Landau (2010)
argues that experiencer nominals in sentences like *The idea appealed
to Julie* are governed by a preposition even in those languages in which
no overt counterpart of *to* is present. This preposition, referred to as
$\emptyset_\psi$, assigns dative case to its complement. To illustrate, the VP in the
Russian sentence (23) below will have the structure in (24), based on
Landau (2010:(12b), p.8). (The tree represents the stage of the derivation before movement outside of the VP takes place, for instance, for
Extended Projection Principle reasons).

(23) Lene   nravitsja   éta   ideja.
      Lena$_{DAT}$ likes   this$_{NOM}$ idea$_{NOM}$
      'Lena likes this idea.'

(24)

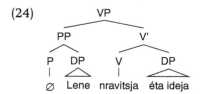

What looks like a "bare" dative nominal is thus a PP, headed by
a phonologically null preposition. It is from this preposition that the
nominal *Lena* receives inherent dative case.

Crucially, Landau treats experiencers as mental locations, with the
null preposition fulfilling a locative function. Following (in part),
some of the previous literature (e.g. Jackendoff 1990, Bouchard 1995,

Arad 1998), Landau analyzes the experiencer as the locus of emotion. This means that experiencer datives are, in a certain metaphorical sense, locations (e.g. Lena in (23) is the location of the 'liking' emotion; in a certain sense, the liking is IN Lena). Thus, in addition to syntactic motivation, the analysis has a semantic component. Under the experiencer use, the dative case correlates with a locative meaning, although the relation between the case and semantics is not direct. Rather, it is mediated by the null preposition.

Irrespective of the mental location component, the empty preposition analysis of dative nominals is also consistent with Pesetsky's (2013) approach to Russian case. Within the system Pesetsky develops, dative nouns are said to bear a suffix of the P category. Roughly, the dative (similarly to other oblique cases, such as the instrumental) is (systematically) assigned by a preposition. The latter can be either overt or covert.

The empty P approach to experiencers is also adopted in Baker (2015). The presence of the phonologically null P affects c-command relations and, as a result, the availability of dependent case-assignment.

2.3.2 Thematic Roles and Features of Which They Are Composed

2.3.2.1 *'Dative' Theta-Roles and Semantic Relations between Them*

It can be seen from Sections 2.1 and 2.2 that the dative case, however wide the spectrum of its uses may seem, is typically interrelated with a particular set of thematic roles: goal, recipient, experiencer and benefactive/malefactive. In turn, these roles, although not identical, are closely related to one another. For instance, a recipient can be viewed as a special instance of a goal, since the concept of change of location can be metaphorically extended to subsume change of possession. Further, the fact that both goals and experiencers are marked with the dative in a range of languages has been explained via the claim that an experiencer is a type of goal or a locative (see e.g. Mohanan and Mohanan 1990 and the discussion in Landau 2010:13). The treatment of experiencers as metaphorical locations has been discussed in the previous subsection. Also, Rappaport Hovav and Levin (2008) note that within the framework of the Localist Hypothesis, a recipient can be viewed as a kind of abstract goal. An experiencer, in turn, can be regarded as a recipient of an emotion.

Smith (1993), who analyzes the dative and accusative cases in German within the framework of cognitive linguistics, unifies many uses of the dative around the experiencer prototype. These include experiencers, recipients and benefactives, as well as possessor datives.

Dative case-marking in these instances is linked to the notion of **bilateral involvement**: on the one hand, a prototypical experiencer is, in a certain sense, affected by the energy involved in the event; on the other hand, it constitutes a (potential) source of energy on its own (see also Smith 2001).

Dabrowska (1997), who discusses in detail the semantic relations between the different uses of Polish datives, treats recipients as a special case of beneficiary, the latter being a broader, more inclusive category. She also points out that an experiencer argument is affected in the sense that "an event or process takes place in his sphere of awareness" (p. 41), and, as we know from the above discussion, affectedness is strongly interrelated with dative assignment. Indeed, the latter notion plays a crucial role within Dabrowska's account, formulated within the framework of cognitive linguistics. According to her analysis, the dative is assigned to a nominal denoting "the landmark participant [who] is affected by an action or process occurring in his personal sphere" (p. 64). A personal sphere, in turn, "comprises the persons, objects, locations, and facts sufficiently closely associated with an individual that any changes in them are likely to affect the individual as well" (p. 16). Dabrowska links the various functions of the dative to five sub-spheres: sphere of empathy, sphere of awareness, sphere of influence, sphere of potency and private sphere.

Dabrowska also notes that the idea of motion toward a goal could, given a sufficient level of abstraction, cover all the functions of the dative, including the goal/allative one. She argues for a different view of the allative uses of the Polish dative, however, proposing for them a historical analysis. She does suggest that the dative case on complements of the preposition *ku* 'to', 'towards' (which can be inanimate) is licensed due to abstraction: from the canonical concept of a personal sphere we get to a broader and more general notion of a region.

Unification of the dative functions on a highly abstract level is indeed observed in the literature. Levin (2008) points out that for some researchers, the term 'goal' covers, in addition to spatial goals, recipients, benefactives and experiencers. In turn, McFadden (2002), following Maling (2001), proposes that, for the purposes of a syntactic analysis, these thematic roles should be subsumed under a single macro-role, which he refers to as EXP. He states explicitly that this unification is made within the domain of purely syntactic conceptualization, with syntactic theta-roles being "related only in indirect fashion to semantic roles" (p. 6). Still, a semantic basis for such a unification is plausibly available.

It is worth noting that in certain languages, other grammatical cases unify some of the uses that are characteristic of datives. For instance, according to Comrie (2004), in Tsez, the lative (a local case) marks goals, recipients, experiencers and possessors in certain constructions, and also alternates with the ergative on subjects in order to reduce agentivity. Rappaport Hovav and Levin (2008) point out that the allative (a local case whose primary role is to mark a goal) can be extended to mark recipients. These facts suggest that the unification of the thematic roles in question by dative case-marking is not accidental, but rather has a conceptual basis.

DISCUSSION

In what ways can recipients be unified with benefactives?

In addition to analyzing dative case-marking in terms of thematic roles or macro-roles, it is possible to take a different but related direction and concentrate on those features into which such roles can be decomposed. It has been proposed in the linguistic literature that theta-roles should not be regarded as primitives but rather as clusters of features. For instance, agentivity can be analyzed as built of such features as sentience, volitionality and causality. Dowty (1991) substitutes traditional thematic roles by two cluster concepts, Proto-Agent and Proto-Patient, each of which consists of a set of entailments. To illustrate, Proto-Agent entailments include volitional involvement in the event and sentience (and/or perception). Proto-Patient entailments can be exemplified by undergoing a change of state and being causally affected by another participant. While Dowty states explicitly that this system should not be equated with theta-role decomposition, his approach contributes considerably to the understanding of the fine-grained concepts that lie behind traditional thematic roles. A range of different approaches to theta-role decomposition have been proposed, one of which (Reinhart's 2000, 2002 Theta System) will be discussed in some detail in subsection 2.3.3.2.

Grimm (2005) analyzes dative experiencers, as well as dative subjects in Hindi/Urdu, using his more general system designed for the purposes of capturing the semantic correlates of case-assignment across languages and across phenomena. The system Grimm develops involves a set of binary features, largely (but not

exclusively) related to Proto-Agent entailments, such as [+/− voli-
tion], [+/− motion], [+/− existential persistence], [+/− sentience]. In
the spirit of Aissen's (2003) work, he constructs a lattice,
a structure within which the combinations of the properties in
question are partially ordered, with more agent-like/individuated
clusters receiving a higher ranking than the more patient-like/ less
individuated ones.[5]

Let us now turn back to the dative. Grimm points out that this case
canonically marks indirect objects bearing the role of a recipient or
a beneficiary, and that the latter is consciously involved in the event
(i.e. [+sentient]) and qualitatively affected by it. With experiencer
subjects, too, mental involvement of some kind or other is entailed.
Further, specifically in Urdu/Hindi, dative case marks subjects of verbs
denoting "physical sensations and conditions, psychological or mental states, but also those of wanting/needing, obligation or compul-
sion, and events not controlled by, but affecting, a subject, including
such verbs as 'find', 'receive' " (p. 69). It is at least not obvious that the
term 'experiencer' is appropriate in some of these instances (e.g. as the
subject of *find*), but they all seem to be unified by such characteristics
as animacy, mental involvement and lack of control over the event.

Grimm emphasizes that the features involved in the canonical uses
of the dative are also reflected in the instances of its non-canonical
assignment, and links this case to **sentience** and **non-volitionality**.

What we see is that this analysis employs features that contribute to
(proto-)agentivity or its absence, rather than theta-role labels, in order
to unify several uses of the dative and their relation to semantics. In
the following subsections, we consider additional approaches that
take this line of analyzing dative case-marking.

2.3.2.2 *Dative Case and Binary Features: HUNGARIAN (Rákosi 2006)*

Rákosi (2006) puts forward an analysis of dative experiencers in
Hungarian. Her approach is based not on thematic roles as primitives,
but rather on features into which these roles can be decomposed.
Specifically, a crucial role is played by two binary features: [+/−c]
(causes change) and [+/−m] (mental state is relevant).

Rákosi's analysis is formulated within the framework of Reinhart's
(2000, 2002) Theta System. This system classifies the thematic domain
by relating explicitly to the two features mentioned above. The feature
[+/−c] has to do with causality; for instance, the [+c] specification
characterizes those arguments that are traditionally characterized as

---

[5] For Aissen's lattice, see Chapter 5 below.

agents and instruments. The feature [+/–m] is interrelated with sentience and animacy (as only an animate being can be mentally involved in an event); [+m] is characteristic of, for example, agents and experiencers. A predicate may also leave a given feature of its argument underspecified. This renders three specification options for each feature and, as a result, nine possible combinations, called theta clusters. Although original thematic roles are not employed in the Theta System, Reinhart specifies correspondences between the clusters and theta-role labels. To illustrate, an agent (e.g. the external argument of the verb *murder*), is assigned the coding [+c+m], as it is a cause whose mental state is relevant. An experiencer is [–c+m]: its mental state is definitely relevant, but it does not cause any change. In turn, the external argument of a verb like *open* can be an agent, a natural force, or an instrument. All of these share the property of being causes but differ in terms of mental involvement (present, e.g. for an agent but not for an instrument). In such instances, the mental state feature is taken to be underspecified, and we get the cluster [+c]. Ultimately, the interpretation may be [+c+m], as well as [+c–m], depending on the individual sentence and the context in which it is uttered.

Turning back to Hungarian, Rákosi argues for the existence of three types of dative experiencer: arguments, thematic adjuncts and more standard adjuncts, groups which differ from one another both semantically and syntactically. Thematic adjuncts have an intermediate status between an argument and an adjunct, that is, they are optional but (crucially) theta-marked. The three kinds are illustrated in (25) below:

(25) HUNGARIAN (Rákosi 2006:9–11)

    a. Ez   tetsz-ik   Péter-nek.   argument
       this   appeal.$_{3SG}$ Peter.$_{DAT}$
       'This appeals to Peter.'

    b. Ez   jó   nek-em.   thematic adjunct
       this good DAT.1.SG
       'This is good to me.'

    c. Nek-em   szép   ez   a   kép.   real adjunct
       DAT.1.SG beautiful this the picture
       'To me, this picture is beautiful.'

It is worth pointing out that the category of thematic adjunct includes datives that appear with modal predicates, of the type illustrated in Section 2.2.1. Rákosi argues that datives exhibited in such constructions as (26) are not arguments of the adjectival modals but rather their thematic adjuncts.

(26) Ez   lehetséges   nek-em.
      this   possible   DAT.1.SG
      'This is possible to me.'

Let us now turn to the analysis proposed for these three types. Dative arguments like the one illustrated in (25a) are experiencers, meaning that they are specified in the theta-grid of the verb as the cluster [−c+m].

In contrast, dative thematic adjuncts may but need not be interpreted as experiencers: (27) illustrates that these DPs may be inanimate (and thus not mentally involved):

(27) Ez   fontos   a   fá-k-nak.
      this   important   the   tree.-PL-DAT
      'This is important for the trees.'

(Rákosi 2006:10)

Rákosi proposes that they receive the specification [−c], which unifies them with goals/benefactives (note that the latter, too, receive dative case-marking in numerous languages). The idea is that dative thematic adjuncts are not causes and their mental state may but need not be relevant (see (25b) versus (27)), hence no specification of the [+/−m] feature. In addition, Rákosi points out that these DPs may be affected; however, affectedness cannot be directly related to within Reinhart's Theta System. Still, [−c] is compatible with affectedness since affected participants are not causes. Further, Rákosi proposes that the datives under discussion are licensed by those predicates whose subject is coded as [−m]; that is, it is not mentally involved and constitutes a potential cause. If, in a given sentence, the subject does receive a causer interpretation ([−m+c]), the [−c] (dative) participant may become affected by the eventuality that is caused. Thus, the proposed configuration makes the dative thematic adjunct a potential candidate for an affected entity.

Syntactically, dative thematic adjuncts are merged inside the VP.

Finally, real adjuncts (25c), unlike the other two kinds, do not receive a thematic specification and are in principle compatible with any predicate, that is, their licensing does not depend on the semantic nature of the latter. Unlike thematic adjuncts, they are VP-external and tend to appear on the left periphery of the clause.

2.3.2.3 Dative and Binary Features: RUSSIAN

Russian is among those languages in which animacy plays a crucial role in the licensing of semantically motivated datives (as opposed to purely syntactic or idiosyncratic licensing, which will be addressed at the end of this subsection). It thus conforms to Aristar's (1996, 1997) claim that, across languages, the dative case is animacy-oriented. In Russian, both core and non-core datives (arguments as well as thematic adjuncts in the sense of Rákosi) are generally associated with the [−c+m] interpretation. Essentially, these are animate arguments[6] that (unlike agents) do not exhibit control over events. They are mentally involved but do not cause a change in another argument. While this combination of features defines the experiencer role in Reinhart's system, it is also compatible with additional interpretations, such as the benefactive/malefactive and recipient. While Reinhart treats goals and beneficiaries together as [−c], with the value for mental involvement left unspecified, this cluster is compatible with the [−c+m] construal, and the latter is, in fact, typical for beneficiaries if they are to be distinguished from spatial goals. As we will see below, Russian grammar distinguishes between these two thematic roles. Prototypical recipients, too, are animate and do not constitute causes.

Let us consider evidence that animacy does indeed play a significant role in the licensing of the dative case.

First of all, it should be pointed out that inanimate, spatial goals cannot appear in the dative case in Russian (in contrast to many other languages, see Section 2.1). Thus, in (28) below, the goal has to be realized as a prepositional phrase. The dative variant forces a recipient reading, and since the wall and London cannot function as recipients, the sentences become unacceptable:

(28) a. Dima   brosil   mjač   v   stenu / #stene.
        Dima   threw   ball   in   wall$_{ACC}$ wall$_{DAT}$
        'Dima threw a ball to a wall.'
     b. Dina   otpravila   posylku   v   London / #Londonu.
        Dina   sent   parcel   in   London$_{ACC}$ London$_{DAT}$
        'Dina sent a parcel to London.'

In this respect, the Russian construction with a dative DP strongly resembles the English double object construction (as opposed to the *to*-variant, used in the translations of 28):[7]

---

[6] I use the term *argument* in a broad sense, to include not only arguments of the verb but also ones that are taken, within a minimalist analysis, to be introduced by functional heads, such as, e.g. Appl.

[7] See Krifka (2004), Rappaport Hovav and Levin (2008) and references therein for a discussion of the dative alternation in English and its relation to theta-role assignment.

(29)　a.　#John threw the wall a ball.
　　　　b.　#Mary sent London a parcel.

As expected, animate recipients are fine in the dative, and so are benefactives and experiencers:

(30)　a.　Dima　brosil　mjač　Lene.
　　　　　　Dima　threw　ball$_{ACC}$　Lena$_{DAT}$
　　　　　　'Dima threw a ball to Lena.'
　　　　b.　Dima　ispëk　Lene　tort.
　　　　　　Dima　baked　Lena$_{DAT}$　cake$_{ACC}$
　　　　　　'Dima baked a cake for Lena.'
　　　　c.　Dime　　　grustno.
　　　　　　Dima$_{DAT}$　sad$_{NEUT.SG}$
　　　　　　'Dima is/feels sad.'

Second, it has been demonstrated that in certain languages, the recipient and benefactive/malefactive dative can be extended to inanimate objects, as long as they can be conceived of as receiving (getting) an object or as benefiting from (or being harmed by) a certain entity or action. This is illustrated in (31) for recipients in Spanish and for benefactives in Hungarian.

(31)　a.　SPANISH (Cuervo 2003:70)
　　　　　　Le　　　puse　el　mantel　a　la　mesa.
　　　　　　CL.DAT　put$_{1SG}$　the　tablecloth　DAT　the　table
　　　　　　'I put the tablecloth on the table.'
　　　　b.　HUNGARIAN (Rákosi 2006:133)
　　　　　　A　fokhagyma　jó　a　hangszalag-ok-nak.
　　　　　　the　garlic　good　the　vocal.cord$_{PL-DAT}$
　　　　　　'Garlic is good for the vocal cords.'

Cuervo claims that in (31a), dative case is appropriate because the table can be conceptualized as a kind of recipient, an entity that receives the tablecloth. In turn, according to Rákosi (2006), the licensing of a dative DP in (31b) is related to the fact that the vocal cords are treated as a benefactive. It is worth noting, though, that the table in the first sentence can also be analyzed as a goal (which, too, would receive dative marking in Spanish), and that the vocal cords do not constitute a prototypical benefactive.

Crucially, the use of the dative case in analogous Russian sentences is unacceptable. In order for the dative to be licensed, the corresponding argument must be animate or at least personified.

(32) a. Ja   postelila / položila skatert'   na stol /   *stolu.
          I   spread /   put   tablecloth   on table$_{ACC}$ table$_{DAT}$
          'I put the tablecloth on the table.'
      b. Česnok polezen dlja svjazok   /   *svjazkam.
          Garlic useful   for   vocal-cords$_{GEN}$ vocal-cords$_{DAT}$
          'Garlic is good for the vocal cords.'

(32b) can be compared to (33), which contains a prototypical animate
benefactive. In this instance, both a dative DP and a *dlja*-PP constitute
acceptable realizations of the corresponding argument.

(33) Saxar   polezen malen'kim   mal'čikam   /   dlja   malen'kix
      Sugar   useful   little$_{DAT}$ boys$_{DAT}$ for   little$_{GEN}$
      mal'čikov.
      boys$_{GEN}$
      'Sugar is good for little boys.'

The acceptability of (32b) with the PP variant reveals that the predicate
polezen does not impose an animacy requirement on its thematic
adjunct and is compatible with the latter being [–m]. This is in line
with Reinhart's and Rákosi's prediction that predicates of this kind
impose the [–c] requirement on this dependent, leaving the value of its
[+/–m] feature unspecified. The dative, however, turns out to be more
selective. Apparently, it looks not only on the requirements of the
predicate but also on the specific construal involved in a given sentence, and is compatible only with the [–c+m] extension.
Alternatively, one could argue that the dative itself makes
a semantic contribution, marking the DP as [–c+m]. If the argument
is semantically incompatible with the [+m] feature (is inanimate and
cannot be personified), the clash between its semantics and the
requirements of the dative will result in unacceptability.

To some up thus far, the [–cause], [+animate] (or [–c+m]) restriction
does the job of unifying experiencers, recipients and benefactives/
malefactives and excluding the non-prototypical inanimate bearers
of such roles. It also correctly rules out dative case-marking on DPs
fulfilling a range of alternative roles. Thus, instruments and agents are
predicted not to appear in the dative since they are causes, and indeed,
such nominals do not generally receive dative case.[8] Further, spatial
goals are ruled out since they are inanimate and cannot be mentally
involved. Finally, themes are not expected to appear in the dative
since they are unspecified for animacy. Thus far, we have succeeded
in capturing the distribution of dative arguments in Russian.

---

[8] Unless a purely syntactic condition is involved; see discussion below.

As mentioned above, there exist uses of the dative which (arguably) are not dependent on semantics; in these instances, the animacy condition need not be observed. Firstly, certain Russian prepositions require that their complements appear in the dative case. Plausibly, this requirement is idiosyncratic, which is expected when case-checking by a P head is involved (see e.g. Woolford 2006). Thus, the dative is lexical in such instances.

(34) Ivan   šël   po   tropinke.
      Ivan   walked along   trail$_{DAT}$
      'Ivan walked along the trail.'

Still, it is worth mentioning that the preposition which marks animate goals, *k* 'to (the place of)', requires a dative DP, a fact that may be semantically motivated.[9]

(35) Ivan   šël   k   Maše.
      Ivan   walked to   Masha$_{DAT}$
      'Ivan went to (visit) Masha.'

Secondly, it has been argued that dative case is assigned to subjects of Russian infinitival clauses (see e.g. Franks 1995 and references therein). Presumably, in such instances, semantic factors do not play a role. However, the issue requires further investigation since non-finiteness is often closely interrelated with a modal interpretation (see e.g. Stowell 1982, Pesetsky and Torrego 2004, Kondrashova 2009). This link raises the question of whether this use of dative case is related primarily to a syntactic feature or to modality. (See also footnote 2.)

Finally, let us also consider a problem that the animacy (or [+m]) approach raises. Some Russian modals appear with dative arguments (or thematic adjuncts), as they do in Hungarian and a range of other languages. The tendency in Russian is for dative DPs to co-occur with deontic, bouletic and teleological modals, which, in turn, are likely to take animate arguments. In contrast, the basic modals *dolžen* 'must' and *možet* 'may', which are compatible with a range of readings, including the epistemic one, combine with nominative subjects.

(36) a. Ivan   možet   guljat'   po   parku.
          Ivan$_{NOM}$ may   walk   along   park
          'Ivan may be walking in the park (right now)', 'Ivan is allowed to walk in the park.'

---

[9] When used with inanimate complements, the preposition receives the meaning 'towards'. The case of the complement remains dative.

    b. Ivanu   možno   guljat'   po   parku.
        Ivan$_{DAT}$ is-allowed-to walk   along   park
        'Ivan is allowed to work in the park.'

Predictably, the subject of *možet* may be inanimate, but the dative
argument of the deontic *možno* is required to be animate.

(37) a. Étot   stul   možet   zdes'   stojat'.
         This$_{NOM}$ chair$_{NOM}$ may   here   stand
         'This chair may stand here.'
     b. #Étomu   stulu   možno   zdes'   stojat'.
         This$_{DAT}$ chair$_{DAT}$ is-allowed-to   here   stand
         'This chair is allowed to stand here.'

If we look deeper, however, the data turn out to be more complex than
that. For instance, the adjective *objazan* '(is) obliged' takes
a nominative argument, in spite of its deontic nature. And, more
crucially for our purposes, with some modals, an inanimate dative
argument is allowed:

(38) Étomu   domu   trebuetsja   remont.
      This$_{DAT}$ house$_{DAT}$ require$_{REFL}$ renovation$_{NOM}$
      'This house is in need of renovation.'

A detailed analysis of case–modal correlations is required in order
to figure out whether examples like (38) can be reconciled with the
[−c+m] approach to Russian dative or rather force us to reject it.

    In any event, both Russian and Hungarian datives exhibit a strong
tendency toward the [−c+m] pattern. In other words, such nominals
are [+m] like prototypical subjects but [−c] like prototypical objects.
This kind of duality receives a central role in some of the analyses
proposed for the dative case within the cognitive framework (e.g.
Smith 1985, Janda 1993). For instance, Janda (1993), who concentrates
on dative nominals in Czech and Russian, discusses the cognitive
network of different sub-meanings of this case, dividing its functions
into two schemas, one for indirect objects and one for free datives.
Each schema covers various sub-uses of the dative. Crucially, following Smith's (1985) approach to the German dative, Janda treats this
case as unique in the sense of being "both an object of a verb and
a subject of a potential verb, both controlled and controlling" (p. 56).
The idea is that dative nominals combine properties of prototypical
subjects with those of prototypical objects, those of agents with those
of patients. Like patients, datives are affected and do not control the

event described by the clause. But they also constitute potential agents/controllers (Smith 1985) given their agent-like characteristics: after all, they are sentient; further, they are characterized by independent existence (Jakobson 1957/1971), which constitutes a Proto-Agent property (Dowty 1991). Smith points out that in many instances, the dative participant constitutes an implied agent of a further eventuality which is expected to follow the event denoted by the sentence. The schemas provided for datives by Smith (1985) and Janda (1993) represent the dative participant as both a (potential) actor and an entity acted upon. (For the sake of comparison, let us point out that the prototypical nominative is treated under Smith's analysis as acting upon another participant, and the accusative, as being acted upon (by the nominative). The dative combines properties of both.) The idea that dative nominals evoke both agent-like and patient-like properties is further developed in Smith (1993), (2002) and (2005). To sum up, what we see is that the cognitive analyses and the binary features approach, despite the dramatic differences between them, share the feature of treating the dative as combining agent-like and patient-like characteristics.

2.4 CONCLUSION

To sum up this chapter, the dative case poses numerous challenges to the linguistic analysis, but at the same time, it reveals quite clearly that case-marking can be strongly interrelated with meaning, specifically, with thematic roles and strongly associated concepts. Across languages, the sets of theta-roles whose assignment is accompanied by dative case-marking overlap quite significantly. A closer consideration of the Russian and Hungarian data suggests that theta features are particularly useful for the purposes of making generalizations regarding the distribution of the dative. Still, the high number of constructions in which these case is observed makes its investigation quite challenging: in different instances the dative exhibits properties of a structural, inherent and lexical case, sometimes semantically motivated and sometimes purely syntactic or idiosyncratic.

FURTHER READING

Pylkkänen's (2002/2008) book introduces high and low applicatives, their syntactic and semantic properties, and discusses in detail applicative constructions in a range of languages, as different as Hebrew and Japanese, for example. The author also discusses other types of argument introducers.

Cuervo's (2003) dissertation is dedicated to the syntax and semantics of dative nominals, primarily in Spanish. The author considers a wide range of uses of the dative case and relates its properties to the structural position occupied by the corresponding DP. The author adopts (and extends) the approach which links the assignment of the dative case to the applicative head.

Rákosi's (2006) dissertation is devoted to three types of dative experiencers in Hungarian. The author captures the syntax–semantics interface of the phenomenon by relating to binary features [+/–c] (causes change) and [+/–m] (mental state is relevant), as well as to the status of the DP as an argument, an adjunct or a thematic adjunct (in some sense, an intermediate category).

Dative case semantics has received considerable attention in cognitive linguistic literature. Smith (1985, 1993, 2002, 2005) analyzes the various uses of this case in German and discusses dative nominals as involving an interaction of agent- and patient-like characteristics. Janda (1993) discusses this case in Czech and further provides a comparison between Czech and Russian facts. In turn, Dabrowska (1997) concentrates on the dative in Polish.

3 Spatial Cases

3.1 SPATIAL CASES: AN INTRODUCTION

The primary, basic, function of spatial, or local, cases is to mark spatial relations between objects, including directionality of motion and spatial configuration. In many languages, these relations are represented via prepositions, for example in English, *to* and *from* reflect directionality, while *in*, *on* and *above* specify configuration. These theoretical notions will be explored in more detail in the following sections. As a primary illustration of the role of case in the spatial domain, consider the following examples from several different languages:

(1) a. HUNGARIAN (from Hegedüs 2008, as quoted in Lestrade 2010)
   A   ház-ban   állok.
   the   house.$_{\text{INESS}}$ stand$_{\text{1SG}}$
   'I'm standing in the house.'

   b. A   ház-on   állok.
   the   house.$_{\text{SUPER}}$ stand$_{\text{1SG}}$
   'I'm standing on the house.'

   c. HEBREW
   nasati   yeruSalaim-a.
   went$_{\text{1SG}}$ Jerusalem.$_{\text{GOAL}}$
   'I went to Jerusalem.'

   d. LEZGIAN (from van Riemsdijk and Huybregts 2007)
   sew -   re -   q^{h} -   -aj
   bear   AUGM   BEHIND   FROM
   'from behind the bear'

In the Hungarian example (1a), the inessive case suffix *-ban* specifies the position occupied by the speaker relative to the house; specifically, we are informed that the speaker is standing **inside** the house.

In (1b), another (superessive) case is used; as a result, the described configuration is different, and the sentence reports that the speaker is standing **on** the house.

In the Hebrew example (1c), the suffix -*a* marks Jerusalem as the goal toward which motion is directed.

Finally, in the Lezgian example in (1d), two case suffixes provide the same information that is contributed by the English prepositions *from* and *behind* in the translation. The suffix -q^h relates the entity that undergoes motion to a position behind the bear. The suffix -*aj* further specifies that this position constitutes the source of the motion event, that is, motion begins behind the bear and then proceeds away from this place.

For the sake of illustration of a spatial case system of a given language, consider the following sentences in Finnish:

(2) a. Hiiri   juoksi   laatikkoon.
         mouse   ran   box$_{ILL}$
         'A/The mouse ran into the box.'

     b. Hiiri   juoksi   laatikossa.
         mouse   ran   box$_{INESS}$
         'A/The mouse ran in the box.'

     c. Hiiri   juoksi   laatikosta.
         mouse   ran   box$_{EL}$
         'A/The mouse ran out of the box.'

     d. Hiiri   juoksi   laatikolle.
         mouse   ran   box$_{ALL}$
         'A/The mouse ran onto the box.'

     e. Hiiri   juoksi   laatikolla.
         mouse   ran   box$_{ADESS}$
         'A/The mouse ran on top of the box.'

     f. Hiiri   juoksi   laatikolta.
         mouse   ran   box$_{ABL}$
         'A/The mouse ran from on the box.'

Finnish has six spatial cases: illative, inessive, elative, allative, adessive and ablative. All of them are illustrated in (2); note that the sentences are identical except for the case-marking on the noun *laatikko* 'box'. Illative (2a) and allative (2d) mark the noun phrase as a goal. Inessive (2b) and adessive (2e) specify that it fulfills the role of location. Finally, elative (2c) and ablative (2f) mark it as a source. In this way, the spatial cases of Finnish are related to (spatially relevant) thematic roles.

However, this is not the whole story. Within each of these thematic roles (goal, source and location), a further division into two sub-meanings is found, which is why each role is associated with two cases. Specifically, we are dealing with a division into what are sometimes called **internal** versus **external** cases. This contrast is essentially the same as the one observed in the Hungarian examples (1a) and (1b) above. For instance, while both (2b) and (2e) mark the box as the location of the running event, (2b) asserts that the mouse was running **in** the box and (2e) that it was running **on** the box. In other words, the mouse is located internally to the box if the case is inessive and externally to the box if it is adessive. The contrast between (2a) and (2d) is analogous. According to (2a), the motion event is directed to a location inside the box; that is, if the event reaches completion, the mouse gets into the box at its endpoint. In contrast, according to (2d), motion is directed to a position on top of the box. A similar opposition applies to the sources characterized in (2c) and (2f).

The Finnish facts described above are summarized in Table 3.1.

Before turning to a more detailed discussion of the types of meaning components contributed by spatial cases, it is worth noting that the phenomenon is rather widespread in languages of the world. Spatial cases are found in numerous languages belonging to different families, including Finnish, Estonian and Hungarian (Finno-Ugric), Lezgian, Bezhta, Tabasaran and Tsez (Northeast Caucasian, also known as Nakh-Daghestanian), Malayalam (Dravidian), West Greenlandic (Eskimo-Aleut), Armenian, Albanian and Sanskrit (Indo-European), Turkish (Turkic), Basque. This list is merely illustrative and definitely very far from exhaustive. The number of spatial cases in a language varies quite considerably. Thus, Modern Hebrew uses just one spatial case non-productively; Dyirbal has three spatial cases; Finnish has six, while Northern dialects of Tabasaran have either twelve or forty-eight spatial cases, depending on the way in which one performs the counting (more on this in Comrie and Polinsky 1998 and in Section 3.3).

Table 3.1 *Spatial cases in Finnish*

Case	Thematic role (directionality)	Internal/external (configuration)
illative	goal	internal
inessive	location	internal
elative	source	internal
allative	goal	external
adessive	location	external
ablative	source	external

3.2 SEMANTICS OF SPATIAL CASES

The discussion in this section is largely based on Lestrade's (2010) dissertation, which involves a detailed cross-linguistic investigation of spatial case systems. The major notions expressed by spatial cases are **directionality** and **configuration**. These concepts, also referred to as **path** versus **location**, have been assigned great importance in the linguistic literature that deals with the spatial dimension, from both the semantic and the grammatical perspective (see e.g. Hjelmslev (1935/37), Jackendoff (1983, 1990), Talmy (1983), Langacker (1987, 1991), Koopman (2000), van Riemsdijk and Huybregts (2007), Lestrade (2010) and references therein). Each of these notions and its role in the semantics of case is discussed in the following subsections.

3.2.1 Configuration

Configuration deals with the relative position of two objects in space. Note that location is an inherently relational notion. If we want to explain where a certain entity is located, we need to state something about its position **relative to other objects**. *In my room, near the house, on the roof, under the table, on my left* – all of these relate an argument that is being located to another object. The entity whose location is being communicated is called the **figure, theme** or **trajector** (different terms are used within different theoretical frameworks, but the concepts are quite similar), and the object relative to which the location is specified, that is, the entity that is used in order to help locate the figure, is called the **ground, reference object** or **landmark**. (The terms trajectory and landmark were introduced by Langacker, see e.g. Langacker 1987.) Talmy (2000:312) provides the following definitions of the two notions:

> The figure is a moving or conceptually movable entity whose path, site, or orientation is conceived as a variable, the particular value of which is the relevant issue. The ground is a reference entity, one that has a stationary setting relative to a reference frame, with respect to which the figure's path, site, or orientation is characterized.

When we define the location of an object with the help of another one, different spatial relations may hold between the two. To illustrate, let our figure be a ball and our ground a table. While specifying the location of the ball, we are not limited to stating that it is located, roughly, in the area of the table. We can be much more specific. We can state that the ball is **under** the table, **on** the table, **near** the table,

behind the table, etc. These are all different values of the configuration function.

In the above example, the different configuration options are represented by different prepositions, for example *on* versus *under* versus *behind*. But some languages convey information regarding configuration using case. This is illustrated in the Hungarian example (1) above, where the difference between *in a house* and *on a house* is encoded in the case system. The internal meaning is conveyed when the noun appears in the inessive case and the external one obtains when the noun is superessive. Further examples will be provided in what follows.

3.2.2 Directionality

Directionality has to do with a change of location and, more specifically, a change in the relative position of the figure and the ground that takes place in the course of an event. It is here that the contrast between such thematic roles as **goal**, **location** and **source** becomes relevant. Suppose that an event of motion occurs in whose course the figure changes its location. Then a given spatial relation between the figure and the ground may hold at different stages of the event. To illustrate, consider the location *under the bridge*. Suppose further that we are dealing with an event of floating, and the object undergoing motion (the figure) is a boat. The boat may start floating while in a different location and finish floating when it gets under the bridge, that is it may float (to) under the bridge. In this case, *under the bridge* corresponds to the **goal** of the motion event, the location that the boat comes to occupy at the endpoint. Alternatively, the boat could be located under the bridge throughout the floating event. In this case, *under the bridge* constitutes the **location** in which the event takes place. Also, the boat could start floating while under the bridge and then float away from this place. That would mean that *under the bridge* is the **source**.

More generally, exactly the same configuration could correspond to the location occupied by the figure throughout the event, to the location where it starts its motion and away from which it moves, or the location to which motion is directed. Thus, on top of the configuration function we get the directionality distinction between source, location and goal.

In fact, these three options are not the only ones. While Lestrade (2010) proposes that this three-way distinction is indeed the basic one, there do exist additional values of the directionality function, such as VIA, TOWARD and AWAY-FROM (see Jackendoff 1983). Lestrade argues that all these functions are derived from goal and source. For instance, TOWARD and AWAY-FROM constitute atelic versions of goal and source. Consider the contrast in (3):

(3) a. John walked to the castle.
     b. John walked toward the castle.

The event predicate in (3a) is telic: the event is associated with an inherent natural endpoint. The goal phrase provides the path along which John moves with a final boundary. As soon as this boundary is reached, the walking event is completed. In contrast, (3b) is atelic. The *toward*-phrase only supplies direction but does not make the path bounded. The contrast in telicity is strongly related to the fact that the predicate in (3b) is cumulative, whereas the one in (3a) is quantized. Thus, an event of walking toward the castle can be further divided into two sub-events of walking toward the castle. In contrast, an event of walking to the castle cannot contain two proper sub-events of walking to the castle (in the course of both of which the goal is reached).

Lestrade puts forward definitions of TOWARD and AWAY-FROM which are based on the concepts of goal and source. Intuitively, "AWAY-FROM is a path that can combine with a Source to become a Source" (p. 85). Analogously, TOWARD is a path that can combine with a goal and become a goal (i.e. become a bounded path that has a final point).

Further, Lestrade proposes that VIA constitutes a combination of a goal and a source. To illustrate, if a given path lies VIA the crossroads, this means that it can be divided into two sub-paths: one for which the crossroads is the goal and one for which it is the source. First we have a sub-path that starts in a different location and ends at the crossroads. Then we proceed along a sub-path that starts at the crossroads and heads elsewhere.[1]

To sum up thus far, we have listed the following directionality meanings that can be expressed within a case system of a language: location, goal, source, TOWARD, AWAY-FROM and VIA. Additional meanings are occasionally found, such as UP-TO in Hungarian. Lestrade further arranges these on an implicational scale of directionality distinctions:

(4) Place > Goal, Source > VIA, TOWARD, UP-TO, . . .

(4) is to be interpreted in the following way. A case system of a language is predicted to express a given directionality meaning only if it

---

[1] For formal definitions of TOWARD, AWAY-FROM and VIA, see Lestrade (2010:85).

expresses the meanings that appear higher (to the left of it) on the scale. Thus, if a given language has a case for source, it is also expected to have a case for location, but not vice versa. Analogously, meanings like VIA, TOWARD or AWAY-FROM will only be found as long as the case system in question expresses such notions as goal and source.

Crucially, this scale is not purely descriptive. Rather, the predictions it makes have a theoretical explanation: a case system of a language expresses the more complex directionality meanings only as long as it expresses the more basic ones. As discussed above, such meanings as TOWARD and VIA are based on the notions of source and goal. Thus, it is natural for a system that is sensitive, for example, to VIA, to be sensitive to source and goal as well. Analogously, the concepts of goal and source are based on the notion of location. After all, these **are** locations, which stand in certain relations to the path along which the event proceeds.

Cross-linguistic facts seem to support the scale in (4). For instance, most Slavic languages have a locative case without any other spatial cases. In turn, some Indo-European languages have locative as well as ablative, that is, they mark both location and source, which is, again, compatible with (4). This state of affairs was found in Proto-Indo-European as well as Old Latin and is present in Sanskrit. Location and goal are marked by the case systems of, for example, Lithuanian and Malayalam. Further, numerous languages make a three-way directionality distinction between the most basic roles of location, goal and source. These languages include Finnish, West Greenlandic, Dyirbal, Imonda, Mundary, Tabasaran. Finally, there are languages that make additional directionality distinctions, but the case systems of these languages do systematically mark locations, goals and sources as well. To illustrate, Tsez makes a four-way directionality distinction between location, goal source and TOWARD. In turn, Basque marks the VIA relation – and, in addition, distinguishes between source, goal and location. Finally, it is worth noting that many of the languages mentioned above also make configuration-related distinctions in their case systems. The interaction of configuration and directionality is discussed in the next subsection.

A potential counterexample to the hierarchy in (4) is provided by Japanese, which has only one spatial case, lative. Crucially, this is a case of a goal, not location. It thus seems that a case system of a language may mark the former without marking the latter. In fact, the same is observed in Modern Hebrew (see Section 3.1); however, this language does not present a strong counterexample given the non-productive nature of its goal case.

Still, whatever the relative ranking of location on the one hand and source/goal on the other turns out to be, the other directionality values are clearly ranked lower. The presence of location/source/goal seems to constitute a necessary condition for the marking of TOWARD, AWAY-FROM or VIA.

3.2.3 An Interaction of Several Concepts

In the previous subsections, configuration and directionality have been considered separately. In fact, however, the grammatical system of a given language need not select only one of these notions to be encoded. On the contrary, spatial case systems may, and often do, represent an interaction of these two notions.[2] Further, the range of spatial distinctions reflected in a spatial case system may extend beyond directionality and configuration (this point will be raised in Section 3.3).

Lestrade (2010) argues that spatial case systems are most likely to grammaticalize directionality distinctions. Those systems that do represent these distinctions may – but need not – also reflect distinctions in configuration. The data he considers support this claim. All the languages in his sample that reflect configurational contrasts in the domain of case also reflect directionality. A (very small) subset of such languages includes: Alamblak, Finnish, Hungarian, Lezgian, Lithuanian, Kanuri, Tabasaran, Tsez. At the same time, many languages morphologically represent distinctions in directionality but not in configuration. These include, for example, Basque, West Greenlandic, Malayalam, Nivkh. The reversed situation (with configuration but not directionality being encoded by morphological case) does not seem to be observed.

Let us consider the interaction of directionality and configuration in more detail, examining specific examples.

Such an interaction is illustrated in the case system of Finnish (see Table 3.1). For instance, the noun *laatikosta*, 'out of a/the box', which appears in the elative case, is specified for both directionality (source) and configuration (internal, IN). Literally, it means *from in (a/the) box*. The noun *laatikolta* 'from the top of a/the box', which is marked ablative, is, too, specified as a source in terms of directionality, but

---

[2] In fact, according to Lestrade (2010), configuration is always represented in a spatial case system, but a system may not grammaticalize any *distinctions* along this dimension. Thus, we have case systems which distinguish between such directional concepts as goal and location but not between configurational notions like IN versus ON.

differs from the previous example as far as configuration is concerned. The configuration is, in this example, external (ON), and the word can be literally translated as *from on a/the box*. Yet another example of this interaction is the Lezgian noun *sewrekdi* 'to under the bear', where the morpheme -*k* specifies the UNDER configuration and -*di*, goalhood.

The fact that both directionality and configuration can be represented within the same grammatical system is well established and has been discussed in the literature quite extensively (see e.g. Hjelmslev 1935/37, Jackendoff 1983, Talmy 1983, Bierwisch 1988, Koopman 2000, van Riemsdijk and Huybregts 2007, Lestrade 2010 and references therein). Van Riemsdijk and Huybregts consider this interaction as revealed both in the morphology (case system) and in the syntactic domain (the system of prepositions). Concentrating primarily on two particularly rich examples (the case system of Lezgian and the adpositional system of German), van Riemsdijk and Huybregts provide evidence that distinct positions should be posited in the grammar for configuration and directionality markers (**Location** and **Direction** in their terminology). Specifically, they argue for the following structure: $[_V \ V° \ [DIR° \ [LOC° \ [_N \ N°]]]]$.[3] In other words, configurationality markers are claimed to occupy a position that is closer to the N head/root than that of directionality markers. This approach is supported by the order of spatial case suffixes found in Nakh-Daghestanian languages (see e.g. the example *sewrekdi* above). Obviously, suffixes follow, rather than precede, the nominal stem, but, crucially, their proximity to the latter is indeed as predicted by the structure. Configurational suffixes appear closer to the stem than directional ones.

The spatial case systems of Nakh-Daghestanian, or Northeast Caucasian, languages which are particularly rich, are discussed in more detail in the next section.

3.3 ILLUSTRATING RICH SPATIAL CASE SYSTEMS: NAKH-DAGHESTANIAN LANGUAGES

Table 3.1 summarized the spatial case system of Finnish. In this section, we consider in some detail the range of spatial cases found in three additional languages, Tabasaran, Tsez and Bezhta, all of which

---

[3] This representation reflects structure, rather than linear word order (the latter varies from language to language).

Van Riemsdijk (2007) argues that an additional projection, RO (ROUTE), should be inserted between DIR and LOC, as is discussed in Section 3.3 below.

belong to the Nakh-Daghestanian language family. These languages are of interest for our purposes because they exhibit a particularly rich system of spatial cases. Tabasaran has even been mentioned in *The Guinness Book of Records* as a language with the highest number of nominal cases, specifically, forty-eight. Following Comrie and Polinsky (1998), we will raise below the question of whether the appropriate description of the Tabasaran data indeed requires such a high number. However, the fact that this Nakh-Daghestanian language exhibits a rich repertoire of cases, especially spatial ones, is in no doubt.

Before we proceed, it is worth noting that Tabasaran, Tsez and Bezhta are used below as representatives of Nakh-Daghestanian languages, many of which are characterized by rich spatial case systems. Additional examples include Lezgian, Lak, Archi, Tsakhur, Udi, Hinuq (see van Riemsdijk and Huybregts 2007, Forker 2012).

3.3.1 Tabasaran

Let us begin by considering Tabasaran data, discussed in detail by Comrie and Polinsky (1998). This language has only four non-spatial cases: ergative, absolutive, genitive and dative (Blake 1994, Comrie and Polinsky 1998). The remaining cases, whose number is so impressive, are of the spatial nature. (In fact, Comrie and Polinsky point out that even the Tabasaran dative has spatial uses, but we will treat it apart from the purely local case morphemes.)

The spatial case system of Tabasaran marks both configuration and directionality. The morphological system involved in this phenomenon is agglutinative in the sense that each meaning component is contributed by a separate morpheme. Thus, there are suffixes with configurational meanings which combine with suffixes that bear directional meanings.

Starting with configuration, Tabasaran makes a seven- or eight-way distinction (depending on the dialect considered). The meanings contributed by configurational case morphemes include: IN, ON (horizontal), ON (vertical), BEHIND, UNDER, AMONG, AT and NEAR. The latter two are distinguished in some dialects but not in others, which is why we get the difference between seven and eight case series. For the sake of illustration, consider the examples in (5), taken from Comrie and Polinsky (1998:98). (Note that spatial case suffixes systematically attach to a stem which contains the ergative suffix -*i*.)

(5) a. cal-i-?
         wall.ₑᵣ𝒈-ᵢₙ
         'in the wall'

b. cal-i-q
   wall_{ERG-BEHIND}
   'behind the wall'

c. cal-i-kk
   wall_{ERG-UNDER}
   'under the wall'

d. cal-i-h
   wall_{ERG-IN.FRONT.OF}
   'by the wall'

e. cal-i-k
   wall_{ERG-ON(VERTICAL)}
   'on the wall'

Turning to directionality, here a lower number of distinctions is made. Specifically, the system distinguishes between location (essive case), goal (allative case) and source (ablative case). This three-way opposition is illustrated in (6), taken from Comrie and Polinsky (1998:98–99):

(6) a. cal-i-q
        wall_{ERG-BEHIND}
        'behind the wall'

     b. cal-i-q-na
        wall_{ERG-BEHIND-ALL}
        'to behind the wall'

     c. cal-i-q-an
        wall_{ERG-BEHIND-ABL}
        'from behind the wall'

It can be seen that while allative and ablative cases are represented by the suffixes -*na* and -*an*, respectively, essive is not associated with any overt morpheme. This allows two possible interpretations: either the location reading results in the absence of a directionality case (which would mean that, strictly speaking, there is no essive case in Tabasaran), or the location meaning is contributed by a phonologically null suffix Ø.

It can be seen that in Tabasaran, case suffixes with directionality meanings attach on top of case suffixes expressing configuration, in accordance with the structural generalization made in van Riemsdijk and Huybregts (2007). Configuration is represented closer to the stem than directionality.

This is not the whole story, however. On top of the configuration-directionality case combinations, the translative morpheme -*di* can further attach, whose function is "to indicate more general rather than more specific location or motion" (Comrie and Polinsky

1998:99). Specifically, the suffix affects the directionality meaning component of the noun, turning goal into TOWARD, source into AWAY-FROM and location into ALONG/OVER/ACROSS, that is roughly the VIA relation discussed by Lestrade. Thus, essentially, the attachment of *-di* extends the range of directionality distinctions that can be reflected within the Tabasaran case system. We end up with a six-way, rather than a three-way, opposition. To illustrate, consider the following minimal pairs (Magometov 1965:129, Comrie and Polinsky 1998: 99).[4]

(7)　a.　nir-i-q
　　　　river.ERG-BEHIND
　　　　'at the river / on the bank of the
　　　　river'

　　　　nir-i-q-ri
　　　　river.ERG-BEHIND-TRANSL
　　　　'along (the bank of the
　　　　river)'

　　　b.　nir-i-q-na
　　　　river.ERG-BEHIND-ALL
　　　　'to (the bank of) the
　　　　river'

　　　　nir-i-q-in-di
　　　　river.ERG-BEHIND-ALL-TRANSL
　　　　'toward (the bank of) the
　　　　river'

　　　c.　nir-q-an
　　　　river.BEHIND-ABL
　　　　'from (the bank
　　　　of) the river'

　　　　nir-q-an-di
　　　　river.BEHIND-ABL-TRANSL
　　　　'from the direction of (the
　　　　bank of) the river'

To sum up, we can say that the Tabasaran case system exhibits a seven-/eight-way distinction in configuration and a six-way distinction in directionality.

3.3.2　Additional Examples: Tsez and Bezhta

Having considered the spatial cases of Tabasaran, let us now turn to Tsez and Bezhta, two other Nakh-Daghestanian languages with rich local case systems. The information provided below is based on Comrie and Polinsky (1998) for Tsez and on Comrie et al. (2015) and Forker (2012) for Bezhta.

In general, the case systems of these languages are rather similar to that of Tabasaran, but the sets of available distinctions are not purely identical. Below, we concentrate only on those differences that have to do with spatial cases.

Tsez exhibits a seven-way distinction in configuration. The meanings represented in the case system include: IN, ON (horizontal), ON (vertical), AMONG, UNDER, AT and NEAR. The list does not contain

---

[4] It should be noted that some of the examples involve morpho-phonemic changes that are reflected in the transcription. This is not relevant for the present discussion.

BEHIND, a configuration that is represented in Tabasaran by the suffix -*q*. In Bezhta, an eight-way distinction is observed: IN, UNDER, AT, ON, ALOC (animate location), CONT (through, in contact with), NEXT (TO) and COMIT(ative).

Further, both Tsez and Bezhta make a four-way distinction in directionality. In Tsez these cases are: essive (location), allative (goal), ablative (source) and versative (TOWARD). In Bezhta, a certain level of disagreement between different researchers is observed. Forker defines the four cases as: essive (location), lative (goal), ablative (source) and directional. Comrie et al. exclude the directional from the list but add the translative. They also refer to Testelets and Khalilov (1998), who posit five directional cases (including both the directional and the translative) for this language (Comrie et al. 2015:260).

This is not the whole story yet. While in Tabasaran, a translative morpheme is used to create a more general locational meaning, in Bezhta the same role is fulfilled by the approximative case suffix, which appears between the configurational and the directional morpheme (unlike the Tabasaran translative, which is attached on top of the directional suffix). The use of the approximative in Bezhta is illustrated in (8) below:

(8)   q'itsa-t͡ʼa-daːs
       bog.ₛᵤₚₑᵣ.ₐₚₚᵣₒₓ.ₐᵦₗ
       'away from the bog'

(Comrie et al. 2015:271)

In turn, Tsez makes a two-way distality distinction between distal and non-distal forms. The distal is created by the attachment of an additional suffix (which appears immediately after the configurational ones) and, as reported by Comrie and Polinsky, contributes the meaning 'over there'. If the suffix is not added, the non-distal meaning results. The contrast in distality is thus a deictic distinction, with the distal form specifying (similarly to such indexical expressions as *there*) that the referent appears in a place that differs from the location of the speech. As discussed by Lestrade, if a case system of a language specifies both directionality and configuration, additional kinds of distinctions become potentially possible. Tsez constitutes an example of a language where a third (in this instance, deictic) type of spatial opposition is introduced.

3.3.3 How Many Cases?

It can be seen that the case systems of these Nakh-Daghestanian languages are indeed extremely rich. If we count the number of individual case morphemes contributing distinct spatial meanings in Tabasaran, we get, following Comrie and Polinsky, ten or eleven, depending on the dialect. (If we assume that the essive meaning corresponds to a -Ø suffix, one more case morpheme would be added.) Adding the four non-spatial case morphemes, fourteen or fifteen cases are obtained. Turning to Tsez, the number of spatial cases in this language is eleven. If -Ø suffixes are postulated for the essive and non-distal versions of nouns, the number is raised to thirteen. Together with non-spatial case morphemes, Comrie and Polinsky report a total of eighteen suffixes (they do not assume a -Ø for essive and non-distal).

Then how are numbers like forty-eight, reported in *The Guinness Book of Records*, obtained? The answer is simple: it is not individual case suffixes (or meaning components) that are calculated, but rather their combinations. To illustrate, each Tabasaran item in (6) above is assumed to appear in a different case. Taking X to be a nominal stem, the combination X-ergative-BEHIND is taken to represent one case (postessive[5]), X-ergative-BEHIND-allative, another case (post-directive), X-ergative-BEHIND-ablative, a third case (postelative), X-ergative-IN-ablative, yet another case (inelative), and so on and so forth. This way, Comrie and Polinsky point out, depending on the dialect, we get between forty-seven and fifty-three cases in Tabasaran, and a considerably higher number of cases in Tsez. For Bezhta, the same kind of calculation renders a number as high as sixty-four for only local cases (and this result obtains for a relatively "modest" approach which takes the language to contain a four-way, rather than a five-way, directionality-based distinction).

Then which is the right way to calculate spatial cases in a language? The combinatorial approach taken in *The Guinness Book of Records* or the case-per-morpheme (or case-per-meaning-component) approach argued for by Comrie and Polinsky? In fact, the issue is subject to a long-lasting debate. Each approach has its potential pitfalls.

Let us begin by looking at the combinatorial approach, which renders a particularly high number of cases. The results of the calculations are, of course, impressive, but do they adequately capture the real state of affairs?

The main problem of this direction has to do with the fact that it misses generalizations. By treating *caliq*, *caliqna* and *caliqan* (see (6) above for detailed glosses) as the noun *cal* 'river' in three different, separate, cases, one seems to ignore the important fact that all

---

[5] The case names used here are taken from Haspelmath (1993).

these forms contain the same suffix -*q*, which makes a systematic semantic contribution to the spatial interpretation of all three items. One also ignores the fact that, for example, the suffix -*an*, present in *caliqan*, is found in numerous other combinations, in the absence of the preceding -*q*, and makes the same contribution as it does in this form (i.e. it specifies that the noun functions as a source). If we further treat translative and non-translative versions as corresponding (each time) to two separate cases, even further generalizations are missed. However, capturing the generalizations in question is essential for an adequate compositional linguistic analysis.

Note also that the combinatorial approach seems to create an impression that a child acquiring a Nakh-Daghestanian language has to memorize about fifty–seventy distinct case forms, while in reality, the burden on the child's memory is considerably less heavy. What the child needs to learn is about fourteen or fifteen suffixes and the rules for their combination.

Finally, since under the combinatorial approach, a spatial case often corresponds to a combination of several case morphemes, it seems to follow that such a combination constitutes a unit in the morphological structure of the words. After all, a given case form of a noun is created via applying the case-related morphological operation to the nominal stem. In the instance of Tabasaran, Tsez and Bezhta, the operation is one of affixation. Thus, case affix(es) are supposed to be attached to the stem of the noun. In fact, however, the case morphology found in many nouns does not form a single grammatical unit to the exclusion of the stem. To illustrate, *caliqan* is not formed by attaching the unit *-iqan* to the stem *cal*-, nor even by attaching -*qan* to the stem *cali*-. Rather, -*i*, -*q* and -*an* constitute separate suffixes, which attach to the nominal stem one by one, in the order represented in (9).

(9)   [[[cal i] q] an]

The correct morphological decomposition of such nominal forms is consistent with the case-per-morpheme approach but seems to pose a problem to the combinatorial account, which treats the whole string of case morphemes as representing a separate case. As (9) shows, such a string simply does not form a linguistic unit.

At the same time, it is worth noting that the alternative, case-per-morpheme, approach faces a potential problem as well. This problem is of a theoretical nature and has to do with the fact that, under the case-per-morpheme view, it follows that numerous nouns in Nakh-

Daghestanian languages are assigned **more than one case**. For instance, even if we ignore the ergative suffix, the noun *caliqna* appears in both the BEHIND configurational case and the allative directional case. *Nirqandi* appears in an even higher number of cases: BEHIND, ablative and translative. Typically, a nominal phrase is assumed to receive one and only one case. How do we reconcile this view with the Nakh-Daghestanian facts? And via what mechanism can several cases be assigned – or checked – for the same DP?

This problem is not unsolvable, however. In fact, the phenomenon of **case stacking** has been observed in a number of languages, including Korean, where the subject may appear in both dative/locative and nominative case, and Cuzco Quechua, where accusative case is stacked on top of genitive in raising-to-object constructions. Another language that allows case stacking is Lardil (an Australian language) (Richards 2007). Pesetsky (2013) even claims that Russian is a case-staking language, even though this is not revealed morpho-phonologically, since, under his view, all cases get deleted except for the outermost.

Case stacking is in some instances associated with the movement of the DP (with different cases being assigned in different positions it passes on the way; see e.g. Yoon 2004); in other instances, some of the cases is/are assigned by agreement (see e.g. Richards 2007). Richards argues that "[c]ase morphology may be assigned to a DP arbitrarily many times," and this approach can be applied to such languages as the ones discussed in this section.

DISCUSSION

Is it possible to reconcile the combinatorial and case-per-morpheme approaches by assuming a discrepancy between abstract and morphological case?

3.4 NON-SPATIAL USES OF SPATIAL CASES

The discussion of spatial cases would be incomplete without referring to those instances when cases of this type are used in the absence of their literal, locational, semantics. Such uses are attested cross-linguistically and can be divided into at least two groups: metaphorical extension and reduced agentivity.

3.4.1 Metaphorical Extension

The range of uses of spatial cases is sometimes extended beyond the original location-related meanings via metaphor and, possibly, metonymy. To illustrate, in Finnish, the adessive case (corresponding to external location) is employed in the possessive construction. Consider the example in (10):

(10) Minulla   on   kirja.
      I$_{\text{ADESS}}$ is   book$_{\text{NOM}}$
      'I have a book.'

Finnish is a so-called **BE language**, meaning that the possessive construction in this language contains the existential *be*, rather than a possessive verb analogous to the English *have*. This is illustrated in (10), which contains the third-person singular present tense form of the verb *olla* 'be', *on*. Crucially, the possessor-denoting DP appears in a spatial, specifically, adessive, case (*minulla*, literally, *on me*). The sentence meaning 'I have a book' can be literally translated as 'There is a book on me', or, even more precisely, 'On me is a book'.

In this example, the relation of location is metaphorically extended to one of possession. Roughly speaking, the possessor is treated as a (metaphorical) location of the possessed object.

Such a fusion of location and possession is quite widespread in world languages and extends considerably beyond the domain of case. Many languages use the same or almost the same constructions for existential sentences and sentences that ascribe possession (see e.g. Freeze 1992, Partee and Borschev 2008). Compare, for instance, the Russian sentences in (11), which assert or deny the existence of an entity in a particular location, to their counterparts in (12), which report the presence or absence of a possession relation:

(11) a. V   moëm   kabinete   jest'   komputer.
          in   my   office   be   computer$_{\text{NOM}}$
          'There is a computer in my office.'

      b. V   moëm   kabinete   net   komputera.
          in   my   office   NEG-BE   computer$_{\text{GEN}}$
          'There is no computer in my office.'

(12) a. U   menja   jest'   komputer.
          at   me   be   computer$_{\text{NOM}}$
          'I have a computer.'

      b. U   menja   net   komputera.
          at   me   NEG-BE   computer$_{\text{GEN}}$
          'I don't have a computer.'

(11a) consists of a phrase that denotes location, the item *jest'* and the pivot (which is asserted to exist in the place in question). *Jest'* constitutes, historically, a present tense form of the verb *byt'* 'be', which, in Modern Russian, is mainly used in the existential construction. In negated existential sentences, it is substituted by the negative item *net*, and the pivot obligatorily appears in the Genitive of Negation. (See Babby 1980, Borschev and Partee 1998, 2002a for a detailed discussion of Russian existential sentences, and Partee and Borschev 2008 and Kagan in press for the similarity between such sentences and the possessive ones in Russian.) Crucially, the sentences in (12), which express the relation of possession, exhibit the characteristic properties of existential sentences. They consist of the possessor (instead of location) phrase, the item *jest'* or *net*, and the pivot, which under negation obligatorily appears in the genitive.

Moreover, it is worth noting that the possessive phrase in (12), *u menja*, contains the preposition *u* 'at', whose original meaning is locational. Thus, in the domain of prepositions, too, spatial meaning can be metaphorically extended to that of possession.

DISCUSSION

In Urdu/Hindi, locative case is found in experiencer constructions illustrated in (13):

(13) nina=mẽ   bʰay   hɛ
      Nina_F.SG.OBL=LOCin fear_M.SG.NOM be_PRES.3.SG
      'Nina is fearful.' (lit.: 'There is fear in Nina.')
                                      (Mohanan 1994:172, Sulger 2012:3)

This is a phenomenon whereby the experiencer argument of certain psychological predicates can appear in the locative case (alternatively, it can also appear in the dative; see Sulger 2012, Butt 2006b for discussion). Can this use of the locative be explained by analogy with the use of spatial cases in possessive constructions? Does metaphorical extension play a role in such uses? Consider also such English phrases as "the fear **in** me" and "the love **inside of** you."

3.4.2   Reduced and Demoted Agentivity

In addition, in some languages, spatial case can be assigned to (potential) agents under certain conditions. For instance, in Lezgian, the ablative suffix can be attached to the ergative subject, thereby reducing the agentivity of the latter. The ablative contributes a meaning component according to which the event was performed accidentally or involuntarily. This is illustrated in the example from Haspelmath (1993:292), quoted by Lestrade (2010) and provided in (14) below:

(14) a. Zamira-di   get'e   xana.
          Zamira.$_{ERG}$ pot   break$_{AOR}$
          'Zamira broke the pot.'
      b. Zamira-di-waj   get'e   xana.
          Zamira.$_{ERG-ABL}$ pot   break$_{AOR}$
          'Zamira broke the pot accidentally/involuntarily.'

We saw in Chapter 1 that a similar effect is obtained in such languages as Hindi/Urdu when an ergative subject is substituted by a nominative or dative one. But while in those instances, the ergative seemed to contribute agentivity, here, on the contrary, the ablative seems to reduce it.

Why is a spatial case (specifically, ablative, which is the case of a source) used in this situation? How can its attachment result in the cancelation or reduction of agentivity entailments? Lestrade (2010) proposes the following explanation: "by using a spatial case on a constituent with a human referent, the speaker suspends standard Proto-Agent implicatures that are especially inappropriate for grounds." Spatial cases, including the ablative, are normally cases of grounds, and grounds differ dramatically from agents. Prototypical grounds are inanimate, they do not perform any actions, do not exhibit volitionality and do not function as causes. They are just *there*. Therefore, by assigning a case of a ground to the subject, one cancels Proto-Agent characteristics which are otherwise expected, and thereby reduces agentivity.

Yet another possible explanation, proposed by an anonymous reviewer, is based on the notion of separation associated with the source meaning of the ablative (where literal, physical separation in the course of motion is involved). An abstract sense of separation could be involved in (14b), whereby the subject is relieved (separated) from responsibility over the action. This results in the reduction of agentivity.

In addition, in some languages, a spatial case marks the demoted agent in the passive construction, that is, it fulfills the function comparable to that of the preposition *by* in English (see e.g. Lestrade 2010 and references therein). This is illustrated for West Greenlandic in (15), originally taken from Fortescue (1984:212).

(15) Qimmi-mit   aupan-niqar-puq.
      dog.$_{ABL}$ attack$_{PASSIVE.3-INDIC}$
      'He was attacked by the dog.'

Here, in the presence of a passive predicate, the agent appears in the ablative case. Lestrade, again, explains such instances by relating to the properties of grounds, to which spatial cases are typically assigned. But while in (14), the relevant opposition was between grounds and agents, in instances like (15), the tension between grounds and subjects becomes important. (After all, here, it is subject-hood, rather than agenthood, that is being canceled.) "Grounds are very much the opposite of subjects. Grounds typically are back-grounded, inanimate referents, entities of less concern, whereas subjects typically are human and in the center of attention. By giving subjects the form of a ground, that is, by marking them with the spatial case, subjects become more like grounds." In other words, an agent in the case of a ground is marked as a non-subject.

Again, the use of the ablative could also be explained via metapho-rical extension: the agent is conceptualized as a source of the event, in the sense that it causes the event to take place.[6,7]

3.5 CASE-ASSIGNMENT IN SYNTAX: CHALLENGES FOR A FORMAL ANALYSIS

As pointed out by McFadden (2002), spatial case constitutes one of the best candidates for the role of a semantic case. It is clearly associated with semantic content which, moreover, is not independently con-tributed by the predicate (e.g. verb of motion). As such, it poses a challenge to the purely syntactic approach which treats case as an uninterpretable feature. Under this view, case is not expected to make a truth-conditional contribution.

Furthermore, it is not quite clear in what way spatial case is assigned or checked. As noted above, its role is typically quite similar to the role fulfilled by prepositions in languages that lack this morphological phenomenon. Within such prepositional phrases, the case-checking story is rather clear. The preposition carries a case feature, and it checks the case of its nominal complement. However, how is this feature checked on those nominals that appear in a spatial case (alla-tive, ablative, etc.) in the absence of any preposition?

---

[6] I wish to thank an anonymous reviewer for the suggestions of metaphorical extension-based explanations of (14) and (15).

[7] The view of agents as a type of source is formally implemented in the force-dynamic framework developed by Copley and Harley (2015), which will be addressed in Chapter 7. However, the discussion there will not be devoted to agenthood.

The two questions are strongly interrelated: it is at least plausible that the head which is responsible for case-checking also makes the semantic contribution which is intuitively associated with the particular morphological form.

Three candidates for the role of the semantic contributor can be considered: (i) the overt predicate which takes the locative expression as its complement; (ii) a phonologically empty head; or (iii) the case morpheme itself.

Let us begin with the first option. Spatial cases can be treated as instances of inherent case which is lexically selected by the verb. The case is thus checked, or assigned, by the V head itself. As is typically assumed to hold for inherent case, this process is related to theta-role assignment. Here, it is the assignment of such theta-roles as *location*, *goal* and *source*.

For some predicates, this approach seems to be quite appropriate. To illustrate, the verb *return* (and, presumably, its counterparts in other languages) may take a source complement, and it is easily conceivable that in languages with a morphologically rich case system it would select a complement in an ablative case (or some other version of a source case, e.g. elative). However, the problem has to do with the fact that many verbs are compatible with numerous spatial cases. Thus, even *return* is compatible not only with a source but also with a goal phrase (as in *I returned home*), and some other verbs are even less selective. The Finnish examples in (2) above demonstrate, for instance, that the verb *juodaa* 'run' is compatible with all the six spatial cases available in this language. Indeed, the predicate *run* can be followed by location, goal and source phrases, and, of course, it is compatible with both the internal and the external configuration. Again, the problem becomes even stronger in Nakh-Daghestanian languages, in which a verb like *run* may easily combine with nominals appearing in more than ten cases, or several dozens of case–morpheme combinations.

Note that this time the problem is not with the very existence a high number of spatial cases. After all, a language may contain numerous inherent cases. What is troubling is rather the fact that, quite often, **the same predicate** may combine with nouns appearing in any of the available cases (or in most of them). Assuming that a given inherent case is selected by a verb on the lexical level, we would have to conclude that a verb like *run* involves numerous selectional options. Essentially, it is compatible with different subcategorization frames. In principle, a verb may be associated with more than one subcategorization frame. To illustrate, *eat* comes in both a transitive and an intransitive version[8] and *think* can take a clausal complement or a PP complement headed by *about*. However, the existence of ten (or even more) distinct subcategorization frames for a given verb is much less plausible.

If the locative meaning is not contributed by an overt predicate, two alternatives remain: a phonologically null head (plausibly an adposition) or the case-marker. Unfortunately, it is often difficult to distinguish between these two approaches empirically, and the decision is thus largely a theory-internal matter. Still, some discussion of the topic is in order.

The claim that local case suffixes are meaningful has important consequences for the linguistic theory in general. It means that case features may be interpretable. In fact, even though this view is not dominant within the minimalist framework, claims along this line have been made (see e.g. Svenonius 2002, 2006, Richards 2013, Crisma and Longobardi 2018). If we choose this direction, we will claim that some case features are interpretable and others are not. While the latter have to be checked by an appropriate probe, this is not obligatory for the former. Roughly, this approach takes the data at face value: things *are* as they seem to be. Spatial case suffixes are indeed meaningful, just like those adpositions which fulfill analogous functions in a wide range of languages.

The alternative approach takes local case to be checked by a phonologically empty adposition, presumably a postposition in Finnic and Nakh-Daghestanian languages. This postposition carries the locational semantic content that is intuitively associated with the overt suffix, and it also does the job of checking the case of the DP, just as overt adpositions do. This view allows for a uniform treatment of such phrases as *caliqan* (wall.ERG.BEHIND.FROM) in Tabasaran and *from behind the wall* in English.

The empty P analysis is put forward for Finnish by Nikanne (1993) and McFadden (2002). When applied to Nakh-Daghestanian languages, however, it faces a number of problems, which will be briefly discussed below in the context of Bezhta.

The first question has to do with how many empty adpositions are assumed to exist in a given language. In accordance with Emond's (1987) Invisible Category Principle, a null element has to be identifiable on the basis of other elements present in the sentence. In order for this restriction to be satisfied, each spatial meaning must correspond to a different postposition, with the distinct case-markers

---

[8] But see Newman and Rice (2006) for an overview of different approaches to the duality associated with verbs like *eat*.

allowing the identification of the corresponding P. In Finnish, we are dealing with six empty postpositions, which is a plausible number. Turning to Nakh-Daghestanian, we get back to the question of how cases (and, correspondingly, empty postpositions) are to be counted.

One option is to state that each case cluster corresponds to a separate null P. Thus, for instance, there will be separate postpositions meaning 'near X', 'to near X', 'from near X', 'to under X', 'from under X', etc. This means, however, that Bezhta has (at least) sixty-four phonologically empty postpositions (in accordance with the number of spatial case-morpheme clusters, as discussed above). Such a claim is clearly untenable.

The alternative is to conclude that each case suffix corresponds to a separate postposition. If a DP contains several local case morphemes (two or three), then each case is checked by a separate phonologically empty postposition, and each meaning component is contributed by a separate P. The number of phonologically null postpositions per language is then not as high as under the previous hypothesis (about ten–eleven Ps). This approach involves what we may call "empty P stacking," as illustrated in the structure below in (16).[9]

(16)

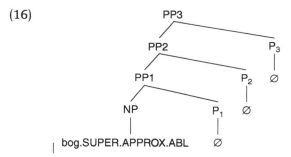

The main problem faced by this analysis has to do with a range of discrepancies between overt postpositions and covert ones. Under the assumption that the latter exist, it follows that both syntactic and semantic characteristics of a postposition differ considerably depending on its phonological properties (specifically, whether it is phonologically realized or not). Several discrepancies of this kind are listed below:

(i) Stacking of overt postpositions is not observed in Bezhta, whereas stacking of covert ones has to be assumed under the present analysis.

[9] Rather than assuming several PPs, we can take the structure to contain only one maximal prepositional projection (the highest one), along the lines of van Riemsdijk and Huybregts (2007).

(ii) Overt postpositions in Bezhta never take a complement in the approximative case (Comrie et al. 2015). However, the approximative suffix is perfectly compatible with the wide range of local case combinations. In the present terms this would mean that a null approximative postposition is **compatible** with all covert Ps but **incompatible** with all the overt ones. But why should its distribution be sensitive to this phonological factor? Potentially, this contrast could be related to a semantic fact: overt postpositions in Bezhta tend to have more precise meanings, which are apparently incompatible with the vagueness contributed by the approximative marker. However, this explanation raises yet another question:

(iii) Why are the meanings of overt postpositions more precise and those of covert ones vaguer? Do we expect such a difference to depend on phonology?

(iv) In addition, any configurational case in Bezhta is compatible with any directional one. This means that covert directional postpositions are free to co-occur with any configurational postpositions. However, the overt directional P that is available in Bezhta (*gisa* 'from') does not exhibit such behavior. It cannot accompany *any* configurational meaning, but rather governs a particular case cluster (IN + ablative). In other words, it selects a specific configurational postposition (IN). Again, we are dealing with different selectional/governing properties of an overt P on the one hand and its covert counterparts, on the other.

Discrepancies of the kind described pose a challenge to an empty postposition approach in a language like Bezhta. More generally, languages with a rich system of spatial cases pose a challenge to a purely syntactic approach to case. In turn, a hypothesis that a case feature may be interpretable allows us to account for the otherwise complicated facts in a relatively straightforward way. Still, ultimately, the choice between a semantic case approach and an empty postposition analysis is likely to be largely governed by theory-internal considerations.

3.6 INTERACTION OF SPATIAL CASE AND PREPOSITIONS

Finally, it is worth pointing out that case may contribute information regarding spatial relations even when it interacts with overt prepositions. This happens when a given preposition is compatible with more than one case on its complement. The choice of case then depends on the spatial relation represented in the sentence.

Let us begin the discussion by considering the following English sentence:

(17)   The boat floated under the bridge.[10]

(17) is ambiguous between two readings. Under one, the boat is located under the bridge throughout the event, and the event is one of floating. According to the other, the boat started floating elsewhere, and, in the course of this event, moved to some place under the bridge. In other words, the *under*-PP may be interpreted as either a goal or a location. The phrase is fully specified for configuration (UNDER) but remains underspecified as far as directionality is concerned. It is compatible with two options: location and goal.

In certain languages, such as Russian, German and Ancient Greek, ambiguity of this kind is resolved with the help of the case that surfaces on the complement of the preposition. Goals, locations and, in Ancient Greek, sources sometimes contain the same prepositions but are distinguished in terms of case-marking. To illustrate, (17) can be translated to Russian in two ways, as represented in (18). Neither of the sentences below is ambiguous.

(18) a. Lodka   plyla   pod   mostom.
         boat   swam   under   bridge$_{INSTR}$
         'The boat floated (while) under the bridge.'   **location**

      b. Lodka   plyla   pod   most.
         boat   swam   under   bridge$_{ACC}$
         'The boat floated (to) under the bridge.'   **goal**

In (18a), the nominal phrase *mostom* 'bridge' appears in the instrumental case, and the PP is unambiguously interpreted as a location. In (18b), the complement of the same preposition is accusative, and the PP is (again, unambiguously) interpreted as a goal.

More generally, Russian contains four prepositions that can take complements in two cases, depending on the thematic role of the PP. Specifically, the complement of *pod* 'under' and *za* 'behind' is instrumental if the phrase functions as a location and accusative if it functions as a goal. In turn, with *na* 'on'

---

[10] See the discussion of this sentence in Higginbotham (1995).

Table 3.2 *Spatial prepositions and case in Russian*

Preposition	Goal	Location
v 'in'	v gorod	v gorode
	in city$_{ACC}$	in city$_{LOC}$
	'to (into) the city'	'in the city'
na 'on'	na stol	na stole
	on table$_{ACC}$	on table$_{LOC}$
	'on (onto) the table'	'on the table'
pod 'under'	pod most	pod mostom
	under bridge$_{ACC}$	under bridge$_{INSTR}$
	'(to) under the bridge'	'under the bridge'
za 'behind'	za dom	za domom
	behind house$_{ACC}$	behind house$_{INSTR}$
	'(to) behind the house'	'behind the house'

and *v* 'in', the form is locative/prepositional with locations and, again, accusative with goals. The facts are summarized in Table 3.2.

Turning to German, here the facts are even more systematic. The number of prepositions that participate in an analogous alternation is higher, and the alternation is always between the same two cases, accusative and dative (see e.g. Jørgensen 1963, Smith 1987, 1993, 1995, Zwarts 2005, van Riemsdijk 2007). This makes sense, given that German has a smaller case inventory. A list of alternating prepositions and the relation between case and spatial meaning is provided in Table 3.3 (the German data are taken from Zwarts 2005); the contrast is further illustrated in (19). In general, it can be stated that complements of the prepositions listed below appear in the accusative case if they function as goals and in the dative if they represent locations.

(19) a. Peter   legt   das   Buch   auf   den   Tisch
       Peter   puts   the   book   on   the$_{ACC}$ table
       'Peter puts the book on the table.'
     b. Das   Buch   liegt   auf   dem   Tisch
        the   book   is-lying   on   the$_{DAT}$ table
        'The book is lying on the table.'

(from van Riemsdijk 2007, ex. 1)

It is important to emphasize that not all spatial prepositions in either German or Russian allow a case alternation.

Table 3.3 *Spatial prepositions and case in German*

Preposition	Case with goals	Case with locations
an 'on'	accusative	dative
auf 'on'	accusative	dative
hinter 'behind'	accusative	dative
in 'in'	accusative	dative
neben 'next to'	accusative	dative
über 'over'	accusative	dative
unter 'under'	accusative	dative
vor 'in front of'	accusative	dative
zwischen 'between'	accusative	dative

Finally, an even more interesting picture is found in Ancient Greek, where the same preposition is sometimes compatible with goal, location **and source** readings, depending on the case form of its complement (here goal corresponds to accusative case, location, to dative and source, to genitive), as discussed by Spyropoulos (2018). Prepositions that allow this three-way distinction include: *epi* 'on', *para* 'at/from/to the side of, by', *peri* 'around/about', *pros* 'towards/at', *hypo* 'under'. In (20) below, the contrast is illustrated for *para*. The examples are taken from Spyropoulos (2018, ex. 7).

(20) a. para+genitive=ablative
           aggeliɛ: hɛ:kei   para   basileos   (Hdt. 8.40)
           message$_{NOM}$ come$_{PAST.3SG}$ PREP   king$_{GEN}$
           'a message came from the king (from the court of the king)'

      b. para+dative=locative
           sito:ntai ... para   tɔ: didaskalɔ: (X.Cyr. 1,#2,#8)
           eat$_{3PL}$ PREP   the   teacher$_{DAT}$
           'they eat ... beside their teacher'

      c. para+accusative=allative
           para   tɛ:n   gephyran   pempsai   (X.An. 2.4.17)
           PREP   the   bridge$_{ACC}$ send$_{AOR.INF}$
           'to send to the bridge (to the sides of the bridge)'

Spyropoulos proposes that the case-assigning properties of the prepositions depend on the functional p$_{CASE}$ head, whose characteristics are, in turn, sensitive to semantic relations.

Case alternations on complements of spatial prepositions will be discussed in more detail in Chapter 4, in the context of the relation between accusative case and boundedness.

Finally, it is worth mentioning that occasionally, the case of the complement of a preposition may be associated with a particular spatial meaning even in the absence of an alternation. For instance, Russian contains several source prepositions, including *iz*, *ot* and *s*. All of these can be translated as 'from', but if we concentrate on the most basic, original sense of the prepositions, it is possible to distinguish between them via the following translations: *iz* 'from (inside)', *ot* 'away from', *s* 'from on (top of)'. They thus differ in terms of configuration, but all specify the directionality of a source. Crucially, all the three prepositions require a genitive complement.[11]

Further, the Russian morpheme *iz* also appears in complex prepositions (which essentially consist of pairs of prepositions) such as *iz-za* 'from behind' and *iz-pod* 'from under'. In these strings, *iz* contributes the directionality value (i.e. source) and the second element, the configuration (*za* 'behind', *pod* 'under'). Crucially, the case selected by such complex prepositions is genitive. In other words, it is determined by *iz*.

What we thus see is that the complement of source prepositions, whether simple or complex, is systematically genitive. This could, of course, be judged as a pure accident, but it is much more likely that we are dealing with an inherent case which is related to the thematic role of a source. This is plausible not only due to the generalization that we can make for Russian prepositions but also given that the genitive is interrelated with the concept of a source in other Indo-European languages (see. e.g. Spyropoulos 2018 for Ancient Greek). We thus conclude that those prepositions which contribute this thematic role also systematically assign, or check, the genitive case on their complements. Note that in such instances, the semantic relation between case and the spatial domain does not pose any problem for the syntactic theory of case licensing.

3.7 CONCLUSION

To sum up, spatial, or local, cases are sensitive to such properties associated with the spatial domain as configuration, directionality and distality. Cross-linguistically, local cases are particularly likely to reflect directionality distinctions, where location, goal and source are the most basic but not the only available notions. Case distinctions

---

[11] Analogously, the Ancient Greek *apo* 'from' can only appear with a genitive complement (Spyropoulos 2018).

along configuration are also quite widespread. Further, the use of spatial cases can extend beyond the literal, locational, meaning, for instance, by virtue of metaphorical extension.

FURTHER READING

Lestrade's (2010) dissertation constitutes a very rich and important source on the nature of spatial case in languages of the world. Lestrade analyzes a wide range of facts, providing data from numerous world languages belonging to different families. His work includes both a thoughtful typological study and a formal semantic analysis based on a careful investigation of a wide range of spatial notions that are relevant for case-marking.

Van Riemsdijk and Huybregts (2007) address the syntactic and morphological representations of location and path, or configuration and directionality.

Comrie and Polinsky (1998) provide an investigation of two languages characterized by a particularly rich spatial case system, Tabasaran and Tsez. They address the issue of how the number of local cases in such languages should be calculated and argue for the more modest approach which counts individual morpho-semantic components, rather than combinations of case morphemes.

Talmy (1983) discusses in detail the linguistic representation of spatial notions. This issue is also addressed in Talmy's (2000) *Toward a Cognitive Semantics*.

4   Case and Aspect

This chapter is devoted to the discussion of the interaction of case and the aspectual properties of a clause. A particularly prominent role in this relation is played by accusative and partitive cases.

The accusative plausibly comes right after the nominative on the list of cases that are assumed to be purely structural, syntactic, associated with a particular grammatical function and position on the tree, rather than with a certain meaning. Indeed, in numerous languages, accusative marks any DP that appears in the direct object position of a transitive verb. It is checked by a particular functional head which is associated with the verbal projection, for example by little v, AgrO or Asp (different approaches can be found in this respect). An accusative object may bear different thematic roles, including theme (1a), experiencer (1b) or stimulus (1c), suggesting that this case is not inherent.[1]

(1)   a. Anton   napisal   pis'mo.
         Anton   wrote   letter$_{ACC}$
         'Anton wrote a/the letter.'
      b. Sobaka   napugala   Ivana.
         Dog   scared   Ivan$_{ACC}$
         'A/the dog scared Ivan.'
      c. Dima   ljubit   Mašu.
         Dima   loves   Masha$_{ACC}$
         'Dima loves Masha.'

Not only is the accusative compatible with different thematic roles, but all these roles are also assigned to DPs that appear in other cases, such as the nominative. Thus, as soon as the predicates in question undergo passivization, the corresponding arguments appear in the

---

[1] Of course, accusative can be inherent when required by a particular lexical head, e.g. there are prepositions that take accusative complements. Also see Danon (2002) for a claim that in Hebrew, transitive verbs systematically assign inherent accusative case to their (indefinite) objects.

nominative case, rather than the accusative (2). Crucially, the thematic role carried by the arguments remains the same. More generally, the argument fulfills exactly the same role in the denoted event independently of whether the predicate is active or passive. Its additional semantic properties (e.g. animacy, referential gender) remain the same, too. It thus seems that accusative case-checking is a matter of functioning as an object of a transitive verb (and occupying the appropriate position in the structure) and is purely structural in nature.

(2) a. Pis'mo   bylo   napisano   (Antonom).
        letter$_{NOM}$ was   written   Anton$_{INSTR}$
        'The letter was written (by Anton).'

     b. Ivan   byl   napugan   (?sobakoj).
        Ivan$_{NOM}$ was   frightened dog$_{INSTR}$
        'Ivan was frightened (by a dog).'

     c. Maša   byla   ljubima   (Dimoj).
        Masha$_{NOM}$ was   loved   Dima$_{INSTR}$
        'Masha was loved (by Dima).'

Further evidence in favor of treating accusative as a structural case comes from the phenomenon of ECM (exceptional case-marking). These are instances when the subject of a subordinate clause (which lacks a finite verb) receives accusative case from the verb of the higher clause (3).

(3) a. John saw Mary/her leave.
     b. Tom considers Jane/her clever.
     c. Dima   sčitaet   Lenu   umnoj.
        Dima   considers Lena$_{ACC}$ clever$_{INSTR}$
        'Dima considers Lena clever.'

The DPs *Mary*, *Jane* and *Lenu* in (3) above do not function as direct objects, nor do they constitute subjects of the immediately preceding verbs. Rather, the verbs take the whole embedded clauses as their complements. To illustrate, in (3a), *Mary leave* is a clausal complement of *saw*. The DP *Mary* constitutes the subject (and argument) of the lower verb, *leave*. Still, the DP appears in the accusative case, as can be seen overtly if the object is substituted by the pronominal *her* (not *she*). The nominative case is not available to it, since the embedded clause is tenseless. The source of the accusative marking is the higher verb *saw*, or, more precisely, a functional head associated with this verb (presumably, little v or AgrO). Exceptional case-marking of this kind is only possible when certain locality constraints are observed;

for instance, a CP (complementizer phrase) projection should not intervene between the embedding verb and the embedded subject.

Crucially, such instances reveal that accusative case can be checked even on a DP which does not constitute an argument of the relevant verb at all. Further, ECM extends the range of thematic roles available to accusative DPs. The latter comes to include roles that are assigned to subjects, such as agent (see 3a). Again, accusative case seems to be sensitive to syntactic restrictions but not to semantic ones.

Despite all these facts, there is evidence that accusative case is, at least under some uses and in some languages, associated with the aspectual meaning of boundedness, or event delimitation. This relation is revealed in at least three domains:

(i) Direct objects. In certain Finno-Ugric languages, including, for example, Finnish and Estonian, accusative case on the object alternates with the partitive. As a result, a nominal does not receive accusative case-marking by virtue of merely appearing in the position of an object of a transitive verb. Rather, the accusative is generally chosen if the predicate is telic and the nominal bounded. For atelic predicates and/or unbounded objects, the partitive is used.

(ii) Adjuncts. Cross-linguistically, accusative case-marking tends to appear on adjuncts of temporal duration, adjuncts measuring distance with verbs of motion, and multiplicative adjuncts, which specify how many times an event of a given kind is repeated. All these phrases contribute boundedness to the clause, as they delimit events, or measure them out.

(iii) Complements of prepositions. In certain Indo-European languages, such as Russian, German and Ancient Greek, some spatial prepositions accept complements in two or three different cases, one of which is accusative. The opposition has to do with directionality: case selection depends on whether the phrase fulfills the role of a goal, a location or a source. While locations are associated with different cases (including locative, instrumental and dative), depending on the language and on the given preposition, and sources are genitive in Ancient Greek and require special prepositions in languages like Russian, goals are systematically accusative. Given that an attachment of a goal phrase (but not of a location) contributes telicity, this use of the accusative can be viewed as an instance of the interaction between case and event delimitation.

In what follows, these three domains (and accusative case-marking in each) will be discussed one by one.

It should also be noted that in still other languages, accusative case is associated with a high degree of individuation. This issue will be addressed in Chapters 5 and 6.

4.1 OBJECTS IN FINNIC LANGUAGES

It is a well-established fact that direct objects often affect the aspectual properties of a clause. This property characterizes so-called incremental theme predicates, whose internal argument undergoes an incremental change over the course of the event. To illustrate, consider the verb *eat*. When it combines with an unbounded object, for example *apples*, the whole VP (*eat apples*) is atelic (lacks an inherent natural endpoint). In turn, if the verb combines with a bounded object, for example *an apple*, the VP (*eat an apple*) is telic. The fact that the object is bounded causes the whole VP to receive an inherent endpoint: once the whole apple is consumed, the eating event is completed. (See e.g. Vendler 1957, Verkuyl 1972 and Krifka 1992 for a detailed discussion.) While this relation between the object and telicity is present with incremental theme verbs, it is absent with many other predicates. For instance, the VP *love John* is atelic, even though *John* is bounded. This is due to the stative nature of the verb *love*.

Still, in numerous nominative-accusative languages, accusative case-marking is totally unrelated to verbal aspect. A nominal phrase receives accusative marking as long as it is base-generated in the object position and accusative case is available (e.g. the clause is not passive). However, Finnic languages form an exception. In these languages, accusative case on the object alternates with the partitive. Case selection strongly depends on the aspectual properties of the clause.

Languages that exhibit such a dependence include Finnish, Estonian, Karelian, Veps, Votic and Livonian (Lees 2015). While some differences between these languages are attested, the general pattern remains the same. The discussion below concentrates primarily on Finnish, which has received most attention in the generative linguistic literature. However, some examples from additional Finnic languages will be provided. I will also refer to certain instances where some Finnic languages differ from Finnish.[2] However, broadly speaking, the picture is rather similar in all these languages.

---

[2] The facts on Finnic languages other than Finnish in the discussion below are taken from Lees (2015), unless specified otherwise.

4.1.1 Types of Partitive Objects

In the discussion of the partitive case in Finnish, a distinction is often made between NP- and VP-related partitive (e.g. Kiparsky 1998, 2005). NP-related partitives are characterized by quantitative indeterminacy (Kiparsky 1998, 2005). These are mass nouns and bare plurals that carry a vague quantificational interpretation along the lines of 'some N' or 'some amount of N'. To illustrate, consider the following example from Kiparsky (2005:4):

(4) a. Jouluksi   satoi   lunta.
        Christmas$_{TRANSL}$ rained$_{3.SG}$ snow$_{PART}$
        'For Christmas, it snowed.'
     b. Jouluksi   satoi   pysyvän   lumen.
        Christmas$_{TRA}$ rained$_{3.SG}$ stay$_{PARTICIP\ ACC}$ snow$_{ACC}$
        'For Christmas, there fell a permanent (amount of) snow.'

In (4a), an unspecified, indeterminate quantity of snow is asserted to have fallen. This is indicated by the choice of the partitive case. In contrast, (4b) asserts the falling of a particular, specified amount of snow. Therefore, the object is accusative.

Accusative case is also acceptable if the quantity associated with the object is specified by the context. To illustrate, (5b) below asserts that the speaker has drunk up the contextually specified amount of water (e.g. all the water in the glass). Contextual specification is sufficient to license accusative case-marking. In contrast, (5a) does not contribute such an entailment; here, the amount of water is undefined, and it is possible, for example, that the speaker drank only half the water in the glass. (The sentence may also have different aspectual readings, an issue that will be discussed later in this section.)

(5) a. Join   vettä.
        drank$_{1.SG}$ water$_{PART}$
        'I drank some water / I was drinking water.'
     b. Join   veden.
        drank$_{1.SG}$ water$_{ACC}$
        'I drank the water.'

A similar use of partitive is also found in other Finnic languages, as illustrated in (6):

(6) a. VEPS (Lees 2015:44, from Kettunen 1943:99)
        mö   šä   meile   vinad.
        sell$_{IMPV.\ 2.SG}$ NOM.1.PL   ALL   alcohol$_{PART}$
        'Sell us some alcohol.'

b. KARELIAN (Lees 2015:44, from Ojajärvi 1950:165)
   maimoa   šoahä   hienuo   kaloa.
   baby-fish$_{SG. PART}$ get$_{3.PL}$ small$_{SG.PART}$ fish$_{SG.PART}$
   'they get baby fish, small fish.'
c. ESTONIAN (Lees 2015:43)
   Ma   tapsin   sääski.
   I   killed$_{1.SG}$ mosquitoes$_{PART}$
   'I killed / was killing (some) mosquitoes.'

This use is also quite similar to the Partitive Genitive in Slavic languages, discussed in Chapter 6. In general, certain parallels between
the partitive/accusative alternation in Finnic and the genitive/accusa-
tive alternation in Balto-Slavic can be observed, which is plausibly
a product of language change due to language contact (see e.g.
Kiparsky 1998, Lees 2015 and references therein).

In turn, VP-related partitive is directly related to verbal aspect. In
this context, verbs can be divided into three groups. Group 1 contains
those verbs whose object is obligatorily partitive (accusative case is, as
a rule, unavailable[3]). These are inherently atelic verbs, such as verbs of
emotion (e.g. *rakastaa* 'love'):

(7) Rakastan   sinua   / *sinut.
     love$_{1. SG}$ you$_{PART}$ / *you$_{ACC}$
     'I love you.'

Note that the partitive case in (7) is not the NP-related partitive. The
object is not quantitatively indeterminate and does not receive a
quantificational interpretation 'some amount of you'. Rather, here,
the choice of case has to do with the unboundedness of the predicate,
which, in turn, is due to the inherently stative, atelic nature of the verb.

The following examples from Lees (2015:71–72) illustrate this phenomenon for five Finnic languages:

(8) a. ESTONIAN
        te   otsite   ristilöödud   Jeesust
        you$_{PL.NOM}$ seek$_{2.PL}$ crucified   Jesus$_{PART}$
     b. LIVONIAN
        tēg   votšõt   rištõ   rabdõtõ   Jēzusõ
        you$_{PL.NOM}$ seek$_{2.PL}$ cross$_{ILL}$ nailed$_{PART}$ Jesus$_{PART}$
     c. FINNISH
        te   etsitte   ristiinnaulittua Jeesusta
        you$_{PL.NOM}$ seek$_{2.PL}$ crucified$_{PART}$ Jesus$_{PART}$
        'you are seeking the crucified Jesus' [the translation of (a)–(c)]

---

[3] But see examples (15b-c) below for an exception.

d. KARELIAN

tüö	ečittö	Iisussua	ristah	nuaglittuu
you$_{PL.NOM}$	seek$_{2.PL}$	Jesus$_{PART}$	cross$_{ILL}$	nailed$_{PART}$

'you are seeking Jesus crucified'

e. VEPS

tö	ecit	Iisusad	kudamb	oli	nagloitu	ristha
you$_{PL.NOM}$	seek$_{2.PL}$	Jesus$_{PART}$	who$_{NOM}$	was	nailed	cross$_{ILL}$

'you are seeking Jesus, who was nailed to the cross'

(Matt. 28:5)

Kiparsky (2005:2) provides the following list of partitive-taking verbs (obviously, the list is non-exhaustive): *halveksia* 'despise', *ihailla* 'admire', *ikävöidä* 'yearn for', *harrastaa* 'be interested in (as a hobby)', *huvittaa* 'amuse', *ik˝avystyttää* 'bore', *inhota* 'feel revulsion towards', *kadehtia* 'envy', *karttaa* 'avoid', *kehua, ylistää* 'praise', *kiinnostaa* 'interest', *kiittää* 'thank', *kunnioittaa* 'honor', *moittia* 'blame, reprimand', *onnitella* 'congratulate', *pelätä* 'fear', *rakastaa* 'love', *sietää* 'tolerate', *siunata* 'bless', *toivoa* 'hope for', *valittaa* 'complain about', *vihata* 'hate', *väsyttää* 'tire', *koettaa, yrittää* 'try', *pyytää* 'ask for', *merkitä, tarkoittaa* 'mean', *ajatella, pohtia* 'think about', *harkita* 'consider', *matkia* 'imitate', *paeta* 'flee', *kysyä* 'ask for', *heiluttaa* 'swing back and forth', *ravistaa* 'shake', *keinuttaa* 'rock', *nyökyttää* 'nod', *suudella* 'kiss', *hyväillä* 'caress', *koskettaa* 'touch', *hieroa* 'rub, massage'.

Group 2 consists of verbs that systematically take accusative objects (unless NP-related partitive is involved). As a rule, these are inherently telic verbs, such as *tappaa* 'kill':

(9) Tapoin   karhun   /*karhua.
     killed$_{1.SG}$ bear$_{ACC}$ / *bear$_{PART}$
     'I killed a/the bear.'

(based on Kiparsky 2005:2)

In (9), the object is count singular, meaning that it is not quantitatively indeterminate. After all, the sentence does not mean 'I killed some quantity/amount of a bear.' We know that we are dealing with a single bear. Therefore, NP-related partitive is unavailable here. Crucially, as a result, a partitive object is not licensed at all (unlike in (7) above), revealing that VP-related partitive is not available either. An example with another accusative-taking verb, *give*, from Lees (2015:70), is provided below for five Finnic languages. As pointed out by Lees, in this example, the speaker is referring to a particular, determined amount of power, "power to do the particular deeds which had been witnessed" (p. 70). This is why NP-related partitive is not used. And, given that the verb is inherently telic (its semantics involves a clear completion point), the object appears in the accusative case.

(10) a. ESTONIAN
          kes   annab   inimestele   säärase   meelevalla
          who   give$_{3.SG}$ men$_{ALL}$ such$_{ACC}$ power$_{ACC}$
      b. LIVONIAN
          kis   seḷḷiz   võimiz   um   rovstõn   andõn
          who   such$_{ACC}$ power$_{ACC}$ be$_{3SG}$ people$_{DAT}$ give$_{PPTCP}$
      c. FINNISH
          joka   oli   antanut   ihmisille   sellaisen   vallan
          who   was$_{3.SG}$ give$_{PPTCP}$ men$_{ALL}$ such$_{ACC}$ power$_{ACC}$
      d. KARELIAN
          kudai   andoi   ristikanzale   nengozen   vallan
          who   gave$_{3.SG}$ man$_{ALL}$ such$_{ACC}$ power$_{ACC}$
      e. VEPS
          kudamb   oli   andnu   mehile   mugoman   valdan
          who   was$_{3.SG}$ give$_{PPTCP}$ men$_{ALL}$ such$_{ACC}$ power$_{ACC}$
          'who gives / gave / has given / had given such a power to men'
                                                                        (Matt. 9:8)

Kiparsky (2005:2) lists the following Group 2 verbs: *saada* 'get', *löytää*
'find', *saavuttaa* 'reach', *ostaa* 'buy', *ottaa* 'take', *säästää* 'save', *pudottaa*
'drop', *suorittaa* 'carry out', *kadottaa, menettää, hukata* 'lose (possession)', *hävitä* 'lose (game, fight)', *löytää* 'find', *hyväksyä* 'accept', *panna,
asettaa* 'put', *tappaa* 'kill', *antaa, lahjoittaa* 'give', *kaataa* 'fell', *mainita*
'mention', *siepata* 'catch', *omaksua* 'appropriate', *ripustaa* 'hang', *istut-
taa* 'plant', *myöntää* 'admit', *kieltää* 'deny'.

Finally, Group 3 contains verbs which allow both partitive and accusative objects (independently of NP-related partitive). These are verbs
that can form part of both telic and atelic event predicates (e.g. incremental theme verbs and degree achievements). Telicity is associated
with accusative case-marking and atelicity with partitive case. To illustrate, let us consider again the incremental theme verb *drink*. This verb is
compatible with both accusative and partitive objects. In the latter case,
both NP-related and VP-related partitive is possible. All these patterns
are illustrated in (5), repeated in (11) below for the sake of convenience:

(11) a. Join   vettä.
          drank$_{1. SG}$ water$_{PART}$
          'I drank some water / I was drinking water.'
      b. Join   veden.
          drank$_{1.SG}$ water$_{ACC}$
          'I drank the water.'

(11b), which contains an accusative object, denotes a bounded drinking event which has reached completion. Obviously, a drinking event

can only be completed if a limited amount of water is involved, and indeed, as mentioned above, the accusative object is necessarily interpreted as denoting a bounded, contextually presupposed quantity. In turn, (11a) may receive an unbounded reading according to which a drinking event was in progress at the reference time but has not necessarily reached completion. This would mean that a VP-related partitive is involved. Alternatively, it could denote an event that has been completed but included an indeterminate, unspecified amount of water. In that case, the meaning is comparable to that of *I drank some water*, and an NP-related partitive is involved.

With *drink*, as well as with other incremental theme verbs, the aspect of the predicate is strongly interrelated with the properties of the object. Therefore, it is not surprising that aspect is reflected in object case. However, the relation between case and aspect extends beyond these verbs. Consider, for example, the pair of sentences in (12). (The sentences are taken from Csirmaz 2006, ex. 1–2.)

(12) a. Hän ajoi autoa.
    he drove car$_{PART}$
    'He drove the car.'
  b. Hän ajoi auton talliin.
    he drove car$_{ACC}$ garage$_{ILL}$
    'He drove the car to the garage.'

Drive the car to the garage is a telic event predicate, in contrast to *drive a car*. However, the car is bounded in both instances. What influences telicity in this example, as well as with many other verbs of motion, is the presence of a **goal phrase**. The goal phrase *talliin* 'to a/the garage' provides the **path** undergone by the car with an endpoint, and as a result, the event predicate becomes bounded. Therefore, the object in (12b) appears in the accusative case. Crucially, it is the boundedness of the path, not of the object itself, that results in accusative case-marking, even though, morphologically, the latter is observed on the DP.

An analogous example from Kiparsky (2005:3) is provided in (13). This time, however, the endpoint of a path is contributed in the (b) sentence not linguistically but rather contextually.

(13) a. Siirsin isoäitiä
    moved$_{1.SG}$ grandma$_{PART}$
    'I moved grandma.' [around, a ways]
  b. Siirsin isoäidin
    moved$_{1.SG}$ grandma$_{ACC}$
    'I moved grandma.' [to another place]

If a potentially unbounded event of motion whose theme is the grandmother is reported, partitive case is used (13a). However, if the grandmother is asserted to have been moved to a particular location, that is, the motion event is bounded, the object appears in the accusative case (13b). Again, boundedness has nothing to do with the properties of the object. It is exactly the same grandmother in both instances, and she is equally bounded. The difference has to do with the path along which the event of motion proceeds and whether or not this path has an endpoint. In (13b), this piece of information is provided contextually, but this is sufficient for case-marking to be affected. And, crucially, the aspectual contrast in (13) is reflected on the object. Thus, we can conclude that in Finnish, object case is sensitive to the boundedness of the whole event predicate, even if the object itself does not contribute to this boundedness.

Resultative phrases constitute yet another way to turn an otherwise unbounded predicate into a bounded one. (The sentences below are taken from Kiparsky 2005:3.)

(14) a. Hieroin   sitä.
         rubbed$_{1.SG}$ it$_{PART}$
         'I rubbed it.'
      b. Hieroin   sen   pehmeäksi.
         rubbed$_{1.SG}$ it$_{ACC}$ soft$_{SG.TRA}$
         'I kneaded it soft.'

Without a resultative phrase, the predicate in (14a) is interpreted as unbounded, and the object appears in the partitive case. However, once a resultative phrase is added (14b), the predicate becomes bounded, and accusative case is licensed.

Additional verbs belonging to Group 3 that are listed by Kiparsky (2005) include: *syödä* 'eat', *leikata* 'cut', *kaivaa* 'dig', *kirjoittaa* 'write', *lukea* 'read', *tutkia* 'investigate', *siirtää* 'move', *sekoittaa* 'mix'.

It should be pointed out, however, that the division of verbs into Groups 1 and 3 (partitive-taking and alternating) is somewhat problematic. In fact, even the most purely atelic (and thus potentially belonging to Group 1) verbs can under certain circumstances appear in a bounded frame and get associated with an endpoint. In this situation, they become compatible with accusative objects. This is illustrated in (15) for *rakastaa* 'love':

(15) a. Rakastan   sinua.
         love$_{1.SG}$ you$_{PART}$
         'I love you.'

b. Rakastan   sinut   kuoliaaksi.
   love$_{1.SG}$ you$_{ACC}$ death$_{TRA}$
   'I love you to death.' (Lees 2015:39, from Sands 2000)

c. Rakastin   **teidät**   rappiolle
   love$_{PST.1.SG}$ you$_{PL.ACC}$ ruin$_{ADESS}$
   'I loved you into ruin.' (Eino Leino, as quoted in Kiparsky 2005, ex 16i)

Even this "purely" unbounded emotive predicate may be turned into a bounded one with the addition of a resultative phrase. And in such a situation, accusative case-marking is licensed. Such facts are very important, as they show that the choice of case is not a matter of lexical, idiosyncratic restrictions of individual verbs (and, consequently, we are not dealing with an inherent case). Rather, structural case is involved, and the choice between the accusative and the partitive frames is governed by aspect-related rules.

Before we proceed to the discussion of these rules and generalizations, it is important to note yet another factor that affects the choice of case – clause polarity. Specifically, Finnic languages exhibit the phenomenon of **partitive of negation**. Under negation, the object appears, as a rule, in the partitive case. This is illustrated for Finnish in (16):

(16) a. Tapoin   karhun   / *karhua.
        killed$_{1.SG}$ bear$_{ACC}$ / bear$_{PART}$
        'I killed a/the bear.'

     b. En   tappanut   karhua   / *karhun.
        NEG$_{1.SG}$ killed   bear$_{PART}$ bear$_{ACC}$
        'I didn't kill a/the bear.'

(16a) is identical to (9) above, which has been shown to allow only accusative marking. The NP-related partitive is ruled out because the object is count singular, and the VP-related partitive because the verb is inherently telic. However, under negation, the case pattern is reversed (16b). Only partitive case is licensed, whereas an accusative object becomes unacceptable.

(17) below, from Lees (2015:75), illustrates partitive of negation in five Finnic languages.[4]

(17) a. ESTONIAN
        keegi   muu   ei   tunne   Poega
        anyone   other   NEG   know$_{CON.NEG}$ son$_{PART}$

---

[4] Some Finnic languages exhibit occasional exceptions to the rule, but the tendency is the same. See Lees (2015:34, 75–76) for discussion.

b. LIVONIAN
mitykš	äb	tund	Puoigõ
nobody	NEG$_{3.SG}$	know$_{CON.NEG}$	son$_{PART}$

c. FINNISH
Poikaa	ei	tunne	kukaan	muu
son$_{PART}$	NEG$_{3.SG}$	know$_{CON.NEG}$	nobody	other

d. KARELIAN
Poigua	ei	tunne	niken
son$_{PART}$	NEG$_{3.SG}$	know$_{CON.NEG}$	nobody

e. VEPS
niken	toine	ei	tunde	Poigad
nobody	other	NEG$_{3.SG}$	know$_{CON.NEG}$	son$_{PART}$

'nobody (else) knows the Son.'

(Matt. 11:27)

(17) shows that the phenomenon of partitive of negation is not limited to Finnish but is also present in Estonian, Livonian, Karelian and Veps.

4.1.2 How Many Object Partitives – One, Two or Three?

The existence of three types of object partitive – NP-related, VP-related and the partitive of negation – naturally raises the question of whether they should be unified. Should all partitive objects receive a uniform account, or should they rather be treated separately? Different approaches are taken in this respect. For instance, Lees (2015:34) notes that partitive of negation "is considered grammaticalized" in Finnic languages. In other words, it is often treated as a purely syntactic case that gets checked on any nominal that appears in the object position in a negative clause, independently of semantics. However, some researchers analyze partitive of negation as an instance of VP-related partitive. The reasoning is along the following lines: VP-related partitive (or partitive in general) is associated with unboundedness, atelicity or incompletion. Negative clauses, too, are inherently characterized by lack of completion. Even if the verb is inherently telic, in a negative sentence, the event is not asserted to be completed. This is why the object appears in partitive case. This approach is taken by Lees, who states in this context: "The action has not been completed, because it never took place" (p. 34). In a similar vein, Vainikka (1989) and Vainikka and Maling (1996) state that "the feature [+COMPLETED] is incompatible with negation; one cannot simultaneously negate a verb and imply that the action has been completed" (p. 194).

Turning to NP-related and VP-related partitive, again, different approaches can be found. For instance, Kratzer (2002) proposes that NP-related partitive is assigned in the presence of a phonologically empty D, by analogy with phrases containing overt numerals, which combine with partitive NPs in Finnish. An analogous approach is proposed by Pesetsky (1982) for Partitive Genitive case in Russian, as will be discussed in detail in Chapter 6. In contrast, the VP-related partitive is analyzed by Kratzer as linked to (a)telicity. Kiparsky (1998), in contrast, treats both VP-related and NP-related partitive as the same phenomenon, whereby partitive case is assigned to objects of unbounded VPs. In turn, a VP is unbounded if it contains an unbounded argument or an unbounded head. In the former case, we get the so-called NP-related partitive. In the latter, a VP-related one. But in both instances, we are dealing with the same phenomenon: partitive case-marking on the object in an unbounded predicate.

4.1.3 Partitive for Unboundedness or Accusative for Boundedness? ▨

Turning back to the relation between case and aspect, the following generalization can be made. Partitive case is strongly associated with atelicity, unboundedness and incompletion. This definitely holds for VP-related partitive, but arguably, this property characterizes partitive objects in general. In turn, accusative case is linked to telicity, boundedness and completion.

This generalization allows (at least) two different interpretations. It is possible that partitive case-checking is related to unboundedness, while the accusative is the 'elsewhere' case, the default case of the object. Alternatively, accusative may be analyzed as a case that is, syntactically and/or semantically, related to boundedness, and partitive – as the default object case.

Again, both approaches are found in the literature. The first approach (one that treats partitive as a semantically special case and accusative as the unmarked one) is quite natural given that the accusative tends to be the default object case cross-linguistically (as long as nominative-accusative languages are considered). As pointed out by Vainikka and Maling (1996), indeed, this is the approach that has traditionally been taken to Finnish. It is often adopted in modern generative linguistics as well. To illustrate, de Hoop (1992) analyzes the Finnish partitive as a weak structural case, with partitive objects functioning as predicate modifiers and thus being of the semantic type $\ll$e,t$>$,$<$e,t$\gg$. Krifka (1992) treats Finnish partitive as an instance of a 'part of' operator. Crucially, the 'part of' relation can hold between both objects and events, as shown in (18). On the event level, it is imposed by the progressive operator (18b). To illustrate, an event of "be eating an apple" constitutes part of an event "eat an apple" (the latter containing the natural endpoint). Analogously, the

Finnish predicate *syödä omenaa* 'eat apple$_{PART}$' denotes a set of events which are parts of *syödä omenan* 'eat apple$_{ACC}$' events.

(18) a. PART = $\lambda P \lambda x' \exists x[P(x) \wedge x' \sqsubseteq x]$
      b. PROG = $\lambda P \lambda e' \exists e[P(e) \wedge e' \sqsubseteq e]$

Kiparsky (1998), too, treats the partitive as a case that is assigned in the presence of a particular semantic property, specifically, unboundedness. As pointed out above, he treats a VP as unbounded if it contains an unbounded verb or an unbounded object (or both). Partitive case is assigned to objects of unbounded VPs.

Quite recently, Huhmariniemi and Miljan (2018) argued that partitive is a marked case. They claim that imperfectivity/unboundedness must be contributed by the partitive case since the alternative perfective interpretation is compatible with different case forms, specifically, nominative and genitive (they disagree with the view that treats the latter two as realizations of the same, abstract accusative, case in different environments). If the bounded reading is attested with different forms, whereas unboundedness is systematically linked to the partitive, this suggests that the latter is semantically marked for aspect.

Further, they claim that the partitive is lexically selected by certain verbs, such as the Finnish *rakastaa* 'love', which makes it impossible to treat this case as unmarked (19).

(19) Pekka   rakastaa   **Merjaa** /   *Merjan.
      Pekka$_{NOM}$ love$_{PRES.3.SG}$ Merja$_{PART.SG}$ / Merja$_{ACC.SG}$
      'Pekka loves Merja.'

                                                (Huhmariniemi and Miljan 2018, ex. 18)

Note, however, that the lexical nature of the partitive with such verbs is questionable. After all, *love* is inherently atelic, and it is plausibly this aspectual property that results in the particular marking on the object. In other words, we are dealing with a systematic pattern. Further, if a bounded interpretation is pushed, an accusative object does become acceptable (which is not what one would predict for lexical case-assignment). This has been shown in (15) above.

Huhmariniemi and Miljan provide further evidence for their approach. They point out that the partitive case has a clear semantic effect when an attempt is made to force it on count singular subjects (with which it is typically not acceptable):

(20) Täällä   pysähtyy   juna /   **junaa.**
     here   stop_{PRES.3.SG}   train_{SG.NOM} /   train_{SG.**PART**}
     'Here stops (a) train / intended: (some part of a/the) train.'
                                          (Huhmariniemi and Miljan 2018, ex. 21b)

The choice of the partitive form in (20) forces the meaning according to which some part of a train stops in the specified location. This looks like a semantic effect contributed by the partitive form.

Analogously, partitive is sensitive to the number of the second noun in pseudo-partitives, to which it is assigned, suggesting that it does not behave like an unmarked case.

(21)   ESTONIAN
       a. Ostsin   hunniku   raamatuid.
          buy_{PST.1.SG}   stack_{SG.GEN}   book_{PL.PART}
          'I bought a pile of books.'
       b. *?Ostsin   hunniku   raamatut.
          buy._{PST.1.SG}   stack_{SG.GEN}   book_{SG.PART}
          lit.: 'I bought a pile of (pieces of) book.'
                                          (Huhmariniemi and Miljan 2018, ex. 22)

The alternative view according to which accusative case is related to semantics, whereas partitive is the unmarked object case, is defended in the literature as well. For instance, this approach is taken in Heinämäki (1984). Also, Vainikka (1989) and, following her, Vainikka and Maling (1996) argue that in Finnish, accusative case is assigned in the presence of the feature [+COMPLETED], while partitive constitutes the default case of complements. They state that "accusative is associated with a resultative aspect, and only occurs when assigned by a verb with a feature [+COMPLETED]" (Vainikka and Maling 1996:194). In contrast to the accusative, which is linked to a particular semantic and syntactic environment, the partitive, they point out, is assigned in a wide range of contexts. We find it with atelic event predicates, with telic ones when it fulfills the quantificational, NP-related function, under negation, with unaccusative predicates and in existential sentences. Further, partitive case is assigned to nominal complements of numerals, as mentioned above, and to complements of prepositions. Last but not least, partitive case is assigned by ECM verbs to the subject of their complement clause (22). If a language has an unmarked object case, it is this case that we expect to find in such a construction. And in Finnish, this is partitive rather than accusative.

(22)   Liisa   pitää   sinua   / ??sinut   älykkäänä.
       Liisa   considers   you$_{PART}$ / you$_{ACC}$ intelligent$_{ESS.SG}$
       'Liisa considers you intelligent.'

                                              (Vainikka and Maling 1996:188)

Partitive case is also treated as default/unmarked by Kiparsky (2001b) and Vainikka and Brattico (2014). Vainikka and Brattico mention the following formal implementations of this approach: "What we might say is that all functional projections have the default option of assigning the partitive – and if all constructions in Finnish have at least one functional projection, then the lowest functional projection c-commanding a local DP would assign the partitive. Alternatively, the partitive is assigned by any lexical complement-taking head" (p. 28). In turn, they take accusative case to be assigned by Asp(ect) head to direct objects that denote participants in completed actions (see also Section 4.2.4.2 for Pereltsvaig's 2000 analysis).

To sum up this subsection, some analyses relate the partitive case to unboundedness and others link the accusative to boundedness. In Section 2, we will see further evidence in favor of the latter approach.

4.1.4   The Problem of Accusative-Assigning Statives

4.1.4.1   Introducing the Problem

Independently of whether a given analysis treats the accusative case as related to boundedness or the partitive as related to its absence, a serious problem is posed by the existence of a set of stative verbs which take **accusative** complements in Finnish. These verbs include, for example, *omistaa* 'own', *tietää* 'know' and *nähdä* 'see'. The longer list provided by Kiparsky (2005:6) contains the following: *omistaa, omata* 'own', *sisältää* 'contain', *käsittää* 'comprise', *muistaa* 'remember', *tietää* 'know', *tuntea* 'know', *ymmärtää* 'understand' (something), *myöntää* 'acknowledge', *katsoa* 'regard, consider', *oivaltaa* 'realize', *uskoa* 'believe' (something), *nähdä* 'see', *kuulla* 'hear', *maistaa* 'taste' (non-agentive), *haistaa* 'smell' (non-agentive) *huomata, havaita, keksiä* 'notice', *tajuta* 'be aware of', *kokea* 'experience', *oivaltaa, hoksata* 'realize'.

This list poses a serious problem for any analysis that is based on the relation between object case and telicity. After all, the predicates listed above are inherently atelic, and still, they take accusative complements. It should be emphasized that Finnic languages do not behave uniformly as far as these predicates are concerned. For instance, the Estonian counterparts of the above-listed verbs generally take partitive complements. Estonian is, thus, more "well-behaved" in this respect, and more easily compatible with a telicity-based approach. Finnish facts, however, raise a question regarding the appropriateness of an aspectual analysis.

4.1.4.2 *Mapping to Events: Kratzer (2002)*

Different attempts have been made to solve the problem. For instance, Kratzer (2002) points out that accusative-taking statives pattern with telic predicates in that they satisfy Mapping to Events, a notion formally represented in (23).

(23) $\forall R[MAP\text{-}E(R) \leftrightarrow \forall e, x, x' [R(e, x) \land x' \sqsubseteq x \longrightarrow \exists e' [e' \sqsubseteq e \land R(e', x')]]]$
                                                                        (from Krifka 1992:39)

Roughly, this means that if a certain relation (presumably, the one contributed by the verb) holds between an event *e* and an object *x*, then for every (relevant) part of *x*, there will be a part of *e* that stands to it in the same relation. To illustrate, consider the telic predicate *eat an apple*. If a (completed) event of eating an apple takes place, this means that for every relevant part of the apple, there is an eating sub-event during which this part is consumed. (Relevant in this case means, roughly, edible.) Kratzer notes that the case is similar with predicates like *contain*. Thus, if a box contains some documents, it also contains all the parts of these documents. Analogously, if a person owns a house, (s)he owns all its parts. This is why the Finnish counterparts of *own* and *contain* pattern with telic predicates in their case-related properties. In contrast, partitive-taking stative predicates like *hate* are different: hating John does not entail hating all the parts of John. I may very well like his eyes and still hate the person.

Kiparsky (2005), however, points to a problem of this explanation. He notes that perception predicates do not satisfy Mapping to Events. To illustrate, seeing a house does not entail seeing all the relevant parts of the house. Still, non-agentive perception verbs take accusative objects in Finnish. For instance, the Finnish counterpart of *see*, *nähdä*, assigns accusative case to its object. Thus, accusative case can be licensed in the absence of Mapping to Events. This means that Finnish statives still pose a problem.

4.1.4.3 *Boundedness and (Non-)Gradability: Kiparsky (1998, 2005)*

Kiparsky (1998, 2005) proposes an alternative explanation for this puzzle. He argues that the object case alternation is based on the notion of boundedness and that **accusative-taking statives are bounded**. He further analyzes boundedness as the absence of gradability. **Bounded VPs denote non-gradable properties**. In turn, a gradable property is one that holds of different individuals to different degrees, the most classical example being an adjective like *tall*. Formally, a gradable predicate takes a degree argument.

Let us first concentrate on states. Those stative verbs that take partitive objects are indeed typically gradable. To illustrate, verbs like *love* and *hate* denote emotions which can be experienced with different degrees of intensity. As a result, it is possible to combine these verbs with degree expressions, for example *John loves Mary very much / strongly, I fear him greatly*. In contrast, stative predicates that combine with accusative objects tend to be non-gradable. We cannot say *The box contains the documents very much / strongly* or *John owns the house considerably*. Either the relation of containment/owing holds or it does not. There is no place for gradability here. No degree argument.

The situation becomes somewhat trickier when we turn to non-statives, however. If gradability is equated with unboundedness, it follows that, for instance, the atelic VP *eat apples* is gradable, whereas the telic *eat an apple* is not. But this is not the way in which gradability is generally treated in the literature on verbal scalarity. Rather, both phrases are taken to be gradable, as both denote events that involve progress along a scale. In this example, it is a volume scale that orders portions of apple(s). In the course of an eating event bigger and bigger portions are consumed. The difference between the two VPs has to do with the fact that with *eat an apple*, the change along the scale is bounded. It is specified which point is reached at the end of the event (the maximal point on the scale, one that represents the apple in its fullness). In other words, the phrase involves a bounded **degree of change**, the degree that represents the difference undergone by an argument between the beginning and the endpoint of the event (Kennedy and Levin 2002). In contrast, with *eat apples*, this degree is unbounded; different events falling under the denotation of this predicate involve different quantities/portions of apples being consumed and are thus linked to different degrees along the scale of volume. In other words, with *eat an apple*, the degree is fixed, the degree variable receives a value. With *eat apples*, the degree is unbounded and is allowed to vary from event to event.

Indeed, this seems to be the crucial point. Telic predicates, even if they are originally gradable like *eat an apple*, have the degree argument saturated, and no longer look for a degree. As such, they denote properties of events, similarly to inherently non-gradable predicates like *kill a bear* – or *own a house*. In contrast, unbounded gradable VPs like *eat apples* denote relations between events and degrees, since they contain an unsaturated degree argument. Following Kiparsky's proposal, we can conclude that accusative case is checked in those VPs that lack an unsaturated degree argument and are non-gradable in this sense. But Djalali (2012) and Acton (2014) point to another problem of the gradability-based analysis. Certain gradable verbs in Finnish appear to take accusative objects. Analogously, there are non-gradable verbs (at least, ones that cannot combine with degree expressions) whose object has to be partitive. Counterexamples of the first type include *tietää* 'know', *tuntea* 'know' and *uskoa* 'believe'. Djalali (2012:137) provides the following examples to show that these predicates are compatible with degree expressions:

(24) a. John knows calculus somewhat more than analysis.
     b. John believes Mary less than most (others).

Acton (2014) adds *loukata* 'injure, wound, hurt' and *ymmärtää* 'understand' to the list. He further provides a list of verbs that represent the second type of counterexamples (non-gradable partitive-taking predicates): *sohia* 'poke', *lyödä* 'hit, strike, knock, beat', *suudella* 'kiss', *läimäyttää* 'slap, smack, slam', *nipistää* 'pinch, tweak' and *nuolla* 'lick'.

4.1.4.4 *Standard Change: Acton (2014)*

Acton proposes an alternative analysis which is also based on the notion of scalarity. He concentrates on a specific class of verbs – 'potential for change' (PFC) predicates. These are predicates that entail some impingement or force exerted upon their arguments (based on Beavers 2011). These predicates include, but are not limited to, verbs that denote a change in their argument that takes place along some scale (**gradual change verbs** in the terminology of Kennedy and Levin 2002), for example *eat*, *heat* and *ascend*. (With *eat*, the change is along the volume scale contributed by the object; with *heat*, along the temperature scale and with *ascend*, along a path scale.) Roughly, Acton proposes that accusative case marks objects of those verbs whose argument is entailed to undergo **standard change**. In turn, standard change is a scalar change in whose course a "goal degree," a lexically or contextually supplied standard value (a standard of evaluation), is reached. Basically, this standard constitutes a certain result or endpoint represented as a degree on a scale. To illustrate, in the case of *eat an apple*, the standard constitutes the maximal degree on the volume scale associated with the object, that is, the degree that corresponds to the apple in its wholeness (rather than one third of the apple, half of the apple, etc.). With the verb *clean*, as in *John cleaned the table*, the standard corresponds to the maximal degree along the cleanliness scale (perfect cleanliness).

Acton's analysis captures the fact that telic predicates take accusative objects (unless NP-related partitive is involved or unboundedness is contributed via imperfectivity). In the literature on verb scalarity, telicity is indeed linked to gradual change which is bounded and in whose course a certain standard value is reached. Recall the above discussion in which it was pointed out that *eat an apple* involves a bounded degree of change, unlike *eat apples*.

But the analysis extends even further. To illustrate, consider the verb *shoot*. Arguably, if we are not dealing with iterativity, *shoot at* (and miss), *shoot* (and hit) and *shoot* (and kill) are all telic. While the former is treated as atelic under some accounts (e.g. Kratzer 2002), the latter two seem to be telic under any approach to telicity. Still, in Finnish, accusative case-marking on the object of *shoot* (e.g. in *shoot a bear*) is typically accompanied by the inference that the bear is shot dead. In other words, the accusative case forces (or at least favors) the third reading. Acton explains this in the following way. The verb itself does not entail killing (or, for that matter, even hitting). However, accusative case-marking contributes an entailment of a standard change along some scale. With this particular verb, a conventionally associated result is death. Therefore, death constitutes the (contextually provided) standard (presumably, on the scale of physical harm), or the "goal degree," which, if the object is accusative, is entailed to be attained.

Importantly, however, Acton's analysis is explicitly limited to a particular subset of predicates. Specifically, he concentrates on PFC predicates in the absence of NP-related partitive and/or progressive and habitual operators. Indeed, Acton successfully captures the case pattern with the predicates under discussion. However, the proposed analysis cannot be extended to accusative-taking statives. After all, these predicates do not entail any change, let alone standard (or bounded) one. Yet their objects appear in the accusative.

4.1.4.5 Existential Commitment: Djalali (2012)

Djalali (2012) takes the opposite direction by concentrating specifically on stative predicates. Having rejected Kiparsky's gradability-based proposal for reasons discussed at the bottom of Section 4.1.4.3, Djalali puts forward an alternative account. Under this approach, the key property on which case-checking of objects of stative verbs depends is **existential commitment**. This is an entail-ment that the object exists (i.e. that it has a referent or quantifies over a non-empty set). Formally, this condition is represented in (25), taken from Djalali (2012:140).

(25) $\forall w \forall x, y \ (R_w(x,y) \longrightarrow \text{Exist}_w(y))$

We are dealing with one of the properties that distinguish intensional predicates from extensional ones. To illustrate, consider the inten-sional verb *seek* and the extensional verb *find*. *John sought a unicorn* does not entail the existence of unicorns. In contrast, *John found a unicorn* entails that there exists a unicorn whom John found. The object of *find* carries existential commitment, whereas the object of *seek* does not.

Crucially, Djalali argues that existential commitment constitutes the property that distinguishes accusative-taking statives from parti-tive-taking ones. Objects of accusative-assigning stative verbs carry existential commitment. To illustrate, if John owns a house, there must exist a house that John owns. Analogously, if a box contains documents, the existence of documents is entailed. Thus, (25) is satis-fied. In contrast, predicates like *love* and *fear*, whose Finnish counter-parts normally take partitive objects, do not contribute existential entailment. It is possible to love or fear something that does not exist in reality.

Indeed, existential commitment seems to divide stative verbs into the right two groups. Further, existential commitment has indepen-dently been argued to affect object case-marking in Russian by Kagan (2009, 2010b, 2013). Kagan claims that objects of negated and strong intensional verbs appear in the genitive case in the absence of exis-tential entailment and/or presupposition. (See Chapter 6 for a detailed discussion.) The possibility that both Russian and Finnish are sensitive to the same semantic property, although in somewhat different ways, is definitely of interest. However, as Djalali acknowledges, it is not clear at this point in what way existential commitment can be unified with the property responsible for case selection with eventive verbs in Finnish. Can we find a way to unify existential commitment with telicity and its absence with atelicity? And how do we explain the fact that specifically with stative predicates, existence, rather that telicity, determines the form of the object?

To sum up this section, meanwhile, accusative-taking statives con-stitute a challenge to an analysis of the partitive/accusative object case alternation in Finnish. Apart from this subset of predicates, however, case selection is rather clearly associated with the notion of bounded-ness (which is, though, defined in somewhat different ways by different researchers). Accusative case-marking is typically observed with bounded predicates and partitive with unbounded ones (where unboundedness may result from the presence of an atelic verb, a quantitatively indeterminate object, a habitual or progressive operator, and/or be associated with an unbounded scalar change, in whose course no independently supplied standard, or "goal degree," is achieved).

With this relation between case and aspect in mind, let us turn to the domain of adjuncts.

4.2 ACCUSATIVE ADJUNCTS

4.2.1 Accusative Case-Marking on Adjuncts across Languages

Cross-linguistically, certain types of adjuncts tend to be realized as accusative nominals rather than prepositional or adverbial phrases. Such adjuncts are illustrated in (26) for Russian:

(26) a. Dima pisal pis'mo dva časa.
       Dima wrote letter$_{ACC}$ two$_{ACC}$ hours[5]
       'Dima was writing a letter for two hours. '

   b. Anton probežal dva kilometra.
      Anton ran two$_{ACC}$ kilometers
      'Anton ran two kilometers.'

   c. Lena stirala éto plat'je pjat' raz.
      Lena washed this$_{ACC}$ dress$_{ACC}$ five$_{ACC}$ times
      'Lena washed this dress five times.'

In (26a), the phrase *dva časa* 'two hours' measures the temporal duration of the writing event. It is realized as an accusative NP. In (26b), the adjunct *dva kilometra* 'two kilometers' specifies the distance that was covered by Anton in the course of the running event. Again, the phrase is accusative and no preposition is used. Finally, (26c) is an iterative sentence that contains an accusative adjunct *pjat' raz* 'five times', which specifies how many times the event was repeated.

---

[5] In Russian nominal phrases that contain numerals, the case of the whole nominal is often realized on the numeral rather than on the noun. The latter appears in the genitive which, in turn, is checked by the numeral (but see Pesetsky 2013 for a different approach to the source of the genitive case).

Russian is far from being unique in assigning accusative case to these types of adjuncts – durational, distance measuring and multiplicative. The same phenomenon is illustrated for several additional languages (belonging to different language families) in (27–29) below. Korean examples are taken from Wechsler and Lee (1996:631–632).

(27) DURATIONAL

  a. Tom-i   kongwu-lul twu sikan-tongan-ul hay-ss-ta Korean
     Tom.$_{NOM}$ study.$_{ACC}$ two hours.period.$_{ACC}$ do$_{PST.DEC}$
     'Tom studied for two hours.'

  b. Maija luki kirjaa   tunnin.   Finnish
     Maija read book$_{PART}$ hour$_{ACC}$
     'Maija read a/the book for an hour.'
                         (Wechsler and Lee 1996:653)

  c. Decem annos   regnavit   Latin
     ten   years$_{ACC}$ reigned
     'He reigned for ten years.'
                         (Wechsler and Lee 1996:657)

(28) DISTANCE MEASURING

  a. Tom-i   isip   mail-ul   tali-ess-ta.   Korean
     Tom.$_{NOM}$ twenty miles.$_{ACC}$ ran.$_{PST.DEC}$
     'Tom ran twenty miles.'

  b. Etiopialainen kestävyysjuoksija Haile Gebrselassie juoksi
     Ethiopian   endurance.runner Haile Gebrselassie ran
     kahden   mailin (3218 m)   uudeksi
     two$_{ACC}$ mile$_{ACC}$ (3218 m)   new$_{TRA}$
     maailmanennätykseksi 8.01,08   Finnish
     world.record$_{TRA}$ 8.01,08
     'The Ethiopian long-distance runner Haile Gebrselassie ran two miles (3218 m) for a new world record in 8.01,08.'[6]

(29) MULTIPLICATIVE

  a. Tom-i   mikwuk-ul twu   pen-ul   pangmwun-hay-ss-ta.
     Tom.$_{NOM}$ America.$_{ACC}$ two   times.$_{ACC}$ visit.do.$_{PST-DEC}$
                                   Korean
     'Tom visited America twice.'

  b. Olen   ollut   siellä yhden   kerran.   Finnish
     be$_{1.SG}$ been   there one$_{ACC}$ time$_{ACC}$
     'I have been there once.'

---

[6] www.mtv.fi/sport/muut-lajit/uutiset/artikkeli/gebrselassie-jai-runsaan-sekunnin-miljoonista/5488014.

Moreover, it turns out that in those languages which lack morphological case (or exhibit it to a highly limited degree), adjuncts of the types specified above are often realized as bare NPs. This is illustrated below for Hebrew and English. Wechsler and Lee (1996) demonstrate that the situation is similar, at least as far as durational adjuncts are concerned, in Bengali, Swedish, French and Mandarin.

(30)   HEBREW

    a. dibarnu   SaloS   Saot.
       talked$_{1.PL}$ three   hours
       'We talked for three hours.'

    b. dani   rac   SloSa   kilometrim.
       Dani   ran   three   kilometers
       'Dani ran three kilometers.'

    c. ruti   hitkaSra   xameS   peamim.
       Ruti   phoned   five   times
       'Ruti phoned five times.'

(31)   ENGLISH

    a. John ran two kilometers.
    b. Jane called me five times.

Durative adjuncts tend to be realized in English as prepositional phrases headed by *for*, for example *for two hours*. However, even here, nominal, rather than prepositional, phrases can be found, as illustrated in (32):

(32)   Wait a minute!

The availability of nominal adjuncts of duration sometimes results in an object/adjunct ambiguity. The latter is employed by Lewis Carroll for the creation of a humorous effect in the passage below:

> 'Would you — be good enough —' Alice panted out, after running a little further, 'to **stop a minute**— just to get — one's breath again?'
> 'I'm *good* enough,' the King said, 'only I'm not *strong* enough. You see, a minute goes by so fearfully quick. You might as well try to stop a Bandersnatch!' (Lewis Carroll, *Through the Looking-Glass*)

An indefinite nominal following the verb *stop* can be either an object (as in *Can you stop a rumor?*) or, if the verb is used intransitively, a temporal adjunct (as in *Can you stop a minute?*). It is indeed important for our purposes that the adjunct is realized here in the same way as a direct object.

Assuming that, by Case Filter, every nominal expression must receive/check case, we conclude that the adjuncts in sentences like (30)–(32) receive abstract case. In the absence of a preposition, it seems quite plausible that the case they receive is structural, and, more precisely, that this is (abstract) accusative. But, of course, this view is theory-internal.

While the three types of adjuncts illustrated above (durational, multiplicative and distance measures) tend to be realized as accusative or bare nominals cross-linguistically, other kinds of adjuncts typically receive a different form. Most often, they are realized as prepositional and adverbial phrases. Below, this is illustrated for adjuncts that locate an event in time, those that locate an event in space and manner adjuncts. The Korean examples are taken from Wechsler and Lee (1996:631–632).

(33) TEMPORAL LOCATION

    a. Tom met Mary at two o'clock.   English

    b. Tom-i   Mary-lul   twu si-ey   mana-ss-ta   Korean
       Tom-$_{\text{NOM}}$ Mary-$_{\text{ACC}}$ two o'clock-at met-$_{\text{PST.DEC}}$
       'Tom met Mary at two o'clock.'

    c. Dima   vstretil Mašu   v   dva   časa.   Russian
       Dima   met   Masha$_{\text{ACC}}$ in   two$_{\text{ACC}}$ hour
       'Dima met Masha at two o'clock.'

    d. dani   pagaS et   dina   be-Stayim.   Hebrew
       Dani   met   ACC Dina   in two
       'Dani met Dina at two o'clock.'

    e. Matti   tapasi Leenan   kahdelta.   Finnish
       Matti   met   Leena$_{\text{ACC}}$ two$_{\text{ABL}}$
       'Matti met Leena at two o'clock.'

(34) SPATIAL LOCATION

    a. John met Helen in the office.   English

    b. Tom-i   siktang-eyse   pap-ul   mek-ess-ta   Korean
       Tom-$_{\text{NOM}}$ restaurant.at   meal$_{\text{ACC}}$ eat-$_{\text{PST-DEC}}$
       'Tom ate meals at the restaurant.'

    c. Dima   poobedal   v   restorane.   Russian
       Dima   ate-lunch in   restaurant
       'Dima ate lunch in a restaurant.'

    d. dani   yaSav   ba-misrad.   Hebrew
       Dani   sat   in office
       'Dani was sitting in the office.'

    e. Hiiri   juoksi   laatikossa.   Finnish
       mouse   ran   box$_{\text{INESS}}$
       'A/The mouse ran in the box.'

(35) MANNER
     a. Tom ran quickly.   English
     b. Tom-i   coyonghi   wa-ss-ta   Korean
        Tom.$_{NOM}$ silently   come.$_{PST\text{-}DEC}$
        'Tom approached silently.'
     c. Ivan   bystro   bežal.   Russian
        Ivan   quickly   ran
        'Ivan ran quickly.'
     d. dani   rac   maher.   Hebrew
        Dani   ran   quickly
        'Dani ran quickly.'
     e. Matti   juoksi   nopeasti.   Finnish
        Matti   ran   quickly
        'Matti ran quickly.'

To sum up thus far, it is specifically durational, multiplicative and distance-measuring adjuncts that appear in the same form as direct objects in a wide range of languages, including ones that are genetically unrelated. The examples provided above contain Indo-European, Finno-Ugric, Semitic and Koreanic languages. It is, of course, quite unlikely that such a cross-linguistic pattern is purely accidental. Rather, it is to be expected that the adjunct types in question are unified by certain syntactic and/or semantic properties.

Two questions therefore emerge:

   (i) What is the nature of these unifying properties?
   (ii) How are these properties related to accusative case-marking?

The answer to the first question turns out to be clearer than that to the second. The difficulty is partly related to the fact that accusative case-checking on adjuncts is similar to the checking of the same case on objects in some respects (and languages) and different in others. Section 4.2.2 addresses question (i). We discuss the common semantic core that is shared by the relevant types of adjuncts, as explained in detail by Wechsler and Lee (1996). In Section 4.2.3, we turn to question (ii) and review different approaches to the phenomenon of accusative case-marking on adjuncts.

4.2.2 Semantic Properties of Accusative Adjuncts

Wechsler and Lee (1996) demonstrate that all the three types of adjuncts under discussion function as **event, or situation, delimiters**. Basically, such adjuncts apply to an atelic or unbounded event predicate and turn it into one that is bounded, or temporally delimited. To illustrate, consider (36) below, which contains a durational adjunct.

(36)   John and Mary talked for two hours.

The predicate *talked* is atelic; it is not associated with any inherent natural endpoint and, on its own, does not carry temporal delimitation. In fact, the attachment of durational adverbials, such as *for two hours* in (36), constitutes a well-known atelicity diagnostic. *For*-adverbials are known to be compatible with atelic event predicates. But, crucially, the attachment of these phrases changes the predicate in an important way. Specifically, the *for*-adverbial provides a previously unbounded event with temporal delimitation. The predicate remains atelic since it is still not associated with any inherent, natural finishing point beyond which the event could not potentially continue. However, the adjunct imposes on it a non-inherent, "external", purely temporally defined endpoint, which specifies when the events falling within the denotation of the VP happen to be over. To illustrate, both *talked* and *talked for two hours* are atelic predicates, but only the latter is temporally delimited. Under the terminology used by Depraetere (1995), the relevant contrast is one between telicity and boundedness. *Talked for two hours* is atelic but bounded. And it is boundedness, or temporal delimitation, that accusative adjuncts contribute.

Let us take a look at the other two types of adjuncts that can appear in the accusative case. (37) below illustrates a spatial measure:

(37)   John ran five kilometers.

Similarly to the predicate *talked*, *ran* on its own is atelic and unbounded. However, the attachment of a spatial measure adjunct provides it with an endpoint. An event of running can continue indefinitely; an event of running five kilometers cannot. Thus, spatial measures, similarly to durational expressions, provide otherwise unbounded events with a boundary. As such, they, too, constitute situation delimiters.

Finally, (38) illustrates a sentence with a multiplicative adjunct:

(38)   Jane called me five times.

Here, the situation is slightly different. Multiplicative adjuncts may (and probably even should) quantify over events each of which is completed and, thus, bounded. For instance, in (38), each calling event is bounded, or temporally delimited. Then how can the adverbial function as a situation delimiter?

The answer has to do with the fact that the sentences in question are iterative. And while each calling event has its own endpoint, a sequence of calling events may potentially continue indefinitely. The function of a multiplicative adverbial is to impose a limit on the sequence. For instance, by specifying that Jane called five times, the speaker delimits the whole series of repeated callings. In this sense, multiplicative adjuncts are similar to spatial and durational measures.

Note further that the other types of adjuncts discussed above, realized as PPs and AdvPs, rather than accusative nominals, do not function as situation delimiters. Several relevant examples are provided in (39):

(39)   a. Tom phoned Mary at two o'clock.
       b. John was reading in his office.
       c. John ran quickly.

The adjuncts illustrated in (39) do not change aspectually relevant properties of the event predicates. They do not provide the events in question with a temporal limit.

Let us now turn back to situation-delimiting adjuncts. Formally, they constitute extensive-measure functions, as argued by Wechsler and Lee (1996). Extensive-measure functions are measures characterized by the property of additivity, defined in (40):

(40)   Additivity
       $m(x \oplus y) = m(x) + m(y)$, if x and y do not overlap
                                          (Wechsler and Lee 1996:645)

A measure function m is additive iff the value obtained as a result of applying m to the concatenation of x and y equals the value of m applied to x plus the value of m applied to y.

To illustrate, consider the measure of weight. The weight of the concatenation of x and y equals the sum of the weight of x and the weight of y. Contrast this measure to temperature. Suppose that the temperature of x is 20°C and the temperature of y is 30°C. Then the temperature of the concatenation of x and y will not be 50°C. Rather, it will be somewhere between 20°C and 30°C. Thus, weight constitutes an extensive-measure function, whereas temperature does not.

Turning to the domain of events, we can see that measure functions associated with the three types of adjuncts under investigation are all extensive (they are all characterized by additivity). Starting with duration, if we take an event of working for one hour and another event of working for one hour, the concatenation of these two events (assuming that they are non-overlapping) will be characterized by the duration of two hours. The same holds for measures of distance. Two non-overlapping events of running one kilometer render together an event of running two kilometers. And, finally, if we take a set of five calling events (as in *John called me five times*) and another set of three calling events (as in *John called me three times*), their concatenation will constitute a set of eight calling events.

To sum up this section, the three types of adjuncts that often appear in the accusative case cross-linguistically are unified by the fact that they function as situation delimiters. These adjuncts apply to unbounded event predicates and supply them with temporal delimitation. Formally, these adjuncts constitute extensive-measure functions and are thus characterized by the property of additivity.

DISCUSSION

1. Does length constitute an extensive-measure function?
2. Provide an example of a measure in the domain of events which does not constitute an extensive-measure function.
3. Wechsler and Lee point out that the acceptability of concatenating two events is subject to pragmatic factors. Which factors play a role? For instance, is temporal adjacency a necessary condition?

4.2.3 Accusative Case on Adjuncts: Inherent or Structural?

The next question to ask has to do with the syntactic nature of the accusative case found on adjuncts. Is this case inherent or structural?[7] Is it of the same nature as the accusative on objects, or is this a totally different, independent accusative case? How is the accusative case of adjuncts assigned or checked?

An easy solution would be to propose that the accusative case is of an inherent nature, and that it is checked by a phonologically empty preposition. This account would explain the case-checking procedure in a simple way; after all, many nominal phrases check their case against the P head in whose complement position they appear. However, a whole range of facts observed in different languages suggests that the situation is more complex. The adjunct accusative case is not inherent but rather structural, and it is at least partly of the

---

[7] I assume that it is not lexical (under the approaches that distinguish between lexical and inherent case, e.g. Woolford 2006) since its availability does not constitute an idiosyncratic property of a given lexical head. Rather, we are dealing with a predictable semantic pattern.

same nature as the accusative on objects. It participates in the same
case alternations and is – at least in certain languages and instances –
subject to the same syntactic restrictions.

The first piece of evidence in favor of this view comes from Korean.
In this language, the adjuncts in question appear in the nominative
case with passive verbs (41a), as well as with those verbs that, for
whatever reason, take a nominative, rather than accusative, object
(41b). In other words, case-assignment to objects and adjuncts is
clearly interrelated. Nominative adjuncts are licensed in those environments in which base-generated objects, too, receive nominative
case. Accusative adjuncts appear in those environments in which
objects, too, are accusative. This strongly suggests that we are dealing
with a structural, rather than inherent, case, which is the same for
adjuncts and complements.

(41) a. Sip-i   Swuni-eyuyhay   pheyinthu-ka   [twu pen-i]
         house$_{NOM}$ Swuni.by   paint$_{NOM}$ twice$_{NOM}$
         chilhay-ci-ess-ta.
         brush$_{PASS. PST.DEC}$
         'The house was painted twice by Swuni.'
                                              (Wechsler and Lee 1996:635)

      b. Ku-ka   cha-ka   sey sikan-i   philyoha-ta.
         he$_{NOM}$ car$_{NOM}$ three hour$_{NOM}$ need$_{DEC}$
         'He needs a car for three hours.'
                                              (Wechsler and Lee 1996:636)

The state of affairs is similar in Finnish. The case of partitive objects is
not affected by passivization in this language. But accusative case is
lost with passive predicates, and base-generated objects appear in the
nominative instead. Crucially, the same happens with event-
delimiting adjuncts: in passive clauses they are marked nominative
rather than accusative:

(42) Kirjaa   luettiin   koko   ilta /   *illan.
      book$_{PART}$ was-read   whole   evening$_{NOM}$ / evening$_{ACC}$
      'Somebody was reading a book for the whole evening.'
                                              (based on Pereltsvaig 2000, ex. 28)

More generally, in Finnish, just as in Korean, the relevant adjuncts
appear in the nominative instead of the accusative in those environments in which direct objects are nominative-marked (see e.g. Mitchell
1991, Maling 1993, Pereltsvaig 2000 and references therein). These
include constructions with modal verbs and imperative sentences.
The (a) sentences below demonstrate that in such constructions, the

object appears in the nominative case and not in the accusative. The (b) sentences show that the same holds for adjuncts.

(43) a. Marian   täytyy   lukea   kirja   / *kirjan.
         Mary$_{GEN}$ must   read   book$_{NOM}$ / book$_{ACC}$
         'Mary must read a/the book.'
                                              (Pereltsvaig 2000, ex. 23b)

      b. Hänen   täytyy   asua   siellä   yksi   vuosi   / *yhden vuoden
         s/he$_{GEN}$ must   live   there   one$_{NOM}$ year$_{NOM}$ / one$_{ACC}$ year$_{ACC}$
         'S/he must live there one year.'
                    (based on Mitchell 1991:206, Pereltsvaig 2000, ex 24b)

(44) a. Lue   kirja   /*kirjan!
         read$_{IMPV}$ book$_{NOM}$ / book$_{ACC}$
         'Read a/the (whole) book!'
                                              (Pereltsvaig 2000, ex. 29a)

      b. Lue   koko   ilta/   *illan!
         read$_{IMPV}$ whole   evening$_{NOM}$ /evening$_{ACC}$
         'Read for the whole evening!'
                                              (Pereltsvaig 2000, ex. 29c)

What we see is that in both Korean and Finnish (languages that belong to different families and are spoken in different geographical areas), extensive-measure adjuncts appear in the accusative case in those environments in which accusative is available for objects and in the nominative in those environments in which base-generated objects, too, are nominative.

Further, Finnish provides an additional piece of evidence in favor of the structural and "object-like" nature of the case found on those adjuncts that function as situation delimiters. In this language, as discussed in Section 4.1, the case of the object is affected by the polarity of the clause. In affirmative clauses, an object can be either accusative or partitive. But under negation, the object obligatorily appears in the partitive case:

(45) a. Join   veden.
         drank$_{1.SG}$ water$_{ACC}$
         'I drank the water'

      b. Join   vettä.
         drank$_{1.SG}$ water$_{PART}$
         'I drank some water / I was drinking water.'

(46) En   juonut   vettä   /*veden.
      NEG$_{1. SG}$ drank   water$_{PART}$ / water$_{ACC}$
      'I didn't drink (the) water / I wasn't drinking water.'

Extensive-measure adjuncts, too, undergo the accusative/partitive
alternation. Under negation, they appear in the partitive case (47–49).

(47) Hän   ei   asinut   siellä yhta   vuotta.
     s/he$_{NOM}$ NEG$_{3.SG}$ lived   there   one$_{PART}$ year$_{PART}$
     'S/he didn't live there for a year.'
                                                      (Mitchell 1991:206)
(48) Ei   hän   juossut kahta   kilometria.
     NEG$_{3.SG}$ s/he   ran   two$_{PART}$ kilometers$_{PART}$
     'He hasn't run two kilometers.'
(49) En   ollut siellä   kahta   kertaa.
     NEG$_{1.SG}$ was   there   two$_{PART}$ times$_{PART}$
     'I haven't been there twice.'

Finally, let us consider evidence from Russian, which belongs to
yet another language family (Indo-European, the Slavic branch).
Note that in this language, unlike Finnish and Korean, the accusative case of adjuncts does not depend on voice or, more broadly,
on the presence of an external argument (while, according to
Burzio's Generalization, the possibility of accusative assignment
to objects goes hand in hand with the availability of an external
theta-role; Burzio 1986). To illustrate, consider the Russian passive
sentence in (50):

(50) Éta   rabota pisalas'   nedelju   / *nedelja.
     this   work   wrote$_{REFL}$ week$_{ACC}$ / week$_{NOM}$
     'This paper was in the process of writing for a week.'

The base-generated object in (50) cannot receive accusative case, given
that the verb is passive. As a result, the object is nominative-marked, and
its case feature is checked against that of a finite T. However, this configuration does not affect the form of the durational adjunct, which is
accusative and cannot appear in the nominative.

This suggests that while accusative case-marking on adjuncts in
Russian and in Finnish and Korean has something in common (in
both instances, the accusative marks situation delimiters), a
uniform analysis is still probably impossible. In Korean and
Finnish, adjuncts receive accusative (and nominative!) case via the
same mechanism as objects. In Russian, adjuncts appear in the
accusative case even when it is unavailable for objects.
Consequently, the case-checking mechanism with these two grammatical functions is not the same.

In fact, Wechsler and Lee point out, following Kim and Maling
(1998), that in Korean, durational adverbials may, in some contexts,

appear in the accusative case even in sentences with passive verbs. They suggest that in these instances, inherent case is involved. We can hypothesize that in certain sentences, Korean exhibits the Russian-like pattern.

Still, although the case of Russian adjuncts does not depend on voice, this language contributes its own piece of evidence in favor of viewing adjunct accusative as structural. The evidence comes from the fact that Russian adjuncts (of the three types under discussion) undergo the genitive/accusative alternation under negation. In other words, like in Finnish, the case of both objects and adjuncts is sensitive to the polarity of the clause. The facts here are not exactly the same as in Finnish, however.

Russian, similarly to many other Balto-Slavic languages, exhibits the phenomenon of Genitive of Negation (GenNeg). This is the phenomenon whereby genitive case-marking is licensed under negation on a VP-internal nominal phrase instead of the accusative. In some languages (e.g. Polish and Lithuanian), the substitution of the accusative case by the genitive under negation is obligatory (i.e. objects are always genitive, just as they are always partitive in Finnish), whereas in others, including Russian (as well as Belorussian, Ukrainian and Latvian), it is optional[8] (see Chapter 6 and Kagan 2013 and references therein). Thus, objects of negated clauses can appear in both accusative and genitive forms. The phenomenon is illustrated in (51):

(51) a. Vadim pil   vodu/   *vody.
         Vadim drank   water$_{ACC}$ water$_{GEN}$
         'Vadim drank water.'
      b. Vadim ne   pil   vodu/   vody.
         Vadim NEG drank   water$_{ACC}$ water$_{GEN}$
         'Vadim didn't drink water.'

While in the affirmative clause in (51a), the object is obligatorily accusative, in its negative counterpart (51b), both the accusative and the genitive versions are acceptable.

Crucially for our current purposes, accusative adjuncts of the types discussed in this chapter can appear in GenNeg, too. In other words, similarly to objects, they undergo the genitive/accusative alternation

---

[8] In fact, the notion of optionality is somewhat misleading here. It would be more precise to state that under negation, case selection depends on a wide range of factors, and also exhibits a certain amount of variation in native speaker judgments. As a result, both genitive and accusative objects are attested. The genitive/accusative alternations in Russian are discussed in detail in Chapter 6.

under negation. This is illustrated for each of the three types (durational, distance-measuring and multiplicative adjuncts) in (52) below:

(52)   a. My   ne   progovorili   dva časa /   dvux časov.
         we   NEG   talked   [two hours]$_{ACC}$ /   [two hours]$_{GEN}$
         'We didn't talk for two hours.'
     b. Boris   ne   probežal dva kilometra /   dvux kilometrov.
         Boris   NEG   ran   [two kilometers]$_{ACC}$ [two kilometers]$_{GEN}$
         'Boris didn't run two kilometers.'
     c. Lena   ne   tancevala   so   svoim mužem   pjat' raz /
         Lena   NEG   danced   with   own husband   [five times]$_{ACC}$
         (i)   pjati raz.
         and   [five times]$_{GEN}$
         'Lena didn't dance with her husband (even) five times.'

Genitive adjuncts are not acceptable in the affirmative counterparts of these sentences. While under negation, both genitive and accusative variants are found, a certain semantic contrast is involved. Specifically, genitive adjuncts are necessarily interpreted within the scope of negation. In turn, the accusative ones may receive both wide and narrow scope. For instance, in (52a), both versions may mean that the conversation lasted for less than two hours. But only the accusative version allows the reading according to which the phrase *two hours* measures the interval during which the subject did NOT talk (i.e. it measures the duration of a break in the conversation). Genitive case, which is licensed by negation, can predictably be interpreted only within its scope. The same pattern is observed for objects (see Chapter 6 for details).

Crucially, verbal complements that receive an inherent or lexical case cannot appear in GenNeg (53a). The same holds for nominals embedded in PP adjuncts, which, too, receive an inherent or lexical case from the P head (53b).

(53)   a. Ivan   ne   vladeet   zavodom /   *zavoda.
         Ivan   NEG   owns   factory$_{INSTR}$ factory$_{GEN}$
         'Ivan doesn't own a factory.'
     b. My   ne   vstretilis'   v   ofise /   *ofisa.
         we   NEG   met   in   office$_{LOC}$ office$_{GEN}$
         'We didn't meet in the office.'

The fact that the accusative adjuncts illustrated in (52) do alternate with genitive ones reveals that their case is not checked by a phonologically empty preposition. Otherwise, the same pattern as in (53b) would be expected. Rather, we are dealing with a structural case, which can alternate with another structural one. Moreover, the fact that accusative adjuncts and objects participate in the same alternation suggests that they receive case of the same nature (although the fact that the adjuncts remain accusative in passive clauses demonstrates that the case-checking mechanism is not identical in the two instances).

It is also worth mentioning that Russian exhibits accusative case-marking on yet another type of adjunct, frequency adverbials, which, crucially, do not constitute extensive-measure functions. To illustrate, the expression *každyj den'* 'every day' in (54) does not turn the clause into a bounded one. The sequence of events is not supplied with an endpoint.

(54) Ja   pišu   pis'ma   každyj den'.
      I   write letters$_{ACC}$ [every day]$_{ACC}$
      'I write letters every day.'

It is worth noting that in Korean, analogous adjuncts cannot receive accusative case. This is unsurprising, given their semantic difference from the other adjuncts under discussion.

As demonstrated above, Russian differs from Korean in this respect. Interestingly, however, unlike the adjuncts illustrated in (52), frequency adverbials **cannot** appear in GenNeg. Even under negation, they must remain accusative:

(55) Ja   ne   pišu   pis'ma /   pisem   každyj den' /
      I   NEG   WRITE   letters$_{ACC}$ letters$_{GEN}$ [every day]$_{ACC}$
      *každogo dnja.
      [every day]$_{GEN}$
      'I don't write letters every day.'

The contrast between (52) and (55) is quite important. It reveals that although all the adjuncts illustrated in these examples can appear in the accusative, the case of frequency adverbials is of a different nature. In other words, these adverbials do not only stand out semantically; rather, they also differ from the three groups illustrated in (52) in their case-related properties. The inability of frequency adverbials to undergo the genitive/accusative alternation distinguishes them from both objects and extensive-measure adjuncts. And this, in turn, means that Russian is not all that different from Korean in the relevant respect.

Further, the fact that frequency adverbials cannot appear in GenNeg suggests that the case they receive may well be inherent rather than structural. In fact, with this class of adjuncts, accusative case-checking by a phonologically empty preposition is much more plausible. This analysis would account for their inability to appear in GenNeg: the same holds for other complements of prepositions (53b).

Thus, both the genitive/accusative alternation and the cross-linguistic comparison (Russian as opposed to Korean) reveal that not all accusative adjuncts are created equal. While the case-related properties of durational, distance-measuring and multiplicative adverbials are strongly interrelated with those of direct objects, frequency adjuncts are subject to a different case-checking process.

To sum up thus far, we see that event-delimiting adjuncts undergo the same alternations as direct objects. Evidence that case-checking in the two instances is at least partly interrelated comes from languages belonging to different families, including Korean (Koreanic), Russian (Indo-European) and Finnish (Finno-Ugric).

4.2.4 Accusative Objects and Adjuncts: Analyses

If accusative case on adjuncts is structural, then how is it assigned/ checked in the syntax? Do the adjuncts receive it in the same way as objects? Is the process identical across languages, or is some kind of parametric variation involved (after all, we have seen certain cross-linguistic contrasts)?

A number of analyses have been proposed for accusative case-marking on adjuncts. Different proposals concentrate on different languages. In what follows, two of these approaches are discussed. We begin with Wechsler and Lee's (1996) analysis of accusative case in Korean. Then we turn to Pereltsvaig's (2000) account of accusative objects and adjuncts in Finnish and Russian. In each case, we will consider the question of whether it is possible to extend the proposed analysis to the additional languages discussed in this chapter.

4.2.4.1 Wechsler and Lee (1996)

Wechsler and Lee (1996) focus primarily on case-assignment in Korean but also discuss accusative marking on adjuncts from a cross-linguistic perspective. An important role in their analysis is devoted to the feature CASE, carried by those nominals which are subject to direct case-assignment (primarily, the assignment of structural accusative and nominative cases). Nominals which lack this feature must receive an oblique case.

Wechsler and Lee formulate the following universal rule:

(56) Case Domain Extension (CDE). Optionally assign the feature CASE
      to a dependent R, where R is a situation delimiter.

                                        (Wechsler and Lee 1996:640)

This rule allows direct case-assignment to adjuncts that function as
situation delimiters. The rule is optional, since such adjuncts do not
always receive direct case (consider, e.g. *for*-adverbials in English,
which contain a nominal and a preposition which assigns to the
former an oblique case).

Further, in order to capture the Korean facts discussed above,
Wechsler and Lee define the following rules of case-assignment in
Korean. (Recall that in this language, situation-delimiting adjuncts
receive the same case as the object, be it accusative or nominative.)

(57) Korean Case Rule.
      (i) Assign ACC to any CASE dependent with an external co-argument.
      (ii) Assign NOM to any CASE dependent lacking an external
      co-argument.

                                        (Wechsler and Lee 1996:640)

CASE dependents include both non-oblique arguments of the verb
and, potentially (by CDE in (56) above), situation-delimiting adjuncts.
Largely, (57) corresponds to Burzio's Generalization, again extended
to adjuncts of the relevant type.

While the analysis accounts successfully for the Korean facts, it
cannot be extended to languages like Russian, in which accusative
case on adjuncts is available even in passive clauses, whereas base-
generated objects are obligatorily nominative. In other words, the
accusative (and not nominative) case is available to the adjuncts
even in the absence of an external co-argument.

In addition, this analysis treats accusative case-assignment as related
to aspect on adjuncts but not on objects. On the one hand, this is
a desirable result, given that all Korean objects receive the accusative
(if it is available), independently of aspect, whereas for adjuncts, this
property is inherently related to situation delimitation. On the other
hand, in Finno-Ugric languages, object case and aspect are definitely
interrelated. And more broadly, it seems to be non-accidental that the
same case that plays an aspectual role in the domain of adjuncts also
appears on objects, which are known to fulfill an important part in
aspectual composition (even though not with all verbs).

Let us now consider an analysis which does capture the relation of
both adjuncts and objects to aspect, and also accounts for the Russian
facts.

4.2.4.2   *Pereltsvaig (2000)*

Pereltsvaig (2000) proposes an analysis of accusative adjuncts and
objects concentrating mainly on Finnish and Russian data.
Pereltsvaig proposes that an object can receive case in two positions:
[spec, VP], in which she takes it to be generated, and [spec, Asp(ect)P],
to which an object can move. As suggested by the very name of the
latter functional projection, it is related to aspectual interpretation.
The object moves to this projection in order to check the [+B(ounded)]
feature. Movement is triggered iff both the object and Asp carry the
feature [+B]. In all other instances, the object remains in situ and
receives case in [spec, VP].

The case checked in [spec, AspP] is, cross-linguistically, accusative.
This is why accusative case is associated with boundedness and event
delimitation. This relation is mediated by the syntax, specifically, by
the AspP projection. The Asp head carries aspectual features, and it is
also responsible for accusative case-checking.

Turning to [spec, VP], the case received in this position depends both
on the verb and on the language involved. If the verb checks an
inherent case, then this is the case the object will receive.
Otherwise, the object receives the so-called **default objective case**
in this position. Pereltsvaig proposes that the morphological realization of the default case is language-specific. In Russian, it is accusative
(which means that the cases checked by V and by Asp look the same).
In Finnish, this case is partitive. This view is in agreement with
Vainikka and Maling's (1996) claim that partitive is the default case
of the object in Finnish ("partitive is the basic unmarked case of the
object, corresponding to the English accusative" (p. 186); see also
Section 4.1.3).

In turn, situation-delimiting adjuncts are base-generated in the
[spec, AspP] position. Therefore, they receive accusative case independently of the more specific properties of Asp. In other words, their
case-checking does not depend on any triggers for movement, in
contrast to that of objects. However, the very fact that they are base-
generated in this position is related to their aspectual semantics (the
function of event delimiters).

How does this analysis capture the facts discussed above? Both
(relevant) adjuncts and bounded objects that form part of telic predicates receive the "semantic," aspectually relevant, accusative case in
[spec, AspP]. (The case is not strictly speaking semantic; rather, it is
structural, but, as mentioned above, it is indirectly related to meaning
via the properties of the functional projection.) Most of the similarities

between objects and adjuncts observed above result from this fact. For instance, Partitive of Negation in Finnish and Genitive of Negation in Russian apply to nominals that occupy this position. (But note that in Finnish, objects that check case in [spec, VP] appear in the partitive, too.) Passivization, too, targets the nominal in [spec, AspP]. This explains the fact that in Finnish, neither objects nor adjuncts can check their accusative case feature in passive clauses. (Again, those objects that appear in situ lack this ability to begin with, as they can only be partitive.) A question emerges, of course, as to what happens with passivization in Russian. After all, in this language, it does not affect adjuncts. The latter remain accusative. Moreover, objects that appear in [spec, VP] (e.g. objects of atelic predicates) can passivize as well. Pereltsvaig accounts for this fact by claiming that in Russian, the rule of passivization is determined lexically and targets theme arguments independently of their case and of the position in which they appear (which can thus equally easily be AspP or VP). Accusative adverbials are not themes and, therefore, do not passivize. In contrast, those in situ objects that receive the theta-role of a theme and an inherent case **do undergo passivization**, even though they are not accusative. This has been demonstrated in detail by Fowler (1996).

Finally, the absence of an obvious relation between the accusative case on objects and boundedness results from the fact that objects can receive accusative case from two sources in Russian. One source (AspP) is related to boundedness, the other (VP) is not. This complicates matters, making it impossible to observe the case–aspect dependence which does, in fact, exist. The dependence can only be observed on adjuncts, which check accusative case in only one position, [spec, AspP]. In contrast, in Finnish, different cases are checked in the two object positions (accusative versus partitive), and this is why the relation between accusative case-marking and aspect becomes observable.

Pereltsvaig succeeds in capturing very impressively both similarities and differences between Russian and Finnish on the one hand and between objects and adjuncts on the other. This goal is achieved by distributing object case-checking over two positions. Both the accusative in Russian and the partitive in Finnish (the latter, in negative clauses) can be checked in different positions; such contrasts are not observable on the morpho-phonological level but have semantic consequences.

Below, I attempt to extend this analysis to the Korean facts and consider the problem that such an extension seems to face.

Roughly speaking, Korean is like Russian in that its default objective case is accusative but like Finnish in that its passivization is not lexicalized. The former is revealed by the fact that in Korean, objects are accusative independently of verbal aspect. The latter follows from the fact that adjuncts are passivized. This means that in this language, passivization is sensitive to a structural position (following Pereltsvaig's analysis, [spec, AspP]) and not thematic role. But if this is the case, passivization is expected to apply to those objects that appear in [spec, AspP] but not to those located in [spec, VP]. This basically means that unbounded objects and/or objects of unbounded predicates (which remain in situ) should not passivize. This prediction is not borne out. Passivization applies in Korean independently of verbal aspect. We have to conclude that in Korean, passivization targets both nominals that appear in [spec, AspP] and those in [spec, VP]. If we take this to be a possible passive rule, subject to parametric variation, then Pereltsvaig's account is extended to Korean quite easily. One could also argue that in Korean, both lexical and "structural" passivization takes place. The former targets themes (including the ones in [spec, VP]) and the latter, nominals in [spec, AspP]. If, in contrast, passivization is systematically linked to a single position or thematic role, the Korean facts pose a problem for Pereltsvaig's line of analysis.

4.3 COMPLEMENTS OF PREPOSITIONS: ACCUSATIVE CASE AND GOALS

4.3.1 Prepositional Accusative and Goals: The Intuition

The third piece of evidence that points to a relation between accusative case and boundedness comes from the domain of prepositional phrases. As discussed in Chapter 3, in Russian, German and Ancient Greek, certain prepositions allow a case alternation on their complement, depending on whether the PP functions as a goal, a location or (in Ancient Greek) a source. The phenomenon is illustrated for Russian in (58):

(58) a. Ivan   bežal   v   park.
         Ivan   ran   in   park$_{ACC}$
         'Ivan was running to the park.'
      b. Ivan   bežal   v   parke.
         Ivan   ran   in   park$_{LOC}$
         'Ivan was running in the park.'

(58a) and (58b) contain the same preposition *v* 'in'. However, the case of its complement is different in the two sentences, which has consequences for the interpretation. In (58a), the complement is accusative, and the PP is interpreted as a goal: Ivan was running to the park. In contrast, in (58b), the complement of the preposition appears in the locative (prepositional) case, and the PP is understood to constitute a location: the running event takes place in the park.

The case associated with the role of location changes from preposition to preposition and from language to language. Thus, in Russian, the prepositions *v* 'in' and *na* 'on' take the locative case, whereas *pod* 'under' and *za* 'behind' select the instrumental. In turn, in German, the role of location correlates with dative case-marking. In Ancient Greek, the case linked to the source role is genitive. Interestingly, the case of goals is (in all these languages) systematically accusative. It therefore seems plausible that the relation between accusative case and goalhood is not accidental. Indeed, the feature [+directional] (/ [+ascriptive]) constitutes one of the defining properties of the accusative case within Jakobson's approach to the Russian case system (Jakobson 1957/1971, 1984).

The impression that the accusative case is related to goalhood in a systematic way becomes even stronger in the context of the phenomena discussed in the previous sections. Cross-linguistically, the accusative is associated with boundedness. In turn, goals (similarly to some direct objects and situation-delimiting adjuncts) provide an otherwise unbounded event description with an endpoint. More precisely, the attachment of a goal phrase makes a motion-event predicate telic. For instance, while the VP *walk* is atelic, *walk to the store* is telic. The goal phrase provides the path covered in the course of the motion event with a boundary. Once the path is bounded, the event is bounded as well. As soon as the end of the path is reached, the event has to be finished.

Semantically, it is thus quite natural to unify accusative case-marking on goal phrases with the accusative case on objects in Finnic and on adjuncts cross-linguistically. In all three instances, accusative marking is clearly linked to boundedness. Syntactically, however, unification does not seem to be easy. Complements of prepositions are expected to receive case in a totally different way from objects. Their case is expected to be inherent or lexical rather than structural. The inherent case view is further supported by the strong relation between the accusative case-marking and the assignment of a specific thematic role, that of a goal.

4.3.2 Generative Linguistics Approaches

Zwarts (2005), who analyzes the relation between prepositions and case in German, argues against a direct link between accusative case-marking on complements of prepositions and boundedness. He points out that even under the goal/location readings of the relevant preposi- tions, an accusative complement need not constitute a goal and a dative one a location. To illustrate, consider the sentence *The boat floated under the bridge* under the goal reading. Crucially, the bridge in this instance is not really the goal. The motion event is not directed to the bridge but rather to a different location (say, a certain part of the river). The bridge merely serves as a reference point helping to deter- mine the place which constitutes the actual goal. A similar problem holds for locations. Under the locational reading of the above sen- tence, the boat floated while under the bridge. Here again, the bridge itself does not constitute the location of the boat. Rather, it functions as a reference object.

Interestingly, the Russian case system does make a difference between true locations and reference objects which help define these locations. Thus, the complements of the prepositions *na* 'on' and *v* 'in' (under the locative reading) are indeed real locations. These complements appear in the locative/prepositional case. In contrast, the complements of *pod* 'under' and *za* 'behind' are not true locations, by the same reasoning as applied above to the sentence *The boat floated under the bridge*. Crucially, such complements appear in the instru- mental case, not the locative. Goal interpretations of all the alternat- ing prepositions, however, are associated with the accusative case- marking, independently of whether the complement is a true goal or a reference object relative to which the goal is determined.

It is my impression that the systematic relation between accusative case-marking and goal directionality is still significant. After all, even with prepositions like *under*, goal PPs do fulfill the delimiting function by supplying an endpoint of the path. In the above example, the endpoint is not the bridge itself, but rather some part of the river under the bridge. But crucially, **the endpoint is there**, it is contrib- uted by the *under*-PP, and this seems to be essential for the (semantics- related) accusative case-marking. The goal is simply contributed by the PP as a whole, rather than by the accusative nominal alone.

Indeed, Zwarts (2005) argues that the prepositional head and the case-marking get interpreted together (while the case of the comple- ment of a preposition does not carry any semantics on its own). "[T]he preposition and the case ... *cooccur* and ... their cooccurrence has a particular meaning" (p. 21, author's emphasis). Still, note that even under this approach, the accusative case remains associated with goalhood (and, therefore, event delimitation) at least as long as alter- nating prepositions are considered. Also, interestingly, the formal analysis that Zwarts provides within the minimalist framework does, in fact, separate the configuration function contributed by the preposition from the directionality function associated with case:[9]

(59) [FP KP$_{DAT}$ F$_{DAT}$ [PP in *t*]] [FP KP$_{ACC}$ F$_{ACC}$ [PP in *t*]]
          IN   TO ° IN

(Zwarts 2005:23)

Under this analysis, accusative case "is checked in the specifier position of some functional projection F for directionality" (p. 23). Thus, configuration is specified by the preposition (here, *in*), whereas the goal directionality is contributed by the accusative-assigning F, to whose specifier position the complement of the preposition moves in order to check its case feature. Thus, the two meaning components (configuration and directionality) *are* separated, and goalhood *is* associated with accusative-checking. Crucially, this analysis solves the above-mentioned problem having to do with the fact that the accusative complement of a preposition does not always constitute the goal (as in the *under the bridge* example). Here, what combines with F, the head that contributes the meaning of goalhood, is not the (accusative) DP but rather the whole PP, in which configuration is already specified. As a result, in the bridge example, it follows that the goal is not *the bridge* but rather *under the bridge*, that is, a place that is located below the bridge.

Under this analysis, the accusative case does not carry meaning of its own. Rather, the relation between case and meaning is mediated by the functional projection F. In this respect, this approach is similar to Pereltsvaig's (2000) account of the relation between accusative marking and the semantics of boundedness in the verbal domain. Case is not taken to be meaningful on its own. But the appearance of an NP or DP in the accusative form allows us to draw conclusions regarding the structure and the features involved in the sentence, which, in turn, makes it possible to interpret the sentence in the (aspectually) correct way.

DISCUSSION

Could the accusative-assigning F constitute the same head which assigns aspectually relevant accusative to objects and adjuncts? Could this be Asp?

---

[9] Of course, such a separation is not expected to hold for those prepositions which, like *durch* 'through', lexicalize both configuration and directionality. Naturally, however, such prepositions are not present among the alternating ones.

It is worth pointing out that Spyropoulos' (2018) analysis of Ancient Greek prepositions and the accompanying case alternations is similar to Zwarts' account in that the case of the DP is taken to be checked by a functional head (p_{CASE} for Spyropoulos), rather than by the lexical P. This view captures the fact that the phenomenon in question does not exhibit the typical properties of a lexical case. However, Spyropoulos does not concentrate on the aspectual side of the phenomenon.

According to van Riemsdijk (2007), who builds partly on Zwarts (2005, 2006), the central notion responsible for accusative case-assignment to complements of German adpositions is **route**. Zwarts demonstrates that the accusative is attested in both goal and route PPs, the latter being headed by such postpositions as *durch* 'through', *entlang* 'along' and *über* 'over'. Van Riemsdijk argues that nominal complements of route adpositions function as measure phrases. The evidence he provides comes from a number of properties that are shared by such nominals and measure phrases of other kinds. These include, for example, accusative case-marking, compatibility with degree modifiers, impossibility to be realized as bare plurals, etc.

Further, van Riemsdijk proposes that goal phrases include a route component in their semantics. Intuitively speaking, a goal specifies an endpoint of a motion event, and the latter proceeds along a route which can potentially be measured. The claim is thus that what unifies goals and routes, both of which are associated with accusative case-marking, is the route meaning component.

Case-assignment is explained syntactically under an analysis which takes different spatial notions to be related to different nodes in the structure. This is an updated version of the approach to spatial cases and adpositions proposed by van Riemsdijk and Huybregts (2007) and introduced in Section 2.2 of Chapter 2. The original analysis involves separate N, LOC and DIR heads, the latter two corresponding to configuration (=location) and directionality (=direction), respectively. Van Riemsdijk (2007) argues that an additional, route, projection is necessary, which results in the following structure:[10]

(60)   [DIR° [RO° [LOC° [DP]]]]

The accusative case, van Riemsdijk claims, is assigned to the nominal that moves to the specifier of RO position, under the specifier-head

---

[10] The labels in (60) are based on van Riemsdijk and Huybregts (2007), except for RO, standing for ROUTE.

agreement relation. In turn, the dative constitutes the default case in oblique domains that the DP receives in situ.

4.3.3   A Cognitive Grammar Approach

In turn, Smith (1995) analyzes the dative/accusative alternation on complements of German prepositions within the framework of cognitive grammar. Building on the traditional location versus goal (or motion) approach but departing from it partially, he proposes the following prototypical meaning for these two cases (when assigned to the complement of a P head):

> Dative designates that the trajector of the preposition is confined to a set of points satisfying the locative specification of the preposition (i.e., the search domain of the preposition). This situation can be interpreted as unchanging with respect to the preposition's search domain.
>
> Accusative designates that the trajector of the preposition is not always confined to the search domain of the preposition, but enters the search domain at some point along a path. This situation can be interpreted as involving change with respect to the locative configuration encoded by the preposition. (Smith 1995:296)

The locative specification of the preposition corresponds to the configurational specification, or the semantics of the LOC-DP constituent, in the terms introduced above. Roughly, we can conclude that the accusative implies a change of location whereby the moving object (the trajector) enters this location in the course of a motion event. In contrast, the dative does not imply such a change. At the same time, it does not imply the absence the change. Rather, it forces us to concentrate on the eventuality that takes place within the relevant location. However, it does not contribute an entailment that there has been no change of location immediately preceding the (part of) the eventuality that is in focus.

The latter point allows Smith to account for those instances in which the dative can, or even has to, be used despite the fact that a change of location is entailed or presupposed by the sentence in question. Such uses, which, according to Smith, constitute evidence against the location versus motion approach to the case alternation, are illustrated below:

(61) a. Er brachte   die   Lampe   an der   Decke an.
         he brought   the   lamp   at the$_{DAT}$ ceiling on
         'He attached the lamp to the ceiling.'

b. ?Er brachte die Lampe   an die   Decke an.
   he brought the lamp   at the$_{ACC}$ ceiling on
   'He attached the lamp to the ceiling.'   (p. 305)

(62) a. Er stellate   das Gepäck   auf dem   Bürgersteig ab.
        he put   the luggage on the$_{DAT}$ sidewalk   off
        'He put/dropped off his luggage on the sidewalk.'
     b. *Er stellte   das Gepäck   auf den   Bürgersteig ab.
        he put   the luggage on the$_{ACC}$ sidewalk   off
        'He put/dropped off his luggage on the sidewalk.'   (p. 316)

Literally, (61) involves the lamp being brought to the ceiling, and seems to entail a change of location undergone by this object. Still, the dative case is acceptable; moreover, some speakers dislike the accusative version (61b). For those speakers who do accept both variants, Smith reports a difference in meaning. (61a) is associated with a situation in which the lamp is already in contact with the ceiling, and final adjusting is taking place. In other words, the dative forces us to focus on the part of the event which follows (and thus excludes) the change of location. In contrast, (61b) is more strongly associated, on the intuitive level, with the process whereby the lamp comes to be attached to the ceiling; in other words, here the change of location is the center of one's attention.

Similarly in part, (62) entails a change of location: the luggage comes to be on the sidewalk. Still, only the dative version (62a) is possible. Smith argues that this time, the case requirement is related to the meaning of the verb *abstellen* 'put', analyzed as a restricted-profile verb. Such predicates profile the final point of the path which is implicitly present in their meaning, the part of the path which lies within the configuration specified by the prepositional phrase. Consequently, they force us to focus on the final part of the event which is confined to this final part of the 'path' and is thus located within the corresponding configuration. Hence what looks like a 'location', rather than a 'goal', interpretation, and hence the dative-marking requirement.

Interestingly, the Russian counterparts of the verb *put*, *položit'* 'put in a lying position' and *postavit'* 'put in a standing position', do license Ps with accusative objects and actually require the accusative form under the change of location meaning. Under Smith's account, this would probably mean that these verbs are semantically different from *abstellen* in the sense that they do not constitute restricted-profile predicates. In contrast, the Russian *prjatat'* 'hide' disprefers the accusative version (even though the latter is allowed in some instances), which makes it closer to its German counterpart *verstecken*.

Finally, Smith demonstrates that the accusative is also licensed under the broader notion of a change (of which change of location constitutes a special case). This, of course, takes us back to the interrelation between this case and telicity. For instance, a change and metaphorical, rather than literal, motion is involved in (63):

(63) Hans hat den Brief ins(indas) Deutsche übersetzt.
     Hans has the letter in-the$_{Acc}$ German translated
     'Hans translated the letter into German.'   (p. 313)

4.4 CONCLUSION

In this chapter, we have considered three domains in which accusative case-marking is interrelated with aspect. More specifically, the accusative case is associated with such notions as boundedness, telicity and completion. The relation between case and aspect is observed in the domain of objects in Finnic languages, in the domain of adjuncts cross-linguistically and in the domain of prepositional phrases in some Indo-European languages, including Ancient Greek, German and Russian. It is likely that, in all these instances, accusative case is not meaningful per se. Rather, the relation between case and meaning is mediated by the syntax. Accusative marking signals that the nominal phrase appears in a particular syntactic position (e.g. the specifier of a particular functional head), which, in turn, reveals certain semantically relevant features of the nominal and/or interpretational properties of the head in question. It is not obvious, however, whether a unified syntactic analysis can be provided that would cover all the three instances as well as cross-linguistic variation. This issue still has to be resolved. It is also important to emphasize that accusative case-marking is not always semantically motivated. In many languages, direct objects appear in the accusative independently of the aspectual properties of the clause and of the role that the object plays in aspectual composition. Therefore, some notion of default objective case, which is not semantically motivated and may be realized as the accusative, is needed, along the lines of Pereltsvaig (2000), for example.

FURTHER READING

Kiparsky (1998) provides a very thorough discussion of the partitive/accusative alternation on Finnish objects and its relation to the notion of boundedness. Kiparsky (2005) further provides a wide range of highly relevant examples which reveal the interrelation between case selection, boundedness and gradability.

Lees' (2015) book is a very helpful resource for the purposes of extending the discussion of object case beyond Finnish to additional Finnic languages. Specifically, the book deals with Estonian, Finnish, Livonian, Veps and Karelian, and also, to a lesser extent, Votic. It includes both a synchronic and a diachronic investigation, contains corpus studies and deals with a range of environments in which the base-generated object may appear in different case forms. The discussion is largely descriptive and relatively theory-neutral.

Wechsler and Lee's (1996) paper constitutes an important source on accusative case-assignment to adjuncts. While the main focus of the paper is Korean, in which the relevant adjuncts and objects behave in a highly uniform way, the phenomenon is also considered from a cross-linguistic perspective. A detailed discussion of the semantic characteristics of those adjuncts that cross-linguistically appear in accusative case is provided.

Pereltsvaig (2000) makes an important step in developing a formal analysis which deals with case-checking on both objects and adjuncts in Finnish and Russian. Crucially, the analysis successfully explains both similarities and contrasts in the nature of the accusative case observed on objects and adjuncts.

Chesterman's (1991) book *On Definiteness: A Study with Special Reference to English and Finnish* includes a thorough discussion of the semantic and pragmatic nuances associated with partitive case-marking and its alternatives.

5 Differential Object Marking

Differential object marking (DOM) is a phenomenon whereby, in certain languages, the object of a verb can be either marked or unmarked for morphological case, depending on a number of factors. This phenomenon is observed in more than three hundred languages belonging to different families (Bossong 1985), including (but not limited to) Turkish, Tatar and Uzbek (Turkic), Hebrew (Semitic), Spanish, Romanian and Catalan (Romance), Kannada (Dravidian), Pintjatjara (a Pama-Nyungan language spoken in Australia), Mongolian (Mongolic) and Komi-Zyrian, Mordovian and Udmurt (Finno-Ugric). While the specific conditions under which the object receives case vary from language to language, the major semantic properties to which the phenomenon is sensitive include definiteness, specificity, animacy and the +/–human distinction. To illustrate, in Hebrew, definite objects are preceded by the accusative marker *et*, whereas indefinite ones are morphologically caseless:

(1) a. raiti *(et)   ha-yeled.
       I.saw ACC   the-boy
       'I saw the boy.'
    b. raiti (*et)   yeled.
       I.saw ACC   boy
       'I saw a boy.'

Hebrew facts will be discussed in more detail in Section 5.1.1.

Further, a generalization can be made that cross-linguistically, within DOM languages, case-marking is observed on those objects that are characterized by a higher degree of prominence or individuation. Thus, definite nominals are more individuated than their indefinite counterparts, animate objects are higher in individuation than inanimate ones, etc. In general, animacy, definiteness, specificity and the [+human] feature constitute properties that enhance the likelihood of

147

accusative[1] case-marking in the cross-linguistic perspective. An individual language may be sensitive to only one of these properties, or to an interaction of several features (e.g. animacy, definiteness and specificity).

This chapter is organized as follows. First, several individual DOM languages are discussed in some detail. We will consider the picture that emerges in these languages, thereby illustrating the phenomenon of differential object marking. Second, in Section 5.2, the reasoning behind DOM is discussed. Why would languages case-mark some objects but not others? Section 5.3 addresses the role that the lexical semantics of the verb plays in the phenomenon. Is there a direct relation between the entailments contributed by the predicate and the form of the DP? Section 5.4 is devoted to a review of several analyses proposed for DOM as a cross-linguistic phenomenon. Finally, Section 5.5 concludes the discussion.

5.1 DOM SYSTEMS EXEMPLIFIED

5.1.1 Hebrew: Definiteness

In Modern Hebrew, definite nominals that appear in the object position are preceded by the marker *et*, whereas their indefinite counterparts are not, as illustrated in (1) above.[2] *Et* is often treated in the literature as an accusative case-marker (e.g. Taube 2015), even though alternative approaches have also been proposed. For instance, Danon (2001) argues that *et* is a preposition whose function is to assign case to an otherwise caseless object. Indeed, *et* shares a number of phonological and syntactic properties with certain Hebrew prepositions. In turn, Danon (2002) proposes that *et* constitutes a type-shifting operator. It is worth noting that the latter approach does not contradict the case analysis of this marker, as it has been argued independently that the assignment of certain cases correlates with particular semantic types of the resulting nominals (see e.g. de Hoop 1992 for Finnish, Bleam 2005 and López 2012 for Spanish and Kagan 2013 for Russian). Further, de Swart and de Hoop, building in part on Aristar (1997), argue that animacy distinctions are reflected in the domain of

---

[1] The term *accusative* is used here in the broad sense as an object marker. In fact, in many languages the marker used in DOM is identical to another case morpheme, e.g. a dative suffix in Hindi or a prepositional dative marker in Spanish.

[2] This is the commonly accepted view, although some counterexamples (apparently resulting from language change) will be mentioned below.

semantic types. More precisely, they argue for a sortal distinction within the domain of individuals (type e) between e_{human}, $e_{animate}$ and $e_{inanimate}$. They further state that certain case-markers constrain the type of the nominal to which they are attached. This may account for the fact that accusative case-assignment is limited to animate or human objects in certain DOM languages.

Turning back to Hebrew, it is a descriptive fact that objects can appear in two forms in Hebrew, either marked by *et* or unmarked, and the choice between these two options is determined (mainly) by the definiteness of the nominal. *Et* is obligatory with proper names, pronouns and nominals containing the definite marker *ha-*.

(2) a. pagaSti   et   dani / oto /   et   ha-yalda.
       I.met   ACC   Dani   he$_{ACC}$ ACC   the-girl
       'I met Dani / him / the girl.'

   b. *pagaSti   dani / hu /   ha-yalda.
       I.met   Dani   he$_{NOM}$ the-girl
       'I met Dani / him / the girl.'

In contrast, it is typically unacceptable with indefinite objects:

(3) a. pagaSti   yalda   axat / šloša   yeladim   / mišehu.
       I.met   girl   one   / three   children / somebody
       'I invited one girl / three boys / somebody.'

   b. *pagaSti   et   yalda   axat   / et   šloša yeladim   / et
       I.met   ACC   girl   one   / ACC   three children / ACC
       mišehu.
       somebody
       'I invited one girl / three boys / somebody.'

As argued convincingly by Danon (2001), the phenomenon is sensitive to the syntactic definiteness feature rather than to semantic/pragmatic definiteness. While the two properties typically co-occur, Danon demonstrates instances in which semantic and syntactic definiteness do not go hand in hand. For instance, depending on the register, a nominal that contains a demonstrative may appear either with or without the definiteness marker *ha-*:

(4) a. ha-iS   ha-ze
       the-man   the-this
       'this man'

   b. iS   ze
       man   this
       'this man'

Both (4a) and (4b) constitute grammatical DPs, although the former is more likely to be used in spoken language and the latter in a formal register, in a newspaper, for instance. Note that Hebrew involves definiteness agreement; therefore, in (4a), the morpheme *ha-* is attached both to the head noun and to the demonstrative.

Due to the presence of the demonstrative *ze* 'this', both phrases are clearly semantically definite. However, Danon argues that only the former carries the syntactic definiteness feature. Crucially for our purposes, *et* is compatible (and obligatory) with the (4a) type of objects, but not with the (4b) kind:

(5) a. pagaSti et   ha-iS   ha-ze.
         I.met ACC   the-man   the-this
         'I met this man.'
     b. pagaSti iS   ze.
         I.met   man   this
         'I met this man.'

Following Danon, we can conclude that syntactically definite objects are obligatorily preceded by the marker *et*, whereas those objects that lack the syntactic definiteness feature remain unmarked. There are, however, a few exceptions to this generalization, as we will see immediately below.

Firstly, Danon (2002, ex. 5) demonstrates the following optionality:

(6) a. ma   kanita?
         what   bought$_{2.SG}$
         'What did you buy?'
     b. et   ma   kanita?
         ACC   what   bought$_{2.SG}$
         'What did you buy?'

The *wh*-item *ma* 'what' is, presumably, inherently indefinite. Still, the marker *et* may optionally be attached to it (even though by default, it will be absent). Crucially, Danon points out that (6b) is possible as long as there is a presupposed set of entities out of which the answer is to be selected. In other words, *et ma* forces a **partitive** reading.

In fact, additional examples of partitive indefinites preceded by *et* can be observed in spoken Modern Hebrew. Such sentences typically contain inherently proportional quantifiers, such as *xeci* 'half', or the word *xelek* 'part', as well as an overt partitive PP headed by the preposition *me-* 'from', 'of'.

(7)　a.　mitbarer Se-hem makirim　**et**　　**xeci me-ha-anaSim** Sam.
　　　　turns.out that-they know　ACC　half from-the-men there
　　　　'It turns out that they know half of the people there.'[3]

　　b.　po　　**et**　　**xeci me-ha-anaSim**　ani　lo　　mevin.
　　　　here　ACC　half from-the-men　　　I　　NEG　understand
　　　　'I don't understand half of the people here.'[4]

　　c.　kal　　haya　leSaxnea ...　**et**　**xelek**　**me-ha-anaSim**
　　　　easy　was　convince$_{INF}$　ACC　part　　from-the-men
　　　　'It was easy to convince ... part of the people.'[5]

Crucially, the marked objects illustrated above are indefinite, in contrast to *me*-PP phrases they contain. This suggests that in addition to marking definite objects (a well-known fact about Hebrew), *et* can also mark certain indefinite partitives. This fact is particularly important from the cross-linguistic perspective, given that in some languages, such as Turkish, accusative case is obligatorily assigned to both definite and partitive nominals (e.g. Enç 1991, see also discussion in Section 5.1.3).

Still, it should be emphasized that, unlike Turkish, Hebrew is far from marking **all** partitives with the accusative case.

To sum up, assuming that *et* constitutes an accusative case morpheme, DOM in Modern Hebrew is sensitive primarily to syntactic definiteness, but also, to a limited degree, to partitivity. Syntactically definite nominals are obligatorily accusative, partitive indefinites may appear in the accusative case in the presence of certain proportional quantifiers and *xelek* 'part', and all the other types of objects are obligatorily caseless.

5.1.2　Definiteness: More Fine-Grained Distinctions

While in Hebrew, DOM is sensitive to the general distinction between (syntactically) definite and indefinite nominal, in certain languages, additional, more fine-grained distinctions have to be made within the domain of definiteness in order to account for case-marking patterns. Thus, there exist languages in which some types of definite objects are case-marked, whereas others are not. As discussed by Aissen (2003), these languages include Catalan and Pitjantjatjara.

In Catalan, the marker *a* obligatorily precedes strong personal pronouns that appear in the object position (8a). However, it does not

---

[3]　https://travelingelkins.wordpress.com/2007/07/08/94/, accessed August 17, 2016.
[4]　www.fxp.co.il/showthread.php?t=16157657&page=5, accessed August 17, 2016.
[5]　http://uv-tlv.com, accessed August 17, 2016.

precede other kinds of definite objects, such as proper names and definite descriptions (8b).[6]

(8) a. Él te telefoneará a ti.
he CL will.phone ACC you
'He'll phone you.'   (Aissen 2003, ex. 20b)
b. No havien vist l'alcalde.
NEG they.have seen the-mayor
'They had not seen the mayor.'   (Aissen 2003, ex. 21)

Indefinite objects remain caseless.

Thus, DOM in Catalan is sensitive to definiteness: only definites receive the marker *a*. However, here, in contrast to Hebrew, case is assigned not to all definite objects but only to their subset, specifically, to those nominals that are especially highly individuated and, as we will see below, appear on top of the definiteness scale. Other definite objects pattern together with indefinites.

In turn, Pitjantjatjara further extends object case-marking to proper names. Thus, in this language, object case appears on proper nouns and pronouns but not on other types of definite nominals, nor on indefinites.

(9) a. Tjitji-ngku Billy-nya / ngayu-nya nya-ngu.
child.ERG Billy.ACC / I.ACC see.PST
'The child saw Billy / me.'   (Aissen 2003, ex. 23)
b. Billy-lu tjitji nya-ngu.
Billy.ERG child see.PST
'Billy saw the child.'   (Aissen 2003, ex. 24a)

To sum up thus far, languages in which DOM is sensitive to definiteness may involve different cut-off points between types of nominals that are marked and ones that are unmarked.

5.1.3 Turkish and Uzbek: Specificity

DOM in a wide range of languages is also known to be sensitive to the property of specificity (although the precise definition of this notion as the one determining case-marking is far from obvious[7]). In this

[6] The examples in (8) and (9) are taken from Aissen (2003), who in turn quotes them from Rigau (1986) and Comrie (1979) for Catalan and Bowe (1990) for Pitjantjatjara.
[7] Types of specificity mentioned in this context include, for example, partitivity, epistemic specificity, wide scope, choice functions and relational specificity (see e.g. Enç 1991, von Heusinger and Kornfilt 2005, Lidz 2006, López 2012 and references therein).

section, I discuss two Turkic languages, Turkish and Uzbek, whose DOM-related properties are quite similar. Turkish has received much closer attention within generative linguistic literature (e.g. Erguvanlı-Taylan 1984, Enç 1991, Kornfilt 2003, von Heusinger and Kornfilt 2005, Göksel and Kerslake 2005, Öztürk 2005, Özge 2011) than the various dialects of Uzbek (Guntsetseg et al. 2008, von Heusinger and Kornfilt 2017 and Levy-Forsythe 2018 constitute important exceptions). However, most approaches proposed for Turkish DOM are equally relevant for Uzbek data, and below, examples from both languages will often be provided in order to enrich the descriptive data.

Let us begin with the fact that in both Turkish and Uzbek, similarly to Hebrew, definite objects are obligatorily case-marked. This is illustrated in (10) for Turkish and in (11) for Uzbek.

(10)   TURKISH (Enç 1991:9)

    a. Zeynep Ali-yi / on-u / adam-i / o masa-yi gördü.
       Zeynep Ali-acc / he.$_{ACC}$ / the-man.$_{ACC}$ / that table.$_{ACC}$ saw
       'Zeynep saw Ali / him / the man / that table.'
    b. *Zeynep Ali / o / adam / o masa gördü.

(11)   UZBEK

    a. Anvar   bu   rasm-*(ni)   chiz-di
       Anvar   this   picture.$_{ACC}$ draw.$_{PST.3.SG}$
       'Anvar drew this picture.'   (Levy-Forsythe 2018:59)
    b. Anvar   Madina-*(ni)   chiz-di
       Anvar   Madina.$_{ACC}$ draw.$_{PAST.3.SG}$
       'Anvar drew Madina.'   (Zarina Levy-Forsythe, p.c.)
    c. Anvar   Ra'no-ning   rasm-i-*(ni)   chiz-di
       Anvar   Ra'no.$_{GEN}$ picture.$_{1.SG.GEN-ACC}$ draw.$_{PST.3.SG}$
       Anvar drew Rano's picture.'   (Levy-Forsythe 2018:59)

Thus, for example, in (10), we can see that a proper name, a pronoun, a definite description and a nominal that contains a demonstrative obligatorily receive accusative case in the object position. Absence of accusative marking results in ungrammaticality.

Further, in both these languages, the accusative is assigned to specific indefinites. According to Enç (1991), the notion of partitivity plays a crucial role. Partitive specifics obligatorily appear in the accusative.

This is revealed in a number of ways. Firstly, Enç claims, overt partitives, which contain an analogue of the English *of*-phrase (as in *three of the boys*), obligatorily appear in the accusative. This is illustrated in (12) and (13) (from Enç 1991, ex. 10). These sentences demonstrate that the superset can be represented in Turkish as either an ablative (12) or a genitive (13) nominal. Both versions are unacceptable without accusative case-marking.

(12) a. Ali kadin-lar-dan   iki-sin-i   taniyordu.
          Ali woman-$_{PL\text{-}ABL}$ two-$_{AGR\text{-}ACC}$ knew
          'Ali knew two of the women.'
      b. *Ali kadin-lar-dan iki-si   taniyordu.

(13) a. Ali kadin-lar-in   iki-sin-i   taniyordu.
          Ali woman-$_{PL\text{-}GEN}$ two-$_{AGR\text{-}ACC}$ knew
          'Ali knew two of the women.'
      b. * Ali kadin-lar-in   iki-si   taniyordu.

Secondly, weak nominals in the object position may be either accusative or caseless, but, crucially, accusative case-marking is accompanied by the specific/partitive reading. To illustrate, Enç points out that each of the sentences in (15) could be used following (14):

(14) Odam-a   birkaç   çocuk   girdi.
      my-room-$_{DAT}$ several   child   entered
      'Several children entered my room.'

(15) a. Iki   kiz-i   taniyordum.
          two   girl-$_{ACC}$ I-knew
          'I knew two girls.'
      b. Iki   kiz   taniyordum.
          two   girl   I-knew
          'I knew two girls.'

                                              (Enç 1991:6)

In (15a), the phrase 'two girls' appears with the accusative marking; as a result, its referent is understood to be included in the set of children mentioned in (14). In other words, the object is interpreted partitively, even though it does not have an overt partitive structure. In contrast, (15b) is interpreted as a statement about two different girls who do not belong to the previously introduced set.

Thirdly, objects containing inherently strong/proportional quantifiers, for example the universal one, are obligatorily accusative:

(16) TURKISH (Enç 1991:10)

  a. Ali her   kitab-i   okudu
     Ali every book.$_{ACC}$ read
     'Ali read every book.'
  b. *Ali her kitap okudu.

(17) UZBEK (Levy-Forsythe 2018:59)
    Anvar hamma rasm-*(ni)/ har bitta rasm-*(ni) chiz-di
    Anvar every picture.$_{ACC}$ every one picture.$_{ACC}$ draw.$_{PST.3.SG}$
    'Anvar drew every picture.'

Enç explains this restriction by treating universally quantified nominals as inherently partitive since such phrases always involve quantification over a contextually supplied set.

Thus, Enç (1991) argues that in Turkish, definite and indefinite partitive objects receive accusative case, whereas other types of indefinites remain unmarked. How is definiteness unified with partitivity? Enç points out that both types of nominals impose the condition that "their discourse referents be linked to previously established discourse referents" (p. 9). Definites refer to (sets of) individuals that are **identical** to referents that have been previously introduced in the discourse. In turn, indefinite partitives refer to individuals that are **included** in a previously established set. Thus, in both instances, we are dealing with the relation of inclusion '⊆', which is compatible with both proper inclusion '⊂' and identity '='. This makes definites a special case of partitives. It is also worth noting that under some (although definitely not all) approaches to specificity, definite nominals are assumed to be inherently specific. Under this view, definites and partitives are unified by the property of specificity.

While, intuitively, specificity does indeed play a crucial role in Turkish and Uzbek DOM, it is less clear whether this property should be equated with partitivity. The view under which DOM is sensitive only to partitivity has been challenged in the linguistic literature, for instance by von Heusinger and Kornfilt (2005) and Özge (2011). To illustrate the problem, consider first the Turkish minimal pair in (18) and its Uzbek counterpart (19):

(18) TURKISH (von Heusinger and Kornfilt 2005, ex. 6b–c)

  a. (Ben) bir kitap oku-du-m.
    I   a   book read.$_{PST-1.SG}$
    'I read **a** book.'

b. (Ben) bir kitab-ı oku-du-m.
I a book.ACC read.PST-1.SG
'I read **a certain** book.'

(19) UZBEK (Zarina Levy-Forsythe, p.c.)

a. (Men) bir/bitta kitob o'qi-di-m.
I a book read.PST-1.SG
'I read **a** book.'

b. (Men) bir/bitta kitob-ni o'qi-di-m.
I a book.ACC read.PST-1.SG
'I read **a certain** book.'

Intuitively, (18b) and (19b) receive a specific reading, comparable to that of *a certain*-phrases in English. In contrast, the caseless objects in (18a) and (19a) get a non-specific interpretation. But, crucially, the objects in the (b) sentences need not be interpreted as partitive. This is a possible reading (i.e. the sentences may be understood, roughly, as 'I read a book from a previously introduced set'), but it is definitely not obligatory. This suggests that the notion of specificity which is relevant for DOM in Turkic languages is not identical to partitivity. The set of specific nominals includes partitive ones but is not limited to them. In other words, not all specifics are partitive.

In fact, it is even questionable whether all partitives are specific. While the tendency for partitive objects to appear in the accusative case in both Turkish and Uzbek is very strong, counterexamples have been provided in the literature. Contrary to Enç, von Heusinger and Kornfilt (2005:32) claim that explicitly partitive indefinites of the type illustrated in (12a) above, namely the ones that contain an ablative *of*-phrase, need not be accusative. Rather, they may be either marked or unmarked, depending on the nature of the head of the object and on the interpretation. (20) below illustrates a minimal pair of sentences that differ in the marking of the partitive DP:

(20) TURKISH (von Heusinger and Kornfilt 2005, ex. 57, 57')

a. Ali kadın-lar-dan **iki kişi** tanı-yor-du.
Ali woman.PL-ABL **two individual** know.PROG-PST
'Ali knew two individuals of the women.'

b Ali kadın-lar-dan **iki kişi-yi** tanı-yor-du.
Ali woman.PL-ABL **two individual.ACC** know.PROG-PST
'Ali knew two (specific, particular) individuals of the women.'

Even though the object is overtly partitive in all the above examples, it is case-marked in (20b) but not (20a). This has consequences for meaning: according to (20b), the identity of the women in question is known (plausibly to the speaker), whereas the women are not identified in (20a). In both instances, however, the women belong to a familiar set. In other words, a specific/non-specific contrast is possible even within the domain of partitives, and it correlates with object case-marking.

Von Heusinger and Kornfilt propose that in Turkish, accusative objects exhibit relational, or anchored, specificity, a concept which is also discussed by Enç (1991) and is analyzed in detail by von Heusinger (2002). Roughly, a nominal phrase is specific iff its referent is linked to another, already established, discourse referent via a salient function/relation. In the case of partitive specifics, the link is to the previously established superset. In the case of epistemic specificity, when the nominal is specific in the sense that its referent is known/identified, the link is to the person who bears the knowledge (often the speaker).[8]

It is also important to point out that in some instances, the form of the object is governed by syntactic, rather than semantic, considerations. As pointed out by von Heusinger and Kornfilt (2005), in Turkish, unmarked objects are only possible in the canonical object position of this language, namely, immediately preceding the verb. In other positions, for example when separated from the verb by an adverb, the object is obligatorily accusative-marked. Interestingly, it is interpreted as specific, but, crucially, the absence of the accusative suffix leads to ungrammaticality rather than to a non-specific interpretation.

To sum up this subsection, specificity clearly plays a significant role in Turkish and Uzbek DOM, although additional factors may intervene, affecting the choice of case.

5.1.4 Kannada: An Interaction of Specificity and Animacy

In certain languages, DOM is sensitive both to specificity/definiteness and to animacy. These languages include (but are not limited to) Spanish, Romanian, Hindi and Kannada. In this section, the Kannada data are briefly introduced, based on Lidz (2006).

Firstly, in Kannada, animate objects obligatorily receive accusative case-marking. The absence of the accusative case-marker results in ungrammaticality (21a), independently of whether the nominal is interpreted as specific or non-specific. In other words, for animate NPs, there is no correlation between accusative case and specificity.

---

[8] For detailed, in-depth discussions of various types of specificity, see e.g. Farkas (2002), von Heusinger (2002) and references therein.

(21) a. *nannu **sekretari** huDuk-utt-idd-eene
      I_{NOM} secretary   look.for.$_{NPST}$-be.$_{-1.SG}$
      'I am looking for a secretary.'

   b. naanu **sekretari-yannu** huDuk-utt-idd-eene
      I_{NOM} secretary$_{ACC}$ look.for.$_{NPST}$-be.$_{-1.SG}$
      'I am looking for a secretary.' (Lidz 2006, ex. 2)

For instance, whether the speaker is looking for a particular secretary
or for any secretary, the object in (21) has to be marked by *-yannu*.

In contrast, with inanimate objects, accusative case-marking is
optional. More precisely, it correlates with the specificity of the nominal. In sentences like (22), accusative inanimate objects can only
receive specific readings. In contrast, their caseless counterparts are
compatible with both specific and non-specific interpretations.
Specificity, in this instance, seems to be very close to the property of
scope (but Lidz argues that in sentences like 22b, choice functions are
involved).

(22) a. naanu **pustaka** huDuk-utt-idd-eene
      I_{NOM} book   look.for.$_{NPST}$-be.$_{-1.SG}$
      'I am looking for a book.'

   b. naanu **pustaka-vannu** huDuk-utt-idd-eene
      I_{NOM} book$_{ACC}$ look.for.$_{NPST}$-be.$_{-1.SG}$
      'I am looking for a book.'   (Lidz 2006, ex. 1)

Thus, (22b) entails that there is a particular book which the
speaker is looking for. In other words, the object has to receive
wide scope relative to the intensional verb. In turn, (22a) is compatible with two readings. It may have the same meaning as (22b)
(with the object taking wide scope), or it may mean that the
speaker is looking for, roughly, any book (wide scope of the
intensional predicate).

It may seem that unmarked inanimate objects are compatible with
any scopal interpretation, but it turns out that this is not always the
case. This is revealed in sentences which contain more than two
operators and, as a result, allow more than two interpretations
which differ in terms of relative scope. If an object can potentially
receive narrow, wide and also intermediate scope, the following configuration is observed. Accusative nominals are compatible with wide
and intermediate scope readings. Unmarked nominals are compatible
with intermediate- and narrow-scope readings. Thus, intermediate
scope constitutes the overlap area. These facts are summarized in
Table 5.1 and illustrated in (23).

Table 5.1 *Case-marking and scope in Kannada*

	Narrow scope	Intermediate scope	Wide scope
Accusative object	X	V	V
Unmarked object	V	V	X

(23) a. pratiyobba vidyaarthi **pustaka** huDuk-utt-idd-aane.
          every   student   book   look.for.$_{\mathrm{NPST}}$-be.$_{\mathrm{3.SG.M}}$
          'Every student is looking for a book.'
      b. pratiyobba vidyaarthi **pustaka-vannu** huDuk-utt-idd-aane.
          every   student   book.$_{\mathrm{ACC}}$ look.for.$_{\mathrm{NPST}}$-be.$_{\mathrm{3.SG.M}}$
          'Every student is looking for a book.'

(Lidz 2006, ex 5)

(23) is associated with (at least) three readings, paraphrased in (24):

(24) a. There is a particular book such that every student is looking for
          it.
          widest scope of the object: $\exists > \forall >$ look-for[9]
      b. For each student, there is a specific book (s)he is looking for.
          (These may be different books for different students.)
          intermediate scope: $\forall > \exists >$ look-for
      c. Every student is looking for some book or other.
          narrow scope: $\forall >$ look-for $> \exists$

The caseless version (23a) is compatible with the readings in (24b) and
(24c). The accusative one in (23b) can receive readings (24a) and (24b).

   Finally, it is important to point out that, as in Turkish, DOM interacts with the syntactic position of the object in Kannada. However, the
effect is not the same. In Kannada, unlike Turkish, both accusative and
caseless objects can appear both inside and outside the VP (as revealed
by their position relative to a VP-level adverb). It is the resulting
interpretation of caseless objects that is affected by syntax. When
these nominals appear in the relatively high position outside the VP
(as revealed by the linear order subject – object – adverbial phrase –
verb), they receive wide scope, similarly to their accusative counterparts. Thus, (25) entails that Rashmi bought the same book repeatedly,
however strange this interpretation may be.

---

[9] The relative ordering of the universal quantifier and the intensional verb does not
   seem to play a role.

(25)   Rashmi pustaka   **matte-matte**   koND-aLu
       Rashmi book   repeatedly   buy.$_{\text{PST-3.SG.F}}$
       'Rashmi repeatedly bought a book.'   (Lidz 2006, ex. 14a)

Lidz accounts for this fact by proposing that the object has moved outside of the scope of existential closure (Diesing 1992), to the domain in which nominals receive presuppositional and specific readings. In contrast, he claims that the semantics of accusative nominals involves choice functions (along the lines of Reinhart 1997 and Kratzer 1998) and, for this reason, their specificity is independent of the syntactic position and not even sensitive to island effects.

For more recent detailed discussions of the role of animacy in case-marking from a cross-linguistic perspective, see Malchukov (2008) and de Swart and de Hoop (2018).

5.1.5   Additional Properties of the Object

De Swart (2003) points out that in some languages, additional properties of the object affect DOM. For instance, in Palauan, an Austronesian language, number plays a role, in addition to animacy and specificity. Thus, a non-human object will be case-marked only if it is both specific and singular:

(26)   PALAUAN (Austronesian; Woolford 1995)

       a. Ak   ousbech   er   a bilas   er a   klukuk.
          I   need   PREP   boat   tomorrow
          'I need the boat tomorrow.'

       b. Ak   ousbech   a bilas   er a   klukuk.
          I   need   boat   tomorrow
          'I need a boat/the boats tomorrow.'
                                           (quoted from de Swart 2003:26–27)

In fact, the examples from Woolford (1995) suggest that it may be more precise to formulate the generalization in the following way: a non-human object will be interpreted as specific and singular if it is case-marked. If it is not case-marked, it will be understood as nonspecific, plural or both.

In turn, in Albanian, DOM is affected by number as well as gender (in addition to definiteness) (Moravcsik 1978). Thus, an object will only be marked if it is definite, singular and **not neuter** (but rather masculine or feminine).

Thus, while the impact of animacy and definiteness/specificity on DOM is much more widespread, in certain languages, number and gender play a role as well.

5.2 THE REASONING BEHIND DOM?

Is there any reasoning behind the case-marking tendencies that have been illustrated in Section 5.1? Why is object marking affected specifically by such properties as animacy and definiteness/specificity? And why do these properties systematically affect DOM in the same direction, for example, definite nominals are more likely to be case-marked than indefinite ones and not vice versa, and so on? Below, two approaches to this system are discussed. The first locates DOM in a wider schema of transitivity parameters. The second is a functional approach which relates DOM to (non-)prototypicality of the direct object.

5.2.1 DOM Signals Higher Transitivity

Hopper and Thompson (1980) relate DOM to the broader notion of transitivity. Transitivity, they point out, "is traditionally understood as a property of an entire clause, such that an activity is 'carried-over' or 'transferred' from an agent to a patient" (p. 251). The authors discuss a range of properties that contribute to a higher (or lower) transitivity of a clause. They build a list of so-called "parameters of transitivity," properties that affect the degree to which a given clause possesses this property. The parameters include characteristics of the subject, the object and the clause more broadly. To illustrate, the presence of two or more participants that include A and O (an agent and an object) contributes to higher transitivity, as opposed to the presence of only one event participant. Telicity and realis mood are additional properties that make the degree of transitivity higher, as well as a volitional agent. And, crucially, for our present purposes, the individuation of the object contributes to the transitivity of the clause as well. Individuation, in turn, is decomposed into a set of properties, as listed in (27) below:

(27) INDIVIDUATED   NON-INDIVIDUATED
      proper   common
      human/animate   inanimate
      concrete   abstract
      singular   plural
      count   mass
      referential, definite   non-referential
                                (from Hopper and Thompson 1980:253, ex. 2)

It can be seen that individuation is built in part from those characteristics which are known to affect DOM, such as definiteness, referentiality/specificity and animacy. Objects that are more likely to be case-marked in DOM languages are also more individuated.

Essentially, under the approach developed by Hopper and Thompson, high individuation of the object contributes to higher transitivity of the clause. Definite, specific, animate objects make the sentence more transitive in the classical sense of carrying an event over from an agent to a patient. In turn, highly transitive clauses are more likely to receive various kinds of transitivity marking (as determined by the characteristics of the individual language), such as, for example, transitive marking on the verb, ergative marking on the subject and/or, crucially, for our purposes, case-marking on an object in a DOM language.

In turn, non-individuated, unmarked objects are associated with low transitivity and, at least in the extreme case, even lose their object status, undergoing incorporation into the verb instead. Indeed, in the recent literature on some DOM languages, unmarked objects have been analyzed as, in some sense or other, incorporated. (See e.g. López' 2012 account of DOM in Spanish. Lidz 2006, too, considers the incorporation option for unmarked objects in Kannada, but ultimately rejects it.)

Many of Hopper and Thompson's parameters of transitivity are incorporated into Grimm's (2005) lattice, developed with the goal of accounting for case-marking patterns in various languages. (See Chapter 2 for more detail on Grimm's approach.)

5.2.2 Marking a Non-Prototypical Object (Disambiguation)

While for Hopper and Thompson, DOM essentially signals a **prototypical**, classical transitive relation, Comrie (1979) and Aissen (2003) hold, in a certain sense, an opposite view. Under their approach, case-marking in a DOM language is essentially a signal of **atypicality**. It appears on NP/DP complements which, in terms of their individuation-related properties, resemble classical subjects rather than classical objects. After all, animacy, definiteness and specificity all characterize **prototypical subjects**. In contrast, **prototypical objects** are inanimate, indefinite and non-specific. This is illustrated in a sentence like (28), which seems to constitute a very typical transitive clause:

(28)   John wrote a letter.

Accusative marking is thus found on those objects which are less prototypical and more subject-like. A configuration that is non-prototypical and, in this sense, **marked**, comes hand in hand with morphological **marking** on the object. This notion of markedness plays a central role in the analysis developed by Aissen (2003) (see Section 5.4.1).

The relevance of number and gender is addressed less often in this context. However, generalizing across the more specific properties, we can state that prototypical subjects are highly individuated, whereas prototypical objects are, in contrast, low in individuation. Singular nouns are often treated as more individuated than plural ones (e.g. Timberlake 1986), which makes the Palauan and Albanian number-related facts fit neatly into the general picture. Turning to gender, it is worth noting that although, cross-linguistically, there is no one-to-one correspondence between grammatical gender and the sex and/or animacy of the referent, certain correlations still hold. A prototypical neuter noun is inanimate, in contrast to feminine and masculine ones.[10] This, in turn, explains the higher individuation of masculine and feminine nominals and the higher likelihood of such objects to be marked.

Functionally speaking, the strategy described above can be viewed as playing a disambiguating, or discriminatory, role.[11] It helps the hearer figure out that the nominals in question are **objects**, despite their subject-like properties. An indefinite, non-specific, inanimate object is prototypical (cf. the example in (28) above); it is less likely to be confused with the subject, and so object marking is (in many languages) not required. But once an object is, for example, animate, it becomes more similar in its characteristics to the subject. As pointed out by Grimm (2005), such objects may be characterized by certain agentivity-related characteristics, like motion and sentience, which makes it more difficult to discriminate them from subjects. Here, it is

---

[10] Again, it should be emphasized that we are dealing with prototypicality and not with a rule. Obviously, in a language that makes a two-way gender distinction between masculine and feminine (e.g. French or Hebrew), these gender values are equally compatible with animate and inanimate nominals. And even in a language that adds the neuter value to the list, masculine and feminine nouns need not be animate, nor is neuter gender restricted to inanimate nominals. To illustrate, in Russian, which exhibits the three-gender system, *stol* 'table' is masculine, *kartina* 'picture' is feminine, and *čudovišče* 'beast' is neuter in spite of its animacy (although it is still non-human). But despite the existence of exceptions, the tendency of neuter nouns to be inanimate is quite strong.

[11] The discriminatory approach to case-marking is discussed by Song (2001) and Grimm (2005), for example. Under this view, the function of case is to mark a distinction between the different arguments of a predicate.

useful to case-mark such objects, making it absolutely clear and explicit what their grammatical (and, correspondingly, thematic) status is.

The hypothesis according to which the logic underlying DOM is
disambiguation is further supported by certain syntactic facts. As
discussed in Section 5.1.3, in Turkish, objects that do not occupy the
canonical object position obligatorily receive the accusative case suffix. This could potentially be due to the fact that it is particularly
important to explicitly identify such nominal as objects.[12]

A partly similar dependence between object position and the
optionality of case-marking is observed in Spanish. The following
example is quoted by de Swart (2003:31):

(29) SPANISH (Romance; De Jong 1996)
    a. el entusiasmo   vence   (a) la   difficultad.
       the enthusiasm   conquer$_{3.SG}$ (to) the difficulty
       'Enthusiasm conquers difficulties.'
    b. A la   difficultad   vence   el entusiasmo.
       to the difficulty   conquer$_{3.SG}$ the enthusiasm
       'Enthusiasm conquers difficulties.'

The two sentences differ only in the fact that in (29a), the object
occupies the canonical object position (it follows the verb) whereas
in (29b), it appears sentence-initially (i.e. in terms of word order, in
a position that is much more strongly associated with the subject).
Crucially, while in (29a) object case-marking is optional, in (29b) it is
obligatory.

Once again, we see that the likelihood of overt marking increases if
the object is non-prototypical in a certain respect.

Finally, de Swart (2003) points out that "case marking of objects is
used in different languages not only when the object resembles the
subject, but also when the subject resembles the object" (p. 38). This is
revealed in the contrast between the following Malayalam examples:

(30) MALAYALAM
    a. tiiyyə   kuṭil   naʃippiccu
       fire$_{NOM}$ hut$_{NOM}$ destroy$_{PST}$
       'Fire destroyed the hut.'
    b. veḷḷam   tiiyyə   keṭutti
       water$_{NOM}$ fire$_{NOM}$ extinguish$_{PST}$
       'Water extinguished the fire.'
                (from Asher and Kumari 1997, quoted by de Swart 2003:32)

---

[12] But see von Heusinger and Kornfilt (2005) for arguments against the functional
approach.

(31) MALAYALAM

   a. kappal   tiramaalaka[e   bheediccu
       ship   wave$_{PL.ACC}$ split$_{PST}$
       'The ship broke through the waves.'

   b. tiramaalaka[kappaline   bheediccu
       wave$_{PL}$ ship$_{ACC}$ split$_{PST}$
       'The waves split the ship.'
       (from Asher and Kumari 1997, quoted by de Swart 2003:32)

Typically, inanimate objects are unmarked in Malayalam. We see this in (30). However, in (31), potential ambiguity arises: the ship could affect the waves and the waves could affect the ship. The ambiguity is resolved via accusative case-marking, which makes it clear which of the two nominals is the object and, consequently, which of them is the theme (rather than the cause). Note that the potential ambiguity arises not only due to the properties of the object (i.e. its inanimacy) but also due to those of the subject (which is inanimate, too), as well as the lexical meaning of the verb. Such examples show clearly that DOM at least **may** be used for the purposes of disambiguation.

It is worth noting that, arguably, analogous disambiguation reasoning stands behind certain instances of differential subject marking (DSM). Consider the following contrast in Dani (West Papuan):

(32) a. (ap)   palu   na-sikh-e
          man   python   eat-$_{RM.PAST-3SG.SUBJ}$
          'The man ate the python.'

      b. ap   (palu-nen)   na-sikh-e
          man   python-$_{ERG}$ eat-$_{RM.PAST-3SG.SUBJ}$
          'The python ate the man.'
          (Foley 2000:375, as quoted by Palancar 2011:566)

Ergative marking appears on the subject in (32b) but not (32a). Foley (2000) and Palancar (2011) relate this to the unexpectedness of the former: a man is more likely to eat a python than vice versa. The contrast could also be related to the fact that *man* is more highly individuated than *python* (both are animate, but only the former is also human). Hence *man* is a better candidate for subjecthood. Once a different subject is chosen, a non-prototypical situation is created, and this is reflected in subject marking (rather than in object marking as in the instances of DOM). Indeed, de Swart (2007) unifies DSM and DOM, arguing that within both these phenomena, the distinctness of the subject from the object (or one between two predicate structures) plays a crucial role.

5.3 VERBAL INFLUENCE: DIRECT OR INDIRECT?

Meanwhile, we have seen that DOM is affected by the properties of the object (and its distinctness from the subject). The next question to ask is whether this phenomenon is sensitive to the properties of the verb as well. The latter is in line with Hopper and Thompson's (1980) discussion of different degrees of transitivity: after all, transitivity, obviously, depends on the properties of the verb, which makes the latter a potential candidate for affecting DOM. Along this line, Grimm (2005:57) suggests "that while the qualities of nominals are indeed the key component which gives rise to DOM, this is within the larger context of the argument structure in which the nominal is involved" – and the argument structure is determined by the predicate.

How can the lexical meaning of a verb play a role in DOM? Different verbs assign different thematic roles to their internal arguments, thereby affecting in some sense the interpretation of the latter. Further, if we consider theta-role decomposition (see e.g. Reinhart 2000, Grimm 2005 and references therein, as well as Section 2.3.2 of Chapter 2) and concentrate on individual features from which theta-roles are built, more fine-grained distinctions between verbs can be formulated. Here is a brief illustration: the object of *kill* is entailed to be affected; moreover, its existence depends on the event denoted by the verb (if the event takes place, the killed individual no longer exists). (Both being causally affected and lacking independent existence constitute Proto-Patient properties according to Dowty's 1991 seminal work.) Neither of these properties holds of the object of *read*. Such contrasts make *kill* higher in transitivity than *read*. Objects of verbs that are high in transitivity are, in turn, more strongly expected to receive accusative case within Hopper and Thompson's approach and more recent accounts inspired by it. The question is: do such semantic properties, contributed by the verb rather than by the object itself, really affect case-marking?

To list just a few recent examples, the claim that transitivity in general and properties of the verb in particular affect DOM has been made by Guntsetseg et al. (2008), von Heusinger et al. (2008) and von Heusinger and Kaiser (2011) for such different languages as Mongolian, Uzbek and (historically) Spanish. In other words, evidence has indeed been provided that in some DOM languages, objects of different verbs exhibit degrees of likelihood of appearing in the accusative case. To illustrate, accusative objects of *kill* are judged better by native speakers of Mongolian than accusative objects of *read*

(Guntsetseg et al. 2008:3). This could potentially result from the contrast in transitivity discussed above. Another example of the interrelation between DOM and the choice of verb is Udmurt (a Finno-Ugric language). For instance, according to Serdobolskaya and Toldova (2006), verbs meaning *break*, *pour out* and *lose* are more likely to take accusative objects in this language than *build*, *pour into* and *find*.

But does the lexical semantics of the verb truly affect DOM? Is there a direct relation between verb transitivity and case-marking? In spite of the observations illustrated above, this is not trivial to decide because the relation between verb and case could turn out to be indirect, **mediated by the properties of the object** itself. For the sake of illustration, consider the verbs *invite* and *read*. The object of the former is required to be animate; the object of the latter has to be, on the contrary, inanimate. As a result, in a language whose DOM is determined by animacy, complements of *invite* are predicted to be accusative and those of *read*, caseless. This could very well result from the properties of the nominals themselves. The [+animate] feature would bring about accusative-ness, the [–animate] feature, caseless-ness. The relation between case and verb semantics would be indirect. The verb determines whether its object is animate or not, but ultimately, it is the animacy of the object that affects case. In other words, the question is: does case (ever) depend on the semantic, theta-related properties of verb, or rather on the actual characteristics of a particular object involved?

For instance, von Heusinger (2008) conducts a corpus study of the historical development of Spanish between the fourteenth and twentieth centuries. He shows that DOM is sensitive to the difference between verbs like *kill*, whose object is obligatorily animate, *see* (indeterminate in this respect) and *put* (whose objects are typically inanimate). On the one hand, we see that case-marking correlates with lexical properties of the predicate. On the other hand, these properties are relevant by virtue of the fact that they interact with the object's animacy. Therefore (on the basis of these facts only), we could conclude that what really matters for DOM is animacy, an inherent property of the object, and not verb semantics. We will see below, however, that this is not the whole story.

The conclusion that the role of verb semantics in DOM is only secondary, or indirect, seems to follow from Serdobolskaya and Toldova's (2006) investigation of several Turkic and Finno-Ugric languages, including Udmurt, Mari, Kazakh and Uzbek. Under the authors' view, case is determined by definiteness (and/or specificity). But some verbs are more likely to take definite objects than others, which creates an impression that it is the verb that affects case. More precisely, those verbs whose complement is presupposed to exist combine more easily with accusative nominals.[13] For instance, the object of *extinguish* (a fire) is more likely to be accusative than that of *light* (a fire), since the former but not the latter is presupposed to exist. But, in fact, case is determined by properties of the object (definiteness and presuppositionality), rather than directly by the verb.

The contrast between *kill* and *read* in Mongolian could be accounted for in a similar manner. Mongolian DOM is sensitive to animacy (Guntsetseg et al. 2008). Since the object of *kill* is animate and that of *read* is not, it is to be expected that the former will be more likely to combine with case-marked nominals. As discussed above, this prediction is borne out. It seems that we do not have to relate to affectedness in order to account for the contrast in case: inherent properties of the nominal are sufficient. The fact that *invite* shows more or less the same results as *kill* suggests that the relevant property is indeed animacy (the object of *invite* must be animate, but it is not entailed to be affected).

This is not the whole story, however. Other examples suggest that verb semantics does contribute to object markedness. For instance, in Mongolian, *write* complicates the picture. Experimental evidence collected by Guntsetseg et al. (2008) suggests that objects of this verb are better in the accusative case than those of *read*. Animacy cannot be responsible, as internal arguments of both verbs are inanimate. Transitivity, in contrast, may very well play a role: *write* is higher in transitivity since it is a creation verb (the existence of its object is dependent on the action – which is not true for *read*). This small piece of data demonstrates how complex the configuration may be. A range of properties may interact with case-marking, in which case it is not always trivial to figure out which of them affect the choice between ACC and Ø directly and which do not.

Von Heusinger and Kaiser (2011) conduct a study of the historical development of the Spanish DOM whose results suggest that affectedness and other entailments contributed by the verb do play a role in the phenomenon. They show, for instance, that DOM is sensitive to "the competition of agentivity between the participants in the event" (p. 31 of the manuscript). Specifically, in those instances when the object receives from the verb properties that are typically

---

[13] The extent to which presuppositionality coincides with definiteness remains to be determined, however. The two properties, although related, are clearly not equivalent.

characteristic of subjects (Proto-Agent properties), its likelihood of being accusative-marked increases.

To illustrate, *querer* 'to like' and *temer* 'to fear' exhibit considerably different results despite the fact that both are taken to appear on the same level on the affectedness scale. *Temer* is much more likely to take accusative objects, both when the latter are definite and (especially) when they are indefinite.[14] The authors explain this contrast by the fact that the object of 'fear' may be viewed as a cause (which is an agentive property). This is an instance where a stimulus causes a change in the other event participant. The object of 'like', in contrast, is not regarded as a cause. Yet another interesting contrast is observed between *ver* 'see' and *mirar* 'look at', on the one hand, and *oír* 'hear' and *escuchar* 'listen', on the other. The latter two are much more likely to take accusative objects; again, the contrast is particularly striking with indefinite nominals. The authors attribute this to the fact that the object of 'hear/listen' must actively produce a noise; whereas the object of 'see/look' need not really do anything: it must merely appear within the field of perception of the subject. Again, this makes the former more agent-like and, as a consequence, more likely to be case-marked.

Note that such contrasts, make a lot of sense within the functional, disambiguation view of DOM discussed in Section 5.2.2. We have seen that cross-linguistically, prototypical objects are less likely to be marked than objects characterized by subject-like properties, such as animacy or definiteness. Examples like *temer/querer* and *oír/ver* exhibit the same principle, although here, we are dealing with subject-like characteristics that are not inherent to the nominal but rather stem from the lexical semantics of the verb. Once again, objects that are relatively subject-like appear with accusative marking, which makes it clear for the addressee what their grammatical status is.

DISCUSSION

Suppose that affectedness per se (and not via its interrelation with additional factors) increases the likelihood of accusative case-marking. Would this generalization support the disambiguation view of DOM presented in Section 5.2.2 or, on the contrary, provide evidence against it?

(Hint: Affectedness is a Proto-Patient property, i.e. it is typical of objects, not of subjects.)

[14] The study concentrates on human nominals.

To conclude this section, the relation between verb semantics and DOM is definitely present, but it is not easy to determine when the verb affects case directly and when this relation is mediated by the properties of the object (e.g. the verb selects an animate object, and case-marking is determined by animacy). Apparently, both types of relations are observed. The investigation of this topic is quite important and may have consequences for our broader understanding of DOM. For instance, it may provide evidence for or against the disambiguation approach to this phenomenon.

5.4 CROSS-LINGUISTIC ANALYSES OF DOM

The above discussion reveals that despite the considerable amount of cross-linguistic variation, a uniform picture of DOM can (and probably should) be discerned. Indeed, a number of analyses have been proposed whose goal is to account for this phenomenon not just in an individual language but rather cross-linguistically. Several such analyses are reviewed below.

5.4.1 Aissen (2003)

A very prominent approach in this direction has been put forward by Aissen (2003). Aissen discusses a range of languages in which an object can be either marked for case or remain morphologically caseless. The investigated languages include Hebrew, Turkish, Hindi, Spanish and Yiddish, among many others. Aissen shows that these alternations are sensitive to the position occupied by the nominal on two prominence scales: the scale of animacy and the scale of definiteness (the latter incorporates both definiteness and specificity). In other words, cross-linguistically, the three properties discussed above play a critical role in DOM. We can say that the unifying concept is individuation. Although the different languages place the boundary between accusative and caseless objects on different scales and in different places in the hierarchies, caseless nominals are systematically less individuated than accusative ones.

Let us begin by considering the two prominence scales in more detail. The corresponding hierarchies can be represented as follows:

(33)   Definiteness scale: Pronoun > Name > Definite > Indefinite Specific > Non-Specific

(34)   Animacy scale: Human > (non-human) Animate > Inanimate
                                                    (based on Croft 1988)

In fact, first- and second-person pronouns can arguably be ranked higher on the definiteness scale than third-person ones.

The higher an object is on a scale, the more prominent or individuated it is. Thus, humans are more individuated than inanimate objects, and definite nominals are more prominent than their indefinite counterparts.

Grimm (2005) follows Aissen in relating to the above-mentioned distinctions; however, he reformulates them by using several binary features and introduces certain changes in the course of this shift. For the definiteness scale these are: [+/−utterance context], [+/−given], [+/−referring] and [+/−singular term] (the latter corresponding to the property of being uniquely referring). Animacy scale distinctions are represented using three binary features: [+/−motion], [+/−sentient], [+/−human]. The former is needed in order to distinguish between inanimates that are capable of motion (e.g. *wind*) and ones that are incapable of motion (e.g. *house*). Case-marking depends on the kinds of features that characterize a given object.

But how do such prominence contrasts affect case-marking? It is here that Optimality Theory (OT) comes in to play an essential part within Aissen's analysis. The formal account of DOM proposed by Aissen is formulated within the OT framework. The phenomenon is viewed as a product of the tension that arises between two distinct principles, having to do with iconicity on the one hand and economy, on the other. Roughly, iconicity requires overt case-marking (and the higher the prominence of the object, the stronger the requirement), whereas economy, in contrast, penalizes overt case-marking. Let us consider this approach in more detail.

Aissen makes an assumption that "audible expression of case must involve a positive specification for morphological case, while zero expression need not, and often does not." In other words, when a nominal expression carries a certain value for the feature CASE (e.g. dative or accusative), this value is typically accompanied by an audible exponent. However, such an audible exponent may be (and often is) absent if the feature CASE is left with no value. The constraint in (35) penalizes the absence of case specification:

(35) $*\emptyset_C$ 'STAR ZERO': Penalizes the absence of a value for the feature CASE.[15]

Roughly, this constraint requires for nominal arguments to have a value for the feature CASE, which, in turn, also means that case will be morphologically realized.

---

[15] Subscripted C in $*\emptyset_C$ stands for CASE.

The constraint in (35) is in tension with the requirement in (36), which is dictated by the principles of economy.

(36)   *STRUC$_C$: penalizes a value for the morphological category CASE.

Roughly, this constraint says that a nominal should not have morphological case, for reasons of economy.

Different languages resolve the tension between (35) and (36) in different ways, depending on language-specific constraint ranking. In particular, instead of universally applying to all objects, (35) is restricted to the more prominent ones (i.e. objects that appear higher on the prominence scales introduced above).[16] In contrast, the less prominent objects are subject to (36). Technically, this relation between the prominence scales and STAR ZERO is achieved via Local Constraint Conjunction (Smolensky 1995). The point at which (35) is forced to apply, overruling (36), depends on the individual language. In other words, languages differ in the cut-off point that they set between case-marked and non-case-marked objects. Roughly speaking, the more individuated objects will be systematically case-marked, whereas the less individuated ones will lack cases. However, languages differ in the particular cut-off point which they treat as a boundary between what counts as individuated and what counts as non-individuated (for case purposes).

Let us illustrate this with the definiteness scale. For instance, in Hebrew, the cut-off point appears between definite NPs and indefinite specifics:[17]

(37)   Personal pronoun > Proper name > Definite NP > / Indefinite specific NP > Non-specific NP

Objects that are higher than this point (i.e. definite ones) receive accusative case (STAR ZERO wins); objects that are lower do not (the economy principle wins).

In Turkish, the cut-off point distinguishes non-specific indefinites from all the rest. But just as in Hebrew, the part that appears below such a point remains caseless, whereas the higher part is case-marked.

---

[16] The reason for the association between (35) and iconicity is the following. As discussed in detail in Section 5.2, an object that is characterized by high prominence or individuation is marked (since such a property is more characteristic of a subject). The application of (35) therefore results in the morphological *marking* of objects that are *marked* in terms of their semantic properties.

[17] Assuming that we ignore, for the sake of the current discussion, instances of accusative-marked partitives discussed in the subsection on Hebrew above.

(38)   Personal pronoun > Proper name > Definite NP > Indefinite specific NP > / Non-specific NP

In turn, in Catalan, the cut-off point appears very high on the scale: immediately below personal pronouns.

(39)   Personal pronoun > / Proper name > Definite NP > Indefinite specific NP > Non-specific NP

Here, only personal pronouns are case-marked in the object position.

DISCUSSION

Can those languages in which all objects are case-marked fit into the above-described system? What about languages in which an object is never overtly marked for case?

(Hint: The cut-off point may be located at a scale boundary, with all the objects being located below (or above) this point.)

The situation is analogous for those languages in which DOM is determined by the animacy scale.

Turning to languages like Kannada and Spanish, in which an interaction of definiteness/specificity and animacy plays a role, Aissen creates partial ranking of composite properties by crossing the two scales. This is illustrated in Figure 5.1.

The general idea is the same as with unidimensional DOM: objects that are higher in prominence/individuation are more likely to

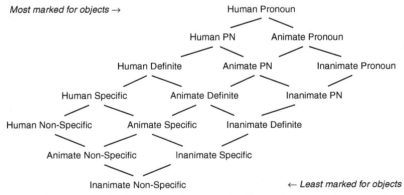

Figure 5.1   Relative markedness on the dimensions of animacy and definiteness (from Aissen 2003:459)

receive overt case-marking. Human pronouns are the most prominent; inanimate non-specific DPs, the least prominent. Again, different languages draw the cut-off line in different places. In fact, we sometimes even get two cut-off lines (resulting in three types of nominals), since with some objects, overt case is obligatory (the highest prominence), with others, optional (intermediate prominence) and with yet others, impossible (the least prominent). To illustrate, in Hindi, ko-marking is obligatory with all human objects unless they are non-specific, as well as with animate pronouns and proper names. It is unacceptable with inanimate indefinites, and optional with everything else. (For further detail, see Aissen 2003:29.) Given that ranking in Figure 5.1 is partial, it is up to a given language to decide whether clusters of properties appearing on the same level will bring about the same case-related behavior or will rather contrast in this respect. For instance, in Hindi, case-marking of both human definites and animate proper names (which appear on the same level) is obligatory. In contrast, with inanimate pronouns it is optional, even though they are characterized by exactly the same degree of prominence. This kind of configuration is allowed by the system.

5.4.2   De Swart (2003)

De Swart (2003) puts forward a different analysis, although it incorporates certain elements of Aissen's approach. He departs from the account provided by Aissen for several reasons, including the following. Firstly, he points out that DOM is sensitive to a range of properties of the object which are not limited to animacy, definiteness and specificity. For instance, in some languages, object case-marking depends on number and gender, as pointed out in Section 5.1.5. Secondly, and this is probably a more important issue, in certain instances, properties of the object per se are not sufficient in order to predict the emerging case pattern. Rather, de Swart claims, it is essential to look at a broader picture which includes additional elements present in the sentence. A very considerable role is devoted in his approach to **the comparison between the object and the subject**.

Aissen's analysis captures the generalization that subject-like objects are more likely to receive overt case-marking (e.g. Comrie 1979). De Swart, however, argues that what matters is whether, in a given sentence, **the subject is more subject-like than the object**. For instance, recall the Malayalam example in (31), repeated below as (40):

(40) a. kappal   tiramaalakaļe   bheediccu.
          ship   wave$_{PL.ACC}$ split$_{PST}$
          'The ship broke through the waves.'

      b. tiramaalakaļ kappaline   bheediccu.
          wave.$_{PL}$ ship$_{ACC}$ split$_{PST}$
          'The waves split the ship.'

While normally, in Malayalam, inanimate objects remain caseless, here, accusative marking is present. Intuitively, this helps resolve ambiguity. De Swart (2003, 2007) emphasizes that the overt marking is due to the fact that the subject and the object do not differ in animacy (the property that is relevant for object case-marking in this language) "the object is not lower in animacy than the subject" (de Swart 2003:61). Thus, what plays a role is not only the animacy feature specification on the object but also the relative ranking of the object and the subject along the corresponding scale.

In order to account for this observation de Swart (2003) defines the notion of **Minimal Semantic Distinctness**:

(41) MINIMAL SEMANTIC DISTINCTNESS: the two arguments of a semantic transitive predicate must be minimally distinct. If they are not minimally distinct this must be marked in the realized structure.

The reasoning behind this principle has to do with potential ambiguity: "if two arguments resemble each other to a greater extent the chance of a potential ambiguity arises and this potential ambiguity can be solved through the overt marking of the subject and/or object argument" (p. 71).

Languages differ in terms of the dimension(s) along which distinctness is assessed, such as animacy, definiteness, specificity, etc. De Swart proposes the following list of relevant features, based on Comrie's (1979) discussion of natural transitive constructions and Hopper and Thompson's (1980) transitivity parameters.

(42)

	α	β
	agent	*patient*
animacy	animate	inanimate
definiteness	definite	indefinite
specificity	specific	non-specific
number	singular	plural
volitionality	volitional	non-volitional
discourse status	high prominence	low prominence
topicality	topic	comment

(de Swart 2007:72)

In (42) α corresponds to the external argument of the predicate, which is mapped as the subject, and β, to the internal argument, realized as the object. Thus, we are dealing with a transitive construction P(α, β).

Here, it is important to point out that de Swart's goal is to capture not only DOM but also differential subject marking across languages. Hence the inclusion in the table of such properties as volitionality. However, since the present chapter is devoted to DOM, we will concentrate on object case-marking.[18]

Formally, de Swart proposes an analysis that is based on Blutner's (2000) Bidirectional Optimality Theory, which relates to optimality in production and comprehension and involves determining optimal form–meaning pairs. A central role in de Swart's proposal is devoted to the constraints in (43).

(43)   Constraints on Form and Meaning (p. 88):
       (i) 'Star Structure': *STRUC: penalize morpho-syntactic structure
       (ii) MINIMAL SEMANTIC DISTINCTNESS: the α-argument should
       minimally outrank the β-argument.[19]

Here, (i) is an economy restriction based on the corresponding constraint in Aissen (2003). While (i) represents morpho-syntactic unmarkedness, (ii) is a constraint on semantic unmarkedness (roughly, in the unmarked case, the subject is more prominent than the object), based on (41) above. According to de Swart's optimality account of case alternations, the two types of markedness (or unmarkedness) should go together. In other words, semantically unmarked structures will be unmarked morpho-syntactically (e.g. the object will remain caseless), whereas semantically marked structures, the ones in which the subject does not outrank the object along the relevant dimension(s), will involve morpho-syntactic marking, for example overt accusative case. Essentially, de Swart's analysis predicts that the two rules in (43) will go hand in hand; morpho-syntactic structure is expected to be penalized when the subject minimally outranks the object. An optimal form–meaning pair will result when the object does not minimally differ from the subject and is marked for case, or when the object does minimally differ from the subject and is morphologically unmarked.

In fact, Malchukov (2008), following Feldman (1986), points out that in Awtuw (another DOM language), an object obligatorily appears in

---

[18] It is also worth noting that for the purposes of illustrating the application of his analysis, de Swart uses mainly examples of DOM.
[19] As we will see below, de Swart introduces two additional semantic constraints.

the accusative case not only when it is equal to the subject in terms of animacy but also if it appears higher than the subject on the corresponding scale. For instance, the object will be accusative if it is [+animate], [+human] whereas the subject is [+animate], [−human]. These facts are accounted for straightforwardly under the disambiguation approach. They are also predicted by Minimal Semantic Distinctness since the subject does not outrank the object (in fact, the two **are** distinct, but in the opposite direction).

De Swart's object of investigation is not restricted to asymmetric DOM; rather, his goal is to provide an analysis that would encompass the broad range of subject and object case alternations. He points out that minimal distinctness is not the only meaning-related constraint that is needed for this purpose. In order to account, within the same analysis, for such predicate-oriented alternations as the boundedness-based partitive/accusative contrast in Finnish (see Chapter 4), de Swart formulates the **Avoid Predicate Ambiguity** principle:

(44)   If two predicate specifications (a) and (b) differ in one of the features [below] this difference should be expressed morpho-syntactically.

(45)   aspect: telic, atelic
tense: present, past, future
punctuality: punctual, non-punctual
affirmation: affirmative, negative, imperative, question
mode: realis, irrealis

(p. 76)

The features are adopted from Hopper and Thompson (1980).

For example, this principle accounts for the fact that in Finnish, the case of the object depends on the aspectual properties of the predicate.

Finally, de Swart points out that in certain instances, the two principles formulated above are insufficient, and our knowledge of the world and information lexically associated with certain linguistic items should also be taken into consideration. This constraint, called Lexical Information, is more vaguely defined as stating that "we must obey our lexical and world knowledge" (p. 92). The purpose of this constraint is to capture such facts as lack of case-marking in (46):

(46)   MALAYALAM (Dravidian; Asher and Kumari 1997)
tiiyyǝ   kuṭil   naʃippiccu.
fire$_{NOM}$ hut$_{NOM}$ destroy$_{PST}$
'Fire destroyed the hut.'

Given that both the subject and the object are inanimate here, and DOM in Malayalam is sensitive to animacy, Minimal Semantic Distinctness predicts that *kuṭil* 'hut' should be accusative-marked. This is not what we observe, however. De Swart explains this via Lexical Information since, roughly, world knowledge tells us that typically, fires destroy huts but not vice versa. Thus, disambiguation takes place due to world knowledge, and morphological markedness is not needed for this purpose.

De Swart's analysis has the advantage of accounting for the fact that DOM is sensitive not only to the properties of the object per se but also to the relative prominence of the object and the subject. But at the same time, it raises questions regarding those languages in which properties of the subject appear to be totally irrelevant for this phenomenon.

For instance, in Hebrew, object marking depends on the property of definiteness. As demonstrated in Section 5.1.1, definite objects are marked by *et*, whereas, typically, indefinite ones are not. Crucially, the definiteness of the subject does not play any role in object case-marking. To illustrate, consider (47). Both the subject and the object are indefinite in this example. Further, they are not distinguished in terms of animacy (both are +animate, +human) and need not differ in terms of specificity. Thus, by Minimal Semantic Distinctness, one would expect the object to be marked by *et*. The marking, however, would result in ungrammaticality, due to the fact that the nominal *yeled* 'child' is indefinite (and not overtly partitive either).

(47) Ish   ra'a   (*et)   yeled.
      man   saw   ACC   boy
      'A man saw a boy.'

What (47) reveals is that Hebrew DOM is sensitive to the properties of the object only, not to its prominence relative to the subject. Such empirical facts, predicted by Aissen's analysis, pose a problem for de Swart's approach. It actually seems that we are dealing with a parameter across which DOM languages are allowed to differ. In some languages, case-marking depends on the object per se, whereas in others, the subject plays a role as well. It is in the languages of the latter type that the Minimal Semantic Distinctness principle applies.

5.4.3 De Swart (2007)

In his (2007) dissertation, de Swart concentrates on differential object marking and puts forward an analysis which, too, emphasizes the importance of distinguishability in this phenomenon. However, he also provides treatment of the problem specified at the end of the previous subsection.

De Swart (2007) proposes that in such sentences as the Malayalam examples in (40) and (46) above, the speaker considers the perspective of the addressee while choosing which form of the object to use. Will the addressee successfully understand the intended meaning if overt case-marking is omitted? Or will this rather result in undesirable ambiguity, or even in a wrong interpretation on the part of the addressee? Formally, de Swart puts forward an analysis formulated within the framework of Bidirectional Optimality Theory (also employed in the formal system in his (2003) approach), which involves both production and interpretation constraints. Roughly, this means that a given alternative may be rejected if it does not convey the intended meaning – even if it is optimal from the production perspective.

The model includes the following four constraints:

(i) **Economy**: avoid the use of overt case-marking. (p. 94) This production constraint, inherited from Aissen's (2003) STAR ZERO, gives preference to morphologically unmarked objects for economy reasons.

The remaining constraints constitute restrictions on interpretation:

(ii) **FaithInt**: make use of available morpho-syntactic information. (p. 94) The purpose of this constraint is to rule out instances in which there is a mismatch between morpho-syntactic information and interpretation, as in accusative-marked subjects, for example.

(iii) **Bias**: interpret a sentence according to the regularities in Table 3.1 (p. 94; the table is provided here as Table 5.2). The table lists several prototypical properties of subjects and objects, and the constraint states that a sentence is to be interpreted in accordance with these properties. For instance, according to de Swart, prototypical subjects are animate, whereas the object prototype is equally compatible with animacy and inanimacy (in the latter respect, de Swart differs from Aissen, who takes prototypical objects to be inanimate). Hence, in the presence of an animate argument and an inanimate one, Bias will direct us to interpret the former as the subject and the latter as the object. On the basis of de Swart's discussion, I conclude that it depends on the individual language which of the properties

Table 5.2 *Properties of subjects (A) and objects (O) (from de Swart 2007:95)*

Transitive subject (A)	Direct object (O)
+ animate	± animate
+ definite	± definite
given	± given
pronominal	± nominal
topic	comment

listed in the table is going to play a role. Crucially, the Bias constraint is relatively weak, ranked below FaithInt and Selection (formulated below).

(iv) **Selection**: obey the selectional restrictions of the verb. (p. 96) Selection is violated if a sentence is interpreted contrary to the restrictions imposed by the argument structure of the verb.

De Swart shows in detail how the model sketched above accounts for case patterns in such sentences as (40) and (46). Roughly, the speaker will adhere to Economy and use an unmarked object unless this results in a non-intended interpretation or undesirable ambiguity.

De Swart further acknowledges that in many instances (unlike in the above-mentioned Malayalam examples), case-marking of objects is independent of potential ambiguity. For instance, in some languages, including Malayalam, all animate objects are accusative-marked, even if there is no chance of the subject–object ambiguity arising. In other languages, accusative marking is obligatory for all definite or specific objects (e.g. Hebrew and Turkish), independently of the corresponding properties of the subject.

In order to capture such facts while accounting, at the same time, for the distinguishability-related data discussed above, de Swart proposes that an additional constraint is to be added into the bidirectional model. For a language like Malayalam, in which animate objects are obligatorily case-marked, this will be the production constraint ANIM→ACC, which rules out unmarked animate objects. Crucially, this constraint is ranked above Economy and, therefore, wins despite the morphological price that has to be paid.

De Swart further argues that in a given language, distinguishability-based DOM, whose main function is to resolve ambiguity, may develop into prominence-based DOM. He proposes that this is what happened with the Spanish marker *a*.

5.4.4 Malchukov (2008)

Malchukov (2008) puts forward an analysis of DOM and DSM (differential subject marking) which also employs an OT-like framework in which different constraints may require different patterns, in which instance the language-specific ranking of the constraints is at play. This paper concentrates mainly on animacy, which constitutes an important contribution to the discussion of DOM, as papers on this topic often dedicate more attention to definiteness/specificity issues.

Malchukov points out that an asymmetry can be observed between DOM and DSM. DOM is more consistent cross-linguistically: systematically, the more prominent objects (e.g. ones located higher on the animacy scale) are more likely to be case-marked. In turn, the DSM pattern is non-uniform. In some languages, the ergative marking (and here we are dealing largely with the ergative/unmarked distinction) is more likely to be observed on the less prominent subjects, which are less prototypical and thus more likely to be confused with objects. This direction is in line with the disambiguation approach to case alternations. For instance, in Mangarayi, animate subjects (masculine and feminine) do not receive ergative marking, whereas their inanimate counterparts (neuter) appear in the ergative form. Further, in some languages (e.g. some Tibetan and Caucasian languages), pronominal subjects do not receive the ergative, unlike those subjects that are lower in prominence. In other languages, however, the reverse pattern is observed (and as far as I can tell, the reverse pattern has received considerably more attention in the literature). Specifically, animate subjects are more likely to be ergative than their inanimate counterparts. In many instances, the ergative marking is linked to agentivity and such properties as volitionality and intention, all of which, again, characterized animate nominals. (See Chapter 1 for a more detailed discussion and references.)

Malchukov explains this pattern by relating to two potentially conflicting constraints (corresponding to two case-marking functions), DIFF and INDEX:

- DIFF: The arguments (A and P) must be distinguishable.
- INDEX: Encode semantic roles (A and P).

(Malchukov 2008:209)

DIFF follows the same principle as Aissen's (2003) markedness and requires for the subject and the object in a transitive clause (A and P) to be distinguishable. It thus favors case-marking on **animate objects** and **inanimate subjects**, whose presence may potentially give rise to confusion and/or ambiguity. Case-marking is one of the means to make it clear which of the arguments is A and which is P. In turn, INDEX takes the case-marking function to be one of encoding semantic roles. It favors case-marking on those arguments that constitute "good," typical, agents and patients.

The interaction of these two constraints renders an interesting result, which captures correctly the cross-linguistic empirical pattern briefly described at the beginning of this section. In DOM, DIFF and INDEX act uniformly: both favor case-marking of the prominent, animate objects. DIFF does so for the reason addressed in the previous sections: an animate object is relatively subject-like, and case-marking helps distinguish such objects from subjects. INDEX makes the same choice but for a different reason: an animate object constitutes a more prototypical patient and is therefore a good candidate for semantic-role-based marking. (Note that the interaction of these two constraints makes the system combine the insights of Hopper and Thompson's transitivity approach, addressed in Section 5.2.1, and the markedness/disambiguation view, see Section 5.2.2.) Thus, in DOM, case-marking is predicted to be consistently favored for those nominals that are relatively high in animacy/prominence, which is indeed what we observed.

The situation with DSM is different since here, DIFF and INDEX are in conflict. DIFF disfavors case-marking of prominent, animate subjects, since they do not give rise to a potential ambiguity. These are classical, typical subjects, which do not require a differentiating mechanism. Rather, DIFF "wants" for non-prominent, inanimate subjects to be marked (so that they are not confused with objects). In contrast, INDEX imposes reverse requirements. In favors case-marking on animate subjects, since they constitute "good" agents (and should therefore be marked as such). Thus, the two constraints favor opposite patterns. Which of them will win depends on the language-specific constraint ranking. As a result, we observe both DSM patterns, depending on the individual language.

5.4.5   Klein and de Swart (2011)

Klein and de Swart approach the phenomenon of DOM from a somewhat different perspective. Their goal is not to explain the reasoning behind the phenomenon but rather to formulate those rules that allow two object-marking options and capture a range of cross-linguistic as well as language-specific observations. Their approach does not relate to hierarchies in such properties of specificity, animacy or individuation. Further, while in de Swart's (2003) analysis, languages in which DOM depends on the relative ranking of the object and the subject play a crucial role, Klein and de Swart concentrate on those languages in which case is determined by (or sometimes, as the authors suggest, determines) the prominence of the object.

Central to their approach to DOM are two closely related distinctions: one between factors that **trigger** object marking versus those that **result** from object marking (de Swart 2007, de Swart and de Hoop 2007) and one between **split** and **fluid** case alternations (de Hoop and Malchukov 2007).

Let us begin by concentrating on the first distinction. Roughly, the question is whether a given semantic property triggers case-marking or, rather, we infer from the presence of case-marking that the DP has this property. In other words, what is primary – the semantic characteristic or the morphological marking? In this respect, animacy is claimed to differ dramatically from specificity (unless the latter constitutes a purely formal property marked in a language, for instance, within the system of articles). The animacy value of the noun does not depend on case in any way. Thus, consider the example (21) from Kannada repeated below:

(48) a. *nannu **sekretari** huDuk-utt-idd-eene.
          I_{NOM} secretary look.for.$_{NPST}$-be.$_{-1.SG}$
          'I am looking for a secretary.'

      b. naanu **sekretari-yannu** huDuk-utt-idd-eene.
          I_{NOM} secretary.$_{ACC}$ look.for.$_{NPST}$-be.$_{-1.SG}$
          'I am looking for a secretary.'

The nominal *sekretari* 'secretary' is animate (and human) independently of whether it is accusative or zero-marked. The property is inherent to the head noun. However, it contributes to the grammar by requiring an accusative suffix. In other words, animacy **triggers** case-marking.

Let us now compare this example to (22), taken, again, from Kannada and repeated as (49) below:

(49) a. naanu **pustaka** huDuk-utt-idd-eene.
          I_{NOM} book look.for.$_{NPST}$-be.$_{-1.SG}$
          'I am looking for a book.'

      b. naanu **pustaka-vannu** huDuk-utt-idd-eene.
          I_{NOM} book.$_{ACC}$ look.for.$_{NPST}$-be.$_{-1.SG}$
          'I am looking for a book.'

Recall that in (49b), the book is interpreted as specific, whereas in (49a) it may be specific or not. Here, the DP *pustaka* 'book' does not inherently carry any specificity value. Rather, when we see (or hear) that it is accusative-marked, we conclude that a specific interpretation is involved. If the same DP appears without overt marking, we do not draw such a conclusion. This is a situation where a particular reading **results** from a particular object marking: the choice of the accusative form brings about the specific interpretation. Of course, one may disagree and argue that specificity originally characterizes the nominal (if not formally, then at least pragmatically), and this brings about case-marking. While the correlation is clear, the decision regarding cause and effect is much less trivial in such instances. But within the trigger/result approach, the assumption is that the specific interpretation in examples like (49) is a **result** of case-marking.

The distinction between split and fluid alternations draws essentially the same line. A split case alternation makes a split between DPs that receive different values along a certain dimension (e.g. between animate and inanimate ones). For example: all animate objects are obligatorily accusative, whereas with inanimate objects, the situation is different (either they are all caseless or a further division takes place inside that group). This state of affairs is observed in Kannada. Or vice versa: all inanimate objects are obligatorily caseless (a claim made e.g. for Spanish and Mongolian), whereas with animates, a different rule applies. A violation of a restriction involved in such a split alternation results in **ungrammaticality**. For instance, a caseless animate object in Kannada makes the sentence ungrammatical (see (48a) above).

In turn, a fluid case alternation is illustrated in (49). Here, "the use of case applies within a category and has an effect on a dimension different from that category" (Klein and de Swart 2011:5). For instance, consider the category of inanimate nominals. Such an object can be either accusative or unmarked, and that has consequences for a different property, namely, specificity. A choice of one form over the other does not result in ungrammaticality but rather affects interpretation.

Klein and de Swart point out that triggers are systematically present in split case alternations, and results, in fluid ones.

A very important contribution of Klein and de Swart's paper, which involves universal predictions, is the claim that split case alternations always take priority over fluid alternations. (Obviously, this is relevant only for those languages in which DOM is multidimensional, i.e. case-marking is sensitive to more than one property.) In other words, "fluid alternations can only occur in those areas of the grammar where split alternations leave room for them" (p. 5). To illustrate, let us again consider Kannada. In this language, first, a split alternation in animacy applies (with all animate objects being accusative, independently of specificity) and then, within the domain that is left unfixed with respect to case (i.e. inanimates), a fluid alternation in specificity comes into play (non-specific inanimates are caseless, specific inanimates can be both). The prediction is that in no language can the situation be reversed.

Some languages, however, involve more than one split alternation. For instance, in both Mongolian and Spanish, DOM is sensitive to animacy, (formal) definiteness and specificity. The first two alternations are split in both languages, the third one is fluid. The prediction is that the relative ordering of split alternations is determined language-internally and, thus, different priorities can be observed in different languages. This is indeed what we observe. Thus, in Spanish, the first DOM-related division is based on animacy (inanimate objects are obligatorily unmarked for case,[20] whether definite or not), the second one, on definiteness (animate definites are always *a*-marked) and the third one, on specificity (animate indefinites can be either marked or unmarked but can be specific only in the former case). In contrast, in Mongolian, definiteness takes priority over animacy. All definites are accusative (independently of their animacy), all inanimate indefinites are caseless, and then within the domain of animate indefinites, the fluid alternation in specificity applies (accusative animate indefinites are specific; the unmarked ones can be interpreted as specific or non-specific). The prioritizing in the two languages is schematized in Figures 5.2 and 5.3.

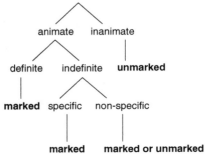

Figure 5.2 Prioritizing in Spanish *(based on Klein and de Swart 2011)*

---

[20] But see García 2007 for a discussion of exceptions.

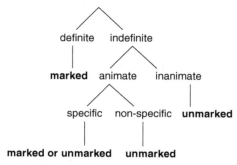

Figure 5.3 Prioritizing in Mongolian *(based on Klein and de Swart 2011)*

In order to formally capture the phenomenon of DOM, Klein and de Swart propose that the languages in question have two rules for combining a verb with a direct object. In one rule, the verb combines with an accusative/marked nominal, in the other, with an unmarked one. Each rule specifies what kinds of DPs it applies to (i.e. includes restrictions regarding the nature of the DP). When the two rules involve different restrictions on the object (i.e. apply to different types of noun phrases), we get a split alternation. For instance, Hebrew has one rule for combining a verb with an *et*-marked definite object and another rule which combines a verb with an unmarked indefinite object. There is no "optionality," no overlap. A definite unmarked object will result in ungrammaticality, and so will an indefinite *et*-marked object (again, if we slightly simplify the picture by excluding overt partitives in the modern spoken variety of the language).

We get a fluid alternation when both rules apply to the same kind of DP (e.g. a human indefinite in Spanish or Mongolian). As a result, the verb may (grammatically) combine with the DP in either a case-marked or a zero-marked version (depending on which of the two rules applies). Even in such instances, however, the rules differ in the nature of the conditions they impose on the DP. To illustrate, in Spanish, the rule for combining a verb with an unmarked human indefinite further specifies that the nominal is non-specific. In contrast, the rule for combining a verb with an accusative (*a*-marked) human indefinite does not involve any specification of this kind, as a result of which such nominals can be interpreted as both specific and non-specific in this language.

Crucially, specificity does not constitute an inherent property of any lexical item within the DP. Therefore, the information that an object is [+specific] or [−specific] is only contributed by the combination rule that is applied. Thus, the specificity information can be viewed as **a result of the application of a particular rule**. In contrast, a property like animacy is inherently specified as characterizing the noun. It does not result from applying a rule; rather, on the contrary, it **triggers the application of a particular rule** (e.g. a rule for combining verbs with case-marked animate nominals). This way, the contrast between trigger and result is captured.

5.5 CONCLUSION

Differential object marking is observed in more than 300 languages (Bossong 1985). Despite the existence of cross-linguistic variation, sometimes quite considerable on the surface, it is also characterized by substantial uniformity: systematically, we are dealing with an alternation between objects which are marked and unmarked for case, with the marked nominals being higher in terms of individuation or prominence than the caseless ones. More specific properties to which DOM is sensitive include animacy, definiteness, specificity, number and gender. Numerous analyses have been proposed for this phenomenon in the literature, only a small proportion of which could be discussed in the present book for reasons of space. Some of the accounts concentrate on a specific language and others attempt to capture the broader cross-linguistic picture. Further, some analyses place more weight on the syntactic side of the phenomenon, deriving the semantic contrasts between the two types of objects via the syntax–semantics interface (e.g. López 2012), whereas others focus primarily on the nature of the semantic and pragmatic concepts involved (e.g. Enç 1991). Phenomena argued to be involved in DOM include, among many others, object incorporation, scrambling, partitivity, scope, relational specificity. It has been argued that DOM is sensitive not only to the properties of the object but also to those of additional elements in the sentence, such as the subject and the verb.

This chapter has concentrated on so-called asymmetric DOM, in which a marked object is contrasted with an unmarked one. In addition to this phenomenon, we find alternations in which both types of objects are marked but appear in different cases. This variation can be referred to as symmetric DOM, and its consideration increases considerably the range of languages and linguistic properties that require investigation. One such alternation, between accusative and partitive case in Finnish, which is sensitive largely to aspect, has been discussed in the previous chapter. Chapter 6 is devoted to yet another object case alternation, the one between accusative and genitive nominals, observed in Balto-Slavic languages. This phenomenon, as we will see below, differs in certain respects from (asymmetric) DOM, but at the same time shares with it a number of important properties.

FURTHER READING

Aissen's (2003) seminal work addresses DOM from a cross-linguistic perspective. Aissen develops an OT framework analysis according to which the alternation in case is a product of the tension between two principles, one of which requires case-marking and the other penalizes it. The resolution of the tension is interrelated with the ranking of the object on the definiteness or animacy scale. In some languages, both scales play a crucial role, and Aissen shows in detail how the form of the object is determined in such instances.

De Swart (2003) supplies a detailed overview of both differential object marking and differential subject marking, discusses the previously proposed accounts of the phenomena and puts forward a unifying approach for these two types of case alternations. The central role in his analysis is devoted to the relative prominence of the subject and the object.

López' (2012) book presents a detailed analysis of DOM in a specific language, Spanish. The analysis is primarily syntactic in nature, but semantic contrasts between marked and unmarked objects are accounted for via the syntax–semantics interface.

6 The Genitive/Accusative Alternation in Balto-Slavic

In the previous chapter, we discussed differential object marking (DOM) and those semantic, pragmatic and syntactic properties to which it is sensitive. In (asymmetric) DOM, we are dealing with an alternation between a case-marked object and an unmarked one. The next natural question to ask is what happens when an accusative object alternates with an object **in a different case form**. In other words, morphological case is present in both variants, but the marking is not the same. Are we dealing with essentially the same phenomenon as DOM, one that is sensitive to the same characteristics? Or is this a contrast of a totally different kind?

In fact, in Chapter 4, we have already considered one example of such an alternation: the partitive/accusative contrast in Finnic languages. As we have seen, this phenomenon differs from DOM quite considerably, as it is sensitive primarily to aspectually relevant notions such as telicity and boundedness. Specificity is intuitively relevant in certain instances, but the relation seems to be indirect. Thus, the so-called **NP-related partitive**, illustrated in the Finnish example in (1), typically marks indefinite and non-specific nominals, but this is apparently a by-product of the unboundedness of such nominals – a property which, in turn, has consequences for the aspectual characteristics of the whole VP. (See Section 4.1 of Chapter 4 for details.)

(1) Jouluksi   satoi   lunta.   (Kiparsky 2005:4)
     Christmas$_{\text{TRANSL}}$ rained$_{3.\ \text{SG}}$ snow$_{\text{PART}}$
     'For Christmas, it snowed.'

Thus, in (1), the nominal *lunta* 'snow' appears in the partitive case, indicating that we are dealing with an unspecified, indeterminate quantity of snow. This, in turn, is associated with a non-specific reading of the object.

However, it is easy to see that the Finnic partitive is very far from being a non-specificity (or even indefiniteness) marker. For instance, consider the Finnish (2) and an example from the Bible in five Finnic languages in (3).

(2) Siirsin   isoäitiä.   (Kiparsky 2005:3)
     moved$_{1.SG}$ grandma$_{PART}$
     'I moved grandma.' [around, a ways]

(3) a. ESTONIAN
         te   otsite   ristilöödud   Jeesust
         you$_{PL.NOM}$ seek$_{2.PL}$ crucified   Jesus$_{PART}$
     b. LIVONIAN
         tēg   votšõt   ristõ   rabdõtõ   Jēzusõ
         you$_{PL.NOM}$ seek$_{2.PL}$ cross$_{ILL}$ nailed$_{PART}$ Jesus$_{PART}$
     c. FINNISH
         te   etsitte   ristiinnaulittua   Jeesusta
         you$_{PL.NOM}$ seek$_{2.PL}$ crucified$_{PART}$ Jesus$_{PART}$
         'you are seeking the crucified Jesus'
     d. KARELIAN
         tüö   ečittö   Iisussua   ristah   nuaglittuu
         you$_{PL.NOM}$ seek$_{2.PL}$ Jesus$_{PART}$ cross$_{ILL}$ nailed$_{PART}$
         'you are seeking Jesus crucified'
     e. VEPS
         tö   ecit   Iisusad   kudamb oli   nagloitu   ristha
         you$_{PL.NOM}$ seek$_{2.PL}$ Jesus$_{PART}$ who$_{NOM}$ was nailed cross$_{ILL}$
         'you are seeking Jesus, who was nailed to the cross'
         (Matt. 28:5)   (Lees 2015:71–72)

Here, the DP *isoäitiä* 'grandmother' is under the most plausible reading definite and specific, and so is the proper name *Jesus*. Still, both appear in the partitive due to purely aspectual properties of the sentences.

This chapter is devoted to yet another object case alternation phenomenon, specifically, the genitive/accusative (and sometimes genitive/nominative) contrast in Balto-Slavic languages. This phenomenon, which has interested and puzzled linguists for many decades, is in a certain sense closer to DOM[1] than the corresponding Finnish alternation. Genitive case-marking on objects in certain Balto-Slavic languages exhibits strong sensitivity to the same kinds of properties that cross-linguistically affect DOM, such as specificity, definiteness, animacy and number. But at the same time, it seems to differ from DOM in at least two ways. First, it involves a very complex interaction of a wide range of factors, which are not limited to the ones mentioned above and also involve, for example,

---

[1] It can also be referred to as an instance of a symmetric DOM, i.e. DOM in which both alternants are case-marked.

the abstract/concrete, mass/count and perfective/imperfective distinctions. Second, it seems to be somewhat more flexible than DOM, in the sense that it is virtually impossible to draw a clear line between, for example the kinds of objects for which accusative marking is obligatory and those for which it is optional, or those for which the accusative is optional as opposed to those for which the accusative is totally unacceptable (and genitive, obligatory). To illustrate, even though proper names very strongly tend to appear in the accusative case, they can be genitive in certain environments.

These characteristics make the genitive/accusative alternation an interesting candidate for a comparison with DOM. Therefore, in this chapter the phenomenon is considered in some detail and the question of which patterns unite it with DOM and which distinguish the two alternations is addressed.

6.1 IRREALIS GENITIVE IN BALTO-SLAVIC

Three main types of genitive case-marking on objects have been distinguished in the literature on Balto-Slavic languages: Partitive Genitive, Genitive of Negation and Intensional Genitive. This section is devoted primarily to the latter two types, which have been unified in Kagan (2007, 2010b and 2013) under the term *Irrealis Genitive*.[2] Partitive Genitive will be discussed separately in Section 6.4.

6.1.1 Genitive of Negation

Genitive of Negation (GenNeg) is a well-documented phenomenon which has received very considerable attention in the linguistic literature (see e.g. Lomonosov 1952, Jakobson 1957/1971, Babby 1978, Pesetsky 1982, Timberlake 1986, Neidle 1988, Bailyn 1997, 2004, Franks 1995, Padučeva 1997, Pereltsvaig 1999, Brown 1999, Borschev and Partee 2002a,b, Harves 2002a,b, Babyonyshev 2003, Borschev et al. 2008, Kagan 2013 and references therein). This is a phenomenon whereby a non-oblique, argument of a verb is assigned genitive case under sentential negation, even if genitive case-marking is not licensed in the corresponding affirmative clause. Arguably, the argument is always internal, although this point is subject to debate (see e.g. Babby 2001 for an alternative view). GenNeg can be assigned to objects of transitive verbs, in which instance it alternates with the accusative (4), to the argument of some passive and intransitive verbs,

---

[2] The discussion in Sections 6.1–6.3 is largely based on Kagan (2013).

in which instance the genitive/nominative alternation is observed (5), or to the pivot in negated existential sentences (6). In the latter instance, the genitive is obligatory, therefore, no alternation in case is observed. While (4)–(6) are Russian examples, (7) illustrates GenNeg for additional languages.

(4) a. Ja   ne   pil   vodu.
         I   NEG   drank$_{IMP}$ water$_{ACC}$
         'I didn't drink (the) water / I wasn't drinking water.'

     b. Ja   ne   pil   vody
         I   NEG   drank$_{IMP}$ water$_{GEN}$
         'I didn't drink (any) water.'

(5) a. Otvet   ne   prišol.
         Answer$_{NOM.M.SG}$ NEG   arrived$_{M.SG}$
         'The answer did not arrive.'

     b. Otveta   ne   prišlo.
         Answer$_{GEN.M.SG}$ NEG   arrived$_{NEUT.SG}$
         'No answer arrived.'   (Babby 1978:13)

(6) V   bol'nice   ne   bylo   nejroxirurga.
     In   hospital   NEG   was   neurosurgeon$_{GEN.SG}$
     'There was no neurosurgeon in the hospital.'

(7) a. UKRAINIAN (Pugh and Press 1999)
         Vin   ne   prodav   stola.
         he   NEG   sold   table$_{GEN.SG}$
         'He did not sell a table.'

     b. BELORUSSIAN (Mayo 2002:932)
         Ja   ne   čytau   hetaha   ramana
         I   NEG   read   [this   novel]$_{GEN.SG}$
         'I haven't read this novel.'

     c. POLISH (Błaszczak 2007:129)
         Ewa   nie   czyta   gazet.
         Ewa   NEG   reads   newspapers$_{GEN.PL}$
         'Ewa does not read / is not reading newspapers.'

     d. LATVIAN (Nau 1999:59)
         Bet   viņ-š   ne-kā   ļaun-a   ne-darīj-a
         but   he   NEG-what$_{GEN}$ bad$_{GEN}$ NEG-do$_{PST.3}$
         'But he didn't do anything bad.' (ak-323)

In the following sections, I concentrate mainly on the genitive/accusative alternation on objects, unless specified otherwise.

Balto-Slavic languages can be divided into three groups on the basis of the presence of GenNeg:

Group 1: languages in which GenNeg is obligatory (i.e. accusative case-marking is ungrammatical under negation)

Group 2: languages in which GenNeg is optional (i.e. under negation, a genitive/accusative alternation is present, with various factors affecting case selection, **including e.g. definiteness and specificity**)

Group 3: languages in which GenNeg is virtually absent (i.e. accusative case is virtually obligatory under negation, except for frozen expressions, phrases that contain negative concord items, and the like).

Group 1 includes such languages as Lithuanian and Polish.[3] Group 2 contains Latvian and Russian, for example, and Group 3, Czech and Serbo-Croatian. For our current purposes, Group 2 is of particular interest, since it is in these languages that we find a **case alternation** under negation. Therefore, the discussion in the following sections will concentrate primarily on Russian as representative of this group.

The state of affairs in Balto-Slavic is partly reminiscent of languages like Finnish, which, too, contain Partitive of Negation. The similarity is especially strong when we consider Group 1 languages like Polish, in which GenNeg is obligatory, just like Partitive of Negation. But the genitive case cannot receive the same atelicity/unboundedness treatment as its Finnic counterpart, as it lacks an analogue of VP-related partitive, with verbal aspect depending in Slavic on verbal morphology (perfective versus imperfective) rather than on object marking. Indeed, both the Balto-Slavic genitive and the Finnic partitive exhibit the negative and the partitive/NP-related uses (the latter will be shown for Russian in Section 6.4). However, it is the VP-related use that constitutes the glue which allows them to be unified under the aspectual approach. In Balto-Slavic, this glue is absent, and an aspectual account cannot be maintained. For instance, a VP with a perfective verb will always be bounded, no matter whether the object is accusative or genitive (or what type of genitive it exhibits).

6.1.2 Intensional Genitive

Intensional Genitive is a phenomenon whereby genitive case appears on objects of certain intensional verbs, independently of whether the clause is affirmative or negative. In Russian, these verbs include *xotet'* 'want', *zasluživat'* 'deserve', *trebovat'* 'demand', *prosit'* 'ask', *ždat'* 'wait',

---

[3] The nominative/accusative facts are more complex in Polish: here, the case alternation is indeed present (see e.g. Błaszczak 2007).

among others. All these verbs belong to the class of *weak intensional predicates* in the terminology used by Farkas (2003). Both genitive and accusative case-assignment with these predicates is exemplified in (8):

(8) a. On   ždal   čuda   / Dimu.
        He   waited$_{IMP}$ miracle$_{GEN.SG}$ / Dima$_{ACC}$
        'He was waiting for a miracle / for Dima.'
     b. On   prosit   vnimania   / knigu.
        he   asks$_{IMP}$ attention$_{GEN}$ / book$_{ACC.SG}$
        'He is asking / asks for attention / a book.'
     c. Ty   zasluživaeš   medali   / medal'.
        You   deserve$_{IMP}$ medal$_{GEN.SG}$ / medal$_{ACC.SG}$
        'You deserve a medal.'

In Russian, genitive case-marking turns out to be obligatory with some verb–object pairs (e.g. *ždat' čuda$_{GEN}$* 'wait for a miracle'), optional in others (e.g. *zasluživat' medali$_{GEN}$* 'deserve a medal') and yet in others is unacceptable (e.g. **ždat' Dimy$_{GEN}$* 'wait for Dima').

If we look at other Balto-Slavic languages, it turns out that they can be divided into approximately the same three groups as those introduced in the previous subsection. In fact, there is a strong correlation between the presence and optionality of Genitive of Negation on the one hand and of Intensional Genitive on the other. The tendency is the following. In those languages in which GenNeg is obligatory, the intensional verbs in question consistently take genitive objects as well. In those languages in which GenNeg is "optional," as it is in Russian, in the sense that under negation, both genitive and accusative case-marking is possible, intensional verbs also license both genitive and accusative objects. Finally, if GenNeg is essentially absent in a language, Intensional Genitive is also absent, with most intensional verbs taking accusative or PP complements. The two exceptions I have found include Polish, in which GenNeg is obligatory and Intensional Genitive obligatory with some verbs but optional with others, and Slovenian, in which GenNeg is obligatory and Intensional Genitive optional. The cross-linguistic comparison is summarized in Table 6.1, taken from Kagan (2010b:22).

6.2 UNIFYING GENNEG AND INTENSIONAL GENITIVE

The cross-linguistic parallel discussed above suggests that the two alternations in question are strongly interrelated. Indeed, Neidle (1988) and later Kagan (e.g. 2005, 2013) and Partee and Borschev (e.g.

Table 6.1 *Genitive of Negation and Intensional Genitive across languages*

Language	Genitive of Negation	Intensional Genitive
Old Church Slavonic	obligatory	obligatory
Lithuanian	obligatory	obligatory
Russian	optional	optional
Ukrainian	optional	optional
Belarusian	optional	optional
Latvian	optional	optional
Serbo-Croatian	essentially absent	essentially absent
Czech	essentially absent	essentially absent
Slovenian	obligatory	optional
Polish	obligatory	?obligatory / ?optional

2004) propose that we are dealing, in fact, with two instances of the same phenomenon. Below, I briefly list arguments that have been provided in favor of this claim. More detailed information can be found in the above-listed references.

a. Both phenomena involve a genitive/accusative alternation in the case of the object.
b. Within both alternations, genitive marking is licensed by (and within the scope of) a non-veridical operator.
c. The alternations pattern together cross-linguistically, as summarized in Table 6.1.
d. In Russian, both alternations exhibit considerable variation in native speakers' judgments, which is at least partly a by-product of the process of language change taking place in the language. As pointed out by Neidle (1988), within both phenomena, accusative case is now being used with increasing frequency.
e. In those languages in which both genitive and accusative marking is possible, the two alternations are sensitive to the same range of semantic factors. To illustrate just a few tendencies, both GenNeg and Intensional Genitive are more likely to appear on:
   i. abstract nouns, rather than concrete ones (9–10)
   ii. plural nominals, rather than singular ones (11–12)
   iii. indefinite nominals, rather than definite ones (13–14)
   iv. common nouns, rather than proper names (15–16)[4]
   v. nominals that take narrow scope and are indefinite/non-referential/non-specific (17–18).

---

[4] Definite nominals are relatively unlikely to appear in the genitive, but if they do, the likelihood of a proper name being genitive is particularly low.

(9) a. On   ne   našol   ???sčast'je /sčast'ja.
        he   NEG   found   happiness$_{ACC/GEN}$
        'He didn't find happiness.'

     b. On   ne   našol   cvetok/???cvetka.
        He   NEG   found   flower$_{ACC.SG/GEN.SG}$
        'He didn't find a/the flower.'   (based on Timberlake 1986:342)

(10) a. Dima   ždjot   čuda / *čudo.
        Dima   waits   miracle$_{GEN.SG /ACC.SG}$
        'Dima is waiting for a miracle.'

     b. Dima   ždjot   posylku / *posylki.
        Dima   waits   parcel$_{ACC.SG/GEN.SG}$
        'Dima is waiting for a parcel.'

In (9) above, the abstract object of a negated verb (*ščastje* 'happiness')
prefers the genitive case, whereas its concrete counterpart (*cvetok* 'flower')
is better with the accusative. A similar contrast with even clearer judgments is revealed in (10), which contains an intensional predicate *ždat'*
'wait'. Here, Intensional Genitive is obligatory for the abstract nominal
čudo 'miracle', but only the accusative is possible with the concrete *posylka*
'parcel'.

(11) a. Ja   ne   našol   cvetov.
        I   NEG   found   flowers$_{GEN.PL}$
        'I didn't find (the) flowers.'

     b. Ja   ne   našol   ???cvetka.
        I   NEG   found   flower$_{GEN.SG}$
        'I didn't find a/the flower.'   (Timberlake 1986:342)

(12) a. Ja   ždu   cvetov.[5]
        I   wait flowers$_{GEN.PL}$
        'I am waiting for flowers.'

     b. ??? Ja   ždu   cvetka.
            I   wait flower$_{GEN.SG}$
        'I am waiting for a flower.'

Both (11) and (12) show that a concrete count plural object is more
easily assigned the genitive case (whether GenNeg or Intensional
Genitive) than its singular counterpart.

(13) a. Lena   ne   kupila   éti   ukrašenija / ??? étix ukrašenij
        Lena   NEG   bought   [these   jewels]$_{ACC.PL / GEN.PL}$
        'Lena didn't buy these jewels.'

---

[5] (12a) tends to be judged acceptable under the reading according to which the
speaker is waiting for a plant to blossom.

    b. Lena   ne   kupila   novyje   ukrašenija / novyx ukrašenij.
       Lena   NEG   bought [new   jewels]$_{\text{ACC.PL / GEN.PL}}$
       'Lena didn't buy new jewels.'

(14) a. Lena potrebovala éti   ukrašenija /??? étix ukrašenij
       Lena demanded   [these jewels]$_{\text{ACC.PL / GEN.PL}}$
    b. Lena potrebovala novyje ukrašenija / novyx ukrašenij.
       Lena demanded   [new   jewels]$_{\text{ACC.PL / GEN.PL}}$

While the indefinite DP *novyje ukrašenija* 'new jewels' can choose between the genitive and the accusative, its definite counterpart *éti ukrašenija* 'these jewels' strongly prefers accusative marking.

(15) a. Ja ne   pomnila   Lenu / *Leny.
       I   NEG remembered Lena$_{\text{ACC/GEN}}$
       'I didn't remember Lena.'
    b. Ja ne   pomnila   étot razgovor / etogo razgovora.
       I   NEG remembered [this conversation]$_{\text{ACC.SG / GEN.SG}}$
       'I didn't remember this conversation.'

(16) a. Ivan ždjot Annu / *Anny.
       Ivan waits Anna$_{\text{ACC/GEN}}$
       'Ivan is waiting for Anna.'
    b. Ivan ždjot ???etu vstreču / etoj vstreči.
       Ivan waits [this   meeting]$_{\text{ACC.SG / GEN.SG}}$
       'Ivan is waiting for this meeting.'

In both (15) and (16), the proper name must appear in the accusative case. In contrast, a definite description is perfectly acceptable in the genitive. (The fact that definite DPs with a demonstrative can be assigned genitive in 15–16 but not (or not equally easily) in 13–14 is related to the abstract nature of the former, as well as to additional semantic properties to be discussed below.)

(17) a. Anna ne   kupila   knigi.
       Anna NEG bought   books$_{\text{ACC.PL}}$
       'Anna didn't buy the books.' / 'There are specific books that Anna didn't buy.'
    b. Anna ne   kupila   knig
       Anna NEG bought   books$_{\text{GEN.PL}}$
       'Anna didn't buy (any) books.' (Harves 2002b:38)

(18) a. Dima iščet   švedskije   marki.
       Dima seeks   [Swedish   stamps]$_{\text{ACC.PL}}$
       'Dima is looking for any Swedish stamps.' / 'There are Swedish stamps that Dima is looking for.'

   b. načal'nik   trebujet   pribyli.
      boss   demands   profit$_{GEN}$
      'The boss requires profit.'

In (17), the accusative object is likely to receive a definite or specific reading. In contrast, the genitive one requires the indefinite, non-specific, narrow-scope interpretation. In (18a), the accusative object is ambiguous between a wide and a narrow-scope interpretation. (18b), in contrast, requires a narrow-scope reading according to which the profit in question does not even exist at the speech time; roughly, according to this sentence, the boss requires that the employees work in such a way that there be profit.

   The role of animacy in the genitive/accusative alternations is somewhat less striking, given that in most instances, animate nouns have identical accusative and genitive forms. Due to this syncretism, we cannot know which abstract case they receive in each instance (if both cases are available in the given position). But those animate nouns that do have a special accusative form are quite reluctant to appear in the genitive:

(19) Lena   ne   zametila   svetofora /   ???krysy.
      Lena   NEG   noticed   traffic.lights$_{GEN}$ rat$_{GEN}$
      'Lena didn't notice a/the traffic lights / a/the rat.'

These tendencies are discussed in much detail by Timberlake (1986), Neidle (1988) and Kagan (2013), among others. It can be seen that the genitive/accusative alternation is sensitive to the definiteness scale, which accounts for tendencies (iii)–(v), and probably to animacy (19), similarly to DOM. At the same time, the range of factors affecting the choice of case in Slavic seems to be wider. Still, it is worth noting that DOM has also been claimed to be sensitive to number at least in some languages, as discussed in the previous chapter.

   Given the above-mentioned parallels between Genitive of Negation and Intensional Genitive, Kagan (2013) coins the term *Irrealis Genitive*, by analogy with irrealis mood, in order to unify them. Recall that the genitive objects in question are licensed only by non-veridical operators (which license subjunctive mood as well). Further motivation for this term will be introduced in the next section, in which the notion of existential commitment is discussed.

6.3 THE SEMANTICS OF IRREALIS GENITIVE

Genitive of Negation and Intensional Genitive, jointly or separately, have received a range of both syntactic and semantic analyses. The main semantic notions to which these case alternations have been linked include specificity, semantic type and existential commitment. The corresponding approaches are addressed in the following subsections. It is important to emphasize that the semantic and pragmatic characteristics in question are compatible with each other and, thus, it is possible that all these properties are indeed relevant for case selection.

6.3.1 Specificity

Specificity and/or referentiality is often claimed to play a crucial role in the genitive/accusative contrast, which, of course, unifies this phenomenon with DOM. Let us reconsider the example in (17) above. (17a), the accusative version, is more likely to receive a reading according to which Anna did not buy a particular set of books, possibly ones that have been previously specified, or ones that the speaker has in mind. Under this reading, the object takes wide scope relative to the negative operator: there is a set of books that Anna did not buy (although maybe she intended to). In contrast, the genitive version (17b) is most plausibly understood as an assertion that Anna did not buy any books. The object takes narrow scope and gets an indefinite, non-specific interpretation.

Indeed, such notions as specificity and referentiality constitute important components of certain analyses proposed for the genitive/accusative alternation. For instance, interestingly, the relevance of these properties has been argued for in syntactic analyses of Genitive of Negation, via the syntax–semantics interface. Under these approaches, the case of a nominal is taken to depend on the structural position it occupies. For instance, Bailyn (1997) claims that genitive and accusative cases in negative clauses are checked in different structural positions. Accusative is checked in the specifier of Object Agreement Phrase [spec, AgrOP], and genitive, in the specifier of Negation Phrase [spec, NegP]. Crucially, the former is located higher on the tree than the latter. Following Diesing's (1992) Mapping Hypothesis, Bailyn divides the tree into two parts. Nominals that appear above the NegP projection (either at Spell-Out or possibly after Spell-Out, at the stage when the sentence is interpreted) will get specific, presuppositional readings, whereas their counterparts that stay lower than NegP will be interpreted as indefinite and non-specific. This is due to the fact that only the material in the lower part of the tree falls within the domain of existential closure.

This means that the [spec, NegP] position is accessible to existential closure, in contrast to [spec, AgrOP]. As a result, genitive objects systematically get bound by an existential quantifier, hence their existential, indefinite interpretation. In contrast, accusative objects are born below NegP (inside the VP) and then move to a position above NegP ([spec, AgrOP]), where their case is checked. This is why they can receive both specific and non-specific readings, depending on whether the head or the tail of the chain determines the interpretation.

Harves (2002a,b) provides a somewhat different configurational analysis, which does not depend on the Mapping Hypothesis. Following Beghelli and Stowell's (1997) approach to scope-checking, she claims that referential nominals carry the [+Ref] feature, which they check in the [spec, RefP] position, RefP being a functional projection located immediately above CP. Accusative objects can carry this feature and move to the corresponding position successfully. In contrast, genitive nominals cannot be [+Ref]. This limitation is due to the fact that they check their case feature against the Neg head, which, in turn, carries the [+NQP] (negative quantifier phrase) feature. Once the object enters into an agreement relation with Neg, [+Ref] clashes with [+NQP], and the derivation crashes. (Roughly speaking, [+Ref] signals specificity, whereas [+NQP] requires its absence, hence the incompatibility.)

Additional configurational analyses of GenNeg have been proposed, for example by Brown (1999) and Babyonyshev (2003). A unifying feature of these approaches is that the genitive case feature is taken to be checked by the Neg head, which, in turn, is responsible for the indefinite, non-specific, existential interpretation of the object.

A considerably different account of GenNeg is put forward by Pereltsvaig (1998, 1999). Following Pesetsky (1982), she proposes that this case is always assigned by a phonologically empty quantifier q.[6] She further argues that q is a strict negative polarity item (NPI), since it cannot appear in other downward-entailing environments, such as antecedents of conditionals, relative clauses headed by universal quantifiers, etc. Pereltsvaig accounts for the semantic properties of genitive objects by proposing the Referentiality Constraint, formulated in (20):

---

[6] For other approaches to (certain types of) genitive case that are based on an empty quantifier head or a [+/−Q] feature, see Neidle (1988), Franks (1995) and Bailyn (2004). The empty quantifier account of Partitive Genitive is discussed in Section 6.4.3 below.

(20) REFERENTIALITY CONSTRAINT:
      If the object participant is individuated/referential, it cannot be
      quantified over, and is thus assigned Accusative. On the other
      hand, if the object participant is non-individuated/non-referential,
      it can be quantified over, and is thus assigned Genitive.
                                           (Pereltsvaig 1998, page 21 of the manuscript)

According to Pereltsvaig, referential nominals are nominals that cannot be quantified over. Since GenNeg is assigned by a quantifier, then,
naturally, it can be assigned only to those NPs that can be quantified
over – thus, non-referential ones.

Specificity/referentiality-based approaches definitely capture an intuitive contrast between genitive and accusative objects, both under negation and following intensional verbs. One problem, however, has to do
with the fact that while the tendency is present, the division is not clear-
cut. In certain instances, Irrealis Genitive seems to be compatible with
nominals which are both definite and presumably specific, as illustrated
in (21) below:

(21) a. Tvoj   otčot   ne   soderžit   étix   faktov.
         Your   report NEG   contain   [these facts]$_{GEN.PL}$
         'Your report doesn't contain these facts.'

      b. Ja ne   pomnju   etogo   razgovora.
         I   NEG   remember [this   conversation]$_{GEN.SG}$
         'I don't remember this conversation.'

Of course, whether or not such objects are to be treated as specific
depends on the definition of specificity that one adopts. After all, this
concept has been used in the literature to refer to a wide range of
possibly related but non-identical phenomena, including scope (e.g.
Ioup 1977), speaker's knowledge or the epistemic state of another
salient individual (e.g. Groenendijk and Stokhof 1980, Farkas 1994,
Kagan 2011), noteworthiness (Ionin 2006), partitivity and D-linking
(Enç 1991, von Heusinger and Kornfilt 2005), and more (see e.g. Farkas
2002, von Heusinger 2002 for discussion). Approaches to the semantics of genitive objects discussed in the following subsections can, in
fact, be viewed as attempts to capture the notion of specificity/refer-
entiality that is relevant for the genitive/accusative contrast.

6.3.2 Property-Type Hypothesis

According to the property-type analysis, genitive objects denote properties, and are thus of the semantic type $<e,t>$ (functions from individuals to truth values), or $<s,<e,t>>$ – if possible worlds are introduced
into the picture, which is particularly relevant with intensional verbs.

In contrast, their accusative counterparts are either individual-denoting (type <e>) or quantificational (type <<e,t>,t>). This account was independently proposed by Partee and Borschev (2004) and Kagan (2005). In their later work, Partee and Borschev considered arguments for and against the property-type approach (2007) and then argued for this analysis (e.g. Borschev et al. 2008). This account is also discussed in Kagan's (2013) book.

The property-type approach accounts for a whole range of characteristics associated with Irrealis Genitive, including the indefinite and non-specific nature of genitive objects. Definite and referential nominals are generally individual-denoting. Therefore, it is not surprising that they appear in the accusative case. At the same time, a definite DP may in principle undergo a type-shift to the property type as well (Partee 1986). Thus, we can also account for those exceptions where definite nominals appear in the genitive. (See also Kagan in press for a discussion of type-shift with genitive nominals in negated existential sentences.) Proper names are even less likely to denote properties and are as a rule of type <e>; thus the unlikelihood of genitive case-assignment to nominals of this class is captured as well. Further, property-denoting objects are expected to be scopally inert and thus, essentially, to be interpreted within the scope of such operators as negation or an intensional predicate. Therefore, the narrow-scope interpretation of genitive nominals is accounted for as well. In addition, the claim that objects of intensional verbs denote properties has been made in the literature for independent reasons (Zimmerman 1993, van Geenhoven and McNally 2005). Genitive case-assignment to complements of such predicates is therefore to be expected, as soon as the property-type approach to Irrealis Genitive is assumed.

The analysis captures the fact that in some sentences, the meaning of the accusative and genitive variants seems to be very close (with the choice of case often subject to variation in native-speaker judgments). After all, objects of <e,t> (property) and <<e,t>,t> (quantificational) type often ultimately render the same truth conditions.[7] Also, the property type can be viewed as a special case of non-specificity, which relates this analysis to the specificity approach.

Finally, it is worth noting that the approach under discussion is partly in the spirit of de Hoop's (1992) distinction between weak and strong case, the former illustrated, for instance, by the Finnish

---

[7] See Borschev et al. (2008), Kagan (2013) and references therein for a discussion of different ways in which an extensional verb can combine with a property-type complement.

partitive. Nominals bearing the two types of case are argued to be of different semantic types. However, for de Hoop, the type of weak-case objects (a group that would presumably include the Russian genitives) is that of predicate modifiers (<<e,t>,<e,t>>), rather than properties.

6.3.3 Existential Commitment

Kagan (2005, 2009, 2013) further argues that Irrealis Genitive is assigned to objects that lack existential commitment (EC). Grimm (2005), too, proposes that commitment to existence plays a central role in the assignment of Intensional Genitive. According to Kagan, a nominal carries commitment to existence *if the sentence in which it appears either entails or presupposes that the nominal has a referent or quantifies over a non-empty set.* If the nominal is property-denoting, existential commitment would mean existence of an entity that instantiates the property. By default, it is existence in the actual world that plays a role. However, in certain environments, it gets shifted, or relativized, to an alternative set of possible worlds or to a particular spatio-temporal location.

Below I consider examples that illustrate the relevance of EC (both default and relativized) for the choice of case. The notion of existential commitment is less discussed in the linguistic literature than specificity and property type and for this reason receives a somewhat more detailed discussion below.

Let us begin with negative sentences. First of all, let us reconsider briefly the minimal contrast in (17), repeated below:

(17)   a. Anna   ne   kupila   knigi.
          Anna   NEG   bought   books_{ACC.PL}
          'Anna didn't buy the books.' / 'There are specific books that Anna didn't buy.'
       b. Anna   ne   kupila   knig.
          Anna   NEG   bought   books_{GEN.PL}
          'Anna didn't buy (any) books.'

As we already know, (17a) is more likely to receive a meaning according to which there are specific books that Anna did not buy, whereas according to (17b), she did not buy any books. Notice that while (17a) entails and/or presupposes the existence of the books in question, (17b) does not. In fact, the genitive variant does not guarantee the existence of any books in the world. Our pragmatic knowledge tells us that books do exist in reality, but the sentence itself does not contribute such an entailment, given that the negative operator takes scope over the existential quantifier over books. Thus, the object in (17a) must have a referent, whereas the object in (17b) may potentially quantify over an empty set. The former carries EC, but the latter does not.

So far, so good. But is the difference in EC not merely a by-product of the fact that the object in (17a) takes wide scope and is specific, whereas the one in (17b) takes narrow scope and is non-specific? In what follows, I provide evidence that EC is linguistically relevant independently of such notions as scope.

It has been noted, for example by Timberlake (1986), that the availability of GenNeg depends, among other factors, on the lexical meaning of the verb. Thus, creation verbs facilitate GenNeg marking (Pereltsvaig 1999, Kagan 2013):

(22) a. ???Ja ne   čitala knigi.
        I   NEG   read   book$_{GEN.SG}$
        'I wasn't reading a book.' / 'I did not read a book.'
     b. ?Ja   ne   pisala pis'ma.
        I   NEG   wrote   letter$_{GEN.SG}$
        'I wasn't writing a letter.' / 'I didn't write a letter.'

Acceptability judgments of both sentences above vary across speakers.[8] Most speakers, however, consider (22a) unacceptable. In turn, (22b) is often judged as either perfectly or at least marginally acceptable and tends to be considered better than (22a). Note that in both sentences it is possible to interpret the object as non-specific and taking narrow scope. Still, (22b) is more acceptable than (22a), and the question emerges as to what causes this contrast.

The relevant difference has to do with the fact that *pisat'* 'write' is a verb of creation, whereas *čitat'* 'read' is not. Zucchi (1999) claims that objects of creation verbs are intensional. They need not have a referent in the actual world. The existence of an object of a creation verb depends on whether or not the event of creation successfully takes place. Thus, the existence of a letter depends on whether I write it or not, whereas the existence of a book does not depend on my reading it. If a creation event is not asserted to have taken place, one cannot be committed that the object of the creation verb has a referent (or quantifies over a non-empty set). As a result, negating an event of writing a letter, as in (22b) above, strongly suggests that the letter did not come into existence – at least not in

---

[8] The fact that both examples in (17) may be considered unacceptable apparently results from the tendency for count singular nominals to appear in the accusative case.

the process of the event described in the sentence. Negating an event of reading a book, in contrast, is not associated with a similar conclusion. Thus, in (22b), the possibility that the object does not have a referent is much more prominent than in (22a). Apparently, this interpretational contrast makes the assignment of Irrealis Genitive much more easily acceptable in (22a). More generally, objects of creation predicates are especially likely to lack EC under negation, which is why they are also especially likely to appear in Irrealis Genitive.

Verbs that presuppose the existence of their complement, in contrast, favor accusative objects:

(23)   a. On   ne   polučil   otveta.
          He   NEG   received   answer$_{\text{GEN.SG}}$
          'He didn't receive an answer.'
       b. *On   ne   perečital otveta.
          He   NEG   reread   answer$_{\text{GEN.SG}}$
          'He didn't reread a/the answer.'

The verb *polučit'* 'receive' does not contribute a presupposition that its object has a referent. Thus, it is possible that an answer was not received because no answer had ever been written. In contrast, *perečitat'* 'reread' does contribute an existential presupposition. (23b) presupposes that the subject did read the answer for the first time, and it can therefore be concluded that the answer exists. Thus, the nominal complement carries EC, due to the properties of the verb. For this reason, genitive case-marking is unacceptable in (23b), in contrast to (23a).

Let us now turn to *ni*-phrases, negative concord (or strong negative polarity) items, illustrated by the phrase *ni odin student* 'no student'.[9] Borschev and Partee (2002), among others, claim that *ni*-phrases have to appear within the scope of negation. Such a restriction could be explained by the need of negative concord items to check their features against the Neg head in syntax.

Unsurprisingly, given their inherently non-specific and negative nature, *ni*-items functioning as objects typically appear in the genitive case. However, certain exceptions can be found. Consider the following contrast:

(24)   a. Serby   ne   načinali   ni   odnu   iz   vojn
          Serbs   NEG   started   not   one$_{\text{ACC}}$ from   wars
          'Serbs did not start a single war.'

---

[9] Properties of these phrases are discussed by Pereltsvaig (1999), Harves (2002a) and Borschev and Partee (2002b), among others.

www.ng.ru/world/2002-02-15/6_miloshevich.html
b. Serby   ne   načinali   ni   odnoj   vojny
   Serbs   NEG   started   not   [one   war]_GEN
   'Serbs did not start a single war.'

The fact that the *ni*-phrases exhibited in (24) cannot take wide scope is further supported by the interpretation of these sentences. Neither (24a) nor (24b) may mean that there is a (particular) war that was not started by Serbs. Rather, the sentences assert that Serbs started no war / none of the wars. Thus, the object in both sentences takes narrow scope relative to negation and gets a non-specific, indefinite interpretation, as it is not identifiable to the speaker and not familiar from the context. Still, the nominals do differ in terms of EC.

(24a) contains a partitive nominal and thus presupposes that there were a number of wars in which Serbs participated. The sentence further asserts but **none of these wars** started on their behalf. (24b) could be uttered in the same context as well, but, in contrast to (24a), it is also compatible with a model in which Serbs did not participate in any wars at all, and thus, naturally, did not start any. In other words, the object in (24a) carries EC, whereas in (24b), this property is absent. Recall that partitive objects are predicted to be (in a certain sense) specific under Enç's (1991) approach to specificity and generally receive accusative marking in Turkish and Uzbek. Again, we see that a property that is relevant for DOM (in this instance, partitivity) plays a role in the genitive/accusative alternation as well.

Borschev and Partee (2002b) demonstrate that the same kind of semantic contrast holds between genitive and nominative arguments in existential sentences. Thus, while *ni*-phrases strongly tend to be genitive, this tendency may be overruled if EC is present.

Further, we already know that definite objects are relatively likely to appear in the accusative case, but certain exceptions are available. As it turns out, these exceptions are based primarily on EC facts. As a rule, definite nominals carry existential presupposition (see e.g. Frege 1892, Strawson 1950). As such, they are predicted to appear in the accusative, rather than genitive, case, which is indeed what we observe. Still, there are instances when definite nominals lose an existential presupposition under negation, and in such cases, GenNeg is easily assigned to the nominals:

(25) Ja   ne   pomnju   etogo   razgovora.
     I   NEG   remember [this   conversation]_GEN.SG
     'I don't remember this conversation.'

Note that this sentence is perfectly compatible with the possibility that the conversation in question never took place and this is why, naturally, the speaker cannot recall it. Thus, the nominal lacks EC and therefore GenNeg is perfectly acceptable.

Finally, proper names are particularly likely to carry EC and indeed, in Modern Russian, they tend to be incompatible with Irrealis Genitive. However, the latter case becomes possible in those environments in which presence in a particular spatiotemporal location (rather than existence in a world in general) becomes particularly salient. Following Borschev and Partee's (1998, 2002a) 'Existence is Relative' Principle, Kagan (2013) proposes that in the corresponding environments, EC gets relativized to the spatiotemporal location in question. In existential sentences, this is the place denoted by the location phrase. In sentences with perception predicates such as *videt'* 'see', this is the field of perception of the subject.

As an illustration, consider the contrast in (26):

(26) a. Mašu   ne   vidno.
         Masha$_{ACC}$ NEG   seen$_{NEUT.SG}$
         'Masha can't be seen.'

      b. Maši   ne   vidno
         Masha$_{GEN}$ NEG   seen$_{NEUT.SG}$
         'Masha can't be seen.'[10]

According to (26a), Masha is in the same location as the speaker but cannot be seen, for instance, because she is hiding behind a tree or because someone tall and fat is standing in front of her. For instance, such a sentence could be uttered by a photographer, who suggests that Masha has to move in order to be seen on the picture. In contrast, (26b) strongly suggests that Masha is absent, and cannot be seen for that reason. A contrast in EC is thus observed, even though in both instances, Masha is presupposed to exist in the world.

The situation with Intensional Genitive is even more complex. On the one hand, it is rather easy to see that genitive objects are interpreted within the scope of intensional verbs and, as such, naturally, lack EC. For instance, the miracle in (27) is not entailed to take place in reality. On the other hand, in many instances, genitive marking is impossible for an object even though the latter is perfectly compatible with a non-specific, narrow scope, non-EC reading. For instance, the speaker of (28) is most likely not to believe in the existence of mermaids, which means that the

[10] The examples are based on an analogous genitive/nominative contrast discussed by Padučeva (1997:106).

object falls within the scope of the intensional predicate *ždjot* 'waits'. Still, accusative case-marking is obligatory in this sentence.

(27) Dima   ždjot   čuda.
     Dima   waits   miracle_{GEN.SG}
     'Dima is waiting for a miracle.'

(28) Dima   ždjot   rusalku / *rusalki.
     Dima   waits   mermaid_{ACC.SG / GEN.SG}
     'Dima is waiting for a mermaid.'

In order to capture such contrasts as the one illustrated in (27)–(28), Kagan (2009, 2013) introduces a distinction between *Instantiation-Oriented* and *Location-Oriented Attitude*. The former type is illustrated in (27) above and (29) below. The latter, in (28) and (30).

(29) a. John is waiting for a miracle.
      b. The committee demands an approval of the government.

(30) a. John is looking for Mary.
      b. The hunter is waiting for a deer.

Roughly, when a person waits for, demands, wants, etc. some entity, essentially, she wants for a certain change to take place in the world. But in fact, two types of change can be desired. One possibility is that the subject is willing for a new entity to come into existence. To illustrate, according to (29a), John is waiting for a new miracle to be instantiated. Such propositional attitude sentences with weak intentional verbs illustrate *Instantiation-Oriented Attitude*.

In contrast, the subject of (30a) is not wanting for Mary to get born. Nor does the hunter in (30b) wait for a (new) deer to come into existence, even under the non-specific, narrow-scope reading of the object. Rather, in such sentences, the subject desires **an already existing entity** to come to occupy the same location as himself. The entity may not exist in reality, but the attitude holder (the subject) must either be committed to its existence or at least believe that its existence is possible. Dima will not be waiting for (or seeking) a mermaid if he is certain that mermaids do not exist. A hunter will not be waiting for a deer if he is committed that there are no deer around. These sentences exhibit *Location-Oriented Attitude*.

A sentence may be also ambiguous between the two readings. For instance, (31), uttered by a reader addressing her favorite author, may mean that the speaker is waiting for new books to be written. In this case, Instantiation-Oriented Attitude is involved. Alternatively, the sentence can be used in a context in which copies of the new books have already been sent to the speaker, and she is waiting for the parcel. Under this reading, we get Location-Oriented Attitude.

(31)   I'll be waiting for your new books!

Crucially, the Instantiation/Location contrast correlates with an existence-related difference. Under Instantiation-Oriented Attitude, EC is absent in every possible sense, even relative to the subject's worldview. Possibly we can even state that commitment to **non**-existence is observed. In contrast, under Location-Oriented Attitude, existence must be present at least in a weak sense, relative to some world that conforms to the subject's vision of reality. Critically, in Russian, Intensional Genitive is typically assigned in Instantiation-Oriented but not Location-Oriented sentences. Kagan (2013) captures this contrast by proposing that in the presence of intensional verbs, EC is relativized to the set of worlds which is introduced by the predicate. With weak intensional verbs such as verbs of desire, this is typically the epistemic set of the subject (the set of worlds that represent his or her knowledge state). (This view is based on Heim's 1992 and Farkas' 2003 treatment of intensional verbs.) Location-Oriented Attitude is accompanied at least by such a relativized version of EC. In contrast, in Instantiation-Oriented Attitude, objects interpreted within the scope of the intensional predicate lack EC even in this weak sense.

It is also worth noting that Instantiation-Oriented Attitude sentences report the subject's desire **for a property to be instantiated**. Thus, the appearance of genitive case-marking in this environment is consistent with the property-type approach to Irrealis Genitive. In addition, the tendency of abstract nominals to appear in the genitive case receives an explanation. Referents of abstract nouns, such as *freedom*, *reason*, *love*, etc., or entities these nouns quantify over, are not normally linked to a particular location in the world. For the same reason, abstract entities are not generally expected to move from one physical location to another. Thus, abstract nominals are unlikely to appear in sentences that exhibit Location-Oriented Attitude, in which accusative case is assigned. Rather, they are strongly associated with the Instantiation-Oriented interpretation, where a person wishes for a property (e.g. that of freedom, love or miracle) to get instantiated. Hence the tendency for genitive case-marking.

Below, I provide several minimal pairs in which the genitive/accusative alternation corresponds to the Instantiation/Location-Oriented Attitude contrast.

(32) Dima   iščet   ubežišče / ubežišča   v   etom   dome.
     Dima   seeks   shelter$_{ACC.SG}$ / $_{GEN.SG}$ in   this   house
     'Dima is seeking shelter / a shelter in this house.'

Under its accusative variant, the sentence means that Dima is trying to locate an already existing shelter (plausibly a bomb shelter) inside the house. Location-Oriented Attitude is thus exhibited. (*Seek* is special in that it is the attitude holder, rather than a desired object, that undergoes a change of location. But still, we are dealing with an attempt to come to occupy the same location as the entity that is searched for.) But the interpretation of the genitive variant differs quite substantially from that of the accusative version. The genitive variant means that Dima wants the house to become shelter for him. Thus, he is not trying to locate an already existing shelter; rather, he wishes for the property *shelter* to come to be instantiated. The genitive variant thus forces an Instantiation-Oriented reading.

Another example is provided in (33):

(33) a. načal'nik   trebujet   pribyli.
        boss   demands   profit$_{GEN}$
        'The boss demands profit.'

     b. načal'nik   trebujet   pribyl'.
        Boss   demands   profit$_{ACC}$

(33a) means that the boss demands that there be profit; namely, he demands for the employees to work in such a way that would afford a profit. (33b), in contrast, means that the boss wants to physically receive the money that has already been gained. Thus, in the second sentence, the complement nominal relates to an entity (money) that exists in the worlds representing the epistemic state of the boss (and, if the nominal takes wide scope, in the actual world). What the boss wants is for this object to move to his location, or to come to be under his possession. This interpretation leads to accusative case-marking. In contrast, the complement in (33a) does not refer to an already existing object (whether in reality or in its version that corresponds to the boss's beliefs). Rather, the boss wishes for new profit to come into existence. The nominal thus denotes a property that the attitude holder wishes to be realized. As a result, it appears in Irrealis Genitive.

The nominal is property-denoting and does not carry even the world-relativized version of EC.

Finally, consider the naturally occurring examples in (34). Note that both contain the verb *trebovat'* 'demand' and the object *zaveščanie* '(last) will'.

(34) a. ...Trebujut   zaveščanie   ili   kopiju   zaveščanija...
          demand   will$_{ACC.SG}$ or   copy$_{ACC.SG}$ will$_{GEN.SG}$
          'They require the will or a copy of the will.'
          Podskažite adres ... notarial'noj kontory ... gde togda bylo zaregistrirovano zaveščanie.
          'Point me towards a notarial office where the will was then registered.'
      b. Ona na 16 let starše ego ... I vsë-taki nastaivaet na tom, čtoby oba ostavili zaveščanie...
          'She is 16 years older than him, and she still insists that both of them write a will.'
          ... ona trebuet ot nego zaveščanija.
          she demands from him will$_{GEN.SG}$
          '... She demands a will from him.'

The context in (34a) makes it clear that the will exists, and it is the actual document (either the original or its copy) that is demanded. The requirement is for an existing object to be provided, and accusative case-marking is chosen. In contrast, (34b) reports a demand to write a will. The requirement is for the property *will* to be instantiated and, thus, Instantiation-Oriented Attitude is involved. The genitive case form is therefore used.

6.3.4 Irrealis Genitive versus DOM

On the one hand, the Irrealis Genitive / accusative alternation on objects seems to differ substantially from differential object marking. The availability of genitive case depends on a wider range of factors, including non-veridicality, the abstract/concrete distinction, semantic type and existential commitment. These factors may overrule the more standard indefiniteness requirement and have a stronger predictive power than the (non-)specificity of the object.

But on the other hand, at a more abstract level, both the genitive/accusative contrast and DOM are sensitive to the property of individuation. Both genitive objects in Slavic and caseless ones in DOM languages are less individuated than their accusative counterparts. Lack of EC and the property type contribute to low individuation, just as indefiniteness and inanimacy do (see Grimm 2005, who categorizes Intensional Genitive nominals as lowly individuated due to the absence of EC).

Moreover, the absence of existential commitment, as well as property-type denotation, may be viewed as special instances of non-specificity. Property-type nominals that lack EC should presumably be analyzed as occupying a particularly low position on the specificity scale. From this viewpoint, the genitive/accusative alternation is no different from DOM in the semantic sense. Objects that are non-specific (in the EC-based sense) are marked with Irrealis Genitive. Otherwise, accusative case has to surface.

Yet another difference between asymmetric DOM and the genitive/accusative alternation has to do with the form of the non-accusative object. In DOM, it is unmarked for case; within the Balto-Slavic phenomenon, it is genitive. Interestingly, however, even in this respect, a unification is not impossible. Genitive marking can be viewed as a kind of default form of a nominal within Pesetsky's (2013) analysis. Pesetsky argues that Russian cases can be reduced to the part-of-speech categories. He proposes that a genitive-marked word is a stem to which an affix of category N is attached (along the line of Marantz 1997, in whose view a category-neutral stem combines with a categorizing morpheme). Analogously, a nominative-marked word is a product of combining a stem with a morpheme of category D, accusative-marked noun is one that combines with a morpheme of category V and, finally, oblique marking results from combining a noun with a morpheme of category P. This means that Russian is analyzed as a case-stacking language. A natural question to ask is why case stacking is not observed overtly. For instance, consider the DP *doroge* 'path' that functions as a complement of the preposition *po* 'along' in (35).

(35) po   doroge
      along   path$_{DAT}$
      'along a/the path'

This DP appears in only one case, the dative, which is associated with the preposition in question. It does not bear in addition the nominative case suffix *-a*, associated with the D category, nor the genitive suffix *-i*, associated with the N category. Pesetsky accounts for this fact by proposing that the One-Suffix Rule, quoted below, holds in Russian:

(36) Delete all but the outermost case suffix. (Pesetsky 2013:5)

In our example with a prepositional phrase, the outermost suffix is the one associated with the preposition. Therefore, the nominative and genitive suffixes associated with the D and N categories, respectively, are predicted to be deleted. This is why we do not see nominative or genitive case morphology on the nominal that functions as the complement of the P.

Crucially for our purposes, it follows from this analysis that genitive is in a certain sense the default form of a noun. This is the form in which every noun is "born." As stated by Pesetsky, "N_{GEN} categorizes a Russian root as a noun (in the lexicon)." Essentially, a nominal will appear in the genitive case *as long as no other case is assigned to it*. "... a noun to which no other case has been assigned will always take the form [[root] N_{GEN}], i.e. it will bear what traditional descriptions call genitive case" (Pesetsky 2013:5). But this makes genitive nouns especially close to unmarked nouns in those languages in which it is possible for a nominal to lack any overt case. From this perspective, Russian genitive objects can be regarded as natural counterparts of unmarked objects in such DOM languages as Spanish, Turkish or Kannada.

6.4 PARTITIVE GENITIVE

6.4.1 Introducing the Phenomenon

Partitive Genitive, illustrated in (37a) and (38a) below for Russian, is intuitively quite close to NP-related partitive in Finnic. The object is interpreted quantificationally, indicating an indeterminate amount of the matter denoted by the noun. Intuitively, it receives the meaning of "some (undefined quantity) of X" and is, consequently, interpreted as indefinite and non-specific. This phenomenon is discussed extensively by Klenin (1978), Pesetsky (1982), Franks (1995), Khrizman (2011) and Kagan (2013), among others. The marking of Partitive Genitive is typically optional, in the sense that it can be substituted by the accusative case. The accusative alternatives do not carry the undefined quantity flavor and are compatible with definite as well as indefinite, specific as well as non-specific readings.

(37) a. Ja vypil vody.
I drank$_{PERF}$ water$_{GEN}$
'I drank some water.'
b. Ja vypil vodu.
I drank$_{PERF}$ water$_{ACC}$
'I drank the water.'

(38) a. Ja kupil   tebe   jablok.
      I   bought$_{PERF}$ you$_{DAT}$ apples$_{GEN.PL}$
      'I bought you some apples.'
   b. Ja kupil   tebe   jabloki.
      I   bought$_{PERF}$ you$_{DAT}$ apples$_{ACC.PL}$
      'I bought you (the) apples.'

Partitive Genitive is assigned only to homogeneous objects, such as bare plurals and mass terms (39).

(39) Ja kupil   tebe   vody /   jablok /   *jabloka.
      I   bought$_{PERF}$ you$_{DAT}$ water$_{GEN}$ apple$_{GEN.PL}$ apple$_{GEN.SG}$
      'I bought water / apples / an apple for you.'

Further, at least in some Slavic languages, its assignment is limited to objects of perfective verbs.

(40) Ja   pil   vodu / *vody.
      I   drank$_{IMP}$ water$_{ACC/GEN}$
      'I was drinking water / I drank water.'

Partitive Genitive is present in almost all modern Baltic and Slavic languages which have kept morphological case, including Lithuanian, Latvian, Russian, Ukrainian, Belorussian, Polish, Serbo-Croatian and Slovenian.

6.4.2 Partitive Genitive versus Irrealis Genitive

Partitive Genitive differs from Irrealis Genitive along a whole range of properties. Firstly (and most obviously at this stage), its appearance is not sensitive to such notions as non-veridicality and the absence of EC, which play a key role in the licensing of Genitive of Negation and Intensional Genitive. For instance, Partitive Genitive is often found with verbs of consumption, such as *pojest'* 'eat' and *vypit'* 'drink', which are purely extensional. For instance, (37a) above entails the existence of (the relevant amount of) water, at least before the drinking event took place. This does not pose a problem to genitive case-assignment.

Secondly, while Partitive Genitive is only acceptable with homogeneous objects, Irrealis Genitive is compatible with count singular ones, which are heterogeneous:

(41) a. Ja ždu   zvonka.
         I   wait$_{IMP}$ call$_{GEN.SG}$
         'I am waiting for a call.'
   b. Ja ne   uvidel   v   komnate kovra
      I   NEG saw$_{PERF}$ in   room   carpet$_{GEN.SG}$
      'I didn't see a carpet in the room.'

Thirdly, while Partitive Genitive typically appears with perfective verbs, Irrealis Genitive is easily licensed on objects of imperfective ones. Fourthly, Partitive Genitive exhibits a cross-linguistic pattern of development that differs from that of Irrealis Genitive (see Franks 1995, Kagan 2013). As shown in Table 6.1 in Section 6.1, Irrealis Genitive is obligatory in some Balto-Slavic languages, optional in others and essentially absent in yet others. In turn, Partitive Genitive exhibits a completely different pattern. It is found in almost all of these languages (with the exception of Czech, in which, according to Franks (1995), it is no longer productive), and it is consistently optional, in the sense that it can always or almost always be substituted by the accusative.

Several additional differences are discussed by Franks (1995) and Kagan (2013), for example. Based on these contrasts, Kagan (2013) draws the conclusion that Partitive Genitive does not constitute the same phenomenon as Irrealis Genitive, even though the two alternations may possibly be unified on a more abstract level. The unification direction is supported by the fact that both phenomena involve a genitive/accusative alternation on internal arguments that is sensitive to the concepts of specificity and individuation, with genitive objects being less specific and individuated than accusative ones. In the following section, we consider two approaches that unify Partitive Genitive with Genitive of Negation (Pesetsky 1982) and Irrealis Genitive more broadly (Khrizman 2011).

6.4.3 Analyses of Partitive Genitive

First of all, it is worth pointing out that despite its similarity to NP-related partitive in Finnic, Partitive Genitive has not been analyzed as an aspectual unboundedness marker. This is due to the fact that Balto-Slavic languages do not have an analogue of the Finnish VP-related partitive, that is, genitive case on objects does not receive the function of marking atelicity or (VP-level) unboundedness. This job is fulfilled instead by verbal aspect (the perfective/imperfective opposition).

A particularly prominent analysis that has been proposed for Partitive Genitive is the empty quantifier approach, also discussed above in the context of Genitive of Negation. The account was originally put forward by Pesetsky (1982) and then adopted and further developed by Yadroff (1995), Franks (1995, 1997) and Bailyn (2004), among others. The basic analysis states that the Partitive Genitive marking surfaces due to the presence of a phonologically empty quantifier.

This approach is supported by a number of similarities that can be observed between the Partitive Genitive construction and constructions that involve overt quantifiers. Firstly, genitive is the case assigned by most quantifiers to the quantified NP:

(42) a. pjat   devoček
         five   girls$_{\text{GEN.PL}}$
     b. mnogo   čašek
         many   cups$_{\text{GEN.PL}}$

Secondly, as noted above, Partitive Genitive is systematically associated with a quantificational, partitive meaning "some X," "some part of X." This interpretational property is exemplified in (37a), repeated below as (43). As indicated in the translation, the genitive nominal is interpreted as *some water*.

(43) Ja vypil   vody.
     I   drank$_{\text{PERF}}$ water$_{\text{GEN}}$
     'I drank some water.'

This fact is naturally accounted for if one assumes that the genitive is assigned by an empty existential quantifier whose semantics is in part similar to that of the English *some*.

Thirdly, the homogeneity requirement could be due to the presence of an empty quantifier by analogy with overt quantifiers, some of which combine with both mass and count plural nominals but not with count singular ones:

(44) a. mnogo vody /   stolov /   *stola
         many   water$_{\text{GEN}}$ tables$_{\text{GEN.PL}}$ table$_{\text{GEN.SG}}$
         'a lot of water / tables / *table'
     b. malo   vody /   stolov /   *stola
         few   water$_{\text{GEN}}$ tables$_{\text{GEN.PL}}$ table$_{\text{GEN.SG}}$
         'a little bit of water / few tables / *few table'

Fourthly, in Russian, a highly restricted number of nouns have a special partitive morphological form consisting of the suffix -*u* added to the stem.[11] This form can always be substituted by a common genitive form, but not vice versa; the use of the partitive suffix is more restricted. In particular, the morphological partitive is available only with quantifiers or nouns denoting quantity:

[11] It is worth pointing out that the -*u* form, also known as "second(ary) genitive," is currently restricted to spoken language (Rozental et al. 2008) and is perceived by native speakers as stylistically marked, colloquial or archaic (Khrizman 2011).

(45) a. bol'še   saxaru / saxara
        more   sugar$_{\text{PART/GEN}}$
        'more sugar'
     b. tarelka supu / supa
        plate   soup$_{\text{PART/GEN}}$
        'a plate of soup'
     c. cvet   *supu / supa
        color   soup$_{\text{PART/GEN}}$
        'the color of the soup'

In the non-quantificational use of genitive case in (45c), the partitive version is unacceptable.

Crucially, the partitive form is possible when Partitive Genitive is used:

(46) Ja vypil   čaju / čaja.
     I   drank$_{\text{PERF}}$ tea$_{\text{PART/GEN}}$
     'I drank some tea.'

This fact is predictable if (46) is analyzed as containing an empty quantifier.

For further similarities between NPs assigned non-canonical genitive case and constructions with overt quantifiers, see Pesetsky (1982) and Franks (1995). Note also that the empty quantifier analysis accounts both for the syntactic case-checking and for some of the semantic properties associated with genitive objects. Syntactically, the genitive case feature is checked by the empty quantifier. In turn, the quantificational nature of partitive genitives, as well as their indefinite, non-specific interpretation, results from the existential semantics of the quantifier.

A different analysis is put forward by Khrizman (2011), who unifies Partitive Genitive and Irrealis Genitive in an important way. Specifically, she argues that objects marked with Partitive Genitive **denote properties** and are of type <e,t>. She develops a formal account which treats Partitive Genitive arguments as instances of a measure construction, by analogy with such overt measure phrases as *three glasses of wine*. Thus, in terms of its semantic structure, (47a) below is taken to be quite close to (47b):

(47) a. Ivan vypil   vina.
        Ivan drank$_{\text{PERF}}$ wine$_{\text{GEN}}$
        'Ivan drank some wine.'
     b. Ivan vypil   dva   stakana vina.
        Ivan drank$_{\text{PERF}}$ two   glasses wine$_{\text{GEN}}$
        'Ivan drank two glasses of wine.'

Table 6.2 *Comparative analysis of Partitive Genitive NPs and measure-classified NPs (Khrizman 2011:61)*

	Feature	Partitive Genitive NP – *vina* 'wine'	Classified-measure NP – *dva stakana vina* 'two glasses of wine'
1	Type of interpretation	expression of quantity	expression of quantity
2	Semantic type	<e,t>	<e,t>
3	Restriction to homogeneity	V	V
4	Semantic type of the argument of the measure expression	<e,t>(GenNP)	<e,t>(GenNP)
5	Explicit classifier-measure phrase	X	V

Khrizman compares Partitive Genitive objects as in (47a) and explicit measure-classified nominals as in (47b) in a table which, slightly adapted, is provided here as Table 6.2.[12]

Note that Feature 2 relates to the semantic type of the whole expression (e.g. *dva stakana vina*) and Feature 4 specifically to the semantic type of the nominal to which the measure function applies (e.g. *vina*). Of course, in the case of Partitive Genitive objects, we do not observe any explicit difference between the two.

While Features 2 and 4 are internal to the analysis proposed by Khrizman, Features 1, 3 and 5 relate to empirical facts. The fact that we are dealing with a genitive-marked nominal in both instances can be taken as an additional empirical similarity on the basis of Feature 4. To summarize, partitive genitives are similar to measure-classified nominals in that they contain a morphologically genitive NP, express a quantificational meaning and must be homogeneous. Khrizman concludes that partitive objects are indeed nominal measure predicates, even though they do not contain an explicit measure phrase in the structure. She proposes the semantics in (48) for Partitive Genitive objects:

(48)   MEAS (λx. NP(x))

---

[12] I have added row numbers for ease of reference and changed the examples at the top of the table.

6.4 *Partitive Genitive*   219

Up to this point, this analysis seems to be compatible with the empty quantifier approach. One could hypothesize that while the object in (47b) contains a measure phrase *dva stakana*, in its (47a) counterpart, this role is fulfilled by a null element Q. However, Khrizman states explicitly that she "[does] not assume the existence of an empty measure phrase" (p. 61). Rather, she argues that "MEAS function has to be supplied by some external element necessarily present in the logical representation of the sentence" (p. 62).

It is here that aspect enters into the picture. As we know, Partitive Genitive is typically available with perfective verbs but not with imperfective ones. Khrizman proposes that a perfective verb is precisely the external element which is needed in order to induce the MEAS operation. She follows the approach to aspect developed by Filip and Rothstein (2006) and Filip (2008), which regards telicity as maximalization of events and analyzes Slavic perfective verbs as involving the MAX_E operator in their semantics. This is a maximality operator which allows us to select the unique maximal event in the situation at hand. To illustrate, (49) below, which contains a perfective verb, entails that a maximal event of house-building took place (which means that the house was fully built).

(49) Dima   postroil   dom.
     Dima   built$_{PERF}$ house$_{ACC}$
     'Dima (has) built a house.'

Abstracting away from formal compositional details, the property type of a genitive object in a sentence like (47a) above does not allow a maximal, bounded, reading. But such a reading is required by the perfective aspect. Therefore, the perfective verb induces the application of MEAS (a function that is present in its semantic structure) to the genitive NP. A measure reading results, and the (vague) quantity that is rendered is treated as maximal in the given event.

Recall the two key semantic characteristics ascribed to Irrealis Genitive objects in the recent analyses:

 (i) property-type denotation
 (ii) absence of existential commitment.

Under Khrizman's analysis, Partitive Genitive objects share characteristic (i) but not (ii). Both facts have certain consequences for the degree of their individuation, an issue that is discussed in the following subsection.

6.4.4　Partitive Genitive, DOM and Individuation ▬▬▬▬

On the one hand, the alternation between accusative and Partitive Genitive objects differs from DOM. Case is determined by a complex interaction of semantic and syntactic factors, some of which are not generally taken to play a role in DOM. Further, the availability of the non-accusative variant may be due to the presence of a phonologically empty but semantically contributing item, which is not how DOM is typically analyzed. On the other hand, a significant parallel between the two phenomena can be observed. In Balto-Slavic, we see a case alternation between accusative and alternatively marked objects in which the latter receive a less individuated interpretation. This characteristic unifies Partitive Genitive with both Irrealis Genitive and DOM.

Specifically, Partitive Genitive is lowly individuated in the following ways. Firstly, as pointed out above, its marking is restricted to homogeneous nouns. Such nominals are indeed characterized by low individuation, since they leave unspecified the boundaries of the referent. Thus, it is rather clear where the boundaries of **a cat** lie, but what about the boundaries of **cats** (there could be two, three, ten, etc.) or **water**? Timberlake (1986), among others, points out that mass nouns are less individuated than count ones and (count) plural nouns are less individuated than their singular counterparts. We can generalize that, everything else being equal, homogeneous nominal phrases are lower in individuation that heterogeneous ones.

Secondly, Partitive Genitives tend to receive non-specific and indefinite readings. This makes them occupy a low position on the definiteness scale, which, in contrast to the previously specified properties, plays a very prominent role in cross-linguistic DOM. It is worth noting, however, that (unlike with Irrealis Genitive) the non-specificity here is not related to narrow scope. Rather, the non-specificity flavor is interrelated with the quantificational interpretation of these phrases. *Some water* is both indefinite and (quite plausibly) non-specific, in contrast to *the water*.

DISCUSSION

The currently presented picture does not seem to do justice to the similarities that are exhibited by the Finnic partitive and the Balto-Slavic genitive. The analyses these cases receive differ quite substantially. The contrasts are indeed striking, but we also know that NP-related partitive shares many properties with

Partitive Genitive, that sentential negation licenses both Partitive of Negation and Genitive of Negation, and that arguably EC, a crucial property of Irrealis Genitive, plays a role in case-assignment to objects of Finnish stative verbs (see Chapter 4, Section 4.1.4.5). Can you think of ways to capture the similarities between the Finnic and Balto-Slavic alternations? For example, would it be desirable to treat VP-related partitive (which is special to Finnic and does not seem to have a Slavic counterpart) separately from the other uses of the partitive case? Would a cross-linguistic account benefit from such a separation? Or would such a separation be harmful for an analysis of the Finnic case system?

6.5 CONCLUSION

This chapter was devoted to genitive/accusative alternations observed in Balto-Slavic languages. We concentrated mainly on case-assignment to direct objects in Russian, a language in which Irrealis Genitive is productive and, at the same time, not obligatory. We considered three types of genitive marking on objects: Genitive of Negation, Intensional Genitive and Partitive Genitive. Evidence was provided for a uniform treatment of the first two phenomena, referred to together as Irrealis Genitive. The key semantic properties that accompany the assignment of these cases constitute non-specificity, absence of existential commitment and the property-type denotation.

Turning to Partitive Genitive, there are reasons both to unify it with Irrealis Genitive and to draw a distinction between the two. All these kinds of genitive objects are associated with indefiniteness and non-specificity and have been argued to be of the property type. But Partitive Genitive does not depend on such properties as veridicality and existential commitment, which play a crucial part in the licensing of Irrealis Genitive.

The case variation in question was compared to two phenomena observed in additional languages: (asymmetric) DOM and the partitive/accusative alternation in Finnish. DOM differs from the genitive/accusative alternations in that (i) in the former, one of the variants is unmarked for case and (ii) a higher number of semantic-pragmatic factors seem to be involved in the latter, at least this is the impression we get on the basis of the existing literature. Still, it has been suggested that the two phenomena are worth unifying given that they both involve a non-accusative marking on objects that are lowly individuated/located low on a specificity scale.

The comparison between genitive objects in Russian and partitive ones in Finnish reveals a very complex picture of shared properties as well as radical distinctions, and further investigation is needed in order to get a better understanding of the relation between the two phenomena. The investigation should probably incorporate both a synchronic and a diachronic perspective.

FURTHER READING

Kagan's (2013) book puts forward an analysis of Irrealis Genitive based on the property-type hypothesis and existential commitment. Both Genitive of Negation and Irrealis Genitive are considered in detail. The book also addresses the relation between these phenomena and subjunctive mood. One chapter is devoted to an overview of previously proposed analyses of genitive objects. The book is based on Kagan's (2008) dissertation.

The property-type approach is argued for by Partee and Borschev (2004) and Borschev et al. (2008). Its advantages and disadvantages are discussed in detail by Partee and Borschev (2007).

Khrizman's (2011) thesis is devoted to Partitive Genitive. The author analyzes Partitive Genitive objects as instances of a measure construction. The phenomenon in question is discussed in the context of the semantics of classified-measure phrases and Russian aspect.

Borschev and Partee (1998, 2002a) and Partee and Borschev (2004) analyze the genitive/nominative alternation in Russian. They put forward a semantic-pragmatic approach with a considerable focus on information structure.

Pereltsvaig (1999) analyses Genitive of Negation in terms of non-referentiality. Syntactically, she follows Pesetsky's (1982) approach according to which this case is assigned by a phonologically empty quantifier. Pereltsvaig's work covers a rich amount of data and discusses in detail the relation between object case and aspect.

7 Predicate Case

The previous chapters have been devoted to the case of arguments and adjuncts. However, in a range of languages, nominal predicates are case-marked as well. In some of these languages, the case of a predicate depends on semantic notions, such as change, temporariness and permanence.

7.1 INSTRUMENTAL PREDICATES IN SLAVIC

7.1.1 An Introduction

In certain Slavic languages, nominal and adjectival phrases that appear in predicative positions often bear instrumental case-marking. Instrumental forms alternate with nominative ones, which surface when the predicate agrees in case with the subject. (Alternatively, in certain constructions, the predicate agrees with the object, and then it is the instrumental/accusative alternation that we get.[1]) Crucially, the choice of case correlates with certain semantic properties, even though the distinctions are sometimes so fine that it is difficult for native speakers to explain the difference between the two variants.

Let us begin by considering the following example from Polish:

(1) a. Jan jest moim   najlepszym przyjacielem.
        Jan is   my$_{INSTR}$ best$_{INSTR}$ friend$_{INSTR}$
        'Jan is my best friend.'
     b. Jan to   mój   najlepszy   przyjaciel.
        Jan PRON my$_{NOM}$ best$_{NOM}$ friend$_{NOM}$
        'Jan is my best friend.'

(Citko 2008:262)

---

[1] See e.g. Babby (2009) and references therein.

As indicated above, both sentences can be translated identically: "Jan is my best friend." However, while in (1a) the predicate *mój najlepszy przyjaciel* 'my best friend' appears in the instrumental case, in (1b) it is nominative, similarly to the subject *Jan*. And, in fact, this is not the only contrast between the two variants. In Polish, the case of the predicate depends on the copula that appears in the sentence. (1a) contains a verbal copula *być* 'be' (or, more precisely, its present tense third-person singular form *jest*), whereas in (1b), we find a pronominal copula *to*, phonologically identical to the demonstrative meaning *this*. The verbal copula requires an instrumental predicative complement, whereas with the pronominal copula, the form of the predicate is nominative.

Citko (2008) further points out that the two copulas may co-occur in the same sentence, in which case the predicate nominal is nominative-marked (i.e. it is the presence of the pronominal copula that seems to play the key role in case selection).

(2) Jan   to   jest   mój   najlepszy   przyjaciel.
     Jan   PRON   is   my$_{\text{NOM}}$ best$_{\text{NOM}}$ friend$_{\text{NOM}}$
     'Jan is my best friend.'

(Citko 2008:263)

Given the interrelation between the choice of the copula and the case of the nominal, it is not easy to determine which of the two factors is responsible for differences in meaning (to which we will turn soon). In this respect, it is useful to look at Russian facts, since in this language, we find predicate nominal sentences that differ in terms of case-marking only:

(3) a. Dima   byl   xorošim   vračom.
         Dima   was   good$_{\text{INSTR}}$ doctor$_{\text{INSTR}}$
         'Dima was a good doctor.'
     b. Dima   byl   xorošij   vrač.
         Dima   was   good$_{\text{NOM}}$ doctor$_{\text{NOM}}$
         'Dima was a good doctor.'

Both examples in (3) contain the same verbal copula *byl* 'was'. Still, the predicate 'good doctor' appears in the instrumental case in (3a) and in the nominative case in (3b). Both sentences are grammatical. Thus, we can compare the meaning of such minimal pairs as (3) and, if any contrasts are found, they will be linked to the case of the predicate, rather than to the choice of the copula.

Another way in which Russian differs from Polish is that in the former, the use of the verb *byt'* 'be' in the present tense is highly limited, and restricted mainly to existential and possessive sentences. This means that predicate nominal sentences in the present tense lack a verbal copula (or at least this copula is not overtly realized). Crucially, instrumental case is unavailable in such sentences, leaving the speakers only with the nominative option:

(4) Dima xorošij vrač   / *xorošim vračom.
     Dima [good   doctor]_{NOM} / [good   doctor]_{INSTR}
     'Dima is a good doctor.'

This suggests that, as in Polish, the presence of a verbal copula is interrelated with the availability of instrumental marking. The latter is possible only in the presence of the former. In contrast to Polish, however, Russian allows nominative marking in the absence of a pronominal copula (3b, 4) and, in fact, in the absence of any overt copula (4). Still, it is worth noting that Russian does have an analogue of the Polish copula *to*. The Russian pronominal copula is *éto*, and it, too, receives the meaning 'this' under its demonstrative use. Just like its Polish counterpart, this copula is compatible with the verbal one, and in its presence, only a nominative predicate is possible. As mentioned above, the difference between the two languages has to do with the fact that in Russian, nominative marking is possible even in the absence of *éto*.

(5) a. Dima éto   xorošij vrač   / *xorošim vračom.
         Dima this [good   doctor]_{NOM} / [good   doctor]_{INSTR}
         'Dima is a good doctor.'
     b. Dima éto byl xorošij vrač   / *xorošim vračom.
         Dima this was [good   doctor]_{NOM} / [good   doctor]_{INSTR}
         'Dima was a good doctor.'

Before we proceed to the semantics of the alternation, it is worth pointing out that the instrumental/nominative contrast is not limited to predicate nominal sentences of the type illustrated above. It is also observed on secondary predicates (6) and free adjuncts (7) (see e.g. Matushansky 2000, Geist 2006, Babby 2009 and references therein).

(6) a. Ivan tanceval golym.
         Ivan danced   nude_{INSTR}
         'Ivan danced nude.'
     b. Ivan tanceval golyj.
         Ivan danced   nude_{NOM}
         'Ivan danced nude.'

(7) a. Studentkoj,   ja   xodila   v   muzej   besplatno.
    Student$_{INSTR}$ I   walked to museum for.free
    'When a student, I went to museums for free.'

   b. Studentka,   ja   xodila   v   muzej   besplatno.
    Student$_{NOM}$ I   walked to museum for.free
    'As a student, I went to museums for free.'

                                                (Matushansky 2000:294)

7.1.2   Semantic Contrasts

7.1.2.1   Individual- /Stage-Level Distinction

First of all, the instrumental/nominative alternation has been linked to the distinction between temporal and permanent properties, or stage-level and individual-level predicates (see e.g. discussion in Jakobson 1957/1971, Wierzbicka 1980, Smith 1999, Geist 2006, Citko 2008). The terms **stage-level** and **individual-level**, originally introduced by Carlson (1977), relate, roughly, to the temporal/permanent opposition. Stage-level properties characterize not the "whole individual," but rather spatiotemporal "stages" of the individual, that is, they hold of an individual only at a particular time or in a particular event or situation. In contrast, individual-level properties are relatively independent of specific events, hold permanently and are not likely to change (although changes along such properties are not totally impossible). A typical example of a stage-level predicate is *tired*; individual-level ones can be illustrated by such adjectives as *tall* or *wooden*.

   In the literature on Slavic, it has been proposed that instrumental predicates tend to denote stage-level properties and nominative predicates, individual-level ones (see e.g. Jakobson 1957/1971). Given the fine nature of the semantic difference between the two types of sentences, it may not be obvious that the correlation in question exists. However, it has been pointed out that sentences with nominative predicates are characterized by the so-called "lifetime effects," unlike their instrumental counterparts (e.g. Citko 2008). When such sentences appear in the past tense, an implicature arises that the subject to whom the quality is ascribed is no longer alive. This property is known to be characteristic of individual-level predicates. For instance, the Polish example in (8a) suggests that Jan is dead at the speech time (Citko 2008:275). The same conclusion is drawn about the subject of the Russian sentence in (3b), repeated below as (8b).

(8)   a. Jan   to   byl   mój   najlepszy   przyjaciel.
        Jan   PRON   was   my$_{NOM}$ best$_{NOM}$ friend$_{NOM}$
        'Jan was my best friend.'
      b. Dima   byl   xorošij   vrač.
        Dima   was   good$_{NOM}$ doctor$_{NOM}$
        'Dima was a good doctor.'

If, in contrast, one is willing to assert that Dima used to be a good
doctor but later became a bad one, or changed his profession, or
stopped working altogether, the instrumental version (3a), repeated
as (9), is highly preferable:

(9)   Dima   byl   xorošim   vračom.
      Dima   was   good$_{INSTR}$ doctor$_{INSTR}$
      'Dima was a good doctor.'

Further, Citko points out that in Polish, such inherently stage-level
predicates as "*fugitive, passenger, pedestrian* or *spectator*" (p. 274) are
generally infelicitous with the pronominal copula (which, in turn,
requires a nominative complement) (10). However, such sentences
improve considerably if the context supplies the predicates with
a more permanent, individual-level flavor (11).

(10)   #Jan   to   (jest)   zbieg / pasażer / przechodzień / widz.
        Jan   PRON   is   fugitive / passenger / pedestrian / spectator$_{NOM}$
        'Jan is a fugitive/passenger/pedestrian/spectator.'

(11)   Jan   to   (jest)   wieczny   zbieg.
        Jan   PRON   is   permanent$_{NOM}$ fugitive$_{NOM}$
        'Jan is a permanent fugitive.'
                                                        (Citko 2008:274)

In Russian, too, nominal predicates of the above-mentioned type are
much more likely to appear in the instrumental than in the nominative:

(12)   Ivan   byl   passažirom   lajnera   / #passažir   lajnera.
        Ivan   was   passenger$_{INSTR}$ jetliner$_{GEN}$ / passenger$_{NOM}$ jetliner$_{GEN}$
        'Ivan was a jetliner passenger.'

Further, the relevance of temporariness becomes more obvious on the
intuitive level when free adjuncts are considered. The minimal pair in
(7) is repeated in (13) below:

(13)   a. Studentkoj,   ja   xodila   v   muzej   besplatno.
         Student$_{INSTR}$ I   walked   to   museum   for.free
         'When a student, I went to museums for free.'

b. Studentka,   ja   xodila   v   muzej   besplatno.
   Student_NOM   I   walked   to   museum   for.free
   'As a student, I went to museums for free.'

(Matushansky 2000:294)

As can be seen from the translation, the sentence-initial adjunct in
(13a) receives a temporal interpretation: the speaker had free entrance
permission while she was a student. The adjunct defines a temporal
interval during which the state of affairs described in the following
clause held. In contrast, in (13b), the free adjunct is rather interpreted
as a cause: the speaker entered museums for free **because** she was
a student.

To sum up thus far, the nominative/instrumental alternation is
sensitive to the temporary versus permanent nature of the property.
At the same time, this distinction cannot constitute the only factor
affecting the alternation. For instance, it is possible to find naturally
occurring examples in which an inherently individual-level adjective
is instrumental:

(14) Pervyj   grodnensky vodoprovod byl   **derevjannym**   i
      first   Grodno's   water-pipe was   wooden_INSTR   and
      načinalsja vozle   sinagogi.
      began   near   synagogue
      'The first water-pipe in Grodno was wooden and began near the
      synagogue.'[2]

The second complication has to do with the adjectival domain as well.
In Russian (as well as in some other Slavic languages), a predicative AP
may appear in either a long or a short form (e.g. Vinogradov 1947,
Babby 1973, Bailyn 1994, Geist 2010). Short-form adjectives agree with
the subject in number and gender but, unlike their long counterparts,
lack case. The short/long distinction can be illustrated by the pair *bel –
belyj*. Both adjectives mean 'white', are masculine singular and can
appear in a predicative position. As a result of the existence of this
dichotomy, an AP predicate can potentially appear in three forms:
short, long instrumental and long nominative. Indeed, with some
adjectives, we do find such triples:

(15) a. Vasja   byl   spokojen.
         Vasja   was   calm_SHORT
         'Vasja was calm.'

---

[2] http://greenbelarus.info/articles/11–02-2016/pervyy-grodnenskiy-vodoprovod-byl-
     derevyannym-i-nachinalsya-vozle-sinagogi; accessed August 8, 2017.

b. Vasja byl   spokojnym.
   Vasja was calm$_{\text{LONG.INSTR}}$
c. Vasja byl   spokojnyj.
   Vasja was calm$_{\text{LONG.NOM}}$

Crucially, in the linguistic literature, both instrumental predicates (15b) and short AP predicates (15a) have been associated with the stage-level interpretation. Indeed, the stage-level approach is quite prominent in the semantic analyses of short-form adjectives (see e.g. Vinogradov 1947 and Soschen 2002), even though here too, certain counterexamples can be found. One would thus expect (15a) and (15b) to have the same, temporary, interpretation, as opposed to (15c), which should ascribe a permanent property.

In reality, however, the situation is much more complex. All the sentences in (15) differ semantically from each other. Specifically, (15a) asserts that Vasja stayed calm in a particular situation. Here, the ascription of the property is linked to a certain event. This is indeed a prototypical stage-level interpretation. In contrast, both (15b) and (15c) are most likely to be interpreted as statements about Vasja's temperament. In other words, they receive a generic reading. The difference between the two is comparable to the one between (8b) and (9), discussed above. (15c) carries a lifetime effect: it contributes an implicature that Vasja is no longer alive (but while he was alive, he used to be a calm person). In contrast, (15b) asserts that Vasja had a calm temperament throughout a certain temporal interval, but his temperament may have changed since then. The sentence would thus be appropriate if Vasja used to be a calm man but then his character changed and he became irritable and hot-headed. (The change is, of course, not entailed, but such a context is perfectly compatible with the semantics of the sentence.)

The contrast illustrated in (15) raises questions regarding the semantic status of instrumental AP predicates. It is rather clear that the predicate in (15a) is stage-level and the one in (15c), individual-level. But what about (15b)? A more detailed investigation of the three-way distinction is required in order to gain a fuller understanding of both short-form adjectives and their long instrumental counterparts. Still, it is clear that the semantics of the latter does involve temporal delimitation.

7.1.2.2 *Part versus Whole and Relativization*

Geist (2006) does point out that while the individual-/stage-level distinction plays a role in the instrumental/nominative alternation, additional factors contribute to case selection as well. For instance, following Potebnja (1958), she states that the alternation may reflect a **part/ whole** (rather than temporary/permanent) opposition, in the sense that the instrumental predicate in (16) below "implies that the individual has further professions or occupations at the same time" (p. 99). In contrast, the predicate in (16b) "presents the property of being a singer as an exhaustive and identificational property of the person" (p. 100).

(16) a. Katja byla   pevicej.
          Katja was   singer$_{INST}$
          'Katja was a singer.'
      b. Katja byla   pevica
          Katja was   singer$_{NOM}$
          'Katja was a singer.'

                                                    (Geist 2006, ex. 1)

In other words, the semantic contrast between (16a) and (16b) need not be temporal in nature. It may rather be related to the fact that, intuitively, the first sentence only mentions one of Katja's properties, relating to one of the many facets of the subject. In contrast, in (16b), being a singer is taken to constitute the crucial property of the subject (almost a definition), which is sufficient for the purposes of identifying her in a given context.

A contrast between instrumental and nominative free adjuncts can be viewed in a similar way.

(17) a. Soldatom   Boris   ne   imel   žalosti.
          Soldier$_{INST}$ Boris   not   had   compassion
          'When Boris was a soldier he was not compassionate.'
      b. Soldat,   Boris   ne   imel   žalosti.
          Soldier$_{NOM}$ Boris   not   had   compassion
          'Being a soldier, Boris was not compassionate.'

                                                   (Geist 2006, ex. 26)

Geist points out that (17a) makes salient alternative situations in which Boris does not function as a soldier. Thus, again, being a soldier follows to be only one facet of the subject, and the content of the main clause is asserted to hold in those situations in which specifically this facet/role is relevant. (17b) does not contribute a similar delimitation. Note that this contrast may still be regarded as a temporal one: (17a) asserts lack of compassion in particular eventualities / at particular temporal intervals, whereas the statement in (17b) is more general. It is thus not always easy to distinguish between the temporary/permanent and the part/whole oppositions.

In fact, under Geist's analysis, drawing such a distinction is not really necessary. Geist draws a comparison between the case opposition in Russian and the contrast between the copulas *ser* and *estar* in Spanish. The latter, too, is known to be sensitive to the individual-/stage-level distinction, but the relevance of additional properties has been argued for as well. Building on Maienborn's (2005) analysis of the Spanish facts, Geist proposes that the instrumental case is selected when the speaker has in mind a specific discourse/topic situation relative to which the assertion is made. Such a situation could be defined as one that holds at a particular temporal interval but also, for example, as one in which the subject acts as a soldier (or as a singer). Nominative case-marking is, in contrast, semantically neutral: it is indeterminate as far as the specificity of the topic situation is concerned.

Actually, within the formal analysis put forward by Geist, the semantics of all sentences seems to involve topic situations, and it is not obvious in what way specific topic situations can be distinguished from non-specific ones (and in what sense a topic situation may, in general, be non-specific). According to Maienborn's (2005) analysis of the Spanish copulas, a crucial feature is a contrast between different topic situations. *Estar* is only possible as long as the property denoted by the predicate holds relative to the current topic situation as opposed to other topic situations in which it does not apply. Presumably, the same is required for instrumental case-assignment in Russian. While this issue still needs some further clarification, the important generalization holds: instrumental case indicates that predication is in some way **relativized**: to a time, situation, role of the subject, maybe even location or world (see Maienborn 2005: 171–172, Geist 2006: 100–103 for the relevance of the former for Spanish and the latter for Spanish and Russian). The nominative does not involve such a relativization.

7.1.2.3 *Predicational versus Identity Readings*

Additionally, the instrumental/nominative alternation has been associated with the contrast between predicational and so-called identity, or equative, readings of predicate nominal sentences. The distinction between these two types of interpretation, based on Higgins' (1973) classification, is illustrated in (18):

(18) a. John is a doctor.
     b. Zorro is don Diego de la Vega.

In (18a), a certain property is ascribed to the subject. This is a property of being a doctor, the one contributed by the predicative complement. Crucially, this nominal is not referential; rather, it denotes a property and is therefore of the semantic type <e,t>. The meaning of (18b) is somewhat different. This sentence contains two referential DPs, each of which picks up a particular individual in the world. The clause further specifies that the referents of these two phrases are identical. Thus, we do not get a predicate-argument relation in (18b). None of the nominals is property-denoting. In contrast to *a doctor*, *don Diego de la Vega* is a proper name of type <e>. The same holds of the subject *Zorro*.

In fact, originally, Higgins (1973) divided copular sentences into four classes, of which predicational and identity sentences form only a half. The two remaining types are specificational and identificational sentences, illustrated in (19a) and (19b) respectively:

(19) a. The lead actress in that movie is Ingrid Bergman.
          (Mikkelsen 2005:1)
      b. That man is John.

Each type has received considerable attention in the linguistic literature, and different ways of grouping some of the classes together have been put forward (see e.g. Higgins 1973, Heycock and Kroch 1999, Moro 1997, 2000, Partee 1999, Adger and Ramchand 2003, Mikkelsen 2004, 2005, den Dikken 2006). A detailed discussion of this topic falls beyond the scope of the present book, however. Crucially for our purposes, Citko (2008) shows that as far as the distinction between the verbal and the pronominal copula in Polish (or the corresponding instrumental/nominative distinction) is concerned, identity, specificational and identificational sentences exhibit the same behavior. Therefore, following some of the literature on the Slavic predicate case alternation, I will concentrate below on the contrast between predicational sentences on the one hand and identity/equative ones, on the other.

It has been proposed that, in both Russian and Polish, the contrast between these two types of copular clauses affects predicate case. Citko (2008) demonstrates that all types of sentences except for predicational ones require a pronominal copula (and, thus, contain a nominative predicate). In contrast, predicational sentences are compatible with both types on copulas and cases, although the verbal copula and (correspondingly) the instrumental case are more likely.

Pereltsvaig (2001, 2007) proposes that in Russian, copular clauses with a nominative predicate receive an identity interpretation, whereas their instrumental counterparts are predicational and involve an ascription of a property to the subject. Her approach receives substantial support from syntactic data. Pereltsvaig analyzes nominative predicates as DPs and instrumental ones as NPs (or APs), and provides independent and convincing evidence in favor of this claim. Naturally, NPs, which lack a DP projection, will not be interpreted as referential and will rather denote properties. Consequently, we expect them to appear in predicational sentences. In contrast, full DPs can be referential and are thus appropriate in identity clauses.

In turn, it follows from Matushansky (2000) that predicational sentences can co-occur with both case patterns. Matushansky states explicitly that in her paper she concentrates on predicational sentences only. Crucially, this paper does relate to both nominative and instrumental predicates. This is in line with Citko's conclusion for Polish.

It is worth noting that, according to Matushansky, the instrumental constitutes the default case in past and future sentences (recall that the situation with the present tense is different in Russian since, in the absence of an overt verbal copula, only nominative marking is licensed). Matushansky claims that in the past, the nominative case is highly restricted and in the future, almost ungrammatical.

Turning to another relevant similarity to Polish, even in Russian, which in principle allows predicate nominal sentences without an overt copula (see (4) above), the identity reading typically requires the pronominal copula *éto* (20). (Cf. e.g. Geist (2007) who claims that *éto* is required in equative (identity) sentences but disallowed in predicational ones.) And since the pronominal copula requires a nominative predicate, the correlation between nominative case and identity readings naturally follows. A question emerges, however, as to whether the link between case and interpretation is direct or rather mediated via the presence of a pronominal copula (in both Russian and Polish).

(20) Zorro *(éto) don Diego de la Vega.
　　 Zorro this don Diego de la Vega
　　 'Zorro is don Diego de la Vega.'

It seems that we can conclude quite safely that identity sentences indeed require nominative predicates. But what about predicational ones? Recall that Citko reports their compatibility with both verbal and pronominal copulas, and Matushansky discusses both instrumental and nominative predicates in their context. Indeed, consider again the Russian minimal pair below. In both sentences, the predicative nominal can be interpreted as a property of being a good doctor (not as referring to a particular good doctor). Thus, both sentences are presumably predicational, despite the difference in case.

(21) a. Dima   byl   xorošim   vračom.
         Dima   was   good$_{INSTR}$ doctor$_{INSTR}$
         'Dima was a good doctor.'
      b. Dima   byl   xorošij   vrač.
         Dima   was   good$_{NOM}$ doctor$_{NOM}$
         'Dima was a good doctor.'

Recall, however, that such sentences as (21b), a repetition of (3), (i) exhibit lifetime effects and (ii) have an exhaustive flavor in the sense that the property specified in such a clause seems to be sufficient for the purposes of identifying the subject in the current context. These characteristics make sentences with nominative predicates closer to identity-type clauses, even though, strictly speaking, their predicate seems to be property-denoting. Thus, one's definition of identity/equative copular clauses is crucial for the purposes of deciding whether (non-present[3]) sentences with nominative predicates only tend to be equative or are obligatorily equative. If the definition is sufficiently flexible to cover examples like (21b), then the latter is the case. If, however, one goes for a more classical and conservative definition, then (21b) is not equative but predicational and, thus, nominative case-marking is compatible with predicational copular clauses.

DISCUSSION

In what way(s) – if any – is the individual-level/stage-level distinction related to the identity/predicational opposition?

7.1.3 Two Types of Small Clauses

Most analyses that have been proposed for the instrumental/nominative alternation concentrate on the syntax and the syntax–semantics interface of the phenomenon. It is generally agreed that the nominal predicates appear in small clauses (SCs) but the case a given predicate receives depends on the type of SC involved. In such languages as Russian and Polish, copular sentences may contain two types of SCs, one of which is, roughly speaking, deficient in some sense or other.

---

[3] In the present tense, the instrumental case is unavailable, and the nominative is assigned independently of semantic nuances.

Due to this deficiency, instrumental case cannot be checked inside this clause, and the predicate has to receive nominative case by agreement instead.

Details regarding the nature of such clauses vary across analyses. Pereltsvaig (2001, 2007) proposes that the deficient SC is bare, or symmetric: it does not contain a head; rather, the subject and the predicate combine together to form the SC (see Moro 1997 and 2000 for a discussion of such SCs in copular sentences). In contrast, the second type of SC is a projection of a functional head, specifically, little v. The predicate functions as its complement and the subject as the specifier. Matushansky (2000), too, proposes that the "instrumental" clauses involve an extra functional layer. However, she takes both types of SC to be asymmetric, constituting a projection of a (phonologically null) s head. The predicate is its complement and the subject, the specifier. But clauses with instrumental predicates contain an additional functional layer above sP, specifically, Asp(ect)P. In turn, Citko (2008), who analyzes Polish copular sentences, proposes that both types of SC contain the same amount of functional structure. Both are asymmetric and contain a predicational head π (a structure proposed by Adger and Ramchand 2003), but in sentences with the pronominal copula (and a nominative predicate), this head is deficient.

In addition to disallowing instrumental case-checking, the deficient nature of the "nominative" SC has certain interpretational consequences. Again, details depend on the specific analysis. For instance, in the absence of the Asp head, it becomes impossible to temporally delimit the predication relation or make it event-linked, which results in an individual-level reading. According to Citko, the defective π head does not have an event variable. Thus, such a variable can appear in a SC only by the presence of the complete π, in which instance the predicate is instrumental. This, in turn, rules out stage-level readings of clauses with nominative predicates.

7.1.4 Instrumental versus Nominative: A Summary

To sum up the discussion of the instrumental/nominative alternation, instrumental predicates (as well as free adjuncts) have been associated with temporally delimited or otherwise restricted and relativized interpretation. Further, copular sentences with instrumental nominals belong to the predicational type under Higgins' (1973) classification. The instrumental phrases check their case in a small clause that contains an appropriate functional projection. In contrast, nominative predicates appear in small clauses that are in some sense deficient and are strongly associated with individual-level, non-relativized, identity readings. In addition, Pereltsvaig (2001, 2007) proposes that in Russian, the instrumental nominals are syntactically NPs (which makes them natural predicates), whereas their nominative counterparts are full DPs (which makes it possible for them to receive a referential interpretation).

7.2 URALIC LANGUAGES AND THE ESSIVE

The distribution of the Uralic essive case is not identical to that of the Slavic predicate instrumental; however, considerable overlaps and semantic parallels can be noticed. The essive is found in both Finno-Ugric (e.g. Finnish, Hungarian, Votic, Estonian, Saami) and Samoyedic languages (e.g. Forest Enets, Tundra Enets, Nganasan, Selkup) (see de Groot 2017 for a longer list). The examples below are from Finnish, unless specified otherwise.

The essive is particularly famous as a case of temporary properties, that is, it is strongly associated with stage-level predication (see e.g. Niemi 1945, Salminen 2002, Fong 2003, de Groot 2017). Thus, (22a) below reports that Matti is temporarily sick (e.g. has a flu), whereas (22b), in which the predicate is nominative (plausible, just as in Slavic, by agreement with the subject), suggests that his sickness is permanent.

(22) a. Matti   on   sairaana.
        Matti$_{NOM}$ is   sick$_{ESS}$
        'Matti is sick.'
     b. Matti   on   sairas.
        Matti$_{NOM}$ is   sick$_{NOM}$
        'Matti is sick.'

A somewhat more complex example in (23) is taken from Salminen (2002:299).

(23) a. Hän   on   pappi.
        (S)he   is   minister$_{NOM}$
        '(S)he is a minister [by profession, a permanent state or quality].'
     b. Hän   on   pappina   Helsingissä.
        (S)he is   minister$_{ESS}$ Helsinki$_{INESS}$
        '(S)he works as a minister in Helsinki; (S)he holds the office of a minister in Helsinki [at the moment; it may not be permanent].'

Thus, while (23a) reports a profession of the subject (a permanent, individual-level property), (23b) relates to a temporary post. Examples from additional languages are provided in (24):

(24) a. VOTIC
      Minu   sisarə   on   terven.
      1.SG   sister   is   healthy$_{ESS}$
      'My sister is healthy (at the moment).'
   b. KARELIAN
      Tuatto   on   voimattomannu.
      Father   is   powerless$_{ESS}$
      'Father is sick/weak' (at the moment).'

                                         (from de Groot 2017:3)

As with the instrumental in Russian, the syntactic distribution of the essive nominals is not limited to the predicate position of basic copular sentences. The essive is also found, for example, on secondary predicates and free adjuncts:

(25) a. Pidän   katuja   puhtaina.
      Keep$_{1.SG}$ street$_{PL.PART}$ clean$_{PL.ESS}$
      'I am keeping the streets clean.'   (based on Hynönen 2017:43)
   b. Pidin   lapsena   sarjakuvista.
      Liked$_{1.SG}$ child$_{ESS}$ comic$_{PL.EL}$
      'I liked comics as a child.'   (Hynönen 2017:42)[4]

Further, quite similarly to the Russian instrumental, the Finnish essive is not restricted to temporal uses. It is also found in additional contexts in which relativization of some kind or other is salient. For instance, consider the use of the essive in (26), taken from Niemi (1945):

(26) Veljeni   on   säveltäjänä   ainutlaatuinen.
     my.brother   is   composer$_{ESS}$ unique
     'As a composer my brother is unique.'

The sentence reports that the subject is unique specifically as a composer, but possibly not in other respects. Here, it is not temporality that is in focus (being a composer may very well constitute a permanent profession of the subject, even an inherent part of his personality). Rather, the essive is chosen due to the fact that a particular role, or facet, of the subject (rather than the individual in general, as a whole) is described. In this respect, (26) resembles the Russian example in (17a).

---

[4] Within Hynönen's terminology, (25a) and (25b) illustrate an essive predicative complement and an essive temporal secondary predicate, respectively.

238   7 PREDICATE CASE

Yet another example in which the use of essive is not temporal in nature is provided below:

(27) Opettajana   minulla   on   pitkät   kesälomat.
      Teacher$_{ESS}$ I$_{ADESS}$ is   long$_{NOM.PL}$ summer.holiday$_{NOM.PL}$
      'As a teacher, I have long summer holidays.'
                                              (from Hynönen 2017:40)

Hynönen (2017) points out that the sentence above has two readings. First, it can be understood as expressing a causative relation: the speaker has long holidays **because** she is a teacher. This resembles the Russian example (13b) above, in which an instrumental expression is used in a similar way. Under this use, essive phrases are referred to by Hynönen as circumstantial secondary predicates.

Second, (27) may involve a comparison of distinct (but simultaneous) roles of the subject. For instance, the subject has long holidays as a teacher but short holidays as a part-time clerk (Hynönen 2017:41). Under this reading, it resembles (26) above. This reading accompanies a depictive use of the Finnish essive, under which the phrase "expresses a state of a controller that is valid for the predication expressed by the clause" (p. 39).

In addition, Salminen (2002) demonstrates that the use of the essive can be motivated by the presence of salient modal alternatives. The predication relation holds in one salient possible world but (possibly) not in another. On a more intuitive level, different views of reality are contrasted. This is illustrated in (28), taken from Salminen (2002:299):

(28) Ostin   Helmen   aitona.
      I.bought   pearl$_{ACC}$ genuine$_{ESS}$
      'I bought the pearl as genuine = I bought the pearl thinking it was genuine [but later found out that it was not].'

Of course, Salminen points out, the genuineness of the pearl does not change from situation to situation. Thus, we are not dealing with a stage-level property. Rather, the essive in (28) indicates relativization to the subject's worldview at the time of the event. Thus, the world (or, more precisely, the set of worlds) that conforms to the subject's beliefs at the event time is contrasted with the actual world as it is (or else with the speaker's (=subject's) worldview at the speech time, after (s) he has been undeceived). In the former, the pearl is genuine, but in the latter, it is not.

Semantically, this use is apparently interrelated with the complex converbal quasi-construction, which "expresses a pretended state or action" (Hynönen 2017:38). It contains a morphologically complex participle which, among other suffixes, includes an essive one:

(29) Anna on   olevinaan   tietämätön.
      Anna is   be~PTCP-PRES.PL.**ESS**.3.POSS~   uninformed
      'Anna is pretending to be uninformed.'

                                                    (from Hynönen 2017:38)

According to Salminen (2002), this construction, too, involves an opposition between different possible worlds.

To sum up, similarly to the Slavic instrumental, the essive case appears on predicates when the property ascription is in some sense relativized, whether to a temporal interval, a facet/role of the argument, or a specific possible world.

7.3 TRANSLATIVE CASE AND THE NOTION OF CHANGE

7.3.1 Translative Case: Changing and Remaining

Yet another case in which nominal predicates may appear in such Finno-Ugric languages as Finnish, Hungarian and Estonian is **translative**. It is morphologically realized as the suffix -*ksi* in Finnish and -*vá/vé* in Hungarian. Semantically, translative is strongly related to the notion of change (see e.g. Holmberg and Nikanne 1993, Fong 2003, Matushansky 2008 and references therein). Thus, it marks the predicative complements of such change-denoting verbs as *tulla* 'become' and *muuttua* 'change', 'turn (into)' (30), the second (result state-denoting) complement of the causative variant *muuttaa* 'change' (31) and the nominal predicates in resultative constructions (32).

(30) a. Toini tuli   sairaaksi.
          Toini become~PST.3.SG~   ill~TRA~
          'Toini became ill.'   (Fong 2003, ex. 5)

      b. Hän   muuttui   (toukasta)   perhoseksi.
          s/he   change~PST.3.SG~ caterpillar~ELA~   butterfly~TRA~
          'S/he changed (from a caterpillar) into a butterfly.'
                                                   (Fong 2003, ex. 6)

(31) Taikuri   muutti   perhosen   toukaksi.
      magician   change~PST.3.SG~ butterfly   caterpillar~TRA~
      'The magician changed a/the butterfly into a caterpillar.'
                                                   (Fong 2003, ex. 8)

(32)   Ravistin   maton   puhtaaksi.
       Shake$_{PST.1.SG}$ carpet   clean$_{TRA}$
       'I shook a/the carpet clean.'   (Fong 2003, ex. 10)

To illustrate, (30a) denotes a change from not being sick to having this
property. In (31), a butterfly is changed into a caterpillar, and in (32),
the carpet acquires the property of being clean. In all these instances,
the translative marks the adjectival/nominal phrase that denotes the
new, acquired, property.

The generalization regarding the distribution of translative case
thus seems to be simple. However, as Fong (2003) demonstrates, at
least in Finnish, facts are more complicated. Thus, translative is
assigned to predicative complements of the verbs *jäädä* 'remain' and
jättää 'leave':

(33)   Kivi   jäi   vanhaksipojaksi.
       Kivi   remain$_{PST.3.SG}$ old$_{TRA}$-boy$_{TRA}$
       'Kivi remained a bachelor.'   (Fong 2003, ex. 45)

(34)   Lasi   oli   tyhjä.   Jätin   lasin   tyhjäksi.
       glass be$_{PST.3.SG}$ empty   leave$_{PST.1.SG}$ glass   empty$_{TRA}$
       'The glass was empty. I left it empty.'   (Fong 2003, ex. 18)

Crucially, neither (33) nor (34) entails a change of state. Quite the
opposite, (33) is likely to be uttered about an individual who was
a bachelor originally and remained one (i.e. did not get married);
analogously, in (34), the first clause explicitly specifies that the state
of being empty held of the glass originally. In other words, both
examples relate to **an absence of change**. Still, translative case is
possible and even obligatory.

It is worth noting that the verbs in question are also compatible
with a scenario in which a change did take place. For instance,
the second sentence in (34) could be uttered in a context in which
the glass was originally full and the speaker drank the liquid, thereby
leaving the glass empty. In this case, a change from fullness to empti-
ness does take place. But, crucially, such a context is not obligatory in
order for the translative to be licensed. Both the verbs and the translative are perfectly compatible with a no-change context.

In order to pinpoint the special semantic properties of *jäädä*
'remain', Fong compares it to the superficially synonymous verb
pysyä, which, too, can be translated as 'remain', or 'stay'. The nominal
complement of this verb is essive rather than translative. Thus, (33)
minimally contrasts with (35), which is ungrammatical.

(35) *Kivi   pysyi   vanhaksipojaksi.
     Kivi   remain$_{PST.3.SG}$ old$_{TRA}$-boy$_{TRA}$
     'Kivi remained a bachelor.'   (based on Fong 2003, ex. 36)

The acceptable version will be (36), in which the complement is marked with essive:

(36) Kivi   pysyi   vanhanapojana.
     Kivi   remain$_{PST.3.SG}$ old$_{ESS}$-boy$_{ESS}$
     'Kivi remained a bachelor.'   (based on Fong 2003, ex. 36)

The case requirements of the two verbs do not constitute a purely accidental idiosyncratic contrast; rather, they correlate with a semantic difference. Thus, (33), the *jäädä* variant, strongly suggests that Kivi was willing to get married, but for some reason, due to certain circumstances, he did not succeed in doing so – and, thus, remained a bachelor. The *pysyä* variant in (36) does not carry such an implication. It merely specifies that a certain state continued holding. An additional and plausibly related difference has to do with the fact that *pysyä*, unlike *jäädä*, is not compatible with a change context. This is illustrated by the following contrast:

(37) Nevan   suu   jäi   Täyssinän   rauhassa
     Neva$_{GEN}$ mouth   remain$_{PST.3.SG}$ Täyssinä$_{GEN}$ treaty$_{INESS}$
     venäläisille.
     Russian$_{PL.ALL}$
     (i) 'In the treaty of Täyssinä, the mouth of the Neva remained in the possession of the Russians.' (There was no change of hands.)
     (ii) 'In the treaty of Täyssinä, the mouth of the Neva went to the Russians.' (The mouth of the Neva changed hands.)
                                                    (Fong 2003, ex. 37)

(38) Nevan   suu   pysyi   Täyssinän   rauhassa
     Neva$_{GEN}$ mouth   stay$_{PST.3.SG}$ Täyssinä$_{GEN}$ treaty$_{INESS}$
     venäläisillä.
     Russian$_{PL.ADESS}$
     'In the treaty of Täyssinä, the mouth of the Neva stayed in the possession of the Russians.' (There was no change of hands.)
                                                    (Fong 2003, ex. 38)

While (37) is ambiguous between a change and no-change context, (38) is not. (37) may mean either that the mouth of the Neva passed to the Russians as a result of the treaty, or that it was Russian and stayed Russian. (38) is only compatible with the latter kind of interpretation. But even if there is no change in hands, there is a (fine) difference in the meanings of (37) and (38). The former suggests that there was a chance of a change taking place (specifically, the mouth of the Neva could be taken away from the Russians). Maybe the issue was disputed and a change of hands was plausible at some stage. (38) does not require this kind of scenario.

Potentially, the distribution of the translative could be accounted for within the framework of a modal analysis which would link this case to the notion of change realized in a certain (set of) world(s), not necessarily w_0. Essentially, this approach is taken by Fong (2003), although she does not mention modality explicitly. She argues that even *jäädä*-sentences involve a change, whether entailed or presupposed, real or unrealized. Formally, for instances like (33), (34) and (37i), one could define a set of possible worlds which differ from the actual one and represent, for example, the desire state of Kivi or the expectation state of the speaker. A change (e.g. from being a bachelor to being married) is implied to take place in these worlds, which, in turn, is sufficient to license translative case-marking.

One potential problem of this analysis has to do with its vagueness, as the relevant set of worlds will probably be very difficult to define in a relatively precise way. However, an even more immediate problem that we face has to do with the **direction of change**. Taking P to be the predicate denoted by the translative-taking phrase, the change in sentences like (30–32) is **from not-P to P**. For instance, in (30a), this is a change from not being sick to being sick. In contrast, the potential/ expected/desired change in sentences of the (33) and (34) type is **from P to not-P**. Thus, according to (33), Kivi remained a bachelor but he was willing/expected to get married, that is, the unrealized change is one from having the property denoted by the predicate to lacking it (one of stopping being a bachelor). An analogous contrast can be observed between the two readings of (37). Under the (37i) reading, we are dealing with a non-instantiated change from being in the possession of the Russians to being in somebody else's possession. In turn, (37ii) asserts an actual change from belonging to a different country to belonging to the Russians.

Thus, under the modal view, translative case turns out to be compatible with a change in either direction. This leads Fong to state that in its semantics, "the exact ordering of phases in the diphasic structure is left unspecified. The ordering of phases could be not-P<P or P<not-P [. . .] depending on the event structure as determined by the verb and its arguments" (p. 17). However, it remains somewhat unclear how the direction of change is determined in each particular case. For instance, why cannot (30a), repeated below as (39), mean that Toini recovered from sickness? In other words, why doesn't it have a reading

according to which the subject underwent a change from sickness to non-sickness? If the translative is equally compatible with a shift from not-P to P and one from P to not-P, we would expect (39) to be ambiguous. It would assert that Toini either got sick or got healthy. Nothing in the lexical semantics of the individual words that appear in the sentence seems to rule out the second interpretation. Still, it is unavailable.

(39) Toini tuli   sairaaksi.
      Toini become$_{PST.3.SG}$ ill$_{TRA}$
      'Toini became ill.'   (Fong 2003, ex. 5)

The absence of direction-based ambiguity in (39) (as well as in all the examples in 30–32) suggests that translative case is, after all, sensitive to the temporal ordering of P and not-P.

In the remainder of this chapter, I discuss an alternative account of the semantics of the translative case in Finnish. But first, I would like to show that the puzzle demonstrated above is not peculiar to translative marking or specifically to the interaction of the translative and *jäädä*. Rather, we are dealing with a more general phenomenon that has to do with cases associated with the notion of change. Specifically, similar properties are observed with 'goal' cases, illative and allative.

Illative and allative are the two Finnish spatial cases associated with the thematic role of a goal. Illative is an internal directional case (roughly, one corresponding to the meaning of *into*), and allative is an external directional case (*onto*). (See Chapter 3 for a detailed discussion of spatial cases.) Their use is illustrated in (40):

(40) a. Hiiri   juoksi   laatikkoon.
         mouse   ran   box$_{ILL}$
         'A/The mouse ran into the box.'
      b. Hiiri   juoksi   laatikolle.
         mouse   ran   box$_{ALL}$
         'A/The mouse ran onto the box.'

The notion of goalhood is, of course, strongly associated with change. Specifically, this is a particular kind of change: change of location. At the beginning of the event the argument that undergoes motion does not occupy the location denoted by the goal phrase. At the endpoint of the event, it does. Thus, here, too, we are dealing with a kind of change from not-P to P, for example, in (40a), one from not being inside the box to being inside it.

These cases are compatible with such verbs as *laittaa* 'put', *tulla* 'come', *ajaa* 'drive', *juosta* 'run', *mennä* 'walk', etc. But, crucially, they are also found on locational complements of the verb *jäädä* 'remain':

(41) a. Jäin   **kaupunkiin.**
        remained₁.ₛɢ townᵢₗₗ
        'I stayed in town.' (Literally: I stayed to town.)
     b. Merimiehen ei   tarvitse jäädä **merelle**   yksin.
        seaman   NEG.3.SG need   remain seaₐₗₗ   alone
        'A seaman doesn't have to stay at sea alone.'[5]

The sentences in (41) do not entail a change of location; quite the opposite, they assert that such a change did not take place. Still, in both instances, 'goal' cases are used. This state of affairs is, of course, reminiscent of what we have observed with the translative.

The similarity extends further. Once again, *jäädä* differs from the superficially synonymous *pysyä* 'remain'. The latter, more predictably, combines with expressions that appear in local cases, inessive (internal) and adessive (external). These cases correspond to the thematic role of location rather than goal, and can be roughly translated as the English prepositions *in* and *on* (under their locative use).

(42) a. Pysyin   **kaupungissa.**
        remained₁ₛɢ townᵢₙₑₛₛ
        'I stayed in town.'
     b. Merimiehen ei   tarvitse pysyä **merella**   yksin.
        seaman   NEG.3.SG need   remain seaₐᴅₑₛₛ   alone
        'A seaman doesn't have to stay at sea alone.'

Once again, the intuitive difference between sentences with the two verbs has to do with the potential dynamicity of the situation. According to native speakers of Finnish, *jäädä*-sentences create a feeling that the subject was likely to leave the place denoted by the illative/allative DP but, ultimately, stayed there. In contrast, *pysyä*-examples merely assert that a certain locational relation continued to hold.

Here, too, a modal account of "cases of change" (this time – goal cases) is tempting: the illative and allative are licensed as soon as a change of location event takes place in some salient possible world, which does not have to be the actual one. However, now the problem of such an analysis becomes even more striking than with translative case. Just as with the translative, the goal cases are

[5] https://issuu.com/espanjansanomat/docs/es120/4; accessed March 11, 2017.

normally associated with a change from not-P to P (i.e. one whereby the argument comes to occupy the location in question). With *jäädä*, in contrast, the hypothetical change is from P to not-P (e.g. the subject of (41a) was presumably expected to leave the town). But while the translative could in principle be associated with a change in either direction, with the spatial cases this is totally unjustified. Once the (potential) change is from P to not-P, namely, from occupying the location to not occupying it, the location in question is no longer a goal. Rather, it is **a source**. And sources receive different cases in Finnish, specifically, elative and ablative. Thus, if the local case in (41a) reflected the motion away from the town, which was expected but remained non-instantiated in reality, we would predict the noun to appear in the elative form, *kaupungista* 'from the town', and not in the illative as we observe.

To sum up thus far, illative and allative constitute two additional "change cases," which, similarly, to the translative, are compatible with *jäädä* 'remain', thereby challenging an account that is based on the notion of change. In the next section, an approach is put forward that captures the facts described above without assuming that the semantics of *jäädä*-sentences involves alternative possible worlds.

7.3.2 A Force-Dynamic Analysis

Kagan (2019, in progress) proposes that cases of change are sensitive not to the notion of change per se but rather to an inherent component of change: energy being exerted for the purposes of the P-state to hold. In what follows, I concentrate on translative case, but see Kagan (2019, in progress) for an analysis of illative and allative along the same lines (which treats these cases as not strictly those of goal, contrary to the assumption made in Chapter 3).[6]

The intuition behind the proposed account is as follows. Sentences with "cases of change," whether with telic predicates (43a) or with *jäädä* (43b), imply that energy is exerted in order for the P-state (the one denoted by the translative/illative/allative expression) to hold.

(43) a. Hän   muuttui   (toukasta)   perhoseksi.
        s/he   change$_{PST.3.SG}$ caterpillar$_{ELA}$ butterfly$_{TRA}$
        'S/he changed (from a caterpillar) into a butterfly.'
                                                    (Fong 2003, ex. 6)

---

[6] See also Svenonius (2012) for an analysis which treats North Sámi illative not as a goal case but rather as a case of location assigned under conditions related to the semantics of change. Specifically, it marks a nominal which specifies the place occupied by the theme at the endpoint of an event of change.

b. Kivi   jäi   vanhaksipojaksi.
Kivi   remain $_{PST.3.SG}$ old$_{TRA}$-boy$_{TRA}$
'Kivi remained a bachelor.'   (Fong 2003, ex. 45)

In (43a), the energy is required in order for an event of change (from
a caterpillar state to a butterfly state) to take place. In (43b), the energy
is required in order for the state of bachelorhood **to keep holding**. As
pointed out above, the sentence implies that Kivi had a tendency
toward getting married, and energy had to be exerted in order for
this change NOT to take place, that is, in order for Kivi to remain in the
bachelor state. In other words, while a change takes place in (43a) but
not in (43b), energy, or dynamism, is needed in both instances in order
for the P-state to hold.

Here, Kagan follows Talmy's (2000) insight that the semantics of
such verbs as *stay*, *keep* and *remain* (unlike *be*) involves **force
dynamics**. The notion of force has played a substantial role in the
cognitive semantic literature of the last two decades and is also gain-
ing attention in formal semantics (see e.g. Talmy 2000, Wolff 2007,
Croft 2012, Copley and Harley 2015, Goldschmidt and Zwarts 2016).
Copley and Harley (2015) informally define force as "an input of
energy that arises from the objects and properties in a situation."
Roughly, with verbs of remaining, force is entailed to be exerted in
order for the situation to remain unchanged. This makes the above-
listed verbs more dynamic than classical statives. To illustrate, (44) is
compatible with a situation whereby the ball has a tendency to remain
in place, but the tendency is overcome by an external force acting on
it. Alternatively, the ball may, in fact, have a tendency to move which
is opposed by external factors, by stiff grass for, example. The sentence then asserts that the ball **overcomes**[7] these factors. Under both
types of scenario, force/energy is exerted in order for the rolling event
not to stop.

(44)   The ball kept (on) rolling along the green. (Talmy 2000:412)

Analogously to the first scenario, Kagan proposes, the use of *jäädä* in
(43b) suggests that Kivi has a tendency/desire to get married, but other
circumstances (for instance, girls saying "No") force him to remain in
the bachelor state. In other words, action/force/energy is needed for
the purposes of maintaining this state. This is what licenses (and even

---

[7] This notion of overcoming certain tendencies also plays an important role in
Goldschmidt and Zwarts' (2016) analysis of what they refer to as *force verbs*.

requires) translative case-marking.[8] In contrast, *pysyä* is purely stative. It implies no force or dynamics and is used merely to assert that no change of state took place.

More generally, "cases of change"-marking signals that force is exerted in order for the P-situation to hold (i.e. in order for the argument to have the property denoted by the case-marked predicate). This may happen in two types of situations. The prototypical case is one whereby originally, the argument lacks the property P and force is exerted in order for it to come to have this property. In other words, a change from not-P to P takes place. Naturally, this is the configuration that is most closely associated with both the translative and goal cases. However, another type of situations is compatible with the required configuration as well: ones in which force is exerted in order for the argument to remain in the state in question and NOT to undergo a change. This happens when a change is for some reason expected or natural, there is a tendency toward a change, and then force/energy exertion is needed in order to overcome this tendency. Such a configuration is signaled by *jäädä*, and this is why this verb is accompanied by a translative, illative or allative complement.

To summarize:

"Cases of change"-marking signals that force is exerted in order for the P-situation to hold. This happens in two types of situation:

(i)   A **change** from not-P to P takes place.
(ii) Energy is exerted in order for the argument to **remain** in the P-state.

Note that under this approach, the direction is never reversed as it is within the modal analysis. The force is always exerted in order for a P-situation to hold.

Kagan (2019, in progress) further proposes a semantic analysis of the phenomenon within the formal force-theoretic framework

---

[8] It may seem, on the basis of the above discussion, that *jäädä*-sentences involve a force exerted for the purposes of the P-situation being terminated, and not in order for it to keep holding. After all, (43b) suggests that Kivi wishes to get married and, presumably, takes some steps for this purpose. Quite plausibly, in many instances, this is indeed true: some force is present that could potentially bring about the not-P state (an intuition that lies at the basis of the modal account). But, crucially, if force f_1 is exerted toward not-P but P keeps holding, this means that there is also a force f_2 which overcomes f_1. There must be a "counter-force" which makes it possible for P to persist. It is, I argue, the presence of such a force (independently of the (non-)existence of f_1) that licenses those cases which we have originally conceived of as implying change.

developed by Copley and Harley (2015). Within this framework, forces are represented as functions from situations to situations, type <s,s>. The input is the original situation *s* (the **initial situation** of force *f*) and the output, a (potentially different) situation *s'* which is brought about by the exertion of **the net force** of *s* (the force that arises from all the individuals and properties in *s*). *s'* is referred to as the **final situation** of force *f*. Stage-level stative predicates, which are (truly) non-dynamic, are defined as predicates of situations of type <s,t>. In turn, dynamic predicates constitute predicates of forces and as such are of type <f,t>.

Following Copley and Harley's analysis of verbs of maintaining, such as *keep* and *stay*, and change-of-state predicates such as *opened* in *The door opened*, Kagan proposes the following condition on the licensing of the translative case in Finnish:

(45)   The nominal/adjectival predicate P (type <e,st>) will appear in translative case iff the sentence entails that
       ∃f [p(fin(f))]
       (where *p* is the predicate of situations that is obtained by applying P to its individual-type argument)

The translative is assigned when the final situation (e.g. the situation of Toini being sick or Kivi being a bachelor) is entailed to hold by virtue of force exertion. However, this case is indeterminate regarding the nature of the original (initial) situation: it could be a P-situation, as with *jäädä*, or a not-P-situation, as with, for example, *muuttua* '(undergo a) change'. For the sake of illustration, consider again the following sentences:

(46)   a. Toini   tuli   sairaaksi.
          Toini   become$_{PST.3.SG}$ ill$_{TRA}$
          'Toini became ill.'   (Fong 2003, ex. 5)
       b. Kivi   jäi   vanhaksipojaksi.
          Kivi   remain$_{PST.3.SG}$ old$_{TRA}$-boy$_{TRA}$
          'Kivi remained a bachelor.'

In (46a), the initial situation of the force is one whereby Toini is healthy. A change takes place, and the final situation of the force is one in which Toini is sick. Toini's sickness thus characterizes the final but not the initial situation of the force. But crucially for translative case licensing, there is a force at whose final situation Toini is sick.

In (46b), the state of affairs is somewhat different but the components crucial for the licensing of the translative are the same. Here, Kivi is a bachelor both at the initial and at the final situation of the force. But, importantly, the force is there, and it is due to this force that bachelorhood still holds of the subject at the final situation. There is a force at whose final situation Toini is a bachelor. Therefore, the translative is used.

As for the *jäädä/pysyä* contrast, Kagan proposes that while the former entails force exertion, the latter does not. For *jäädä*, Kagan adopts the analysis Copley and Harley (2015) put forward for *keep*:

(47) [[*jäädä*]] = λpλf. p(fin(f))
      presupposed: p(init(f))

A sentence with *jäädä* entails that a force f is exerted due to which p holds of the final situation of f. It further presupposes that p holds of the initial situation of f. For instance, (46b) above entails the existence of a force whose final situation is one of Kivi being a bachelor. In addition, it presupposes that the initial situation of this force is one whereby Kivi is a bachelor, too.

Crucially, sentences of this kind conform to the conditions specified in (45) above for the licensing of the translative case. This is why translative predicates are compatible with *jäädä*.

In contrast, the semantics of *pysyä* does not involve force. This is a function of type <st,st> (it takes a predicate of situations as an input and renders a predicate of situations as an output). The entailment part is quite simple: a p-situation s holds. In addition, the verb presupposes that the temporal trace of s begins before reference time (this captures its 'continuation' flavor):

(48) [[*pysyä*]] = λpλs. p(s)
      presupposed: $BEG(s) < τ(s_R)$
      where BEG is the function from situations to times that returns
      a situation's beginning point[9], and s_R is reference time.

Since the semantics of *pysyä* does not relate to forces, the verb predictably does not license the translative case.

The reader is referred to Kagan (2019) and Kagan (in progress) for further details of the formal analysis and for a force-dynamic account of additional uses of the translative, as well as of the spatial illative and allative cases.

---

[9] Based on the BEG function from events to times (see e.g. Kennedy and Levin 2002, Kagan 2015).

7.4 CONCLUSION

To conclude this chapter, case-marking on predicate nominals is sensitive to a number of semantic components. These include the individual-/ stage-level distinction and, more broadly, relativization of the predication relation to a particular event/time/situation/location/ possible world etc., as well as the partly related notion of change and/or force. Further, case is sensitive to the distinction between predicational and identity/equative sentences.

FURTHER READING

The volume *Uralic Essive and the Expression of Impermanent State* by Casper de Groot, published in 2017, constitutes a valuable resource on the intricacies of the syntax and semantics of the essive and the essive-translative case in different Uralic languages. It contains chapters devoted to the distribution and functions of this case in both widely studied and under-investigated languages, including Finnish, Hungarian, Mansi, Tundra Nenets, Nganasan and many others. For those languages in which the essive and the translative are represented by different forms (e.g. Finnish), the distinction between the two cases is addressed. In those languages which employ the same form for both functions (e.g. Mansi), the contrast between the essive and the translative senses is considered.

Pereltsvaig's (2007) book, based on her (2001) dissertation, puts forward a detailed syntactic analysis of the nominative/instrumental alternation on Russian predicates. The alternation is linked to the existence of two types of copular sentences (ones containing a symmetrical versus an asymmetrical small clause), as well as to the distinction between nominal phrases containing a different amount of functional structure (DPs versus NPs). The book also discusses additional uses of the instrumental case in Russian.

8   Generalizations and Conclusions

To sum up, in this book, we have discussed a range of phenomena within which case gets interrelated with meaning. We began, in Chapter 1, with a general discussion of case types, inventories and alternations, as well as the interdependence of case distinctions with theta-roles and theta features. Examples of the latter included, for instance, the relation between the ergative and agentivity/control/volitionality and the link between the instrumental and instrument/means/causation. Chapters 2–7 have addressed, respectively, the cross-linguistic intricacies of the dative, spatial cases, the relation between case and aspect, differential object marking, non-canonical genitive case in Balto-Slavic languages and, finally, a range of cases that mark nominal (and adjectival) predicates.

On the basis of the above discussion, case can be related to the following three semantic areas (broadly defined):

(i)   thematic roles and related concepts
(ii)   individuation
(iii) aspect and tense.

In (i), the notion of "related concepts" plays a significant role. Talking about thematic roles in the strict sense, the relation to case is illustrated, for example, by instrumental-marked instruments, ergative-marked agents and dative-marked goals, recipients and benefactives. However, as discussed above, it is the features into which thematic roles can be decomposed that play in certain instances a central role in case selection. Thus, the dative case is associated in some languages with the [+sentient, −cause] cluster and the ergative with the feature [+volition]. Moving on to the spatial domain, we can see that cases reflect such thematic roles as goal, source and location, but this is not the limit: local case systems are often sensitive to a whole range of partially related spatial concepts, including additional directionality specifications (e.g. TOWARDS), configuration and distality.

Area (i) is associated primarily with instances of inherent or lexical case; however, in some situations, the classification is not trivial. For example, the dative is treated as an inherent case by Woolford (2006) but as purely structural under those approaches that relate its assignment to some version of a VP-shell (along the lines of Larson 1988) or to the Appl(icative) head (Pylkkänen 2002/2008). Spatial cases can be analyzed as lexical (if they are assigned by phonologically empty adpositions) or semantic (if they are interpretable and contribute meaning of their own).

Turning to individuation (ii), this property affects a number of case alternations. We systematically observe its relevance in DOM, with animate, human, definite, specific and, in general, highly individuated objects being more likely to receive overt marking than less individuated ones. In the genitive/accusative alternation on objects, which can be viewed as an instance of symmetric DOM, individuation is crucial as well. Here, the genitive case marks property-denoting NPs that lack existential commitment. Prominence (including, e.g. the contrast between first- and second-person pronouns as opposed to third-person pronouns) also plays a role in differential subject marking (see Aissen 1999, de Swart 2003).

Finally, (iii) covers a whole range of phenomena involving the interaction of case with notions which are, in one way or another, sensitive to the tense/aspect characteristics of the clause. Most obviously, this includes the partitive case on Finnic objects and its alternation with the accusative (and also the related partitive/nominative alternation on subjects). Here, the partitive case correlates with unboundedness, atelicity and incompleteness, and the accusative, correspondingly, with boundedness, telicity and completion. The debate on which of the two cases is meaningful and which rather constitutes "the elsewhere option" is still going on in the recent linguistic literature.

However, the interrelation between case and aspect extends beyond Finnic languages. Cross-linguistically, adjuncts that provide an eventuality with a boundary tend to be realized as accusative nominals. Further, goals are arguments that often turn an atelic verbal predicate into a telic one, and the accusative case is linked to the goal interpretation of a complement of a preposition in certain Indo-European languages, such as German, Russian and Ancient Greek.

Leaving aside telicity and boundedness, the marking of nominal predicates and of subjects is sometimes sensitive to the individual-level / stage-level distinction or, more generally, to the relativization of the predication to a particular time/event/situation/world. Such notions, too, are sensitive to temporality and the aspectual characteristics of a clause. Also, translative case-assignment depends on such aspectually relevant concepts as change and dynamics. Further, the availability of the ergative case depends in some languages on verbal aspect (perfective versus imperfective).

Summarizing a range of phenomena discussed or briefly addressed in this book, we can list the following semantic correlates of various cases:

Accusative	–	boundedness, goalhood, individuation (in DOM)
Genitive	–	low individuation / property type, source[1]
Essive	–	stage-level / relativized predication
Instrumental	–	stage-level / relativized predication, instrumenthood, [+cause]
Dative	–	goalhood, [+sentient, –cause]
Ergative	–	agency, [+volition]
Translative	–	change / force dynamics
Comitative	–	accompaniment, togetherness
Illative	–	goalhood, internal
Allative	–	goalhood, external
Inessive	–	location, internal
Adessive	–	location, external
etc.		

This is not an exhaustive set: only a sample of spatial cases is provided above; further, the present study could not include *all* cases in *all* world languages that are interrelated with meaning in some way or other.

The relation that holds between case and meaning is often indirect; moreover, defining the nature of this relation is, in many instances, subject to theory-internal considerations. The semantic component associated with a particular marking may be contributed in different ways. Within the minimalist framework, we can define the following four types of contributors:

1. A lexical head, typically, V or P. As a rule, this is the head that is responsible for checking the case in question. To illustrate, consider the example in (1). As pointed out in Chapter 3, Russian source prepositions check genitive case on their complement. The source

---

[1] In fact, adnominal genitive observed in such expressions as *John's* in *John's book* can be analyzed as a purely structural DP-internal case or as a lexical/inherent case related to meaning. Indeed, Vainikka and Brattico (2014) argue for the existence of both types in Finnish.

meaning in such phrases as (1) is presumably contributed by the preposition.

(1) iz/   ot/   so   škafa
     from   away-from   down-from   wardrobe
     'out of / away from / from the top of the wardrobe'

2. A functional head. This view is taken, for example, in the analysis whereby non-core datives are checked by Appl. The benefactive/malefactive/affectedness meaning component is taken to be contributed to the truth conditions by the applicative head rather than by dative case-marking. Analogously, under those analyses that associate boundedness-related accusative with the Asp(ect)P projection, it is the Asp head that carries the corresponding aspectual meaning.

3. The (case-marked) DP. This is what we observe in DOM. The form of the object depends on individuation, which, in turn, depends on the characteristics of the DP itself. For instance, such properties as [+/–human] and [+/–animate] typically characterize the head already on the level of the lexicon.[2] (This is why Malchukov 2008:210 points out that "it is redundant to mark animacy *per se*.") Definiteness, in those languages whose DOM is sensitive to this feature, is often specified by an article (or is inherently present in proper names and pronouns). The state of affairs with specificity may seem less obvious: after all, it is often precisely case-marking that helps the hearer determine whether a specific or a non-specific reading is intended. Here, one could argue that specificity is contributed by the case-marker. (This view would be in line with de Swart 2007 and Klein and de Swart 2011, see Chapter 5.) Such an approach captures processing-related facts (the way in which the addressee gets the sentence interpreted) well and may account for the more general state of affairs in individual languages. However, from a cross-linguistic perspective, it is doubtful that specificity in DOM is contributed to truth conditions by the case-marker.[3] In many languages, DOM is sensitive not only to

---

[2] In fact, in Malayalam, inanimate objects appear in the accusative case when they denote fairy-tale characters and are thus personified (Egger 2016, de Swart and de Hoop 2018). Arguably, in this situation, case contributes animacy-related information that is not available otherwise (e.g. in the lexicon). However, it is also plausible that the animate-like nature of such objects is known from the context, and this shift, although reflected in case-marking, is not triggered by it.

[3] The facts discussed immediately below are still compatible with the view that a particular (e.g. specific) reading may, under certain circumstances, **result** from a given case-form in examples like (2b), as argued by de Swart 2007 and Klein and

specificity but also to additional properties, such as animacy. Consider, for example, the following sentences in Kannada:

(2)   a. naanu   **sekretari(*-yannu)**   huDuk-utt-idd-eene
          I_NOM   secretary-ACC   look.for-NPST-be-1SG
          'I am looking for a secretary.'
      b. naanu   **pustaka-vannu**   huDuk-utt-idd-eene
          I_NOM   book-ACC   look.for-NPST-be-1SG
          'I am looking for a book.'

(from Lidz 2006, ex. 1–2)

Note that in (2a), accusative marking is obligatory independently of whether the object takes wide or narrow scope. The examples in (2) reveal that in Kannada, both a **non-specific animate** object and a **specific inanimate** one can appear in the accusative. Thus, the accusative case requires/entails neither animacy nor specificity (Lidz 2006). It seems plausible that specificity is contributed by additional semantic and contextual factors, while the marking in examples like (2b) (or its absence) helps the addressee figure out whether a specific or a non-specific reading is involved. Thus, case-marking helps the addressee by contributing information as to which specificity value is available. We could say that accusative marking is sensitive to individuation in general, while the particular individuation-related features (such as animacy, specificity, etc.) characterize the DP for independent reasons, which could be lexical, grammatical or context-based. In the presence of such features, object marking surfaces, which, in turn, may help the addressee select the right (intended) reading.

Why would case reflect internal properties of the DP to which it attaches, if it is supposed to deal with the **relation** that holds between this DP and other elements in a sentence? As we know from Chapter 5, the state of affairs in DOM is somewhat more complex. Under the transitivity-based approach to this phenomenon, the individuation of the object contributes to the degree of clausal transitivity; thus, it can no longer be treated as a purely DP-internal property. Under the markedness approach, DOM reflects the non-prototypicality of the object and its relative similarity to a subject (recall that subjects tend to be more highly individuated). Thus, we are comparing the actual object to the prototypical one. We are also comparing it to the proto-typical subject. In fact, the comparison can even be to the actual

---

de Swart 2011. But, crucially, a specific reading is not **entailed** by the same form, as revealed by (2a), where the accusative does not trigger specificity.

subject. Thus, as pointed out by de Swart (2003), in some languages, DOM is sensitive not to the prominence of the object per se, but rather to the relative prominence of the object and the subject. This is reflected in (3) below. While normally, in Malayalam, inanimate objects remain caseless, the accusative is assigned in this example since the subject and the object do not differ in animacy.

(3) a. kappal   tiramaalakaḷe   bheediccu
         ship   wave$_{PL.ACC}$ split$_{PST}$
         'The ship broke through the waves.'
     b. tiramaalakaḷ kappaline   bheediccu
         wave$_{PL}$ ship$_{ACC}$ split$_{PST}$
         'The waves split the ship.'
                 (from Asher and Kumari 1997, quoted by de Swart 2003:32)

In other words, even though DOM reflects primarily the properties of the object DP, it does have a relational nature.

4. Finally, a semantic contribution can be made by the case-marker (e.g. case suffix) itself. The availability of this option is subject to debate, based largely on theory-internal considerations. The choice between assigning a particular meaning to a case-marker or to a silent functional head / phonologically null adposition is often difficult to make on the basis of empirical facts. Still, we have seen above that the complex spatial case system of Daghestanian languages is probably best accounted for if local cases are assumed to be meaningful.

If cases are allowed to be semantic, the next question would be where the boundary between interpretable and uninterpretable cases lies. Among the best candidates for truly semantic cases would be those that mark DP adjuncts, which do not receive a thematic role either from the verb or from a preposition. It is possible that in such instances, the semantic relation between such adjuncts and the remainder of the clause is indeed specified by the case-marker. In fact, as argued in Chapter 2, even the semantics of dative arguments cannot always be reduced to the theta-related requirements of the verb.

The question of the borderline between semantic and non-semantic cases is thus a very intricate one and depends substantially on theory-internal considerations. I leave further investigation of this issue to future research.

Terminology

A-movement – the movement of a phrase from one argument position to another (more precisely, to a subject position). Examples: movement from the object position to the subject positions in passive sentences, or movement from one subject position to another under raising.

Bouletic modality – the expression of necessity and possibility that is based on a person's desires.

Bounded, see boundedness

Boundedness – in the verbal domain, this is an aspectual notion strongly related to telicity and event delimitation. Sometimes, boundedness is used interchangeably with telicity. If the two terms are distinguished (as e.g. in Depraetere 1995 or Kearns 2011), boundedness can be conceptualized as a property of having temporal delimitation. A bounded event predicate would then encode an event that has a temporal endpoint, but this endpoint need not be inherent in the sense specified for telicity. For instance, the predicate *ran for fifteen minutes* is atelic but bounded. There is no inherent endpoint beyond which a running event cannot continue (and the presence of a temporal adjunct does not affect this fact). However, the prepositional phrase does provide the reported eventuality with temporal delimitation: an endpoint is there, even though it is not "inherent" or "natural" in the sense that is typically linked to telicity.

Case – the grammatical marking of a nominal that reflects its relation to other elements in the sentence. The concept of **morphological case** has to do with the morphological form of a nominal which varies depending on the position this nominal occupies in the sentence, the grammatical function it fulfills and/or the semantic role it receives. In turn, **abstract case** is applicable even to those languages that lack overt case morphology and constitutes a syntactic feature of a nominal phrase. Its checking is typically understood to be a crucial condition on the licensing of the nominal.

Case alternation – a phenomenon whereby a phrase can appear in two (or more) distinct case forms, while at least superficially it seems to occupy the same position in a sentence.

Case-checking – checking off the case feature of an NP (or DP). Case-checking takes place in the Spec(ifier)-head configuration.

Case Filter – a grammatical requirement stating that every overt NP must be assigned case or have its case feature checked.

Choice function – a function that applies to a non-empty set and selects a member of that set.

Configuration – a dimension that concerns the relative position of two objects in space. Examples of prepositions that express configuration are: *in, on, above, below*. Each of these prepositions specifies a particular spatial relation in which one entity (figure) is located relative to another entity (ground).

Configurational case – case whose assignment is determined by a purely syntactic configuration, with no dependence on semantic relations.

Cumulativity – an expression is cumulative iff as soon as it applies to two entities, it applies to their collection as well. For example, *water* is cumulative: a collection of two entities each of which can be described as *water* counts as water as well.

Degree achievements – verbs of gradual/scalar change, often derived from gradable adjectives, such as e.g. *widen, lengthen, cool*, etc. These verbs denote an increase that an argument undergoes along some scale. Crucially, the verbs are characterized a kind of aspectual ambiguity: they can be understood in a process/activity-like manner (a dynamic eventuality takes place which is not associated with any inherent end-point) or as accomplishments (the change is up to a particular degree, and the latter indicates a boundary beyond which the event cannot continue). Roughly, *cooled* may mean 'underwent a decrease in temperature (= an increase along the property of coolness)' (an activity reading) or "underwent a decrease up to the desirable temperature" (an accomplishment reading).

Degree of change – the degree that represents the difference undergone by an argument between the beginning and the endpoint of the event.

Deontic modality – an expression of necessity and possibility that is based on moral responsibilities or social norms. It deals with notions of obligation, permission and prohibition.

Directionality – a dimension that concerns a change of location; more specifically, the change in the relative position of the figure and the ground that takes place in the course of an event. In other words, directionality deals with a change of configuration over time. The most basic directionality specifications include *goal* (movement into a particular configuration), *source* (movement out of a particular configuration) and *location* (no change in terms of configuration).

Divisibility – an expression is divisible iff as soon as it applies to an entity, it applies to its proper part as well. For instance, a proper part of water is also water.

DOM (symmetric and asymmetric) – differential object marking, a phenomenon whereby the object of the verb can appear in different morphological forms, depending on its properties. Two kinds of DOM are distinguished, symmetric and asymmetric. Within symmetric DOM, the contrast is between two different morphologically realized cases, e.g. genitive versus accusative in Russian, or partitive versus accusative in Finnish. In turn, within asymmetric DOM, the object is either morphologically marked for case or remains unmarked. The term DOM is often used in the literature specifically for asymmetric DOM; this approach is followed in the present book.

Downward-entailing environment – an environment in which the entailment relation holds from a superset to a subset. For instance, the negative operator creates a downward-entailing environment. As a result, *John didn't buy apples* entails *John didn't buy green apples* (where *green apples* form a subset of *apples*). In contrast, in an upward-entailing environment, a reverse entailment relation (from a subset to a superset) holds. For instance, *John bought green apples* entails *John bought apples*.

D-structure (deep structure) – within transformational generative grammar, the original structure of a sentence before any movement takes place. Deep structure reflects thematic relations.

Epistemic modality – the expression of necessity and possibility that is based on one's knowledge or beliefs.

Epistemic specificity – specificity that is based on the concept of knowledge: the referent of a DP is specific because it is identified by the speaker (or, possibly, by some other salient individual).

Event-delimiting adjuncts – adjuncts that apply to an atelic or unbounded event predicate and turn it into one that is bounded or temporally delimited.

Existential closure – a default semantic operation that existentially binds any variable within its domain if it does not get bound by another operator.

Existential commitment (EC) – an entailment or presupposition that a nominal phrase has a referent or quantifies over a non-empty set.

Extensive-measure functions – measures characterized by the property of additivity.

Figure – the entity whose location is being communicated or which undergoes a change of location.

Force – an input of energy that can affect a patient and/or induce a change.

Free adjunct – defined by Stump (1985) as a non-finite predicative phrase with the function of an adverbial subordinate clause. For example: **As a soldier**, Boris knew no pity.

Genitive of Negation (GenNeg) – a phenomenon observed in Slavic and Baltic languages, whereby an internal argument of the verb, normally marked nominative or accusative, appears in the genitive case under sentential negation. The genitive marking is obligatory for some languages and grammatical functions (e.g. Polish objects) and optional for others (e.g. Russian objects).

Gradable adjectives – adjectives that denote a property which holds of different individuals to different degrees. A classic example is the adjective *tall*: different individuals are characterized by different degrees of tallness.

Gradual change verbs – verbs that denote a change in their argument that takes place along some scale.

Ground – the entity relative to which the location of the figure is specified, the entity that is used in order to help locate the figure.

Heterogeneous – a heterogeneous expression is not homogeneous.

Homogeneous – within the nominal domain, an expression is homogeneous if when it applies to two non-overlapping entities, it also applies to their sum, and when it applies to an entity, it also applies to its proper part. Homogeneous predicates are thus cumulative and divisive. Homogeneity applies analogously in the verbal domain: for instance, two running events together constitute a running event, and a proper part of a single running event is a running event, too.

Imperfective, see perfective

Incremental theme verbs – verbs whose internal argument undergoes an incremental change over the course of the event, and there is a homomorphic relation between the progress of the event and the change in the argument. To illustrate, in the VP *eat an apple*, the object is an incremental theme argument of the verb. Parts of the eating event are mapped onto parts of the apple that are being consumed.

Inherent case – case whose assignment is strongly interrelated with the assignment of a certain thematic role. An example would be the dative case assigned in many languages, such as Russian and Icelandic, to recipient arguments.

Inherent endpoint, see telicity

Intensional Genitive – a phenomenon observed in Slavic and Baltic languages, whereby an object argument of an intensional verb appears, either optionally or obligatorily, in the genitive case.

Irrealis Genitive – a cover term for Genitive of Negation and Intensional Genitive. The underlying assumption is that these constitute two instances of the same phenomenon.

Island – an island to movement is an expression out of which it is impossible to extract a *wh*-phrase.

Lexical case – case whose assignment is idiosyncratic, irregular and lexically selected by individual lexical heads, typically V or P.

LF (logical form) – a formal representation of the logical structure of a sentence. In syntax, the (covert) level of syntactic representation on which the semantic interpretation of a sentence is based.

Local cases – cases that express spatial relations, e.g. illative, allative, inessive, etc.

Negative concord – a phenomenon whereby more than one negative element appears in a clause but the latter is interpreted as containing only one negative operator.

Negative concord item – a negative element which co-occurs with clausal negation and does not contribute negative semantics of its own. Rather, a kind of agreement relation holds between this item and clausal negation.

Negative polarity items (NPIs) – expressions like *any, ever* and *lift a finger*, which are only licensed in special contexts such as negation and semantically related environments (their use is often restricted to downward-entailing environments). For instance, compare the ungrammatical *He will ever eat meat* to *He won't ever eat meat* or *Will he ever eat meat?*

Partitivity – a property of nominal phrases that denote a subset of another set, thereby, intuitively, expressing the notion of partiality. An example is the DP *three of the boys*, which denotes a subset of the contextually familiar set of boys. An overt partitive expression contains an *of*-phrase or its analogue in another language which explicitly refers to the superset. A covert partitive does not contain a phrase that refers to the superset explicitly but is still semantically interpreted as a part of a set that is contextually supplied. For instance, consider the following text: *Ten children entered the room. Two boys were very sad.* Here, the expression *two boys* is likely to be understood as referring to boys who belong to the group of children mentioned in the first sentence. Under this reading, *two boys* receives a partitive interpretation. Since it does not contain an *of*-phrase, this is a covert, rather than overt, partitive.

Perfective – grammatical aspect, generally used to mark an eventuality as completed or at least temporally delimited. Contrasts with imperfective aspect, which does not contribute the delimitation entailment and is often used to express progressive, iterative and habitual meanings. In Slavic languages, such as Czech and Russian, the perfective/ imperfective distinction is reflected in the morphological form of the verb, e.g. *jel* 'ate' (imperfective) – *s'jel* 'ate (up)' (perfective).

PF (phonetic form, phonological form) – the level of representation at which only phonological and phonetic information is encoded.

Pivot – the post-verbal nominal expression in existential sentences, also referred to as *theme* or *thing*, e.g. *a chair* in the sentence *There is a chair in the room*. In turn, the optional locative expression, such as *in the room*, is referred to as the coda. Obviously, the order of these elements in a sentence is language-dependent.

Predicate modifier – a linguistic expression of type $<<e,t>,<e,t>>$. This is a function that applies to a one-place predicate and renders as an output another one-place predicate. Typical examples are adverbial phrases that attach to VPs or adjectival phrases that function as NP-modifiers. For instance, in nominal the phrase *clever girls*, the AP *clever* combines with a one-place predicate *girls*, type $<e,t>$, and renders another one-place predicate *clever girls*, again, type $<e,t>$.

Quantization – a quantized expression is not cumulative: if it applies to a certain entity, then it cannot apply to a proper part of that entity. For instance, a proper part of *two apples* is not *two apples* (but rather, for example, *one apple, half an apple*). The concept of quantization is employed in certain analyses of telicity.

Reference time – a time which is employed as a reference point in determining the temporal location of an event. Contrasts with event time (the time when an event takes place) and speech time (the time when the sentence is uttered).

Secondary predicate – a predicate that ascribes a property to the subject or the object in a sentence but does not constitute the main predicate of a clause. An example is the predicate *nude* in the sentence *John danced nude*.

Spatial cases, see local cases

Specificity – a semantic or pragmatic property of a DP. Intuitively speaking, a specific DP is one that has a particular/identifiable referent. More precise definitions vary dramatically across specificity (sub) types and linguistic analyses. Specific DPs have been defined as DPs that take wide scope; partitive DPs; DPs whose referent is familiar to the speaker; DPs whose referent is, in some way or other, linked or anchored to the context.

S-structure (surface structure) – within transformational generative grammar, the structure that a sentence obtains after transformations / overt movements take place.

Standard change – a scalar change in whose course a "goal degree," a lexically or contextually supplied standard value (a standard of evaluation), is reached.

Strong nominal phrases – nominal phrases that cannot appear in existential sentences (as the theme/pivot), e.g. *There are **both boys** in the room. Originally, the distinction was defined as one between strong and weak quantifiers, but later literature has shown that at least in some instances, the acceptability in the existential construction depends not only on the quantifier but rather on the properties of the whole nominal expression.

Strong personal pronouns – non-clitic forms of personal pronouns.

Structural case, see configurational case

Telicity – an aspectual property of a verb, a verb phrase or a clause which is related to the existence of a natural, inherent, endpoint beyond which an event cannot continue. A telic predicate denotes a set of events that have such an inherent endpoint. An atelic predicate denotes an event without such an endpoint. To illustrate, *eat an apple* is a telic predicate: once the apple is consumed, the event cannot continue any further. In contrast, *eat apples* is atelic: an event that falls under the denotation of this predicate can, in principle, continue indefinitely.

Teleological modality – the expression of what is necessary or possible for the purposes of achieving a particular goal.

Thematic roles – general classes of arguments, based on the way in which an individual or an entity may participate in an event. Some examples include: *agent, patient, experiencer, goal, instrument,* etc.

Theta-roles, see thematic roles

Unbounded, see boundedness

Veridical operator – an operator for which it holds that $Op\ p \rightarrow p$. In other words, the truth of p is retained after a veridical operator is applied to p. Otherwise, the operator is non-veridical. For instance, negation is a non-veridical operator: *John didn't smile* does NOT entail *John smiled*.

Weak nominal phrases – nominal phrases that can appear in existential sentences (as the theme/pivot), e.g. There are **two boys** in the room.

Bibliography

Acton, Eric K. 2014. Standard Change and the Finnish Partitive-Accusative Object Distinction. In *Empirical Issues in Syntax and Semantics* 10, ed. Christopher Piñón, 1–18.

Adger, D. and G. Ramchand. 2003. Predication and Equation. *Linguistic Inquiry* 34: 325–360.

Adler, Julia. 2011. *Dative Alternations in German*. Ph.D. dissertation, Hebrew University of Jerusalem.

Aissen, Judith. 1999. Markedness and Subject Choice in Optimality Theory. *Natural Language and Linguistic Theory* 17(4): 673–711.

Aissen, Judith. 2003. Differential Object Marking: Iconicity vs. Economy. *Natural Language and Linguistic Theory* 21: 435–483.

Amritavalli, R. 2004. Experiencer Datives in Kannada. *Typological Studies in Language* 60: 1–24.

Arad, Maya. 1998. *VP-Structure and the Syntax–Lexicon Interface*. Doctoral dissertation, University College London.

Aristar, Anthony R. 1996. The Relationship Between Dative and Locative: Kuryìowicz's Argument from a Typological Perspective. *Diachronica* 13: 207–224.

Aristar, Anthony R. 1997. Marking and Hierarchy: Types and the Grammaticalization of Case-Markers. *Studies in Language* 21: 313–368.

Asher, R. E. and T. C. Kumari. 1997. *Malayalam*. London: Routledge.

Babby, Leonard H. 1973. The Deep Structure of Adjectives and Participles in Russian. *Language* 49: 349–360.

Babby, Leonard H. 1978. *Negation and Subject Case Selection in Existential Sentences: Evidence from Russian*. Bloomington: Indiana University Linguistics Club.

Babby, Leonard H. 1980. *Existential Sentences and Negation in Russian*. Ann Arbor: Karoma.

Babby, Leonard H. 1987. Case, Prequantifiers, and Discontinuous Agreement in Russian *Natural Language and Linguistic Theory* 5(1): 91–138.

Babby, Leonard H. 2001. The Genitive of Negation: A Unified Analysis. In Steven Franks, Tracy Holloway King and Michael Yadroff, eds., *Annual Workshop on Formal Approaches to Slavic Linguistics: The Bloomington Meeting*. Ann Arbor: Michigan Slavic Publications.

Babby, Leonard H. 2009. *The Syntax of Argument Structure*. Cambridge: Cambridge University Press.

Babyonyshev, Maria. 2003. The Extended Projection Principle and the Genitive of Negation Construction. In Sue Brown and Adam Przepiorkowski, eds., *Negation in Slavic*. Bloomington: Slavica Publishers.

Babyonyshev, Maria and Brun, Dina. 2002. Specificity Matters: A New Look at the New Genitive of Negation. In J. Toman, ed., *Proceedings of Tenth Annual Workshop on Formal Approaches to Slavic Linguistics: The Second Ann Arbor Meeting*. Ann Arbor: Michigan Slavic Publications.

Baerman, Matthew. 2008. Case Syncretism. In Andrej Malchukov and Andrew Spencer, eds., *The Oxford Handbook of Case*. Oxford: Oxford University Press, pp. 219–230.

Bailyn, John F. 1994. The Syntax and Semantics of Russian Long and Short Adjectives: An X'-Theoretic Account. In J. Toman, ed., *Formal Approaches to Slavic Linguistics. The Ann Arbor Meeting*. Ann Arbor: Michigan Slavic Publications, pp. 1–30.

Bailyn, John F. 1997. Genitive of Negation Is Obligatory. In W. Browne, E. Dornisch, N. Kondrashova and D. Zec, eds., *Annual Workshop on Formal Approaches to Slavic Linguistics: The Cornell Meeting*. Ann Arbor: Michigan Slavic Publications.

Bailyn, John F. 2001. The Syntax of Slavic Predicate Case. *ZAS Papers in Linguistics* 21: 1–23.

Bailyn, John F. 2004. The Case of Q. In O. Arnaudova et al., eds., *Annual Workshop on Formal Approaches to Slavic Linguistics 12*. Ann Arbor: Michigan Slavic Publications. www.ic.sunysb.edu/Clubs/nels/jbailyn/JFBailyn.html.

Bailyn, John F. and B. Citko. 1999. Case and Agreement in Slavic Predicates. In K. Dziwirek et al., eds., *Annual Workshop on Formal Approaches to Slavic Linguistics. The Seattle Meeting*, Ann Arbor: Michigan Slavic Publications, pp. 17–37.

Baker, Mark. 1988. *Incorporation: A Theory of Grammatical Function Changing*. Chicago: University of Chicago Press.

Baker, Mark. 2015. *Case: Its Principles and Its Parameters*. Cambridge: Cambridge University Press.

Baker, Mark and Jonathan Bobaljik. 2017. On Inherent and Dependent Theories of Ergative Case. In Jessica Coon, Diane Massam and Lisa Demena Travis, eds., *The Oxford Handbook of Ergativity*. Oxford: Oxford University Press.

Balasch, Sonia. 2011. Factors Determining Spanish Differential Object Marking within Its Domain of Variation. In Jim Michnowicz and Robin Dodsworth, eds., *Selected Proceedings of the 5th Workshop on Spanish Sociolinguistics*. Somerville, MA: Cascadilla Press.

Bar-Asher Siegal, Elitzur A. and Nora Boneh. 2014. Modern Hebrew Non-Core Dative in Their Context. *Ləšonénu* 74: 461–495.

Bar-Asher Siegal, Elitzur A. and Nora Boneh. 2015a. On Discursive Datives in Modern Hebrew. In *Catalonia-Israel Symposium on Lexical Semantics and Grammatical Structure in Event Conceptualization.* The Linguistics Department at The Hebrew University of Jerusalem.

Bar-Asher Siegal, Elitzur A. and Nora Boneh. 2015b. Decomposing Affectedness: Truth-Conditional Non-Core Datives in Modern Hebrew. In Nurit Melnik, ed., *Proceedings of IATL 30.*

Barðdal, Jóhanna. 2011. The Rise of Dative Substitution in the History of Icelandic: A Diachronic Construction Grammar Account. *Lingua* 121: 60–79.

Barðdal, Jóhanna and Shobhana L. Chelliah. 2009. *The Role of Semantic, Pragmatic, and Discourse Factors in the Development of Case.* Edited volume. Amsterdam: John Benjamins.

Bayer, J. 2004. Non-Nominative Subjects in Comparison. In P. Bhaskararao and K. V. Subbaraou, eds., *Non-Nominative Subjects.* Amsterdam: John Benjamins, Vol. 1. pp. 49–76.

Beavers, John. 2008. Scalar Complexity and the Structure of Events. In Johannes Dölling, Tatjana Heyde-Zybatow and Martin Schäfer, eds., Event Structures in Linguistic Form and Interpretation. Berlin: Mouton de Gruyter, pp. 245–265.

Beavers, John. 2011. On Affectedness. *Natural Language and Linguistic Theory* 29: 335–370.

Beghelli, F. and T. Stowell. 1997. Distributivity and Negation: The Syntax of each and every. In A. Szabolcsi, ed., *Ways of Scope Taking.* London: Kluwer, pp. 71–107.

Belletti, Adriana. 1988. The Case of Unaccusatives. *Linguistic Inquiry* 19(1): 1–34.

Bhat, D. N. S. and M. S. Ningomba. 1997. *Manipuri Grammar.* Munich: Lincon.

Bickel, B. 2004. The Syntax of Experiencers in the Himalayas. In P. Bhaskararao and K. V. Subbaraou, eds., *Non-Nominative Subjects.* Amsterdam: John Benjamins. Vol. 1, pp. 77–112.

Bierwisch, M. 1988. On the Grammar of Local Prepositions. In M. Bierwisch, W. Motsch and I. Zimmermann, eds., *Syntax, Semantik, und Lexikon: Rudolf Rčñi.ka zum 65. Geburtstag.* Berlin: Akademie Verlag, pp. 1–65.

Bittner, M. 1994. *Case, Scope, and Binding.* Dordrecht: Kluwer.

Blake, Barry. 1994. *Case.* Cambridge: Cambridge University Press.

Blake, Barry. 2001. *Case*, 2nd edition. Cambridge: Cambridge University Press.

Błaszczak, Joanna. 2007. The NOM/GEN "Subject" Puzzle in Polish. In Peter Kosta and Lilia Schurcks, eds., *Linguistic Investigations into Formal Description of Slavic Languages.* Frankfurt am Main: Peter Lang, pp. 127–145.

Bleam, Tonia. 2005. The Role of Semantic Type on Differential Object Marking. *Belgian Journal of Linguistics* 19: 3–27.

Blutner, R. 2000. Some Aspects of Optimality in Natural Language Interpretation. *Journal of Semantics* 17: 189–216.

Boneh, Nora and Léa Nash. 2010. A Higher Applicative: Evidence from French. In *Proceedings of IATL 25*. http://linguistics.huji.ac.il/IATL/25/ Boneh_Nash.pdf.

Borschev, Vladimir and Barbara H. Partee. 1998. Formal and Lexical Semantics and the Genitive in Negated Existential Sentences in Russian. In Z. Boskovic, S. Franks and W. Snyder, eds., *Annual Workshop on Formal Approaches to Slavic Linguistics* 6. Ann Arbor: Michigan Slavic Publications.

Borschev, Vladimir and Barbara H. Partee. 2002a. The Russian Genitive of Negation in Existential Sentences: The Role of Theme-Rheme Structure Reconsidered. In E. Hajieova and P. Sgall, eds., *Travaux de Circle Linguistique de Prague (novelle serie)* 4. Amsterdam: John Benjamins.

Borschev, Vladimir and Barbara H. Partee. 2002b. Genitive of Negation and Scope of Negation in Russian Existential Sentences. In J. Toman, ed., *Proceedings of Tenth Annual Workshop on Formal Approaches to Slavic Linguistics: The Second Ann Arbor Meeting*. Ann Arbor: Michigan Slavic Publications.

Borschev, Vladimir, Elena V. Paducheva, Barbara H. Partee, Yakov G. Testelets and Igor Yanovich. 2008. Russian Genitives, Non-Referentiality, and the Property-Type Hypothesis. In A. Antonenko et al., eds., *Formal Approaches to Slavic Linguistics: The Stony Brook Meeting (FASL 16)*, Ann Arbor: Michigan Slavic Publishers.

Bossong, Georg. 1985. *Empirische Universalienforschung: Differentielle Objektmarkierung in den neuiranischen Sprachen.* Tübingen: Narr.

Bouchard, Denis. 1995. *The Semantics of Syntax: A Minimalist Approach to Grammar.* Chicago: University of Chicago Press.

Bowe, Heather. 1990. *Categories, Constituents and Constituent Order in Pitjantjatjara.* London: Routledge.

Brecht, Richard D. and James S. Levine. 1986. Case and Meaning. In R. D. Brecht and J. S. Levine, eds., *Case in Slavic*. USA: Slavica Publishers.

Brown, Sue. 1999. *The Syntax of Negation in Russian: A Minimalist Approach.* Stanford: CSLI Publications.

Burzio, Luigi. 1986. *Italian Syntax*. Dordrecht: Reidel.

Butt, Miriam. 2006a. *Theories of Case.* Cambridge: Cambridge University Press.

Butt, Miriam. 2006b.The Dative-Ergative Connection. In P. Cabredo-Hofherr and O. Bonami, eds., *Empirical Issues in Formal Syntax and Semantics.* The Hague: Thesus.

Butt, Miriam. 2012. From Spatial to Subject Marker. Handout of talk given at the Workshop on Non-Canonically Case-Marked Subjects, Iceland, June 2012.

Butt, Miriam and Tracy Holloway King. 1991. Semantic Case in Urdu. In Lisa Dobrin, Lynn Nichols, and Rosa M. Rodriguez, eds., *Papers from the 27th Regional Meeting of the Chicago Linguistic Society*, pp. 31–45.

Butt, Miriam and Tracy Holloway King. 2005. The Status of Case. In Veneeta Dayal and Anoop Mahajan, eds., *Clause Structure in South Asian Languages*. Berlin: Springer Verlag.

Caha, Pavel. 2009. *The Nanosyntax of Case*. Ph.D. dissertation, University of Tromsø.

Carlson, Gregory N. 1977. Reference to Kinds in English. Doctoral dissertation, University of Massachusetts.

Chelliah, S. L. 1997. *A Grammar of Meithei*. Berlin: Mouton de Gruyter.

Chesterman, Andrew. 1991. *On Definiteness*. Cambridge: Cambridge University Press.

Chomsky, Noam. 1981. *Lectures on Government and Binding: The Pisa Lectures*. Dordrecht: Foris.

Chomsky, Noam. 1985. *Knowledge of Language: Its Nature, Origin and Use*. New York: Praeger.

Chomsky, Noam. 1986. *Barriers*. Cambridge: MIT Press.

Chomsky, Noam. 1995. *The Minimalist Program*. Cambridge: MIT Press.

Chomsky, Noam and Howard Lasnik. 1977. Filters and Control. *Linguistic Inquiry* 8: 425–504.

Citko, Barbara. 2008. Small Clauses Reconsidered: Not So Small and Not All Alike. *Lingua* 118: 261–295.

Comrie, Bernard. 1979. Definite and Animate Direct Objects: A Natural Class. *Linguistica Silesiana* 3: 13–21.

Comrie, Bernard. 2004. Oblique-Case Subjects in Tsez. In Peri Bhaskararao and Karumuri Venkata Subbarao, eds., *Non-Nominative Subjects*. Amsterdam:John Benjamins, Vol. 1, pp. 113–127.

Comrie, Bernard and G. G. Corbett. 2002. *The Slavonic Languages*. London: Routledge.

Comrie, B. and M. Polinsky. 1998. The Great Daghestan Case Hoax. In Anna Siewierska and Jae Jung Song, eds., *Case, Typology, and Grammar*. Amsterdam: John Benjamins, pp. 95–114.

Comrie, Bernard, Madzhid Khalilov and Zaira Khalilova. 2015. *A Grammar of Bezhta*. Leipzig-Makhachkala: ALEPH.

Copley, Bridget and Heidi Harley. 2015. A Force-Theoretic Framework for Event Structure. *Linguistics and Philosophy* 38(2): 103–158.

Crisma, P. and G. Longobardi. 2018. A Unified Theory of Case Form and Case Meaning. Talk given at the workshop *On the Place of Case in Grammar (PlaCiG)*, Rethymno, Greece.

Croft, William. 1988. Agreement vs. Case Marking and Direct Objects. In M. Barlow and C. Ferguson, eds., *Agreement in Natural Language: Approaches, Theories, Descriptions*. Stanford: CSLI Publications, pp. 159–179.

Croft, William. 2012. *Verbs: Aspect and Causal Structure*. Oxford: Oxford University Press.

Csirmaz, Aniko. 2006. Interface Interactions – Aspect and Case. Handout of talk given at the 8th Seoul International Conference on Generative Grammar.

Cuervo, M. C. 2003. *Datives at Large*. Ph.D. thesis, Massachusetts Institute of Technology.

Dabrowska, Eva. 1994. Radial Categories in Grammar: The Polish Instrumental Case. *Linguistica Silesiana* 15: 83–94.

Dabrowska, Eva. 1997. *Cognitive Semantics and the Polish Dative* (Cognitive Linguistics Research 9). Berlin/New York: Mouton de Gruyter.

Dahl, Osten. 1971. The Genitive and the Subjunctive in Russian. *Scando-Slavica* 17: 135–139. Copenhagen: Munksgaard.

Dambriunas, Leonardas. 1980. *Introduction to Modern Lithuanian*. New York: Franciscan Fathers.

Danon, G. 2001. Syntactic Definiteness in the Grammar of Modern Hebrew. *Linguistics* 39(6): 1071–1116.

Danon, G. 2002. The Hebrew Object Marker and Semantic Type. In *Proceedings of IATL 17*.

Davison, Alice. 2004. Structural Case, Lexical Case and the Verbal Projection. In Veneeta Dayal and Anoop Mahajan, eds., *Clause Structure in South Asian Languages*. Dordrecht: Kluwer, 199–225.

De Jong, J.J. 1996. *The Case of Bound Pronouns in Peripheral Romance*. Groningen Dissertations in Linguistics 16.

Deal, Amy Rose. 2017. External Possession and Possessor Raising. In Martin Everaert and Henk C. van Riemsdijk, eds., *The Wiley Blackwell Companion to Syntax*, 2nd edition. John Wiley & Sons. DOI:10.1002/9781118358733.wbsyncom047.

Depraetere, Ilse. 1995. On the Necessity of Distinguishing between (Un)Boundedness and (A)Telicity. *Linguistics and Philosophy* 18: 1–19.

Diesing, Molly. 1992. *Indefinites*. Cambridge: MIT Press.

den Dikken, M. 2006. *Realtors and Linkers: The Syntax of Predication, Predicate Inversion and Copulas*. Cambridge: MIT Press.

Djalali, Alex. 2012. If You Own It, It Exists; If You Love It, That Says Something about You, Not It: Semantically Conditioned Case in Finnish. In Nathan Arnett and Ryan Bennett, eds., *Proceedings of the 30th West Coast Conference on Formal Linguistics*. Somerville, MA: Cascadilla Proceedings Project, pp. 131–141.

Dowty, David R. 1979. *Word and Meaning in Montague Grammar*. Dordrecht: Reidel.

Dowty, David. 1991. Thematic Proto-Roles and Argument Selection. *Language* 67(3): 547–619.

Egger, Julia. 2016. Asking the Magic Mirror: Fairytales and Animacy in Malayalam. Nijmegen: Radboud University term paper.

Emonds, Joseph. 1987. The Invisible Category Principle. *Linguistic Inquiry* 18: 613–632.

Enç, Mürvet. 1991. The Semantics of Specificity. *Linguistics Inquiry* 22: 1–25.

Erguvanlı-Taylan, E. 1984. *The Function of Word Order in Turkish Grammar*. Berkeley: University of California Press.

Erguvanlı-Taylan, E. 1986. Pronominal Versus Zero Representation of Anaphora in Turkish. In D. I. Slobin and K. Zimmer, eds., *Studies in Turkish Linguistics*. Amsterdam: John Benjamins, pp. 209–231.

Espinal, M. T. and L. McNally. 2011. Bare Nominals and Incorporating Verbs in Spanish and Catalan. *Journal of Linguistics* 47(1): 87–128.

Evans, Nicholas. 1995. *A Grammar of Kayardild: With Historical Notes on Tangkic*. In George Bossong and Wallace Chafe, eds., *Mouton Grammar Library 15*. Berlin: Mouton de Gruyter.

Farkas, Donka F. 1985. *Intensional Descriptions and the Romance Subjunctive Mood*. New York: Garland.

Farkas, Donka F. 1994. Specificity and Scope. In L. Nash and G. Tsoulas, eds., *Langues et Grammaires 1*. Paris: University of Paris 8, pp. 119–137.

Farkas, Donka F. 2002. Specificity Distinctions. *Journal of Semantics* 19: 213–243.

Farkas, Donka F. 2003. Assertion, Belief and Mood Choice. Paper presented at the *Workshop on Conditional and Unconditional Modality*, ESSLLI, Vienna.

Farkas, Donka F. and Henrieta de Swart. 2003. *The Semantics of Incorporation*. Stanford: CSLI Publications.

Feldman, H. 1986. *A Grammar of Awtuw*. Canberra: Australian National University.

Filip, Hana. 1999. *Aspect, Eventuality Types and Nominal Reference*. New York: Garland.

Filip, Hana. 2000. The Quantization Puzzle. In C. Tenny and J. Pustejovsky, eds., *Events as Grammatical Objects*. Stanford: CSLI Publications.

Filip, Hana. 2003. Prefixes and the Delimitation of Events. *Journal of Slavic Linguistics* 11(1): 55–101.

Filip, Hana. 2008. Events and Maximalization. In Susan Rothstein, ed., *Theoretical and Crosslinguistic Approaches to the Semantics of Aspect*. Amsterdam: John Benjamins, pp. 217–256.

Filip, Hana and Susan Rothstein. 2006. Telicity as a Semantic Parameter. In James Lavine, Steven Franks, Hana Filip and Mila Tasseva-Kurktchieva, eds., *Formal Approaches to Slavic Linguistics (ASL 14)*, The Princeton University Meeting. Ann Arbor: University of Michigan Slavic Publications, pp. 139–156.

Foley, W. A. 2000. The Languages of New Guinea. *Annual Review of Anthropology* 29: 357–404.

Fong, Vivienne. 2003. Resultatives and Depictives in Finnish. In Diane Nelson, and Satu Manninen, eds., *Generative Approaches to Finnic and Saami Linguistics*. Stanford: CSLI, pp. 201–234.

Forker, Diana. 2012. Spatial Relations in Hinuq and Bezhta. In Luna Filipović and Katarzyna M. Jaszczolt, eds., *Space and Time in Languages and Cultures: Linguistic Diversity*. Amsterdam: John Benjamins, pp. 15–34.

Fortescue, M. 1984. *West Greenlandic*. London: Croom Helm.

Fowler, George. 1996. Oblique Passivization in Russian. *Slavic and East European Journal* 40: 519–545.

Franks, Steven. 1995. *Parameters of Slavic Morphosyntax*. Oxford: Oxford University Press.

Franks, Steven. 1997. Parameters of Slavic Morphosyntax Revisited: A Minimalist Retrospective. In Z. Boskovic, S. Franks and W. Snyder, eds., *Annual Workshop on Formal Approaches to Slavic Linguistics: The Connecticut Meeting*. Ann Arbor: Michigan Slavic Publications.

Freeze, R. 1992. Existentials and Other Locatives. *Language* 68(3): 555–595.

Frege, Gottlob. 1892. On *Sinn* and *Bedeutung*. In Michael Beaney, *The Frege Reader* 1997. Oxford: Blackwell.

Fukuda, Shin. 2007. Object Case and Event Type: Accusative-Dative Object Case Alternation in Japanese. *Berkeley Linguistic Society* 33(1): 165–176. DOI:http://dx.doi.org/10.3765/bls.v33i1.3525.

García, Marco. 2007. Differential Object Marking with Inanimate Objects. In Georg Kaiser and Manuel Leonetti, eds., *Proceedings of the Workshop "Definiteness, Specificity and Animacy in Ibero-Romance Languages"*, Arbeitspapier 122. Konstanz: Universität Konstanz, Fachbereich Sprachwissenschaft, pp. 63–84.

van Geenhoven, Veerle. 1998. *Semantic Incorporation and Indefinite Descriptions: Semantic and Syntactic Aspects of Noun Incorporation in West Greenlandic*. Stanford: CSLI Publications.

van Geenhoven, Veerle and Louise McNally. 2005. On the Property Analysis of Opaque Complements. *Lingua* 115: 885–914.

Geist, Ljudmila. 2006. Copular Sentences in Russian Vs. Spanish at the Syntax-Semantics Interface. In *Proceedings of the Sinn und Bedeutung 10: 10th annual meeting of the Gesellschaft für Semantik*, October 13–15, 2005, Zentrum für Allgemeine Sprachwissenschaft, Berlin; ZASPil Vol. 44, pp. 99–110.

Geist, Ljudmila. 2007. Predication and Equation in Copular Sentences: Russian vs. English. In Ileana Comorovski and Klaus von Heusinger, eds., *Existence: Semantics and Syntax*. Berlin: Springer, pp. 79–105.

Geist, Ljudmila. 2010. The Argument Structure of Predicate Adjectives in Russian. *Russian Linguistics* 34(3): 239–260.

Göksel, A. and C. Kerslake. 2005. *Turkish: A Comprehensive Grammar*. London: Routledge.

Goldschmidt, Anja and Joost Zwarts. 2016. Hitting the Nail on the Head: Force Vectors in Verb Semantics. In Mary Moroney, Carol-Rose Little, Jacob Collard and Dan Burgdorf, eds., *Proceedings of SALT 26*. Austin: University of Texas at Austin, pp. 433–450.

Grice, H. Paul. 1975. Logic and Conversation. In Peter Cole and Jerry L. Morgan, eds., *Syntax and Semantics*, vol. 3, Speech Acts. New York: Academic Press.

Grimm, Scott M. 2005. *The Lattice of Case and Agentivity*. M.Sc. thesis, University of Amsterdam.

Groenendijk, Jeroen and Martin Stokhof. 1980. A Pragmatic Analysis of Specificity. In F. Heny, ed., *Ambiguity in Intensional Contexts*. Dordrecht: Reidel.

De Groot, Casper. 2017. Discovering the Assignment: An Uralic Essive Typological Questionnaire. In de Groot, ed., *Uralic Essive and the Expression of Impermanent State*. Amsterdam: John Benjamins, pp. 1–28.

Guntsetseg, Dolgor. 2009. Differential Object Marking in (Khalkha)-Mongolian. In R. Shibataki and R. Vermeulen, eds., *Proceedings of the Fifth Workshop on Altaic Formal Linguistics*. MIT Working Papers in Linguistics.

Guntsetseg, Dolgor, Klaus von Heusinger, Udo Klein and Dildora Niyazmetowa. 2008. Differential Object Marking in Mongolian and Uzbek. Paper presented at SFB 732, Stuttgart, Germany.

Harves, S. 2002a. Genitive of Negation and the Syntax of Scope. In M. van Koppen, E. Thrift, E. J. van der Torre and M. Zimmerman, eds., *Proceedings of ConSOLE 9*, pp. 96–110.

Harves, S. 2002b. *Unaccusative Syntax in Russian*. Ph.D. dissertation, Princeton University.

Haspelmath, M. 1993. *A Grammar of Lezgian*. Berlin: Mouton de Gruyter.

Hedberg, Nancy, Emrah Görgülü and Morgan Mameni. 2009. On Definiteness and Specificity in Turkish and Persian. In *Proceedings of the 2009 Annual Conference of the Canadian Linguistic Association*.

Hegedüs, V. 2008. Hungarian Spatial PPs. *Nordlyd: Tromsø Working Papers in Linguistics* 33(2): 220–233.

Heim, Irene. 1992. Presupposition Projection and the Semantics of Attitude Verbs.*Journal of Semantics* 9: 183–221.

Heinämäki, O. 1984. Aspect in Finnish. In C. de Groot and H. Tommola, eds., *Aspect Bound: A Voyage into the Realm of Germanic, Slavonic and Finno-Ugrian Aspectology*. Dordrecht: Foris.

Higgins, R. 1973. *The Pseudo-cleft Construction in English*. New York: Garland.

von Heusinger, Klaus. 2002. Specificity and Definiteness in Sentence and Discourse Structure. *Journal of Semantics* 19: 245–274.

von Heusinger, Klaus. 2008. Verbal Semantics and the Diachronic Development of Differential Object Marking in Spanish. *Probus* 20: 1–31.

von Heusinger, Klaus and Georg Kaiser. 2003. The Interaction of Animacy, Definiteness and Specificity in Spanish. In Klaus von Heusinger and Georg Kaiser, eds., *Proceedings of the Workshop Semantic and Syntactic Aspects of Specificity in Romance Languages*. Konstanz: Universität Konstanz, pp. 41–65.

von Heusinger, Klaus and Georg A. Kaiser. 2011. Affectedness and Differential Object Marking in Spanish. *Morphology* 21(3–4): 593–617.

von Heusinger, Klaus and Jaklin Kornfilt. 2005. The Case of the Direct Object in Turkish: Semantics, Syntax and Morphology. *Turkic Languages* 9: 3–44.

von Heusinger, Klaus and Jaklin Kornfilt. 2017. Partitivity and Case Marking in Turkish and Related Languages. *Glossa: A Journal of General Linguistics* 2(1): 20, 1-40.

von Heusinger, Klaus, Udo Klein and Dildora Niyazmetowa. 2008. Transitivity and the Diachronic Development of Differential Object Marking. Paper presented at the Workshop *Transitivity and Case Alternations*, Stuttgart, Germany.

von Heusinger, Klaus, Udo Klein and Dolgor Guntsetseg. 2011. The Case of Accusative Embedded Subjects in Mongolian. *Lingua* 121: 48-59.

Heycock, C. and A. Kroch. 1999. Pseudocleft Connectedness: Implications for the LF Interface Level. *Linguistic Inquiry* 30: 365-398.

Higginbotham, James. 1995. *Sense and Syntax*. Oxford: Clarendon Press.

Hjelmslev, L. 1935/37. *La catégorie des cas*. Facs, edition 1972, Munich: Wilhem Fink Verlag.

Hole, Daniel, André Meinunger and Werner Abraham. 2006. *Datives and Other Cases: Between Argument Structure and Event Structure*. Amsterdam: John Benjamins.

Holmberg, A. and U. Nikanne. 1993. Introduction. In Anders Holmberg and Urpo Nikanne, eds., *Case and Other Functional Categories in Finnish Syntax*. Berlin: Mouton de Gruyter, pp. 1-20.

de Hoop, Helen. 1992. *Case Configuration and Noun Phrase Interpretation*. Ph.D. dissertation, University of Groningen.

de Hoop, Helen and Andrej L. Malchukov. 2007. On Fluid Differential Case Marking: A Bidirectional OT Approach. *Lingua* 117 (9): 1636-1656.

de Hoop, Helen and Joost Zwarts. 2008. Case in Formal Semantics. In Andrej Malchukov and Andrew Spencer, eds., *The Oxford Handbook of Case*. Oxford: Oxford University Press.

Hopper, Paul J. and Sandra A. Thompson. 1980. Transitivity in Grammar and Discourse. *Language* 56(2): 251-299.

Horn, L. R. 1989. *A Natural History of Negation*. Chicago: The University of Chicago Press.

Huhmariniemi, S. and M. Miljan. 2018. Finnish and Estonian Partitive Case: in-Between Structure and Semantics. Talk given at the workshop *On the Place of Case in Grammar (PlaCiG)*, Rethymno, Greece.

Hynönen, Emmi. 2017. The Essive in Finnish. In Casper de Groot, ed., *Uralic Essive and the Expression of Impermanent State*. Amsterdam: John Benjamins, pp. 29-56.

Ionin, Tania. 2006. This Is Definitely Specific: Specificity and Definiteness in Article Systems. *Natural Language Semantics* 14: 175-234.

Ioup, G. 1977. Specificity and the Interpretation of Quantifiers. *Linguistics and Philosophy* 1: 233-245.

Isačenko, Aleksandr V. 1960. *Grammatičeskij stroj russkogo jazyka v sopostavlenii s slovackim. Morfologija, čast vtoraja* [The grammatical structure of Russian in comparison with Slovak - Part two: morphology]. Bratislava: Izdatel'stvo akademii nauk.

Jackendoff, Ray. 1983. *Semantics and Cognition*, 8th edition. Cambridge: MIT Press.

Jackendoff, Ray. 1990. *Semantic Structures*. Cambridge: MIT Press.

Jackendoff, Ray. 1996. The Proper Treatment of Measuring Out, Telicity, and Perhaps Even Quantification in English. *Natural Language and Linguistic Theory* 14: 305–354.

Jakobson, Roman O. 1957/1971. *Selected Writings II*. The Hague: Mouton.

Jakobson, Roman O. 1984. Contribution to the General Theory of Case: General Meanings of the Russian Cases. In Linda R. Waugh, ed., *Russian and Slavic Grammar: Studies 1931–1981*. The Hague: Mouton, pp. 59–103.

Janda, Laura A. 1993. *A Geography of Case Semantics: The Czech Dative and the Russian Instrumental* (Cognitive Linguistics Research 4). Berlin/New York: Mouton de Gruyter.

Jónsson, Jóhannes Gísli. 2000. Case and Double Objects in Icelandic. In D. Nelson and P. Foulkes, eds., *Leeds Working Papers in Linguistics 8*, pp. 71–94.

Jørgensen, Peter. 1963. *German Grammar II. Number and Case*. New York: New York University Press.

Kagan, Olga. 2005. Genitive Case: A Modal Account. In Yehuda Falk, ed., *Proceedings of Israel Association for Theoretical Linguistics 21 (IATL 21)*.

Kagan, Olga. 2007. Property-Denoting NPs and Non-Canonical Genitive Case In Tova Friedman and Masayuki Gibson, eds., *Proceedings of Semantics and Linguistic Theory 17* (SALT 17). Ithaca: CLC Publications, Cornell University, pp. 148–165.

Kagan, Olga. 2009. Intensional Genitive Case and Existential Commitment. In *Annual Workshop on Formal Approaches to Slavic Linguistics (FASL)*: The Yale Meeting. Ann Arbor: Michigan Slavic Publications, pp. 81–96.

Kagan, Olga. 2010a. Russian Aspect as Number in the Verbal Domain. In Brenda Laca and Patricia Hofherr, eds., *Layers of Aspect*. Stanford: CSLI Publications, pp. 125–146.

Kagan, Olga. 2010b. Genitive Objects, Existence and Individuation. *Russian Linguistics* 34(1): 17–39. DOI 10.1007/s11185-009-9051-x.

Kagan, Olga. 2011. On Speaker Identifiability. *Journal of Slavic Linguistics* 19 (1): 47–84. DOI:10.1353/jsl.2011.0008.

Kagan, Olga. 2013. *Semantics of Genitive Objects in Russian: A Study of Genitive of Negation and Intensional Genitive Case*. Dordrecht: Springer.

Kagan, Olga. 2015. *Scalarity in the Verbal Domain: The Case of Verbal Prefixation in Russian*. Cambridge: Cambridge University Press.

Kagan, Olga. 2019. Translative Case in Finnish: A Force-Dynamic Account. In Noa Brandel, ed., *Proceedings of IATL 33*, MIT Working Papers in Linguistics, pp. 107–122.

Kagan, Olga. in press. The Definiteness Effect in Russian Existential and Possessive Sentences. In Jacek Witkoś, Malgorzata Krzek and Gréte Dalmi, eds., *Approaches to Predicative Possession: The View from Slavic and Finno-Ugric*, London: Bloomsbury.

Kagan, Olga. in progress. Change versus Force in the Finnish Case System. Ms., Ben-Gurion University of the Negev.

Kagan, Olga and Asya Pereltsvaig. 2011a. Bare NPs and Semantic Incorporation: Objects of Intensive Reflexives at the Syntax–Semantics Interface. In Wayles Browne, Adam Cooper, Alison Fisher, Esra Kesici, Nikola Predolac and Draga Zec, eds., *Formal Approaches to Slavic Linguistics (FASL 18): The Cornell Meeting*. Ann Arbor: Michigan Slavic Publications, pp. 226–240.

Kagan, Olga and Asya Pereltsvaig. 2011b. Syntax and Semantics of Bare NPs: Objects of Intensive Reflexive Verbs in Russian. In Olivier Bonami and Patricia Cabredo Hofherr, eds., *Empirical Issues in Syntax and Semantics 8 (Proceedings of CSSP 8)*, pp. 221–238.

Karlsson, Fred. 1983. *Suomen Peruskielioppi*. Jyväakylä: SKS.

Kearns, Kate. 2011. *Semantics*, 2nd edition. Basingstoke: Palgrave Macmillan.

Kennedy, C. and B. Levin. 2002. Telicity Corresponds to Degree of Change. Unpublished Ms., Northwestern University and Stanford University.

Kennedy, C. and B. Levin. 2008. Measure of Change: The Adjectival Core of Degree Achievements. In L. McNally and C. Kennedy, eds., *Adjectives and Adverbs: Syntax, Semantics and Discourse*. Oxford: Oxford University Press, pp. 156–182.

Kettunen, L. 1943. *Vepsan Murteiden Lauseopillinen Tutkimus*. Helsinki: Suomalais-ugrilaisen Seuran Toimituksia LXXXVI.

Khrizman, Keren. 2011. Imperfective Aspect and Partitive Case in Russian. M.A. thesis, Bar-Ilan University.

Kim, Minjoo. 2003. The Genitive of Negation in Russian: A Relativized Minimality Account. In B. Partee et al., eds., *Annual Workshop on Formal Approaches to Slavic Linguistics 11*. Ann Arbor: Michigan Slavic Publications.

Kim, Soowon and Joan Maling. 1998. Case Assignment in the Siphta Construction and Its Implications for Case On Adverbials. In Ross King, ed., *Description and Explanation in Korean Linguistics*. East Asia Program, Cornell University, pp. 133–168.

Kiparsky, Paul. 1998. Partitive Case and Aspect. In M. Butt and W. Geuder, eds., *The Projection of Arguments*. Stanford: CSLI Publications.

Kiparsky, Paul. 2001a. Structural Case in Finnish. *Lingua* 111: 315–376.

Kiparsky, Paul. 2001b. The Partitive Revisited. Handout of talk, Ben-Gurion University of the Negev, June 2001.

Kiparsky, Paul. 2005. Absolutely a Matter of Degree. Handout of talk, CLS 41.

Klein, Udo. 2007. Comparing Rule-Based and Constraint-Based Analyses of Differential Object Marking. Handout of talk given at the workshop on *Differential Case Marking*, Stuttgart, Germany.

Klein, Udo and Peter de Swart. 2011. Case and Referential Properties. *Lingua* 121: 3–19.

Klenin, Emily. 1978. Quantification, Partitivity, and Genitive of Negation in Russian. In B. Comrie, ed., *Classification of Grammatical Categories*. Edmonton: Linguistic Research, Inc, pp. 163–182.

Komar, E. S. 1999. Dative Subjects in Russian Revisited: Are All Datives Created Equal? In Katarzyna Dziwirek, Herbert Coats and Cynthia M. Vakareliyska, eds., *Formal Approaches to Slavic Linguistics: The Seattle Meeting*. Ann Arbor: Michigan Slavic Publications, pp. 245–264.

Kondrashova, N. 1994. Agreement and Dative Subjects in Russian. In S. Avrutin et al., eds., *Formal Approaches to Slavic Linguistics: The MIT Meeting*. Ann Arbor: Michigan Slavic Publications, pp. 255–85.

Kondrashova, N. 2009. Licensing Modality in Infinitival Structures. In Jodi Reich, Maria Babyonyshev and Daria Kavitskaya, eds., *Formal Approaches to Slavic Linguistics: The Yale Meeting*. Ann Arbor: Michigan Slavic Publications, pp. 131–146.

Koopman, H. 2000. Prepositions, Postpositions, Circumpositions and Particles: The Structure of Dutch PPs. In H. Koopman, ed., *The Syntax of Specifiers and Heads*. London: Routledge, pp. 204–260.

Kornfilt, J. 2003. Scrambling, Subscrambling and Case in Turkish, Word Order and Scrambling. In S. Karimi, ed., *Word Order and Scrambling*. Oxford: Blackwell, pp. 125–155.

Korpela, Jukka K. 2015. *Handbook of Finnish*. E-painos, Kindle Edition.

Krasovitsky, Alexander, Alison Long, Matthew Baerman, Dunstan Brown and Greville G. Corbett. 2008. Predicate Nouns in Russian. *Russian Linguistics* 32: 99–113.

Kratzer, Angelika. 1994. *The Event Argument and the Semantics of Voice*. Ms., University of Massachusetts, Amherst.

Kratzer, Angelika. 1996. Severing the External Argument from Its Verb. In Johann Rooryck and Laurie Zaring, eds., *Phrase Structure and the Lexicon*. Dordrecht: Kluwer, pp. 109–137.

Kratzer, Angelika. 1998. Scope or Pseudo-Scope? Are There Wide-Scope Indefinites? In S. Rothstein, ed., *Events and Grammar*. Dordrecht: Kluwer, pp. 163–196.

Kratzer, Angelika. 2002. *Telicity and the Meaning of Objective Case*. Ms., University of Massachusetts at Amherst.

Krifka, Manfred. 1992. Thematic Relations as Links between Nominal Reference and Temporal Constitution. In I. Sag and A. Szabolcsi, eds., *Lexical Matters*. Stanford: CSLI Publications, pp. 29–53.

Krifka, Manfred. 1998. The Origins of Telicity. In S. Rothstein, ed., *Events and Grammar*. Dordrecht: Kluwer, pp. 197–235.

Krifka, Manfred. 2004. Semantic and Pragmatic Conditions for the Dative Alternation. *Korean Journal of English Language and Linguistics* 4: 1–32.

Krifka, M. and F. Modarresi. 2016. Number Neutrality and Anaphoric Update of Pseudo-Incorporated Nominals in Persian (and Weak Definites in English). In *Proceedings of Semantics and Linguistic Theory (SALT)* 26.

Kuryłowicz, Jerzy. 1971. Słowiański genetivus po negacij. In *Sesja naukowa międzynarodowej komisji budowy gramatycznej języków słowiańskich*, pp. 11–14.

Landau, Idan. 1999. Possessor Raising and the Structure of VP. *Lingua* 107: 1–37.

Landau, Idan. 2010. *The Locative Syntax of Experiencers*. Cambridge: MIT Press.

Langacker, Ronald W. 1987. *Foundations of Cognitive Grammar, vol. 1: Theoretical Prerequisites*. Stanford: Stanford University Press.

Langacker, Ronald W. 1991. *Foundations of Cognitive Grammar, vol. 2: Descriptive Application*. Stanford: Stanford University Press.

Larson, R. 1988. On the Double Object Construction. *Linguistic Inquiry* 19: 335–391.

Legate, Julie Anne. 2008. Morphological and Abstract Case. *Linguistic Inquiry* 39(1): 55–101.

Lee, In Que. 1997. *Dative Constructions and Case Theory in Korean*. Ph.D. Dissertation, Simon Fraser University.

Lees, Aet. 2015. *Case Alternations in Five Finnic Languages: Estonian, Finnish, Karelian, Livonian and Veps*. Leiden: Brill.

Lee-Schoenfeld, Vera. 2006. German Possessor Datives: Raised and Affected. *Journal of Comparative Germanic Linguistics* 9: 101–142.

Lestrade, Sander. 2010. *The Space of Case*. Ph.D. dissertation, Radboud University Nijmegen.

Levin, Beth. 2008. Dative Verbs: A Crosslinguistic Perspective. *Lingvisticae Investigationes* 31(2): 285–312.

Levin, Beth and Malka Rappaport Hovav. 1995. *Unaccusativity: At the Syntax–Lexical Semantics Interface*. Linguistic Inquiry Monograph 26. Cambridge: MIT Press.

Levin, Lori and Jane Simpson. 1981. Quirky Case and Lexical Representations of Icelandic Verbs. In Roberta A. Hendrick, Carrie S. Masek and Mary Frances Miller, eds., *Papers from the Seventeenth Regional Meeting, Chicago Linguistic Society*. Chicago: University of Chicago, Chicago Linguistic Society, pp. 185–196.

Levinson, Dmitry. 2005. *Aspect in Negative Imperatives and Genitive of Negation: A Unified Analysis of two Phenomena in Slavic Languages*. Ms. Stanford University, California.

Levinson, S. C. 2003. *Space in Language and Cognition: Explorations in Cognitive Diversity*. Cambridge: Cambridge University Press.

Levy-Forsythe, Zarina. 2018. *Object Incorporation in Uzbek*. M.A. thesis, Ben-Gurion University of the Negev.

Lidz, J. 2006. The Grammar of Accusative Case in Kannada. *Language* 82(1): 10–32.

Lomonosov, M. V. 1952. *Rossijskaja Grammatika* [Russian Grammar]. *Polnoje sobranije sočinenij* [Complete Works], vol. 7 (*Trudy po filologii 1739–1758 gg.*).

López, Luis. 2012. *Indefinite Objects: Scrambling, Choice Functions, and Differential Marking*. Cambridge: MIT Press.

Lunt, Horace Gray. 1955. *Old Church Slavonic Grammar*. Gravenhage: Mouton.

Lyutikova, E. and D. Ibatullina. 2015. Case Theory and Case Variation in Tatar. In Е. Лютикова, А. Циммерлинг and М. Коношенко, eds., *Материалы международной конференции Типология морфосинтаксических парам етров 2015. 2.* Moscow: МПГУ, pp. 228–244.

Lyutikova, E. and Asya Pereltsvaig. 2015. The Tatar DP. *The Canadian Journal of Linguistics / La revue canadienne de linguistique* 60(3): 289–325.

Magometov, A. A. 1965. *Tabasaranskij Jazyk (Isledovanie i Teksty)* [The Tabasaran Language (Investigation and Texts)]. Tbilisi: Mecniereba.

Maienborn, C. 2005. A Discourse-Based Account of Spanish *ser/estar*. *Linguistics* 43(1): 155–180.

Malchukov, Andrej L. 2008. Animacy and Asymmetries in Differential Case Marking. *Lingua* 118: 203–221.

Malchukov, Andrej L. and Helen de Hoop. 2011. Tense, Aspect, and Mood Based Differential Case Marking. *Lingua* 121: 35–47.

Malchukov, Andrej. L. and Andrew Spencer. 2008. *The Oxford Handbook of Case*. Oxford: Oxford University Press.

Malchukov, A. L. and P. de Swart. 2008. Differential Case Marking and Actancy Variations. In A. Malchukov and A. Spencer, eds., *The Oxford Handbook of Case*. Oxford: Oxford University Press, pp. 339–355.

Maling, Joan. 1993. Of Nominative and Accusative: The Hierarchical Assignment of Grammatical Case in Finnish. In A. Holmberg and U. Nikanne, eds., *Case and Other Functional Categories in Finnish Syntax*. Berlin: Mouton de Gruyter.

Maling, Joan. 2001. Dative: The Heterogeneity of the Mapping Among Morphological Case, Grammatical Functions, and Thematic Roles. *Lingua* 111: 419–464.

Maling, Joan. 2002. Verbs with Dative Objects in Icelandic. *Íslenskt mál* 24: 31–105.

Manandise, E. 1988. *Evidence from Basque for a New Theory of Grammar*. New York: Garland.

Marantz, Alec. 1991. Case and Licensing. In Germán F. Westphal, Benjamin Ao and Hee-Rahk Chae, eds., *ESCOL 91: Proceedings of the Eighth Eastern States Conference on Linguistics*, pp. 234–253.

Marantz, Alec. 1993. Implications of Asymmetries in Double Object Constructions. In S. A. Mchombo, ed., *Theoretical Aspects of Bantu Grammar 1*. Stanford: CSLI Publications, pp. 113–151.

Marantz, Alec. 1997. No Escape from Syntax: Don't Try Morphological Analysis in the Privacy of Your Own Lexicon. In Alexis Dimitriadis, Laura Siegel, Clarissa Surek-Clark and Alex Williams. eds., *University of Pennsylvania Working Papers in Linguistics* vol. 4.2. Philadelphia: University of Pennsylvania Press, pp. 201–225.

Matushansky, Ora. 2000. The Instrument of Inversion: Instrumental Case in the Russian Copula. *Proceedings of WCCFL 19*.

Matushansky, Ora. 2008. A Case Study of Predication. In F. Marušič and R. Žaucer, eds., *Studies in Formal Slavic Linguistics. Contributions from Formal*

Description of Slavic Languages 6.5. Frankfurt am Main: Peter Lang, pp. 213–239.

Mayo, Peter. 2002. Belorussian. In Bernard Comrie and Greville G. Corbett, eds., *The Slavonic Languages*. London: Routledge.

McFadden, Thomas. 2002. *The Structure of Inherent, Quirky and Semantic Cases.* Ms., University of Pennsylvania.

McFadden, Thomas. 2004. *The Position of Morphological Case in the Derivation: A Study on the Syntax–Morphology Interface.* Ph.D. dissertation, University of Pennsylvania.

McNally, Louise. 1998. Existential Sentences without Existential Quantification. *Linguistics and Philosophy* 21: 353–392.

McNally, Louise. 2004. Bare Plurals in Spanish Are Interpreted as Properties. *Catalan Journal of Linguistics* 3: 115–133.

McNally, Louise and van Geenhoven, Veerle. 1998. Redefining the Weak/Strong Distinction. Expanded version of a paper presented at the *1997 Paris Syntax and Semantics Colloquium*.

Melchuk, Igor. 1986. Toward a Definition of Case. In R. D. Brecht and J. S. Levine, eds., *Case in Slavic*. USA: Slavica Publishers.

Mikkelsen, Line. 2004. *Specifying Who: on the Structure, Meaning, and Use of Specificational Copular Clauses.* Doctoral dissertation, University of California at Santa Cruz.

Mikkelsen, Line. 2005. *Copular Clauses: Specification, Predication and Equation.* Amsterdam: John Benjamins.

Mitchell, Erika. 1991. Case and the Finnish Object. *Cornell Working Papers in Linguistics* 9: 193–228.

Miyoshi, Nobuhiro. 2002. The Genitive of Negation in Slavic: A Minimalist Approach. In J. Toman, ed., *Proceedings of Tenth Annual Workshop on Formal Approaches to Slavic Linguistics: The Second Ann Arbor Meeting.* Ann Arbor: Michigan Slavic Publications.

Mohanan, K. P. and Tara Mohanan. 1990. Dative Subjects in Malayalam: Semantic Information in Syntax. In M. K. Verma and K. P. Mohanan, eds., *Experiencer Subjects in South Asian Languages*. Stanford: CSLI Publications, pp. 43–57.

Mohanan, Tara. 1994. *Argument Structure in Hindi.* Stanford.: CSLI Publications.

Moravcsik, E. 1978. On the Case Marking of Objects. In J. Greenberg, ed., *Universals of Human Language; Volume 4: Syntax.* Stanford: Stanford University Press, pp. 249–290.

Moro, A. 1997. *The Raising of Predicates: Predicative Noun Phrases and the Theory of Clause Structure.* Cambridge: Cambridge University Press.

Moro, A. 2000. *Dynamic Antisymmetry.* Cambridge: MIT Press.

Muller, Claude. 1997. *De* partitif et la negation. In D. Forget, P. Hirschbuhler, F. Martineau and M. L. Rivero, eds., *Negation and Polarity.* Amsterdam: John Benjamins.

Narrog, Heiko. 2011. Varieties of Instrumental. In A. L. Malchukov and A. Spencer, eds., *The Oxford Handbook of Case*. Oxford: Oxford University Press, pp. 593–600.

Nash, Léa. 1996. The Internal Ergative Subject Hypothesis. In Kiyomi Kusumoto, ed., *NELS 26*. Amherst: University of Massachusetts, GLSA, pp. 195–209.

Nau, Nicole. 1999. *Latvian*. Munich: LINCOM Europa.

Neidle, Carol. 1988. *The Role of Case in Russian Syntax*. Dordrecht: Kluwer Academic Publishers.

Newman, J. and S. Rice. 2006. Transitivity Schemas of English EAT and DRINK in the BNC. In S. Th. Gries and A. Stefanowitsch, eds., *Corpora in Cognitive Linguistics: Corpus-Based Approaches to Syntax and Lexis*. Berlin: Mouton de Gruyter, pp. 225–260.

Niemi, Clemens. 1945. *Finnish Grammar*, 3rd edition. Duluth: C.H. Salminen.

Nikanne, Urpo. 1993. On Assigning Semantic Cases in Finnish. In Anders Holmberg and Urpo Nikanne, eds., *Case and Other Functional Categories in Finnish Syntax*, pp. 75–89. Mouton de Gruyter.

Ojajärvi, Aulis. 1950. *Sijojen merkitystehtävistä Itä-Karjalan Maaselän murteissa*. Helsinki: Suomalais-Ugrilainen Seura.

Özge, U. 2011. Turkish Indefinites and Accusative Marking. In A. Simpson, ed., *Proceedings of WAFL 7*. Cambridge: MIT Press, pp. 253–267.

Öztürk, Balkiz. 2005. *Case, Referentiality and Phrase Structure*. Amsterdam: John Benjamins.

Paducheva, Elena V. 1992. O semantičiskeskom podxode k sintaksisu i genitivnom subjekte glagola *byt'*. [On the semantic approach to syntax and the genitive subject of the verb *byt'*]. *Russian Linguistics* 16: 53–63.

Paducheva, Elena V. 1997. Roditel'nyj subjecta v otricatel'nom predloženii: sinaksis ili semantika? [Genitive of subject in a negative sentence: syntax or semantics?]. *Voprosy jazykoznania* 2: 101–116.

Palancar, Enrique L. 2011. Varieties of Ergative. In A. L. Malchukov and A. Spencer, eds., *The Oxford Handbook of Case*. Oxford: Oxford University Press, pp. 562–571.

Parsons, T. 1990. *Events in the Semantics of English: A Study in Subatomic Semantics*. Cambridge: MIT Press.

Partee, Barbara H. 1986. Noun Phrase Interpretation and Type Shifting Principles. In J. Groenendijk, D. de Jongh and M. Stokhof, eds., *Studies in Discourse Representation Theory and the Theory of Generalised Quantifiers*. Dordrecht:Foris.

Partee, Barbara H. 1999. Copula Inversion Puzzles in English and Russian. In K. Dziwirek, H. Coats and C. Vakareliyska, eds., *Formal Approaches to Slavic Linguistics: The Seattle Meeting*. Ann Arbor: Michigan Slavic Publications, pp. 361–395.

Partee, Barbara H. 2000. Some Remarks on Linguistic Uses of the Notion of "Event." In C. Tenny and J. Pustejovsky, eds., *Events as Grammatical Objects*. Stanford: CSLI Publications.

Partee, Barbara H. 2005. Weak Noun Phrases: Semantics and Syntax. Paper presented at *Dialog-21*, Moscow.

Partee, Barbara H. 2008. Negation, Intensionality, and Aspect: Interaction with NP Semantics. In Susan Rothstein, ed., *Theoretical and Cross-linguistic Approaches to the Semantics of Aspect*. Amsterdam: John Benjamins.

Partee, Barbara H. and Vladimir Borschev. 2004. The Semantics of Russian Genitive of Negation: The Nature and Role of Perspectival Structure. Paper presented at *SALT* 14.

Partee, Barbara H. and Vladimir Borschev. 2007. Pros and Cons of a Type-Shifting Approach to Russian Genitive of Negation. In B. D. ten Cate and H. W. Zeevat, eds., *Proceedings of the Sixth International Tbilisi Symposium on Language, Logic and Computation (Batumi 2005)*. Berlin: Springer, pp. 166–188.

Partee, Barbara H. and Vladimir Borschev. 2008. Existential Sentences, BE and the Genitive of Negation in Russian. In I. Comorowski and K. von Heusinger, eds., *Existence: Semantics and Syntax*. New York: Springer, pp. 147–191.

Pereltsvaig, Asya. 1998. Genitive of Negation in Russian. In *Proceedings of IATL 13*, pp. 167–190.

Pereltsvaig, Asya. 1999. The Genitive of Negation and Aspect in Russian. In Y. Rose and J. Steele, eds., *McGill Working Papers in Linguistics* 14, pp. 111–140.

Pereltsvaig, Asya. 2000. On Accusative Adverbials in Russian and Finnish. In Adam Z. Wyner, ed., *The Israeli Association for Theoretical Linguistics. The Proceedings of the 15th Annual Conference (IATL 15)*, Jerusalem, 165–190.

Pereltsvaig, Asya. 2001. *On the Nature of Intra-Clausal Relations*. Ph.D. thesis, McGill University.

Pereltsvaig, Asya. 2007. *Copular Sentences in Russian. A Theory of Intra-Clausal Relations*. Berlin: Springer.

Pesetsky, David M. 1982. *Paths and Categories*. Ph.D. dissertation, Cambridge: MIT.

Pesetsky, David M. 2013. *Russian Case Morphology and the Syntactic Categories*. Cambridge: MIT Press.

Pesetsky, David and Esther Torrego. 2004. Tense, Case, and the Nature of Syntactic Categories. In J. Guéron and J. Lecarme, eds., *The Syntax of Time*. Cambridge: MIT Press.

Podobryaev, A. 2013. Differential Case Marking in Turkic as Intermediate Dependent Case. In U. Özge, ed., *Proceedings of the 8th Workshop on Altaic Formal Linguistics (WAFL8). 67*. MIT Working Papers in Linguistics, Cambridge: MITWPL, pp. 281–292.

Polinsky, M and V. Nedjalkov. 1987. Contrasting the Absolutive in Chukchee: Syntax, Semantics and Pragmatics. *Lingua* 71: 239–269.

Potebnja, A. A. 1958. *Iz zapisok po russkoj grammatike*. Vol. I-II. Moscow: Min. prosv. RSFSR.

Priestly, T. M. S. 2002. Slovene. In Bernard Comrie and Greville G. Corbett, eds., *The Slavonic Languages*. London: Routledge.

Pugh, Stefan M. and Ian Press. 1999. *Ukrainian: A Comprehensive Grammar*. London: Routledge.

Pylkkänen, L. 2000. What Applicative Heads Apply To. In *Proceedings of the 24th Annual Penn Linguistics Colloquium*. Volume 7(1): 197–210.

Pylkkänen, L. 2002/2008. *Introducing Arguments*. Cambridge: MIT Press.

Rákosi, György. 2006. *Dative Experiencer Predicates in Hungarian*. Utrecht: LOT.

Rákosi, György. 2008. Some Remarks on Hungarian Ethical Datives. In Andor József, Hollósy Béla, Laczkó Tibor and Pelyvás Péter, eds., *When Grammar Minds Language and Literature. Festschrift for Prof. Béla Korponay on the Occasion of His 80th Birthday*. Debrecen: Institute of English and American Studies, University of Debrecen, pp. 413–422.

Ramchand, G. 2011. Licensing of Instrumental Case in Hindi/Urdu Causatives. *Nordlyd* 38, ed. Peter Svenonius, pp. 49–85. CASTL, Tromsø.

Rappaport Hovav, Malka and Beth Levin. 2008. The English Dative Alternation: The Case for Verb Sensitivity. *Journal of Linguistics* 44: 129–167.

Reinhart, Tanya. 1997. Quantifier Scope: How Labor Is Divided between QR and Choice-Functions. *Linguistics and Philosophy* 20: 335–397.

Reinhart, Tanya. 2000. The Theta System: Syntactic Realization of Verbal Concepts. *UIL-OTS Working Papers in Linguistics*. University of Utrecht.

Reinhart, Tanya. 2002. The Theta System – an Overview. *Theoretical Linguistics* 28: 229–290.

Richards, Norvin. 2007. Lardil "Case Stacking" and the Structural/Inherent Case Distinction. *lingBuzz/000405*.

Richards, Norvin. 2013. Lardil "Case Stacking" and the Timing of Case Assignment. *Syntax* 16(1): 42–76.

van Riemsdijk, Henk. 2007. Case in Spatial Adpositional Phrases: The Dative-Accusative Alternation in German. In Gabriela Alboiu, Andrei Avram, Larisa Avram and Dana Isac, eds., *Festschrift for Alexandra Cornilescu*. Bucharest: Bucharest University Press.

van Riemsdijk, H., and R. Huybregts. 2007. Location and Locality. In S. Karimi, V. Samiian and W. K. Wilkins, eds., *Phrasal and Clausal Architecture*. Amsterdam and Philadelphia: Benjamins, pp. 339–364.

Rigau, G. 1986. *Some Remarks on the Nature of Strong Pronouns in Null-Subject Languages*. In I. Bordelois, H. Contreras and K. Zagona, eds., *Generative Studies in Spanish Syntax*. Dordrecht: Foris, pp. 143–163.

Round, Erich R. 2009. *Kayardild Morphology, Phonology and Morphosyntax*. Ph.D. dissertation, Yale University.

Rozental, D., I. Golub and M. Telenkova 2008. *Sovremennyj Russkij Jazyk*. Moscow: Airis Press.

Salminen, Taru. 2002. Retention of Abstract Meaning: The Essive Case and Grammaticalization of Polyphony in Finnish. In Ilse Wischer and Gabriele Diewald, eds., *New Reflections on Grammaticalization*. Philadelphia: John Benjamins.

Sands, Kristina. 2000. *Complement Clauses and Grammatical Relations in Finnish*. Ph.D. thesis, Australian National University, Canberra.

Sawicki, Lea. 1988. *Verb-Valency in Contemporary Polish: A Study of the Major Valency-Types*. Tübingen: Gunter Narr.

Schoorlemmer, M. 1994. Dative Subjects in Russian. In J. Toman, ed., *Formal Approaches to Slavic Linguistics: The Ann Arbor Meeting*. Ann Arbor: Michigan Slavic Publications, pp. 129–72.

Serdobolskaya, Natalya and Svetlana Toldova. 2006. Direct Object Marking in Finno-Ugric and Turkic Languages: Verb Semantics and Definiteness of Direct Object NP. Paper presented at the *Workshop on Presupposition Accommodation*, 13–15 October 2006, Ohio State University, Columbus, Ohio.

Sheehan, Michelle. 2017. Parameterizing Ergativity: An Inherent Case Approach. In Jessica Coon, Diane Massam and Lisa Demena Travis, eds., *The Oxford Handbook of Ergativity*. Oxford: Oxford University Press.

Siegal, Elitzur Bar-Asher and Nora Boneh. 2015. Decomposing Affectedness: Truth-Conditional Non-core Datives in Modern Hebrew. In Nurit Melnik, ed., *Proceedings of IATL 30*. www.iatl.org.il/wp-content /uploads/2015/10/IATL30proceedings-01-Bar-Asher-Siegal_Boneh-.pdf.

Smith, C. 1991. *The Parameter of Aspect*. Dordrecht: Kluwer Academic.

Smith, Michael B. 1985. Event Chains, Grammatical Relations, and the Semantics of Case in German. *Chicago Linguistic Society* 21: 388–407.

Smith, Michael B. 1987. *The Semantics of Dative and Accusative in German: An Investigation in Cognitive Grammar*. Ph.D. dissertation, University of California, San Diego.

Smith, Michael B. 1993. Cases as Conceptual Categories: Evidence from German. In Richard A. Geiger and Brygida Rudzka-Ostyn, eds., *Conceptualizations and Mental Processing in Language*. Berlin/New York: Mouton de Gruyter, pp. 531–565.

Smith, Michael B. 1995. Semantic Motivation vs. Arbitrariness in Grammar: Toward a More General Account of the Dative/Accusative Contrast with German Two-way Prepositions. In Irmengard Rauch and Gerald Carr, eds., *Insights in Germanic Linguistics I: Methodology in Transition* (Trends in Linguistics, Studies and Monographs, 83). Berlin/New York: Mouton de Gruyter, pp. 293–323.

Smith, Michael B. 1999. From Instrument to Irrealis: Motivating Some Grammaticalized Senses of the Russian Instrumental. In K. Dziwirek, H. Coats and C. Vakareliyska, eds., *Annual Workshop on Formal Approaches to Slavic Linguistics: The Seattle Meeting*. Ann Arbor: Michigan Slavic Publications, pp. 413–433.

Smith, Michael B. 2001. Why *Quirky* Case Really Isn't Quirky (Or How to Treat Dative Sickness in Icelandic). In Hubert Cuyckens and Britta Zawada, eds., *Polysemy in Cognitive Linguistics*. Amsterdam/ Philadelphia: John Benjamins, pp. 115–159.

Smith, Michael B. 2002. The Polysemy of German *es*, Iconicity, and the Notion of Conceptual Distance. *Cognitive Linguistics* 13: 67–112.

Smith, Michael B. 2005. The Conceptual Structure of German Impersonal Constructions. *Journal of Germanic Linguistics* 17: 79–140.

Smolensky, P. 1995. *On the Internal Structure of the Constraint Component CON of UG*. Handout of talk UCLA, April 7, 1995.

Song, Jae Jung. 2001. *Linguistic Typology: Morphology and Syntax*. London: Longman.

Soschen, A. 2002. *On the Distribution of Copula Elements in Hebrew, Russian and Spanish*. Ms., University of Ottawa.

Spyropoulos, V. 2018. Case, Function and PP Structure in Ancient Greek. Talk given at the workshop *On the Place of Case in Grammar (PlaCiG)*, Rethymno, Greece.

Starke, M. 2017. Resolving (DAT = ACC) ≠ GEN. *Glossa: A Journal of General Linguistics* 2(1): 104. DOI: http://doi.org/10.5334/gjgl.408.

Stowell, Tim. 1982. The Tense of Infinitives. *Linguistic Inquiry* 13: 561–570.

Strawson, P. F. 1950. On Referring. *Mind* 59: 320–344.

Stump, Gregory T. 1985. *The Semantic Variability of Absolute Constructions*. Dordrecht: Reidel.

Sulger, S. 2012. Nominal Argument Structure and the Stage-/Individual-Level Contrast in Hindi/Urdu. In *Online Proceedings of the LFG12 Conference*, Udayana University, Bali, Indonesia. CSLI Publications.

Svenonius, Peter. 2002. Icelandic Case and the Structure of Events. *The Journal of Comparative Germanic Linguistics* 5: 197–225.

Svenonius, Peter. 2006. Interpreting Uninterpretable Features. *Linguistic Analysis* 33(3–4): 375–413.

Svenonius, Peter. 2012. Drowning "into" the River in North Sámi: Uses of the Illative. In Luna Filipović and Katarzyna M. Jaszczolt, eds., Amsterdam: John Benjamins, pp. 73–94.

de Swart, Peter. 2003. *The Case Mirror*. M.A. thesis, University of Nijmegen.

de Swart, Peter. 2007. *Cross-Linguistic Variation in Object Marking*. Ph.D. dissertation, Radboud University Nijmegen. LOT Publications.

de Swart, Peter and Helen de Hoop. 2007. Semantic Aspects of Differential Object Marking. In E. Puig-Waldmüller, ed., *Proceedings of Sinn und Bedeutung 11*, Barcelona: Universitat Pompeu Fabra, pp. 598–611.

de Swart, Peter and Helen de Hoop. 2018. Shifting Animacy. *Theoretical Linguistics* 44(1–2): 1–23.

Talmy, L. 1983. How Language Structures Space. In H. Pick and L. Acredolo, eds., *Spatial Orientation: Theory, Research and Application*. New York: Plenum.

Talmy, L. 2000. *Toward a Cognitive Semantics*. Cambridge: MIT Press.

Taube, M. 2015. The Usual Suspects: Slavic, Yiddish, and the Accusative Existentials and Possessives in Modern Hebrew. *Journal of Jewish Languages* 3(1–2): 27–37.

Testelets, J. G. and M. Sch. Khalilov. 1998. *Bezhtinskij jazyk* [The Bezhta Language]. Moscow Jazyki mira: Kavkazskije jazyki.

Timberlake, Alan. 1986. Hierarchies in the Genitive of Negation. In R. D. Brecht and J. S. Levine, eds., *Case in Slavic*. Bloomington: Slavica Publishers.

Tournadre, Nicolas. 1996. *L'ergativité en tibétain*. Louvain: Peeters.

Ueda, Masako. 1993. Set-Membership Interpretations and the Genitive of Negation. *Russian Linguistics* 17: 237–262.

Uspensky, B.A. 1993. "Davnopreshedshee" i "vtoroj roditel'nyj" v russkom jazyke. ["Plusquamperfect" and the "second genitive" in Russian]. In *Issledovanija po slavjanskomu istoricheskomu jazykoznaniju*. Moscow: Moscow University Press.

Vainikka, Anne. 1989. Deriving Syntactic Representations in Finnish. Ph.D. dissertation, University of Massachusetts at Amherst.

Vainikka, Anne and Joan Maling. 1996. Is Partitive Case Inherent or Structural? In J Hoeksema, ed., *Partitives*. New York: Mouton de Gruyter.

Vainikka, Anne and Pauli Brattico. 2014. The Finnish Accusative: Long Distance Case Assignment Under Agreement. *Linguistics* 52(1): 73–124.

Vendler, Z. 1957. Verbs and Times. *Philosophical Review* 56: 143–160.

Verkuyl, H. J. 1972. *On the Compositional Nature of the Aspects*. Dordrecht: Reidel.

Vinogradov, V. V. 1947. *Russkij jazyk*. Moscow-Leningrad.

Wechsler, Stephen and Yae-Sheik Lee. 1996. The Domain of Direct Case-Assignment. *Natural Language and Linguistic Theory* 14: 629–664.

Wierzbicka, Anna. 1980. *The Case for Surface Case*. Ann Arbor: Karoma.

Wolff, Phillip. 2007. Representing Causation. *Journal of Experimental Psychology: General* 136(1): 82–111.

Woolford, Ellen. 1995. Object Agreement in Palauan: Specificity, Humanness, Economy and Optimality. In J. N. Beckman, L. W. Dickey and S. Urbanczyk, eds., *Papers in Optimality Theory*. University of Massachusetts Occasional Papers 18. Amherst: GLSA, University of Massachusetts, Amherst, pp. 655–700.

Woolford, Ellen. 2006. Lexical Case, Inherent Case, and Argument Structure. *Linguistics Inquiry* 37(1): 111–130.

Yadroff, Michael. 1995. AspP and Licensing of Pro-arb Objects. In *Proceedings of WECOL 94*. Los Angeles: UCLA Press.

Yoon, James. 2004. Non-Nominative (Major) Subjects and Case Stacking in Korean. In Peri Bhaskararao and Karumuri Venkata Subbarao, eds., *Nonnominative Subjects*. Amsterdam: John Benjamins, volume 2, pp. 265–314.

Zimmer, Karl and Eser Erguvanlı. 1994. Case Marking in Turkish Indefinite Object Constructions. In *Proceedings of the Twentieth Annual Meeting of the Berkeley Linguistics Society: General Session Dedicated to the Contributions of Charles J. Fillmore*, pp. 547–552.

Zimmerman, Ede. 1993. On the Proper Treatment of Opacity in Certain Verbs. *Natural Language Semantics* 1: 149–179.

Zucchi, A. 1999. Incomplete Events, Intensionality and Imperfective Aspect. *Natural Language Semantics* 7: 179–215.

Zushi, M. 1992. *The Syntax of Dative Constructions in Japanese*. Ms., McGill University.

Zwarts, Joost. 2005. The Case of Prepositions: Government and Compositionality in German PPs. Paper presented at the *21st Annual Meeting of the Israel Association for Theoretical Linguistics*, Haifa, June 23, 2005.

Zwarts, Joost. 2006. *Case Marking Direction: The Accusative in German PPs*. Nijmegen: Radboud University Nijmegen.

Index